IN HOPE OF GOD'S GLORY

IN HOPE
OF GOD'S GLORY

Pauline Theological Perspectives

CHARLES HOMER GIBLIN, S.J.

HERDER AND HERDER

1970
HERDER AND HERDER NEW YORK
232 Madison Avenue, New York 10016

Nihil obstat: Leo J. Steady, Censor Librorum
Imprimatur: ✠ Robert F. Joyce, Bishop of Burlington
June 11, 1970

CONTENTS

TO MY SISTER, MARY

"Greetings to Mary,
   who has done so much hard work for your benefit."

Romans 16, 6

FOREWORD

This book attempts to present Paul and his message mainly in the context of his own letters, arranged in historical sequence. To grasp Paul's apostolic mind and heart, and the very personal gospel of God which Paul astoundingly calls "his" gospel, one must follow the man himself as he confronts various apostolic situations. In facing these situations, Paul reveals both a personal awareness of his special mission and a pastoral concern for the spiritual maturity of those to whom he transmits his understanding of God's word. By attending to these concrete situations as they involve Paul's personal mission and his pastoral concern for others to whom he communicates his gospel, the reader may expect to grasp more integrally the theological outlook and doctrinal message which Paul has given us.

Thirteen letters have come down to us in his name. The authenticity of a number of these, particularly the last three (1 and 2 Tim. and Tit.) can seriously be questioned. But the first seven letters (1 and 2 Thess., Gal., Phil., 1 and 2 Cor., Rom.) can more readily be judged to represent the heart and substance of Paul's personally formulated theology. All seven letters were written in the nine-year period (51–58 A.D.) covering what are known as Paul's second and third missionary journeys, probably the most intensive period of his apostolic activity. We may expect to find in these seven letters, then, especially in the lengthy and mature work (Rom.) which climaxes the series, a quite adequate basis for coming to grips with the Apostle's fully authentic theological contribution. The earlier letters in this group (1 and 2 Thess., Gal., Phil., 1 and 2 Cor.) deal with a variety of situations which serve to introduce the reader to some of the salient features of Paul's work and thought. In the light of these earlier letters, though mutually clarifying them, the last and reputedly most difficult epistle (Rom.) will emerge as a remarkably readable and intelligible synthesis of Paul's missionary message.

Accordingly, this book has two principal parts. The first part devotes a chapter to each of the seven letters discussed. As a general rule, each of these chapters surveys the occasion for the letter treated and follows this survey with a running commentary that discloses the general structure of the letter and the thrust of Paul's argument. The second part focuses on Romans, notably on the first two-thirds of that key letter, and covers more pointedly certain salient perspectives of the Apostle's thought which we will have discussed apropos of the earlier letters (and Rom. 12–16) treated in the first part. Neither part is a verse-by-verse commentary on Paul's epistles, though both parts may serve as a section-by-section or paragraph-by-paragraph commentary, which more coherently reveals what the Apostle is really talking about and whither he is going. The first part supposes that the reader will use along with the running commentary contained in this book a copy of the *Revised Standard Version of the Bible* (*RSV*). We have provided translations only for a few passages—those which differ notably from the translation in the *RSV*. The second part of the book, however, includes a complete translation of Romans 1–11, schematically arranged to facilitate following Paul's elaborate argument.

Particularly in the first part of the book, the reader will meet constant emphasis on "perspective." One of the main theses of this volume is that nothing is so important for understanding St. Paul as grasping his point of view through a kind of inductive reading. Grasping any man's point of view normally requires a certain familiarity with his way of thinking as seen in instance upon instance. Given this inferred knowledge of a man's consistent point of view, what he says—the "content" of his words —can more properly be construed and synthesized. When the "content" itself is relatively less integrated, as is the case with Paul's writings, thanks to the variety of circumstances that he must treat and the unavoidably elliptical character of epistolary communications, it becomes all the more necessary to seek a synthesis in terms of recurrent and dominant perspectives. To try to achieve this synthesis, however, the reader will feel the need to become familiar with a certain sizeable quantity of Paul's correspondence. It is hoped that he will find in this book an aid to perceiving Paul's consistent point of view and dominant perspectives. But the book supposes that he simultaneously reads Paul himself in a rather literal translation like the *RSV*. To render this twofold reading task less distracting, this book itself is free of notes.

Grasping Paul's point of view even in the first part of the book will also require a certain complexive effort, namely, an attempt to see one major aspect of Paul's thinking in conjunction with another. For Paul's notion of the gospel, his theological line of reasoning (that is, the way in which he grounds his statements in his understanding of the activity of the Father, Christ, and the Holy Spirit), his conception of the apostolic office entrusted to him, and his pastoral approach to different audiences are all basically one. In a sense which is made clear only by assimilating the Apostle's own highly integrated point of view, St. Paul is a most practical mystic. To grasp his solution of any particular problem or principle entails grasping to some degree his total vision, and to grasp his total vision more comprehensively entails grasping each detail in its multiple, concrete relationships. Accordingly, we have tried even in the first part of the book to present outstanding, interrelated features of Paul's basic perspectives. In the first part of the book, however, we have concentrated in particular on Paul's pastoral approach to problems. That is, we have attempted to show how he has tried to adapt his intensely personal missionary message to the various audiences and situations which he confronted, endeavoring to impart to his communities that kind of self-sufficiency in the Lord which is known as spiritual maturity.

In presenting Paul's basic perspectives through a reading of Paul himself, it has proved difficult to balance completeness of general coverage with reasonable sufficiency of exegetical detail, especially where we have had to propose rather new insights (for example, 2 Thess. 2, Gal. 4, 20–5, 1, 1 Cor. 7, Rom. 12, 19–21). In such cases, we have made at least that attempt at justification which is compatible with the space and scope of this book. Whoever tries to understand Paul through a reading of Paul will sooner or later experience the need to integrate everything according to what he himself sincerely and judiciously thinks is the mind of the Apostle. We trust, therefore, that the interpretation of a given passage, even where specific arguments can be adduced to support the interpretation, will have to rest in large measure on a more fruitful over-all interpretation of Paul's thought. Moreover, it would be dishonest and impractical to present an interpretation of Paul's theology simply in robes borrowed from a supposed consensus of scholars. Especially when there is question of enunciating Paul's over-all perspectives, "scholarly consensus" rapidly disintegrates. Then, too, an extended discussion of other scholars' views runs the serious risk of becoming a study of scholarly crosscurrents at the expense of interpreting the Apostle himself. To formulate more clearly and tellingly Paul's over-all perspectives, we must frankly content ourselves with presenting the Apostle "as we read him," and hope that the one who reads Paul along with this book will be enabled to grasp the Apostle's mind more fully as he reads both Paul and this book. For some fuller discussion of scholarly views, to many of which we are clearly indebted, we refer the reader to the items contained in the selected bibliography.

In the final analysis, Paul himself provides the best commentary and synthesis for his own work. Accordingly, the second part of this book treats three basic perspectives mainly in terms of the Apostle's own testimony. The first chapter deals more fully with the account of his conversion as revealing his apostolic consciousness. It features the unity between his personal vocation and the central mystery that he preached. The second chapter discusses apropos of Romans 9–11 Paul's theological line of reasoning, notably the perspective he maintains in grounding his arguments. Against this background, the third chapter presents Romans 1–8 as a synthesis of Paul's gospel. The second part of the book may be read independently of the first, provided one is already quite familiar with the Apostle's writings. The first part, however, will prepare the less initiated reader to appreciate the height and depth and breadth of Paul's theological contribution and will render much more profitable a reading of his *chef d'oeuvre,* Romans 1–11.

Fordham University   Charles H. Giblin, S.J.
New York 10458

IN HOPE OF GOD'S GLORY

PART ONE

CHAPTER ONE

1 THESSALONIANS

Paul's letters, at least as we hear them read in bits and snatches in the liturgy, often convey the initial impression of a man passionately dedicated to the cause of Christ and insistent on felling every sinful practice or moral weakness in the community. This impression is fundamentally correct, but it may soon give rise to considerable perplexity. The reader who knows Paul only from such excerpts may regard him as unduly moralistic and even self-contradictory. He will soon reflect that, for all Paul's opposition to the Mosaic law as the ultimate rule of life, the Apostle seems considerably concerned about legislating norms of conduct for his churches. For, when Paul is read as a liturgical "lesson," he unfortunately does not often stand out as a man who adapts his authoritative but genuinely charismatic guidance to various audiences and situations so as to bring his hearers to act on their own according to the power that God has demonstrated among them rather than to depend simply on his own incisive moral exhortations. But we have only to read attentively the first letters that he wrote in order to revise this impression and learn to appreciate Paul's genuinely personal and non-legalistic pastoral approach.

Before we can examine his warm-hearted and solicitous correspondence with the Thessalonians, however, we shall have to treat the circumstances surrounding the composition of these letters. Besides what we can infer from 1 and 2 Thessalonians themselves, we can find in the Acts of the Apostles, written by Paul's younger contemporary and occasional companion, Luke, valuable data for understanding the circumstances in which Paul found himself when he wrote to the Thessalonians.

THE SITUATION: PREACHING THE WORD UNDER PERSECUTION

Luke represents Paul's first contact with the Thessalonians as the result of guidance by the Holy Spirit (cf. Acts 16, 6–10). Apparently, Luke wants to show how the Apostle was providentially directed towards new missionary territory among the gentiles. He mentions that Paul was deterred from entering certain regions (such as Bithynia, a region to the east of modern Istanbul, where there were a number of important Jewish settlements) and that he received at Troas the vision of a Macedonian pleading for help. In preparation for the Apostle's ever more clearly gentile-oriented mission, a new apostolic group had already taken shape. When he left Antioch on his "second missionary journey" to visit the cities in which he and Barnabas had preached, Paul parted company with Barnabas. Paul then chose Silas (= Silvanus) as his traveling companion and soon thereafter he took along with him Timothy, the son of a gentile father. Paul was now clearly at the head of his own missionary band. He would closely associate Silas and Timothy with himself not only in his initial work at Thessalonica, but in his correspondence as well (1 Thess. 1, 1; 2 Thess. 1, 1). At the time Paul crossed the Aegean from Troas to Neapolis and Philippi in response to a vision of the Macedonian pleading for help, Luke himself seems to have formed part of the group. From the way in which the term "we" is employed or not employed in this part of Acts (Acts 16, 9–17, 1), it seems

4

that Luke joined Paul's party at Troas but remained at Philippi or thereabouts until he rejoined Paul in that city some five years later, towards the end of Paul's third missionary journey (Acts 20, 5). After preaching to the Philippians, the three missionaries, Paul, Silas, and Timothy moved on to other Macedonian cities, notably to Thessalonica.

If we undiscerningly accept the missonary itinerary as given in Acts, the period of evangelization in Macedonia while Paul himself was on the scene was quite brief. For instance, Luke represents Paul's stay in Thessalonica as lasting for only about three weeks (Acts 17, 1–10) and ties it to his preaching in the synagogues. In writing Acts, however, Luke may well have accelerated Paul's journey in Macedonia in order to bring out a twofold picture of Paul's constant movements under persecution —persecution from gentiles and Jews alike, but persecution which brings out the fact that Paul's mission is progressively ordered more and more clearly to its reception by the gentiles (cf. Acts 28, 21–28, which represents the climax of this theme in Acts). A similar, theologically motivated editing of the actual events seems to be at work in the way Luke presents the makeup of the community at Thessalonica. Whereas Paul himself, in his first letter to the Thessalonians, indicates rather clearly that the community in that city was primarily a gentile one ("converted from the worship of idols," 1 Thess. 1, 9), Luke suggests that it was Jewish. Even though Luke adds mention of a sizeable group of gentile converts, he seems to stress their Jewish connections, for he refers to them as "devout Greeks" ("godfearers," Acts 17, 4, that is, gentiles who did not accept circumcision but were at least well-disposed towards the Jewish religion).

The solution to this discrepancy between Paul and Luke on the score of the composition of the Thessalonian community may be discerned by noting the way in which Luke has paired the two main episodes of Paul's preaching in Macedonia. Solution of this problem will in turn allow for a considerably longer stay on Paul's part at Thessalonica. At his first major stop in Macedonia, Philippi, Paul's exorcising a pagan prophetess in the name of Jesus Christ brought down on him the wrath of anti-Semitic Roman citizens (Acts 16, 16–24). Then, in Thessalonica, his next major stop, Paul's preaching of Jesus as the Messiah precipitated a Jewish-inspired accusation that Paul and his companions were proclaiming in "Jesus the King" a rival to Caesar (Acts 17, 1–9). Thus, to show how Paul was falsely accused of sedition by pagans and Jews alike and was consequently forced to move onward under pressure of persecution, Luke may well have deliberately overpainted the picture of the actual components of the Thessalonian community. For purposes of his own theology of the Christian mission, Luke has suggested that the Thessalonian community was primarily Jewish, though it was in reality predominantly gentile. Accordingly, Luke may well have assigned to Paul's preaching at Thessalonica a period shorter than the actual length of the Apostle's stay. Luke speaks of Paul's whole period of preaching in Thessalonica in terms of three weeks' preaching in synagogues, that is, his preaching to the Jews.

Moving on to Beroea, where the Jewish community was more friendly, Paul was again harassed by enemies from Thessalonica, and was hurriedly dispatched to Athens by ship. Silas and Timothy remained behind for a while. Judging from 1 Thessalonians, Paul soon contacted Timothy in or from Athens and sent him back to Thessalonica to confirm the community in that city in their tribulations (1 Thess. 3, 1–5). Timothy and Silas finally returned to Paul when the latter reached Corinth (Acts 18, 5; 1 Thess. 1, 1; 3, 6), probably in the early summer of A.D. 51. Timothy's return with a report on conditions at Thessalonica serves as the occasion for Paul's first letter.

THANKFUL OPTIMISM TEMPERED WITH CONCERN (1, 2—3, 13)

One can sense in the first lines of Paul's opening thanksgiving the personal warmth and fundamental optimism that pervades

6

his first letter to this troubled community. At the same time, the reader can also perceive a certain earnest concern on Paul's part to secure and strengthen what he gratefully and prayerfully acknowledges. Paul feels it necessary to secure the Thessalonians' ties with himself as their model and father in Christ. For these new gentile converts hold no other human link with Christ but that which they have received in and through the Apostle himself, and it is the Apostle's intention to strengthen their bond in Christ by every solidly helpful tie. Paul's converts have received more than an abstract doctrine; they have received in Paul's own words and actions a concrete manifestation of God's power, a mysterious power for which tribulation seems to be a condition of an ever more fruitful joy. Paul strengthens their ties with Christ by recalling their experience of his own apostolic manifestation of God's transforming power and by pointing in turn to their own apostolic effectiveness. Although they have received the word of God, not the word of man (cf. 1 Thess. 2, 13), Paul does not regard the members of the community as autonomous Christians, men free to content themselves with their own individual relationship with Christ. Their lives are radically apostolic because they have been patterned on that of Christ by being patterned on that of his Apostle (1 Thess. 1, 6). Paul strengthens this mutual solidarity in a Christ-centered pattern of life even as he speaks about it. For he endeavors to bolster the bond in Christ by bringing the Thessalonians to a heightened awareness of the apostolic power already manifested and of its apostolic implications, its own power to educate men in Christ. If it is true that the community is not a collection of autonomous Christians, it is likewise true that the community itself is not narrowly self-contained. Paul's healthy converts are to become and indeed have become in their turn an effectively apostolic paradigm for Christians elsewhere (1 Thess. 1, 7–8), as did the churches in Judaea before them (1 Thess. 2, 14).

Paul's pastoral encouragement and concern is therefore closely bound up with a twofold apostolic aim: to encourage the Thessalonians in their effective fervor as an apostolic com-

7

munity and to secure their ties with himself and with the other churches. Both aims are one in that they foster the personally communicated gospel which unites in one life pattern the men empowered by God's word. We shall find that this twofold apostolic aim is reflected in the over-all structure of the first half of the letter (1 Thess. 1, 2–3, 13), which deals alternately with thanksgiving and apologia.

In the first *thanksgiving* (1, 2–10), Paul founds his gratitude and prayer on the concrete manifestation of the Thessalonians' fervor in the vital virtues of faith, love, and hope. He speaks of the *work* of their faith, the *toil,* or *labor* of their love, and the *steadfastness ('ypomonē)* of their hope, that is, their patient endurance in trials. The exercise of these virtues, especially that of hope, finds its lodestone in the Lord Jesus Christ. His coming is the magnet, as it were, which accounts for the dynamism and direction of these basic virtues. Ultimately, however, as verse 3 indicates, faith, love, and hope find their lodestone in the Father, in whose presence they are in a sense already exercised and to whose presence they lead.

Paul proceeds further to ground his thanks and prayer in the personal call which the Thessalonians have received (*eidotes,* "For we know . . . ," v. 4). He speaks of this call quite concretely; it consists in the preaching of the gospel not only by word but by attendant signs of the Holy Spirit. For Paul, the gospel is a dynamic message, a breakthrough of God's power. He expresses what philosophically minded theologians would term its "supernatural character" by presenting it as a special divine work above and beyond normal human experience, that is, beyond what a speculative theologian might term "the proportion of human nature." Although Paul's way of presenting the gospel as a supernatural event is genuinely theological, centered on the mystery of God's personal action, it is not abstractly so. He appeals directly to the concrete manifestation of God's power in Christian experience. His words here suggest some charismatic show of power (miracles or glossolalia come readily to mind as specific possibilities). But, at the same time, he does

8

not focus his attention on the "spectacular" or the "preternatural." Rather, he looks to divine power in its personal impact. For he hurries on to speak of the effect of the gospel as the sense of conviction that his converts had experienced. Nor does he stop with a reference to the fervent conviction that they experienced individually at the time they were converted. *"Accordingly,"* he says, "you know what kind of men *we proved to be* among you for your sake" (1 Thess. 1, 5b). Thus, Paul underscores the fact that the character of the missionaries themselves formed part of the Thessalonians' personal inaugural experience of God's power in their receiving the gospel.

For all its divine power, the gospel comes through other men, and in a personally formative way that serves to set in relief rather than minimize the operative power of God. Three times Paul uses the same Greek verb (*egenēthē,* variously translated by the *RSV* as "came," v. 5a; "we proved to be," v. 5b; and "you became," v. 6) to describe concretely the manner of the Thessalonians' calling: the aspect of divine power and solid conviction (v. 5a), the character of the missionaries (v. 5b), and the way in which the Thessalonians themselves have responded to the missionaries and to the Lord (v. 6a). Their reception of the word in tribulation, with joy from the Holy Spirit, has in turn had a salutary impact on the faithful in the whole of Greece. In fact, Paul sees their own personal call in these concrete circumstances as having a missionary impact even beyond the confines of the Grecian provinces of Macedonia and Achaea. He hails their conversion as an effective missionary contribution along with his own worldwide apostolate. Paul concludes this thanksgiving with a reference to the scope of that apostolate and to its specifically Christian character. Its scope consists in a universal, personal transformation: the conversion of men to the living and true God. Its specifically Christian character is spelled out in apocalyptic terms (that is, in somewhat florid imagery of prophetic provenance which is employed to put things in the supernatural perspective of God's world rule achieved in a final judgment): "to await his Son from heaven,

9

the one whom he raised from the dead, Jesus, who rescues us from the wrath to come."

Thus, at the outset of his letter, Paul thanks God for the Thessalonians' receiving the gospel with recognition of the meaning of his own work among them. Looking to the personal impact of God's power as already shown in their conversion and in Paul's own apostolic activity, the Apostle commends the Thessalonians' fervor in an apostolic life for God which has as its awaited goal the coming of the Lord.

With the first *apologia* (2, 1–12), Paul turns more explicitly to the manner of his preaching among the Thessalonians. His apologia betrays a certain uneasy concern. The Apostle takes care to insist on the selfless conduct and hard work which he exemplified at Thessalonica. He contrasts himself with false-speaking, morally lax, and selfishly motivated teachers (2, 3). One of his reasons for doing this is surely to enable the Thessalonians clearly to distinguish the genuine apostle from the pagan itinerant lecturers—people who might be tagged the "prophetic quacks" of the time. In appealing to his own example, however, and to the Thessalonians' recognition of it, Paul protests too much. Repeatedly, he appeals to their experience (2, 1. 2. 5. 9. 10. 11) and to God's witness (2, 5. 10). He seems to be concerned with a disorderly, even rival, element within the community itself (a concern which will reappear in the second apologia, in concluding passages of the second part of 1 Thess., and also at the end of Paul's second letter to this community). In this first apologia, Paul not only stresses his apostolic restraint in not burdening the Thessalonians when he could have done so legitimately, as, for example, by having them support him, but he also underscores the familial relationships that bind the Thessalonians to himself. He depicts himself as a loving and selfless mother (the wet-nurse who takes care of her own children) and as an attentive and judicious father. The Apostle has exemplified the ideal of fatherly correction in dealing with each one as an individual and in displaying positive encouragement. Once more the section ends with a reference

10

to the final consummation of the Christian's vocation, this time under the more positive aspect of the kingdom and glory of God (rather than under the negative aspect of deliverance from his wrath).

The second *thanksgiving* (2, 13–16) picks up once again the theme of receiving the word of God. It is God himself or, more proximately, the word of God that is at work in the faithful (2, 13). In explaining how it is at work, Paul points out that the Thessalonians have become "imitators" of the churches of God in Judaea.

What is the meaning of "imitation" here? It is surely not mere resemblance in external conduct. Paul sees the notion of "imitation" in a much more profound dimension; he sees it rooted in the corporate structuring of one's life according to the paschal mystery. He already implied as much in writing 1 Thessalonians 1, 6: receiving the word in great tribulation with joy from the Holy Spirit, the Thessalonians have become "imitators" of Paul, whose own apostolic life is stamped by the struggle which is a share in the sufferings of Christ. The Thessalonians' being "imitators" of Paul is mentioned in the same breath with their being imitators of the Lord (1 Thess. 1, 6). In 1 Corinthians 4, 16, Paul will show more clearly that "imitation" involves apostolic formation in Christ through the gospel. Being (or rather, continuing to be, continuing to become: *ginesthe*—present imperative) an "imitator" of Paul means living out by personal communication what the Thessalonians have become in Christ through the gospel. One who is an "imitator" does not make himself the norm of conduct, but becomes a living, communicable pattern of conduct for the salvation of others, looking to the glory of God (cf. 1 Cor. 10, 33; 10, 31). Accordingly, Paul appeals to his converts to be imitators of himself as, indeed, he himself is an imitator of Christ (1 Cor. 11, 1). In Ephesians 5, 1, Paul will exhort Christians to be "imitators of God." This further elaboration of the notion is most expressly based on the fact of belonging to God through Christ's sacrifice. "Imitation" is expected of beloved sons, and

11

consists in walking in love as Christ loved us, giving himself up as a sacrificial offering to God on our behalf (Eph. 5, 2). Where he uses the term in his earlier letters, however, Paul is less directly concerned with moral sanctification of one's personal life. He seems to be more intent on describing a feature of apostolic effectiveness. In 2 Thessalonians 3, 7. 9 for instance, he will appeal to imitation of his apostolic selflessness in work that is ordered to the assistance of others. The disorderly, those not conducting themselves according to the "tradition" of apostolic concern for others, are to be avoided as norms for community life.

In 1 Thessalonians 2, 14, Paul treats "imitation" in the context of a thanksgiving for apostolic effectiveness. The word of God is at work in the Thessalonians. Illustrative proof of this is the way in which their pattern of life is conformed to that of the churches elsewhere in Christ Jesus. This pattern of life is one signed by the cross. The Thessalonians are suffering from their own people as the churches in Judaea, composed of Jews, are suffering from their blood relatives. Paul views this pattern of conformity as rooted in hostility to the Lord and to the message of salvation. He speaks of the Jews in Judaea as those who had killed the Lord Jesus and the prophets, who had persecuted the apostles, and who now impede their preaching to the gentiles.

This apparently anti-Semitic outburst calls for some further interpretation. It is hardly characteristic of Paul's pastoral approach to denounce his own people (cf. Rom. 9, 1–6; 10, 1; 11, 1). Nor need we assume that he intends to do so here. We should attend first of all to his main purpose in this whole passage. He does not intend to denounce any racial or national group, but to thank God for the apostolic effectiveness of the Thessalonians' conversion. He discerns this effectiveness in the very pattern of the passion verified in the life of the Church, wherever it may be, whether newly planted in Greece or situated in its homeland, Judaea. Paul's first comparison lies between the Thessalonians and their persecutors on the one hand, and

12

the Judaean churches and their persecutors, who happen to be the Jews, on the other hand. When he goes on to speak of the Jews in verse 15, it is to elaborate on the basic pattern of persecution which he sees verified in the life of the Church and, ultimately, in the life of Christ himself.

One might say that, since he is writing in the year A.D. 51, Paul can speak of the Jews in Judaea as those who were responsible for the death of Jesus some twenty years previously. But this explanation seems somewhat shortsighted. For Paul moves beyond racial and temporal considerations to situate the pattern of persecution in a world perspective dominated by the theme of God's judgment and expressed in rather forceful and simplistic, "black and white" imagery. That is to say, he situates it in the perspective of apocalyptic. He views the persecutors typologically rather than personally. He shuns qualitative judgments of individual responsibility and depicts in a kind of apocalyptic caricature basic theological "types." Those who slew the Lord are those who slew the prophets (1 Thess. 2, 15a; cf. Mt. 23, 34). This they can be only representatively, even though the accusation is indeed tied to a given historical group. They are the same ones—again representatively, since Paul was scarcely hounded by Jews from Judaea during his travels in Greece—who have persecuted Paul, who do not please God, and who oppose all men (v. 15b). With these latter qualifications, we are clearly on the level of a typological representation of hostility. A concrete, historical group is not judged precisely as a given historical group of responsible individuals, but as a group representative of anti-God activity as a whole. To some extent, abstraction is made from the persons immediately involved and certainly from the Jewish people as a race or religion composed of given individuals. The typological representation reaches its climax in verse 16, with the description of these men as opposing the revelation of salvation to the gentiles through the missionary apostolate of Paul and his companions.

The apocalyptic scope of verse 16b complements this typological representation. In the apocalyptic view, God's universal

13

judgment stands as the ultimate principle of intelligibility in the history of mankind. The present makes sense only in the light of the final consummation in just judgment, of which the bright side is salvation and the dark side judgment or "wrath." The final judgment or "wrath" is already in process for those who are "filling up the number of their sins" through their hostility to the divine plan of salvation. Hence Paul can say that "the wrath of God has already come upon them *for the consummation"* (1 Thess. 2, 16b).

The closing phrase *(eis telos),* which the *RSV* translates inaccurately as "at last," is so condensed that it requires some explication. It refers to the "end" as the climactic point of a whole process of fulfillment. The verb "has come upon them" *(ephthasen)* refers to what has *already* occurred. That is, the verb declares that God's wrath in judgment has to some extent been anticipated. Therefore, Paul is not saying (as the *RSV* suggests) that God's wrath has finally caught up with these sinners, as if it had been pursuing them in the past and had now reached its absolute term. Rather, he is saying that these sinners' conduct has reached a certain eschatological fullness. For it has struck at Christ and the gospel, the heart of the "eschaton" or last, decisive stage of the history of God's dealings with men. Hence God's eschatological wrath (his adverse judgment) has reached from the future, as it were, into the present, that is, from the final pole of the last days to the present pole of the same eschatological period. God's wrath is already upon them and is ordered to make a final end of them in due time, when the eschatological wrath will be fully realized in the final judgment, "the consummation" in the fullest sense.

This apocalyptic view of things, especially when it is presented as succinctly as it is here, lies open to misinterpretation as racist or nationalistic, and even as deterministic. But Christian apocalyptic is neither. As Paul will make clear in Romans 1–3, man's liability or non-liability to judgment is not tied to racial or national affiliation, and the possibility of repentance for one

14

who is at the present time liable to wrath is by no means excluded.

What is especially significant in this passage is that Paul's thanksgiving is based on the dynamic power of the word of God among the faithful. This power is shown in a pattern of life common to the other churches in Christ Jesus, a pattern ordered to the vindication of God's judgment in wrath on those who oppose the word of divine salvation. The negative aspect of the parousia hope is by no means the sole one or the most important one. More reassuring aspects have been brought out at the end of the first thanksgiving (1, 10, deliverance from wrath), and the first apologia (2, 12, God's call to his kingdom and glory). These more consoling aspects will reappear in the course of the second apologia (2, 19, the Thessalonians will be Paul's own joy and crown at the Lord's parousia) and at the end of the thanksgiving which closes the first part of the letter (3, 13, prayer for their strengthening in sanctification for the triumphal coming of the Lord). The negative and positive aspects of Paul's apocalyptic view are both necessary, however, for grasping the pastoral scope of his letter to the Thessalonians. The negative aspect, as we have seen, is consequent on opposition to the message of salvation and thus to the faith which Paul preaches. Salvation, on the other hand, comes through one's reception of the word of God, conversion, and service (1, 9), hearkening to guidance in the living out of one's vocation (2, 12), solidarity with others in Christ in the face of hostility to the faith (2, 14 ff.), adherence to the faith in trials (3, 2), and the increase of love for strengthening their hearts in holiness. In both their negative and positive aspects, Paul's various exhortations and explanations of a pastoral character are set in the context of a doctrinal understanding of the life of faith as a bond of personal communication. The process towards judgment and salvation is radically determined by a living faith which has been transmitted through the Apostle and God's co-workers.

The second *apologia* (2, 17–3, 8) deals not with Paul's first contacts with the Thessalonians but with his present separation from them. His inability to reach them is viewed in the apocalyptic context of satanic opposition (2, 18). Only this, and no lack of personal interest, has prevented him from coming in person to the Thessalonians. But Timothy has exercised the apostle's commitment (3, 3b) to strengthen their faith in trials. On the basis of the Greek phrase in this context and the parallel statement in Philippians 1, 16, 1 Thessalonians 3, 3b should read: "You yourselves know that we are committed to this [the defense of the gospel]." Timothy has just returned with the good news of their faith and love and of their attachment to the Apostle. Although Paul does not equate the reception of the word with personal allegiance to himself, he does maintain a keen personal interest in the spiritual well-being of his converts. Preaching the gospel was no mere task for him, but was, rather, his whole life, and his personal involvement in the faith of his converts can hardly find a stronger voice than in the phrase: "for now we really live if you stand firm in the Lord!" (3, 8).

Concluding the first part of the letter (3, 9–13), Paul restates the *thanksgiving* theme, which reaches its peak in the joy before God which the Thessalonians have brought him. The only further thanksgiving that he could offer would be in fulfillment of his petition to see them face to face and supply whatever may be lacking to their faith; for, firm as it may be, faith can always be strengthened. He closes, then, with a prayer that God himself and the Lord Jesus Christ may bring about this meeting. With characteristic enthusiasm, he prays for a superabundance of spiritual goods. In praying for their strengthening in holiness, for that firm faith and rich love which binds one ever more intensely to God, Paul looks to the coming of the Lord with all his holy ones. The latter expression probably covers all the just Christians as well as angels. In any event, it helps place the concept of "holiness" in its proper eschatological perspective. For Paul, holiness is not just an ornament of Christian life, but the very stuff of which future glory is made. This doctrinal per-

16

spective provides a fitting setting for the exhortations opening the second or "parenetic" (hortatory) part of this epistle. For the keynote of Paul's exhortations in the latter part of this letter is holiness, and the more particular instructions which follow later on take up the eschatological hope and the present conduct of those whom Paul prays God will make fully holy (5, 23).

EXHORTATION TO HOLINESS (4, 1—5, 28)

The note of "superabundance" reappears at the outset (4, 1) of the specifically hortatory or parenetic part of 1 Thessalonians. The superabundance of love for which Paul has prayed (3, 12) is ordered to the strengthening of a living faith in sanctification (becoming holy) (4, 1). Moral conduct, in turn, is simply the practical, personal expression of one's faith and love as a Christian. Or, to put the same truth in existentialist terminology, the "imperative" of Christian life, how one is to act, stems from the "indicative," his new state of life, being vitally united to Christ in faith and love through the Spirit whom he has communicated to us and who grounds our hope for fulfillment. Paul begins his exhortation with a word of encouragement; he desires that they increasingly do what is pleasing to God.

The *first exhortation* (4, 2–8) under the heading of "instructions given through the Lord" requires some special attention, both with regard to the specific point of the exhortation and with regard to Paul's pastoral approach. Commentators have generally regarded this passage as dealing with various abuses, such as fornication, adultery, sharp business practices. More particularly, they have often taken the phrase in 4, 4a *(to 'eautou skeuos ktasthai,* "to acquire one's own vessel") to refer to control over one's own body, that is, continence, and the phrase in verse 6a *(en tō pragmati,* "in the case [matter]") to refer generically to "this matter" (for example, the question of adultery) or to business, rather than to refer specifically to a lawsuit. Baltensweiler, however, has shown that the passage

17

deals not with several topics but with one, a rather specific piece of marriage legislation. What is more important, Baltensweiler's exegesis provides lucid insights into Paul's pastoral approach. Drawing on Baltensweiler's exegesis, we shall present a translation of the text with a brief commentary. The text is as follows:

4, 1a Finally, brothers, we beseech and exhort in the Lord Jesus
   1b that as you learned from us how you ought to walk and to please God
   1c —just as you are doing—
   1d you do so more and more.
   2 For you know what instructions we gave you through the Lord Jesus.
   3a For this is the will of God, your sanctification [becoming holy]:
   3b   that you abstain from immorality,
   4a   that each one of you know how to acquire his own vessel
   4b   in holiness and honor,
   5a   not in the passion of lust [self-centered greed]
   5b   like heathen who do not know God,
   6a   that [one is] not to transgress
             and greedily to take advantage of his brother in a lawsuit
   6b   because the Lord is an avenger in all these things,
   6c   as we solemnly forewarned you.
   7 For God has not called us for uncleanness, but in sanctification [holiness].
   8a Therefore, whoever disregards [these instructions]
   8b   disregards not man,
      but God,
   8c   who gives his Holy Spirit to you.

The end of the exhortation is marked by the conclusion ("therefore") in verse 8. Its structure is further determined by a literary technique known as an "inclusion"—the use of a given thematic word or phrase at the beginning of a given development and its repetition at the end of this development. The structure of this passage is further determined by an inclusion on the word "sanctification" (*'agiasmos,* "becoming holy," in vv. 3a and 7; cf. also v. 8, "Holy [*'agios*] Spirit" and the theme of "holiness," *'agiasmos* in v. 4b). The passage opens with reference to the will of God (v. 3a), proceeds towards references to heathen conduct foreign to the acknowledgment of God

(v. 5) and liable to the judgment of God (v. 6b), then concludes with references to the Christian vocation (v. 7) and to the authority and gift of God (v. 8).

Within this structure, there are three salient noun clauses which seem to specify the sanctification mentioned in verse 3a. The first two of these are infinitives in parallel construction (translated as "that . . .," in vv. 3b and 4a). The term "immorality" *(porneia)* in verse 3b refers rather generically to sexual sins, but it can refer more explicitly to invalid marriages if other elements in the context suggest this sense (as we shall see they do here). The expression in verse 4 must not be translated as "control one's own body" (cf. the *RSV*), in spite of Paul's use of the term "vessel" for weak human nature in 2 Corinthians 4, 7. For in 1 Thessalonians 4, 4a there is precisely the question of *acquiring* a vessel. Hence the proper literal translation is "to acquire his own vessel." The expression "vessel" in this phrase is best taken in the rabbinic sense, as 1 Peter 3, 7, where it refers to a wife. Christian conduct in acquiring a wife is then explicitly contrasted with pagan conduct, "the passion of lust" being a generic phrase which can cover not only sexual sins but the self-interest of greed as well. The contrast with pagan conduct is important, for it distinguishes Christian marriage practice at Thessalonica from that of its environment. We shall return to this point later.

The third noun clause ("that . . .," in v. 6a) is not simply parallel to the two preceding ones in verses 3b and 4a (see text as given above). In Greek, the *third* noun clause contains an infinitive preceded by the definite article. The third clause thus specifies the two preceding ones and does not introduce another topic parallel to them. One might therefore translate verse 6a: "to wit: that [one is] not . . ." This third clause contains an expression that should be taken in the more usual technical sense of lawsuit (*en tō pragmati*) than in a sense that would refer to business matters or to sexual ethics rather generally. What is more, the reference in verse 6b to God's judgment ("avenger," *ekdikos*) and in verse 6c to Paul's attestation (*diemartyrametha*, "solemnly forewarned") strengthens the probability of a juridical reference in verse 6a.

Now, in investigating Greek legal practices that seem to be at variance with Jewish and Christian marriage practices, Baltensweiler has found the background that seems to render Paul's exhortation quite intelligible. There was a Greek "heiress law" which allowed the nearest male relative to claim the hand of a girl whose father had died without leaving any male heir. Thus, even if the nearest male relative were the uncle of the heiress, he could marry her. The purpose of the law, obviously, was to keep the money in the family. Conduct according to this law would normally involve marriage within close degrees of kinship and probably, as Baltensweiler thinks, could entail divorce. Paul is thus alluding to conduct at variance with Christian existence. He opposes a form of marriage within certain degrees of kinship which is motivated by dishonorable greed and entails injustice to another Christian.

What is most striking about the pastoral advice is the way in which Paul formulates the specific admonition. Paul is sufficiently clear for his Greek audience to grasp the point of his allusion to pagan marriage laws. But he does not legislate a solution even while he refers implicitly to Christian laws of conduct and makes use of judicial terminology. He expects the Thessalonians to grasp his point in the light of the whole nature of Christian existence and to act accordingly. The motivation is not ultimately "the regulations which I, Paul, gave to you"— though the regulations were present and Paul was certainly the main human instrument in transmitting them. The instructions given are referred to the authority of the Lord (v. 2). Within the exhortation proper, Paul concentrates on the will of God (v. 3a), on the call of God (v. 7), on the distinctive nature of Christian existence in the acknowledgment of God (v. 5), on the judgment of the Lord (v. 6b), and on the gift of the Holy Spirit (v. 8c), which Paul sees as the interior law of God's sons (cf. Romans 8, 2. 14–16; cf. 2 Corinthians 3, 3; Ezekiel 36, 26). What is disregarded by those who reject Paul's admonitions is not "instructions" as such (the object is missing in v. 8a), nor Paul himself, but God (v. 8b).

The *next admonition* (4, 9–12) is written in the same vein. Paul does indicate what he expects of the Thessalonians, a practical charity which consists in minding one's own affairs and supporting oneself instead of presuming on the charity of others. But he places priority on the interior knowledge which they have received from God. "Taught by God" (*theodidaktoi,* v. 9) is a reference to the law of the spirit which is the new covenant (Jeremiah 31 [LXX 38], 31–34; Ezekiel 36, 24–27; cf. 2 Corinthians 3, 2–3; Romans 8, 12–17). Paul's own concrete admonitions, therefore, are placed in the framework of the law of the spirit which already governs the lives of the Thessalonians as an interior principle of personal understanding and direction. He sees his own apostolic direction as complementing or, rather, as helping to evoke what the Thessalonians already have interiorly from God.

The hope that is consequent on Christian existence becomes the point of departure for the *following reassuring instruction* (4, 13–18), which concerns the lot of those who have died. This hope, in turn, is based on faith in Jesus' own death and resurrection. God will bring "through Jesus" those who have died, that is, Jesus risen will be the divine agent by whom the Father will achieve the resurrection of those united with him, even though they have died. The resurrection of Christians is a corollary of Christ's paschal experience accepted in faith.

In an apocalyptic vignette based (4, 15) on the authority of the Lord (rather than on any quoted word of the Lord) to underscore assurance on a point of faith, Paul enthusiastically depicts the moment of final and everlasting union with the Lord which is the substance of the eschatological hope. No doubt he himself hoped to be among those living at the parousia. But this wishful thinking on his part, which proved to be unfounded, as he himself came to realize more clearly, does not alter the substance of his affirmation. His assurance backed by the Lord's authority is that the faithful will be permanently united with Jesus and that the living are really not better off with regard to the parousia than those Christians who have passed away. Similarly, the apocalyptic expressions ("word of command," "voice of an archangel," "God's trumpet call," "gathering in the clouds," and so forth) are poetic embellishments proper to this genre which Paul may have taken literally, but which do not impair the basic affirmation that he makes. Rather, they are the theological idiom of the time which has to be "demythologized" by a process of theological translation that is interpretative rather than subtractive. These apocalyptic flourishes serve to bring out the fact that the final gathering of the faithful is the moment at which the Lord's will is realized in a supernatural triumph. The physical details are not to be taken literally, as though the literal sense were to be understood, as Origen understood it to be, as that which is grasped by the literal-minded man. The ultimate point of reference for interpreting the constant element in somewhat florid apocalyptic descriptions is the constant affirmations of the kerygma, such as Jesus' coming to judge the living and the dead and the final resurrection. If a criterion for determining the limits of demythologizing can be given, surely the kerygmatic professions of the faith preserved in the living credal formulas of the Church are the most solid and adequate guides.

Paul does not speculate on the nature of life after death. His attention focuses simply on the assurance that those who have died have attained a certain priority in the order of the resurrection. From other passages (for example, Phil. 1, 21–24; 2 Corinthians 5, 1; 1 Thessalonians 5, 10), where he sees the possibility of his own death as an opportunity for being with the Lord, he shows, however, that he did not regard "those who sleep," an accepted euphemism for the dead, as those who were simply in a state of suspended animation. For Paul, life was changed by death, not completely taken away; even those who sleep are alive in Christ (1 Thessalonians 5, 10). A later theology, which would not be marked by a vivid expectation of the parousia, would find grounds for speculating on what the deceased know. But even such a theology must reckon with the absence of time for the departed, whose "knowledge" may be exercised in the equivalent of one or two psychic moments over the period of the world's duration until the resurrection. It is we the living rather than those who have died who must "wait," and this, equivalently, is what Paul tells the Thessalonians.

Those who have died enjoy in Paul's view a priority that approaches the notion of the "first resurrection" in Revelation 20, 4–6, a plane of heavenly existence which is ordered only to a fuller and more general resurrection. The interpretation of the "first resurrection" in the Apocalypse (the Book of Revelation in the *RSV*) is anything but clear, though it might be of some help to suggest that it may be the apocalyptic equivalent for what later Western theology would call the beatific vision and would predicate of all those who had been fully purified, like the martyrs and virgins who typify this state in the Apocalypse. In any event, Paul regards the faithful departed (the dead in Christ, 1 Thessalonians 4, 16), in comparison with those who live on earth, as being in a superior state in point of final personal union with the Lord.

Paul then adds *words of caution and encouragement* (5, 1–11) apropos of the Thessalonians' eschatological hope. He takes care to note—in a tone which indicates that he takes the matter for granted—that the date of the parousia does not pertain to revelation. Paul regularly treats the "Day" not under its quantitative aspects but under its qualitative aspects; he speaks of it as a day of judgment and salvation, not as a zero-hour in clock-and-calendar time. It may be a given date on the calendar, but it is not discussed as such. This distinction is vital for avoiding a literal understanding of Paul which would prove to be as baneful as a literal historicism has proved to be in the study of the gospels. The Day of the Lord comes unannounced, like a thief at night (5, 2), and with inescapable doom for those who falsely think they are secure (5, 3). But for Christians it does not come as a thief. Those who are not in darkness will not be ambushed. The motif of light leads Paul to discuss the difference between those who are *morally* asleep (v. 6) and those who, as children of the daylight, are to be armed with faith, love, and hope of salvation. In speaking of this election for salvation made possible and effective through Jesus Christ, he then once more uses "be asleep" in the sense in which it can refer to Christians, that is, as a euphemism for those who have died. These are nonetheless alive with the Lord. The refrain of strengthening assurance (*paraklēsis*—stronger and deeper than the English "consolation," "comfort," or even "encouragement") is repeated (cp. 5, 11 and 4, 18) with the added exhortation to build up one another. Paul does not intend his encouragement merely for the bereaved individual, but for the "edification" of the whole community, the intensification of their solidarity in Christ. The theme of the Mystical Body is not elaborated here, but its essential feature of union with the risen Christ entailing interdependent strengthening of one another can be felt in Paul's words. Whenever the Lord will come, sudden as his coming will be, the Thessalonians are to have been morally prepared for possessing salvation. Their strengthening assurance lies in the fact that whether they live or die they are to be alive with Christ.

With the *closing admonitions* (5, 12 ff.) we can detect certain problems in the community that threaten to disrupt the present work of edification which the Apostle has just stressed. The community in general is admonished to acknowledge those in charge of correcting members of the community and to hold them in special esteem because of their work. Even this community, on which Paul has heaped so much praise, was affected by a certain factionalism. But the means to secure good order were not wanting. Although the interior law of the spirit was to prevail (cf. 4, 1–8. 9–12) as the basic norm of conduct, and although the community was to encourage the exercise of its charismatic gifts (5, 19–20), the community had been endowed with a certain "structure" by the Apostle. It was by no means a free-wheeling charismatic group without appointed leaders. On the other hand, the role of designated leaders did not mean that the community as a whole was to be passive with regard to the correction and encouragement of its members. All are to share in this task, though they are to be careful to avoid a vindictive spirit (5, 15). The positive dispositions which are urged regard joy, constant prayer, thanksgiving. Paul insists in particular on openness to the impulse of the spirit and on esteeming prophecy, properly moderated by prudent judgment and showing moral integrity. From the second letter, it seems as though certain undisciplined persons had not followed these admonitions, but had seriously upset the community with prophecy or spiritual utterances of a heterodox nature. But even in view of disturbances more serious than those that he senses as he dictates 1 Thessalonians, Paul will not retract his basic principles for dealing with a generally healthy Christian community. He will not resort to harsh, repressive measures in the face of good faith and a cooperative spirit.

The *closing prayer* (5, 23–24) picks up once more the theme of sanctification which was sounded at the end of the first part of the letter and at the outset of the parenetic second part. The passage (5, 23) is chiastically arranged in Greek, as van Stempvoort has shown, and should read:

5, 23a May the God of peace himself
  23b   sanctify your whole selves and your spirit entirely;
  23c   may both soul and body be preserved without blemish
  23d for the coming of our Lord Jesus Christ.

Even in the more traditional translation of the *RSV*, Paul's prayer is not to be construed as grounding a physically tripartite division of man. But in the translation given above, the eschatological perspective in which Paul considers the whole man is brought out more sharply. Paul prays first (5, 23ab) for what is specifically supernatural in their very being, the complete perfection of the whole man (*'oloteleis*) and the full inheritance (*'oloklēron*) of the spirit. The second part of his prayer (5, 23cd) relates this supernatural perfection to the historical and

25

moral realization of human integrity at the parousia. Thus, once again, Paul sees man perfected in the dimension of the spirit, but also in relation to an historical event that will mark the point of human fulfillment. In turn, this historical realization is that of the Christian vocation, the call of the Father who will personally achieve what he has begun (5, 24).

The personal request for prayers (5, 25) is followed by a final salutation, an injunction to have the letter read to all (5, 27—another trace of Paul's concern with the disorderly conduct of some at Thessalonica), and his characteristic greeting (5, 28).

CHAPTER TWO

2 THESSALONIANS

INTRODUCTORY CHAPTER (1, 1–12)
AND GENERAL STRUCTURE

Problems which we have already discerned in 1 Thessalonians seem to have become more acute, prompting Paul to dictate a second letter to the community. The tone of this second letter, which closes by dealing rather explicitly with certain disorderly people in the community, is understandably cooler than that of the first letter. But Paul still shows himself optimistic about the spiritual health of the community as a whole. In the introductory thanksgiving and prayer (2 Thessalonians 1, 3–12), he treats of the Thessalonians' faith and love in spite of persecutions from without. Paul sees in their patient endurance an anticipatory manifestation (*endeigma,* "indication," "evidence," 1, 5) of God's favorable judgment. The trials they are undergoing are already proving them worthy of his kingdom, and the Thessalonians are on the way to being fully proved worthy for the ultimate reception of the kingdom at the final judgment. God's judgment will right the wrongs they have endured by meting out (retributive) justice to those who have opposed the

27

faith (1, 8) when Jesus comes to be glorified in his holy ones (the sanctified community as well as the angels) and to be held in awe among all the believers. This consummation will consist in fulfillment of the faith received through Paul's testimony, and he pauses to stress this fact (v. 10b). He presents the Thessalonians with a vividly apocalyptic scene of awesome glory, an event conditioned on the faith which they have indeed received. The Apostle's prayer (1, 11–12) builds on this vision. Once more, Paul looks to God's counting the Thessalonians worthy of their Christian vocation and to his fulfilling their good resolve and effective faith by Jesus' glorification in them and theirs in him.

But the second chapter looks to a disturbance within the community which Paul earnestly wants to remedy. It is this chapter that forms the heart of his second letter to the Thessalonians. The concluding chapter (2 Thessalonians 3) will take up various other requests and admonitions: prayers for Paul in his own struggles against disbelieving adversaries (3, 1–2); encouragement for their own perseverance in his moral teaching (3, 3–4); specific admonitions regarding unruly members of the community and recalling Paul's own example of selfless interest (3, 10–15); and then another prayer (3, 16), this time for peace. The final salutation (3, 17) contains a caution against forgeries, echoing the warning in 2, 2. 15 and suggesting again the presence of some unsettling elements within the community itself.

BACKGROUND FOR UNDERSTANDING THE PRINCIPAL REQUEST

The nature of these unsettling elements within the community is not easy to determine. But some attempt must be made to discern the *Sitz im Leben* for the difficulty, that is, the "life situation" or concrete set of circumstances that had given rise to the difficulty and that may have influenced the way in which

Paul formulated his response to it. If we can infer this *Sitz im Leben,* we should be able to comprehend in good measure what is otherwise one of the most elliptical and enigmatic passages in Paul's correspondence. The following treatment must needs be considerably detailed, if only because the interpretation that we offer is relatively new. Nevertheless, if we want to acquire a coherent understanding of 2 Thessalonians, we can hardly avoid addressing ourselves seriously to its central request, that in 2 Thessalonians 2. The opening chapter of this letter is little more than a prayerful thanksgiving introducing the perspective of a happy consummation for those who by faith and love in trials will have been proved worthy of their calling to enjoy God's complete world reign. The concluding chapter, on the other hand, contains a variety of requests and admonitions which may become more meaningful in the light of the major problem to which Paul devotes the central third of this letter. Moreover, the central chapter may be found to yield a richer understanding of Paul's pastoral approach as this involves an appeal to his apostolic preaching and relies on apocalyptically formulated theological reasoning.

Paul himself does not seem to have been fully apprised of the situation at Thessalonica, since he indicates various possible occasions for the confusion that he attempts to remedy (2, 2). Nevertheless, his own suggestive remarks about the possible proximate cause of the trouble can provide us with some valuable leads for diagnosing the situation at least as Paul knew it and supposed his readers knew it, so that they could grasp the points of his admonition. The *Sitz im Leben* for the difficulty that prompts Paul to voice his earnest request in 2 Thessalonians 2, 1–15 was most likely a charismatic liturgical gathering. We may recall that, at the close of his first letter, Paul had encouraged the Thessalonians not to quench the spirit or despise prophesying (1 Thessalonians 5, 19–20), but to exercise good judgment and hold fast or seize (*katechein*) what is good (1 Thessalonians 5, 21–22). His encouragement at that time covered at least in large measure (cf. the reference to "prophecies")

29

judicious discernment in the spirit which was expected at liturgical gatherings. Now, when he indicates at the outset of 2 Thessalonians 2 various possible avenues of deception that have caused complete consternation in the community, it is interesting to note that all these possibilities have a common denominator: they point to a liturgical gathering. Any and all of the means of deception that Paul enumerates in 2 Thessalonians 2, 2 would most likely have figured only in such a gathering: an oracular utterance or personal communication of an inspired character (a "revelation" of apocalyptic character; cf. *apokalypsis,* 1 Corinthians 14, 26 ff.), a sermon preached, a letter (originally or interpretatively Pauline) read to the community. Our inference is that someone seems to have put forth at a liturgical gathering a view of the Lord's coming that did not accord with Paul's catechesis. We should also recall that the early liturgical functions were strikingly "charismatic" and that it would accordingly be quite likely that whatever means of deception were employed were presented under "spiritual auspices" of some kind. Even if the authority of the Apostle had been invoked, as Paul seems to think it was, it would have been invoked in a charismatic context, that is, not simply as a humanly authentic communication, but as a spiritually authentic communication.

Not only at the outset of his admonition (2, 2), but again at its close (with a double inclusion, 2, 15), Paul suggests that a pseudo-apostolic communication—and for Paul that would mean a pseudo-charismatic communication—was the proximate occasion for the confusion in the community on a key point of his preaching. He wants the Thessalonians to stand firm and hold to the traditions in which they had been schooled by his own communications, whether oral or written (2, 15). A pseudo-charismatic utterance would account not only for Paul's opening and closing remarks in this chapter but also for the way in which he characterizes the disturbance created. He speaks of the Thessalonians' being "shaken from their wits" (2, 1). Previously (1 Thessalonians 1, 9), Paul had indicated that the community was composed of converts from paganism. We know from what archaeological evidence we have that the predominant pagan religion in that region was Dionysiac worship, a form of worship frequently characterized by ecstatic seizure and loss of one's wits. It seems reasonable to assume that Paul was dealing with some pseudo-charismatic outburst of a pagan stamp, masking itself in good faith or bad—Paul himself does not seem to pronounce on this—as revelation concerning the Day of the Lord (2, 2). Perhaps the *ataktoi* ("disorderly, unruly ones," not simply "idle ones") spoken of in the first letter and mentioned again in 2 Thessalonians 3 were at the source of the trouble.

It seems to be generally agreed that Paul is attempting in 2 Thessalonians 2 to restore the community to equilibrium. But consensus on this point soon divides into quite divergent views on a number of other key features. Some interpreters, like Frame, see in the passage an attempt to reassure the Thessalonians of salvation. Others, like von Dobschütz and Rigaux, find Paul largely concerned to give reasons why the Day of the Lord is not present or imminent as the Thessalonians wrongly imagine. The former approach stresses Paul's pastoral concern; the latter, his theological speculation.

Almost all commentators regard the mysterious figure, the *katechon/katechōn* of 2 Thessalonians 2, 6–7 (appearing successively in the neuter [*-on*] and masculine [*-ōn*] genders) as a "restrainer" that holds off the coming of the antichrist (which, in turn, must precede the coming of Christ on the Day of the Lord) or that directly deters the coming of Christ himself. This "restrainer" is usually identified either as the Roman Empire (and Emperor), or as the apostolic preaching (and Paul himself), or as some mythological figure which binds Satan. It is almost always interpreted as a force neutral in character or benign so far as the Thessalonians are concerned, an element that defers the dread events of the end-time. The interpretation of the passage is further complicated by the fact that the text is always considered to end with 2 Thessalonians 2, 12, whereas we have already seen that it is in verse 15 that Paul concludes his request.

Even a summary discussion of the bewildering variety of

opinions that figure in the interpretation of this chapter would take us beyond the scope of this book. Since a detailed defense of our position is available in English elsewhere, we can content ourselves here with giving solely our own views concerning the interpretation of this text and with drawing some conclusions for understanding Paul's pastoral and doctrinal solution to the problem at Thessalonica. The interpretation differs on a number of key, interrelated points from those given elsewhere, and to some extent these differences are reflected in the translation. The most notable difference both in interpretation and in translation is that the "restrainer" does not appear at all. One will find the term *katechon/-ōn* translated as "Seizing Power" (neuter, v. 6), and "Seizer" (masculine, v. 7). This figure will be found interpreted as referring to a force hostile to the Thessalonians, a pseudo-charismatic, demonic force theologically allied with the archetypal antigod and pseudo-prophetic figure, the Man of Rebellion, but distinguished from that alien figure to come as something that is already present within the community but will be purged from it. Accordingly, a further key difference may be found in the translation of verse 7b. Our translation reads as follows:

2, 1a We implore you, brothers,

    1b   with regard to the Coming of our Lord Jesus Christ

    1c   and our being gathered together to [meet] him

    2a not suddenly to be shaken from your wits

        or let yourselves be alarmed either through an oracular

                                utterance [spirit]

          or pronouncement [word]

          or letter allegedly coming from us

    2b saying in effect that the Day of the Lord has arrived.

    3a Let no one deceive you in any way!

    3b For, unless the great disbelief comes first

    3c   and there be manifested the Rebellious One [the Man of

                                  Rebellion]

          the Doomed One [the Son of Destruction]

    4a   the one opposing himself to and

          exalting himself against every-

          thing called divine or holy

4b   so as to seat himself in God's sanctuary
            passing himself off as divine——
5   Do you not recall that when I was yet with you
            I explained these things to you?
6a   And now you know by experience the Seizing Power
6b   for his being manifested at his own [proper] time.
7a   For the Mystery of Rebellion is already at work.
7b   But the Seizer [is to be, is to seize] for the present
7c   until he is ousted.
8a   And then will the Rebel be "manifested," [the one]
8b   whom the Lord Jesus will destroy
                    with the spirit [breath] from his mouth
8c   and will completely inactivate
                    by the sudden splendor of his own Coming;
9a   whose "Coming" relies on [is according to] the driving
                                                    force of Satan
9b   in every show of power
                and in signs and fake prodigies
10a   and in every distorted deceit
10b   for those who are perishing
10c   because they did not receive the love of truth
10d   so that they would be saved.
11a   And this is why God sends them the driving force of deception
11b   so that they believe the lie:
12a   that all who will not have believed the truth
12b   but who have delighted in wrongdoing may be judged.
13a   But we must give thanks to God at all times concerning you,
13b   brothers loved by the Lord,
13c   seeing that God has chosen you from the beginning
13d   for salvation by [the] sanctification of [the] Spirit
                and by faith in [the] truth [or: faith from the truth]
14a   to which [end] he has also called you through our gospel
14b   to possess the glory of our Lord Jesus Christ
                [or: to be the glorious possession of our Lord Jesus Christ].
15   In a word, brothers, stand firm
            and hold fast to the teachings
                in which you have been schooled
                    whether orally [through word]
                    or through our letter[s].
16   May our Lord Jesus Christ himself
        and God our Father,
            having loved us
            and having given us eternal consolation and sound hope by
                                                        [his] grace,
17   console your hearts
                and strengthen [them] in [your] every sound work and
                                                            word.

EXPLANATION OF THE CENTRAL CHAPTER:
A THREAT TO FAITH (2, 1–17)

Paul earnestly exhorts the Thessalonians not to be thrown off balance by false teaching. What is in danger is a point of faith, Paul's teaching on the parousia. They wrongly assume that the Lord's actual arrival and their being gathered to meet him is taking place or is surely imminent. Their confusion may well involve conceiving the parousia as an event imminent in clock-and-calendar time. Be that as it may, what is in danger is their fidelity to Paul's teaching on the eschaton (the final stage of salvation history), specifically, his teaching with regard to the Lord's coming to achieve it fully by gathering the faithful. As we mentioned earlier, the circumstance giving rise to the trouble was probably a liturgical assembly in which charismatic utterances of a heterodox scope occurred. Whatever may have been the precise character of these utterances, Paul shows himself concerned to rule out deception in any form (v. 3a).

In addressing himself to the problem at Thessalonica, Paul neither affirms nor denies that the Day of the Lord is present or imminent. Even if he has in mind as the conclusion to the condition subsequently given in verses 3b–4 "the Day of the Lord will not have come," he would not understand that coming as the confused Thessalonians probably construed it. The phraseology of verse 2 and the tenor of the whole opening warning sufficiently indicate that he dissociates himself from the sources of misinformation and disapproves of the view of the parousia as held at Thessalonica, where people have "lost their head" on the topic. Judging from the way Paul speaks of the parousia or Day of the Lord elsewhere, namely, as a day of judgment or salvation, not as a date on the calendar of human reckoning, he would not here try to correct the Thessalonian's misconception by pointing to a date other than that which they conjectured. Thus it is improbable that he is about to say simply: "The Day of the Lord is not present or imminent as you wrongly think, but will come when the following temporal signposts have appeared."

What is more, Paul is expressly concerned with the present problem at Thessalonica. If he goes on to speak of future events, it will be not to speculate on the actual time of the parousia but to put the present situation in its proper perspective. We have already seen from 1 Thessalonians (especially 1 Thessalonians 5) that Paul is not concerned with determining the date and hour of the Day of the Lord but with seeing to it that the present state of his converts is one of readiness. The future event is called to mind in order to clarify a man's present position and impart to his life the proper direction. The whole life of faith is determined by the climactic event of the Lord's coming, which Paul sees as precisely that event which renders various trials in the life of faith meaningful. Thus, throughout 1 Thessalonians he has sounded the note of the final consummation in discussing past and present trials to the faith, and in 2 Thessalonians 1 he has situated in the context of the ultimate judgment of God his thanksgiving for the Thessalonians' present endurance of trials from without.

Lastly, we have seen from passages such as 1 Thessalonians 4, 1–8. 9–12 that Paul presents his admonitions in the light of what he has already said and what he expects his converts to know on the basis of their Christian experience. When he can presume a healthy faith on the part of the community as a whole (as 2 Thessalonians 1 and 2, 13 ff. show is the case here), he can make himself clear by *alluding* to the particular abuse that he wants remedied. He does not legislate a solution but prefers that his converts recognize the nature of the situation and therefore the conduct expected of them.

These considerations concerning Paul's way of presenting the Day of the Lord, his viewing the present in the light of the future, and his attempt to bring his converts to recognize the problem and its solution from what they are already expected to know, directly contribute to our understanding of Paul's exhortation in 2 Thessalonians 2.

The summary warning against deception in any form (v. 3a) is followed by an incomplete, compound conditional clause indicating the reasons for not being deceived. These reasons are simply the known conditions for the Lord's coming, conditions known from Paul's catechesis, as he points out somewhat abruptly in verse 5. Now, what Paul had explained to the Thessalonians could not have been precisely "sign posts" of the Lord's coming in the sense of indications for calculating the date or reckoning it in some general way. For he and the other New Testament writers never concern themselves with temporal indications as such in regard to a coming which they affirm is sudden and unpredictable. Even the sign of the fig tree in Mark 13, 28 f. and parallels is a parable of growth rather than a temporal indication of the zero-hour. The scope of the condition in 2 Thessalonians 2, 3b–4a must be explained accordingly. The events depicted in the conditional clause are indeed events that must precede the day of judgment and salvation, but precisely as "conditions" rather than as temporal "signs" of the Lord's coming to requite and reward. Unless there is a manifestation of antifaith, the coming of the Lord as the rewarder of the faithful and the judge of disbelievers cannot occur. For that coming, as 2 Thessalonians 1 has already recalled to mind, will be precisely the climax of a life of faith or disbelief by which men will have been proved worthy of reward or of adverse retribution.

The two conditions of which Paul speaks are complementary. The "great disbelief" (*apostasia*) is a revolt against God that will entail a separation of the wicked from the faithful, a clearer "drawing of lines" between progressively widening moral and doctrinal opposites. It probably refers to the climactic point of something already under way in the apocalyptic view of things. Paul's attention focuses, however, on the second part of the condition, the manifestation of the Man of Rebellion, the one doomed to destruction for self-exaltation at God's expense. This figure is a Pauline construct based on the image of the antigod in Daniel 11, 36. Whether the Man of Rebellion is a collective figure or an individual is beside the point; he is a figure representative of active hostility to God himself. The Rebel is depicted not so much as a persecutor, much less a

36

political figure, but as one who would put himself as judge or teacher in God's stead. If we look ahead to verses 8–10, where Paul refers once more to the manifestation of the Rebel and speaks of his antiparousia, we find that he is characterized as a false prophet or as a parody of an apostle. In verses 3b–4b, Paul simply recalls the conditions for the Lord's coming, the manifestation of antifaith and the figure which represents antifaith: self-assertion in the face of God by an attempt to appropriate what belongs to God alone. Whether or not the sanctuary in verse 4b represents the Church is difficult to determine. If so, the Church is represented not so much as a terrestrial place but as a divine possession which no one but God should dare to appropriate. Whether or not the antigod figure will succeed in his attempt seems to be irrelevant; it is the attempt itself with which Paul is concerned, an attempt that is described so as to characterize the Man of Rebellion as the ultimate antifaith figure.

Paul cuts himself short. Without going on to speak of the actual advent of the Lord as savior and judge, Paul has apparently achieved what he intends to do at this stage of his exhortation. As verse 5 indicates, he supposes that the Thessalonians will recall these conditions and their import from his previous instruction at the time he had converted them (the only face-to-face contact he has had prior to the writing of 2 Thessalonians). Having recalled the futuristic catechesis that gave the Thessalonian Christians the framework for understanding their whole life in faith, Paul can now turn to the present situation in the hope that it will be recognized for what it is in the perspective of his basic catechesis. "And now" (v. 6a) looks both to the present situation and to the precise point that Paul wants to make. He says that they know the *katechon*. As in most of the other instances where Paul uses the term "know," experiential knowledge is in question, not directly speculative knowledge by which the figure may be identified. The knowledge they have of this power (neut.) is ordered to the manifestation of another figure (masc.), the Man of Rebellion, at his own proper time

—whenever that may be. Paul is not concerned with the date of the latter's appearance. He is concerned to relate the object of the Thessalonians' present experience to the antifaith figure to come, and to relate their present experience to a coming manifestation in due time. The connection between these two points (that is, between a and b of verse 6) is then made clear by verse 7a. The Mystery of Rebellion, the antifaith process of deception which is satanic in inspiration (cf. vv. 9–10 and v. 11, where "driving force," *energeia,* reflects the verb "is at work," *energeitai* of v. 7a) is already under way. The *katechon* is thus best taken as a force hostile to the faith and allied to the Man of Rebellion.

We may pause here to ask how Paul expected his enigmatic reference to the *katechon* to be understood and why he used this precise term, which has no clear parallel. The *katechon* was not one of those things that Paul said he had explained to them previously. But it seems to be readily intelligible in the light of several features of Paul's exhortation thus far. First, there is the situation with which he is dealing. In a community recently converted from paganism, especially from Dionysiac worship, and given to charismatic manifestations of the spirit in prophecy, an abuse of the charismata in liturgical gatherings is quite probable. Now, the standard term for one possessed or seized by the god in Dionysiac ecstasy is *katechomenos,* and the corresponding verb in the passive is *katechesthai,* "to be seized," "possessed," "held fast." Paul, of course, is not saying that the Thessalonians are possessed; he obviously regards the community as a whole as being healthy in the faith. Nor is he interested in the phenomenon of possession as such. He is dealing, rather, with a disturbing element experienced by the community. In speaking of the *cause* of the disturbance in these circumstances, he can reasonably expect his hearers to grasp his meaning when he alludes (by the active voice of *katechō*) to an agent of pseudo-charismatic character, the "Seizing Power" which has "shaken them from their wits" (v. 2a).

38

In fact, it is difficult to see how any other interpretation of the *katechon* can stand the acid test of showing how Paul reasonably could have hoped to be understood by his audience when he used this term. An allusion to a pseudo-charismatic force of a pagan stamp seems much more likely than any other interpretation that has been proposed to date. The sense of the very word *katechō,* particularly as used by Paul, confirms the basic sense of "possession," "seizure." The term may be particularly apt for other reasons. For instance, it can connote, especially in Paul's usage, a self-interested grasping (such as in 1 Corinthians 7, 30), which would make good sense here in view of the positive association between the Seizing Power and the Man of Rebellion.

In verse 7b, Paul uses the former term in the masculine, "Seizer." The change of gender is not disturbing if one sees in the *katechon/-ōn,* a demonic power. This is easily personified or even rather easily identified with an offending member of the community. What is more, Paul is about to speak of the ousting of this figure (v. 7c), and in this connection it is more appropriate to represent the Seizer in personal terms. The grammatical construction of verse 7b (initial *monon,* "only," "but") requires that we supply not an object for the term Seizer but a verb in the imperative mood. Paul says that the Seizer "must be" or "is to seize" for the present, for the community is not yet the proved community of the elect. The progression of evil as well as good to the time of the consummation is an attested feature of New Testament apocalyptic (cf. Rev. 22, 10–12). Within the community itself, as Paul will note in 1 Corinthians 11, 19: "It is necessary that there be factions among you, so that those who are proved may become manifest." The precise point in 2 Thessalonians 2 is somewhat different, but the basic principle is much the same. In 2 Thessalonians 2, the Mystery of Rebellion is already at work. The community itself, though it is healthy as a whole, is not wholly free of trouble from within any more than it is secure from persecution from without. It is inevitable, a necessary trial to faith, that the Seizer be for the present, but Paul looks ahead to the point at which the community will be fully purified: "until he is ousted."

Paul himself does not presume to oust the offender. Perhaps he felt that it would be sufficient to threaten him with God's judgment, as he does with a far more disturbing offender or offenders in Galatians 5, 10. It is noteworthy that Paul shows special restraint in dealing with charismatics, and his restraint is somewhat paralleled by early Christian practice, as attested in the *didachê*. Then, too, the offense, while serious enough, need not have been the result of bad faith or open revolt, nor did it apparently corrupt the morals of the community. So there is no need to expect Paul on this occasion to impose a ban as he does in 1 Corinthians 5. But he does look forward to the moment of judgment. This moment has two stages, the ousting of the Seizer, whenever that will be, and the climactic moment at which the Man of Rebellion, the archetypal figure to whom he is spiritually akin, will be manifested and destroyed.

At this juncture (v. 8), Paul resorts to irony or sarcasm in describing the "manifestation" of the Rebel. His manifestation is mentioned directly in connection with his destruction by the Lord. On the one hand, this manifestation is equivalent to a pseudo-parousia (v. 9a) contrasted with the Lord's own parousia (v. 8c). This pseudo-parousia represents the maturing of a process of deception hostile to God's love shown in the truth of the gospel which is ordered to salvation (v. 10cd). On the other hand, the manifestation of the Rebel is placed in conjunction with the end of the threat to faith. For, with the counter-coming of the Lord, he will be destroyed effortlessly by the spirit, the vital power which is had only by the true Lord, Jesus (v. 8b; cf. Ps. 134 [135], 17). The awesome, sudden entry of the Lord in the Holy War, in which God delivers his people from those who threaten their existence, will completely inactivate this archetypal figure of antifaith.

Thus far, Paul has tried to restore the Thessalonians to equilibrium by warning them against deception in any form, and by

40

giving as a reason for not being deceived a partial restatement of the catechesis he had explained to them. In the perspective of this catechesis, they are to recognize that the conditions for the coming of the Lord as savior and judge are manifestations of antifaith. Their present situation is to be seen accordingly. They already know by experience a certain form of the threat to faith, namely, the demonic force which has apparently seized them to the extent of causing severe consternation on a point of Paul's teaching. This disturbing force is positively related to the archetypal figure of rebellion against God. For the process of rebellion is already under way, though its climactic stage has not been reached. The Seizer who is causing the trouble must be for the present, until he is ousted with God's purification of the community. The climactic moment of the consummation of the process of rebellion is the manifestation of the one who epitomizes it, and his destruction, in turn, will mark the end of the whole antifaith process. The coming of the Lord will mean the end of the satanic opposition which they now experience in some limited form.

In verses 11–14, Paul then restates the whole twofold process towards judgment and salvation mainly in terms of God's design. For, if his pastoral aim of restoring the Thessalonians to a stable understanding of his teaching is to succeed, he must do more than get them to see that their present confusion is part of the scheme of things about which he had instructed them. He must further ground this scheme of things in the plan of God which governs the whole process. In other words, he must enrich their theological understanding of the basic point at issue, the providence of God. On the one hand (vv. 11–12), the process of deception is ordered to judgment. Human responsibility in yielding to the spirit of deception is clearly supposed by the phraseology of verse 12. But the whole process of deception is subject to the control of God and is resolved by his judgment. It is not a power which God cannot control. On the other hand (vv. 13–14), Paul can thankfully note that the Thessalonians enjoy God's favor by the fact of their being called

41

"from the beginning," that is, from the first preaching of the gospel among them. Their destiny is not judgment but salvation. As the process towards judgment is worked out by the power of deception and by disbelief, the process towards salvation is mediated by sanctification and faith. The goal of salvation, particularized as the possession of the Lord's glory in the resurrection, is also mediated by the call as voiced through Paul's preaching (v. 14a).

On this hopeful and personal note, Paul can conclude the body of his exhortation with a positive appeal to stand firm and hold fast to the teachings in which they have been schooled by the Apostle himself (v. 15). Only one thing remains, the prayer for divine assistance without which Paul's exhortation would be sterile. The "consolation" and strengthening in the faith for which Paul hopes are predicated of the Lord Jesus Christ and, more immediately, of the Father. But the action of the two is seen as one (the verbs "console" and "strengthen" are in the singular; cf. the same perspective in 1 Thessalonians 3, 11). The prayer somewhat confirms what was previously said about Paul's concern that the Thessalonians thoroughly understand the present situation, seeing it in the light of their presumed knowledge in faith and in the light of their ultimate hope as known by the faith which Paul preached. It is in this way, together with God's ever-present encouragement and advice, given in their hearts, that they will regain their equilibrium. The text closes appropriately on the note of divine strengthening in every sound work and word. Not moral action, but renewed, applied, and enriched understanding of Paul's teaching on a point of faith now threatened is the over-all scope of the Apostle's pastoral admonition.

Reflecting on the interpretation we have offered for 2 Thessalonians 2, one can discern a number of features of Paul's pastoral approach that are relevant to the faithful today, in spite of the apocalyptic garb in which they appear in Paul's text. In effect, Paul reminds the Thessalonians that they should have expected a great test to their faith. He had warned them of this at the time he first preached to them, and now they know by experience an advance indication of the climactic representation of antifaith activity. There is no reason for them to be thrown into consternation, for they have received solid instruction in the faith and enjoy God's favor. Since Paul had already presented the Lord's coming as a triumph over the forces of disbelief, the faithful should have been prepared to recognize coming trials and to endure them without dismay—even worse trials than those they now experience. To have one's faith attacked in some form or other is to be expected, since faith accounts for the whole thrust of Christian life and its whole structure. The peril lies in becoming so alarmed as to become confused. If they can recognize the alarming factor for what it is (and it is to be recognized in the general framework of that with which it is allied), then the Thessalonians should be able to regain stability in the life of faith.

CLOSING REQUESTS AND INJUNCTIONS
(3, 1–18)

In the closing chapter of his letter, Paul first appeals for the Thessalonians' prayers for himself, that the word of the Lord may progress to its final destination as it is indeed doing among the Thessalonians. Paul's own struggles with evil men are seen as struggles among disbelievers (3, 2). But, in recalling God's fidelity in this struggle, Paul turns again immediately to their own need to be strengthened and guarded from the Evil One, and expresses his confidence that they will continue to follow his guidance. To this end he adds another prayer (v. 5), which looks to their inner direction in hastening forward into the way of God's love and the patient endurance shown by Christ. By these latter phrases Paul apparently means that they should persevere steadfastly and wholly in the love of God shown them in the truth they have received (cf. 2 Thessalonians 2, 10c. 13b ff.), and in the patient endurance in undergoing trials of

43

whatever nature in solidarity with the endurance shown by Christ himself.

Becoming more specific, Paul proceeds to give instructions on the authority of the Lord to avoid any Christian who lives an unruly life, which seems to be the equivalent of not following the tradition received from Paul (3, 6). For he goes on to contrast with such conduct the example of his own life among the Thessalonians. It is generally thought that Paul is here giving an example of industriousness expected of a Christian, or at the most that he is indicating the duty of each to work for a living. Paul's expressions, however, are closely parallel to those from the first epistle, where he distinguishes himself from false *teachers*. The disorderly people of whom Paul speaks here (vv. 6. 11) in contrast to himself (v. 7) are hardly just economic parasites. They are "busybodies" (v. 11), who do not adhere to the pattern of apostolic selflessness in the service of others. They probably expected to be supported by the community which they did not help build up.

Once more, the Apostle encourages the community as a whole in their good work (3, 13). He expects them to take gentle but firm corrective measures in segregating themselves from anyone who does not heed what Paul has written them. This exclusion does not seem to amount to formal excommunication, especially since the offender is not to be regarded as an outsider, but corrected as a brother (3, 15). The peace for which Paul hopes is the theme of his closing prayer.

CHAPTER 3

GALATIANS

Paul's epistle to the Galatians is perhaps the most important primary source for discussing Paul's conversion and apostleship. What is more, this epistle is at least a fruitful source for treating the question of his characteristic form of preaching during the early missionary journeys and a key source for determining the chronology of his life and works. In all of these areas, to be sure, Luke's Acts is another source with which we must reckon. To treat these topics more satisfactorily within the scope of this book, however, we shall defer to more appropriate contexts a fuller treatment of a number of them. Paul's conversion and apostleship as represented in his own letters and in Acts will form the first chapter of Part Two of this book. A discussion of Paul's preaching, entailing a brief comparison with some of the speeches attributed to him in Acts, will appear in the second chapter of Part Two. An over-all sketch of the chronology of Paul's life and writings has been appended as a chronological table. Nevertheless, it seems advisable even during a first reading of Galatians that we devote some attention to outstanding problems regarding the Apostle's contacts with Jerusalem, notably those apropos of the "Council" of Acts 15 and its "decrees." For we shall thus be able to grasp more readily Paul's own distinctive theological and pastoral viewpoint. We shall find him much more personally engaged than was Luke with an immediate problem which keenly affected his apostolate among the gentiles, namely, the problem posed by the "Judaizers."

GENERAL BACKGROUND: THE PROBLEM OF THE JUDAIZERS

Three interrelated points call for our attention: a sketch of Paul's relationship to the Judaizers in Galatia, the general circumstances of his preaching and writing to the Galatians, and the main sections of his forthright letter to the communities in Galatia.

What the position of the Judaizers was is difficult to determine, though the damage done by Judaizers in the churches of Galatia is the basic reason for Paul's letter to the communities there. The term "Judaizers" itself, as applied by critics to some of Paul's adversaries in communities other than those in Galatia —that at Philippi, for example—does not seem to admit simple classification except in most general terms. The one thing that does seem to be common to Judaizers was their conviction that adherence to the Mosaic law with its plethora of prescriptions was of decisive importance for salvation. Accordingly, any man who wanted to be saved had to be circumcised. For the Judaizers in Galatia there seem to have been further requirements, but we cannot easily or accurately reconstruct them from what Paul says.

Fortunately, it is not really necessary for us to reconstruct in detail the views of Paul's Judaizing adversaries in Galatia. Fundamentally, the Judaizers had disrupted the faith of the Pauline community. Paul's problem was less what the Judaizers had said than what now had to be done on his part to restore the faith of the community. He never addresses the Judaizers in his letter, and his polemic references to them are always directed to reawakening the faith of the Galatians themselves.

46

Paul sees in the teaching of the Judaizers at Galatia a submission to angelic powers that involves a multiplicity of calendar observances, and he regards the Galatians' subjection to this doctrine as a virtual regression to the paganism from which they had been converted (Galatians 4, 8–10). However, this polemic reference tells us much more about Paul's own definitive rejection of the Judaizers' doctrine, his exclusion of any "second-degree" Christianity, and his pastoral intent to make the Galatians realize the tragedy of their relapse than it can be relied on to form the basis for a theological reconstruction of the Judaizers' position. For, in his exasperation, Paul even represents the Galatians' plight at the hands of the Judaizers as succumbing to the evil eye (bewitching, 3, 1).

Perhaps the Galatians themselves had thought of the Judaizers' doctrine as being less a repudiation of the gospel than simply another (legitimate) gospel; if so, Paul leaves them no refuge in this delusion (1, 6–7). Even angelic powers cannot be invoked to alter what the Galatians have once received (1, 8), so certain and so integral is the faith which comes through God's word. The Judaizers among them seem to have gone beyond proposing a different way of salvation or a new gospel. There are indications that they had attacked Paul personally, impugning his sincerity and representing him as one who had curried men's favor (cf. Galatians 1, 10). They seem to have misrepresented his own teaching as requiring circumcision (cf. 5, 11), and were thus able more easily to sway the whole church in Galatia. Perhaps even forgeries of Paul's writings figured in their tactics. Paul seems to suspect as much when he writes the final lines of the letter in his own bold hand (6, 11).

The Apostle responds to the situation in Galatia by frontally assaulting the Galatians' presumptuous position. The letter contains no thanksgiving. Its argument is intense, heated, and precipitate, with little respite. At times, there are expressions of frustration, where Paul feels that his previous work has been in vain (3, 4; 4, 11) or where he wishes that he could change his voice, that is, use angelic speech, to break through to the Gal-

47

atians in a form of superhuman communication (4, 20). But for all his storming, his biting sarcasm, and his indignation, Paul can plead with heartfelt sincerity and tenderness (4, 12–20). In no other letter, except the closing chapters of 2 Corinthians, does Paul use the diapason of emotion and argumentation that he employs here. His whole pastoral effort among the Galatians and their own salvation is at stake.

Only a few years before, he had successfully planted the gospel in Galatia. The year was probably 50 A.D., shortly after Silas and Timothy had joined him on his second missionary journey. Paul seems to have moved into "northern" Galatia, a region in what is now central Turkey. Acts is silent about Paul's preaching in northern Galatia, though several interrelated reasons may be assigned for this. In the first place, Luke wants to show how Paul separated from Barnabas and came to head his own missionary band while continuing the work which both had begun among the people of southern Galatia (the region of Derbe, Iconium, and Lystra). Secondly, he wants to depict Paul's work as being in accord with the consensus articulated at the Council of Jerusalem (Acts 16, 4; cf. Acts 15, 22–29). Insofar as this consensus, which Luke presents as articulated in "decrees," touched people already evangelized by Paul and Barnabas, the "decrees" might be considered to extend to regions previously covered by Paul. Or they could simply be referred to in connection with Paul's contact of people previously evangelized in order to show how his resumption of missionary work after the consensus articulated at Jerusalem proved to be fully in accord with the mind of the apostles and elders there. In either case, no mention would have to be made of Paul's travels in northern Galatia. Thirdly, Luke wants to show how Paul was providentially directed to an entirely new area of apostolic activity in Macedonia, to the west. Hence, the intervening journey—from the area of southern Galatia where Paul had previously worked to that of northwestern Turkey where Paul's path is directed to Troas and Greece—is simply passed over in silence.

48

Luke's own theological concerns dictate his overpainting of a number of other key features that one must take into account as background for understanding the letter to the Galatians. More is at stake here than identifying the addressees of the letter or determining the chronology of Paul's life and writings. We must recognize that Paul and Luke, each legitimately in the light of his own theological purpose pursued independently of the other's, represent in notably different ways the apostleship and preaching of Paul. We cannot successfully try to reconcile or understand the accounts of Luke and Paul by supposing that both or even one of the two provides simply the actual data in a given instance. A certain general reconstruction of the actual course of events and of other features like Paul's conversion and his early preaching is possible, but only through discerning the theologically motivated selection and repainting of events in each author. Each gives a picture that is true to the author's legitimate intention, an understanding of the data in the light of God's salvific purpose. It would be critically naïve to take one independent account as normative for interpreting the other; likewise, it would be tendentious to pit the view of one author against the other, as if, for example, Luke were trying to correct Paul's impression of his own apostleship or his gospel. Once we can discern and respect the theological purpose of each author, we shall experience neither critical nor dogmatic embarrassment in discussing Paul's preaching and writing to the Galatians.

If Paul had first preached to the Galatians whom he addresses in this letter when he was on Mission II in 50 A.D., he seems to have contacted them a second time (implied by Galatians 4, 13, "the former time," rather than the *RSV* "at first"), that is, on Mission III some four years later, when he passed overland to Ephesus. Perhaps it was shortly after this second visit that Judaizers arrived on the scene in Galatia or began to infiltrate the community there, effectively undoing Paul's work. The writing of this letter is best placed during the earlier part of Paul's two- or three-year stay at Ephesus, about 55 A.D.

Three general parts of the letter can be distinguished, al-

49

though, as we shall see, these overlap. The *first part* (1, 1–2, 21) is mainly an apologia. Paul's gospel is not derived from men. It is an irreplaceable gospel which he received together with his apostolic commission from God through a revelation of Jesus Christ. The self-sufficiency of the Apostle's gospel is attested by Paul's argument that he was not a disciple of the apostles in Jerusalem and that he did not in any essential respect depend on authorization from those in Jerusalem. On the contrary, his gospel was accorded at Jerusalem its due recognition, necessary to further its spread and secure the solidarity of all the churches. Recalling an encounter with Peter at Antioch, Paul then presents the arguments that he had used on that occasion to show that the new bond of faith in Christ, by which alone is effected man's supernatural relationship to God (justification), leaves no room for regarding the law as the norm for Christian life. The *second part* of the letter (3, 1–5, 1) consists primarily of a doctrinal exposition of the relationship between faith and the law, showing how faith transcends the law and brings the freedom of God's sons for their inheritance according to the promised spirit. Building on this doctrinal exposition, the more specifically hortatory *third part* of the letter (5, 1–6, 18) appeals for an exercise of freedom in the spirit which is not license but freedom for a life of service in love. It concludes (6, 11 ff.) with a note in Paul's own hand admonishing the Galatians of the marks of the one whose concern for them is genuine by being not a boast in their personal allegiance to himself, but a boast in the cross of Christ.

OPENING REMARKS: DECLARATION OF APOSTLESHIP (1, 1–5)

In Galatians 1, 1–5, Paul forthrightly presents himself as a plenipotentiary of Jesus Christ and God the Father, though he does not stand alone (1, 2a). This address in the circular letter to the Galatian churches is followed by a greeting (1, 3) which comes from the divine persons who commissioned him. This greeting sounds a kind of keynote for the letter, speaking of the sacrifice of Christ in apocalyptic terms of our deliverance from "the present evil age." By this expression, Paul does not mean something like "these calamitous times." He is referring to a sublevel of human existence which is opposed to the "coming age" of messianic fulfillment, that of justification leading to final salvation in the resurrection. In Jewish thought the age to come lay simply in the future and/or on a heavenly plane. Its realization, which could be conceived at times independently of the hope in one or more messiahs, was not to be found in present human experience. For Paul, however, the age to come, which is the apocalyptic correlative of the present evil age within which God's deliverance is not at work, is already present in a sense. Although its full consummation lies in the resurrection, the age to come is inchoatively realized through the deliverance effected on the cross and made available to men through faith in the risen Christ. Since the transition from the "present evil age" to the "age to come" is effected by faith, not on condition of racial or national affiliation, and since the one on whom this faith centers is in a risen state, a form of human existence no longer tied to race or nation as defined by the flesh as we know it, the two ages can "coexist" temporally. They are specifically distinguished not in terms of clock-and-calendar time but in terms of the new existence of Christ made possible and effective through faith. All of this is not said in these opening lines, but it is implied. The reference in this greeting to the sacrificial death of Christ, whose resurrection is connoted by referring to him as "Lord," and the apocalyptic expression "to deliver us from the present evil age," also provide the necessary framework for understanding much of what Paul says subsequently.

Paul views the whole of Christian life in cosmic but essentially religious and not cosmological dimensions. While the present evil age continues, the age to come has already been opened to those who believe in Christ, the risen Lord. Once they enter this new age, which they do by faith, men have entered upon a new plane of existence which is eschatological, that is, definitive and final. No new or superior order is possible short of the resurrection, which marks the culmination of Christian life on the same eschatological plane. In turn, this eschatological plane is dominated by the perspective of God's salvific will. The self-giving of Christ to deliver us is "according to the will of God our Father." In saying this (v. 5) and in adding the brief doxology, Paul places the whole redemptive order in Christ in its fully theological perspective. His understanding of the final state of things, the eschaton, is not determined by speculation on the "aeons," as Schoeps would have it, but by his understanding in faith of the paternal will of the Godhead.

I. PAUL'S APOLOGIA (1, 6—2, 21)

A. *Paul's Gospel as God's Doing (1, 6—2, 10)*

Paul plunges into his apologia with a *reproof for disloyalty* (1, 6–9) on the part of the Galatians. He bases his reproof on the fact that his gospel is the only gospel. That is, the substance of his preaching is none other than the one message of salvation. As he does elsewhere, the Apostle perceives in the gospel the efficacious word of God, a power for salvation which, though transmitted through men like himself, has an efficacy and integrity which transcends the powers of the human instrument. The word of truth is not weak in itself, and cannot simply prove insufficient to the needs of those who have received it. There must be some other reason which accounts for its loss. Paul finds it hard to believe that the failing would so soon have been the fault of the Galatians left to themselves. He therefore suspects (probably also on the basis of information brought to him at Ephesus from some travelers from Galatia) that there are men alien to the communities that he knew who are trying to change their faith. He attributes to these men the attempt to overturn the gospel of Christ. But, again, the gospel has its own holy strength. Neither Paul himself nor an angel from heaven is to be anything but accursed for preaching a gospel other than what he preached to them originally. No power whatsoever can pretend to alter the gospel of Christ.

The basis for this reproof serves (1, 10) to anticipate a charge apparently leveled against the Apostle by the Judaizers. He does not seek to acquire the Galatians for himself, to persuade men to join his own movement. He is ready to be anathema for the sake of the integrity of the gospel. If he were "still" pleasing men—not that as an Apostle he ever did devote himself to winning the hearts of others for his own personal gratification, but so the charge goes—he would not be the slave of Christ, the one totally devoted to the service of preaching the messianic gospel.

The uniqueness of that one gospel, its authenticity and recognized integrity, form the subject of the following passages in his apologia (1, 11–2, 10). Paul proceeds in four stages. In the *first stage* (1, 11–17), he recounts his conversion in terms of an inaugural prophetic experience. Like the prophetic Servant of Isaiah 49, 1 (and perhaps like the unwilling prophet, Jeremiah, Jeremiah 1, 5), he was called by God. He had not merited this grace, as he would have the Galatians known by recalling how he had excelled as a persecutor. The gospel had been given him through a revelation whose source and especially whose content was Jesus Christ. By this inaugural experience of Jesus Christ he was invested as an Apostle with the special (though obviously not exclusive) task of preaching the gospel to the gentiles. Since this experience was a divine communication and investiture, he did not seek the mediation of human authorities ("flesh and blood") but immediately went off to "Arabia," the Nabataean Kingdom which lay east of the Jordan, to the south of Damascus. He mentions that he returned to Damascus, the area of his conversion, but pointedly omits referring to the mother church at Jerusalem.

Acts says nothing of this trip to the Nabataean Kingdom and seems to telescope the two stays in Damascus which Paul implies (Acts 9, 19–25). Luke's reason for this is probably simple enough. Acts is progressively oriented westward. Jerusalem, Samaria, and the coastal plain, Antioch and Asia Minor, Greece, and finally Rome, the center of the gentile world, progressively occupy Luke's attention. Jerusalem remains a point of return on the eastern circumference of ever-widening circles to the north and west, until at last Paul is taken as a prisoner to Rome, where he preaches unhindered. Besides, Luke is more concerned to show how Paul was brought into contact with the apostolic community through the instrumentality of Barnabas—not to play down the importance of Paul's conversion experience or the integrity of his gospel, but to situate him more clearly in the mainstream of the Church's missionary effort as a whole. For Luke, Paul does not enter the scene like some comet simply to follow his own orbit in a blaze of glory; he figures as a key personage in the total missionary effort of the one, catholic, and apostolic Church whose cradle was in Jerusalem. Paul, on the other hand, must make a complementary point equally clear. He is not a disciple of the Jerusalem community or of another apostle. What is more, Paul's concept of the gospel and of his own apostleship is even more markedly personal and prophetic than that which one will find in Acts, where the Twelve, viewed more symbolically and institutionally, as the new Israel (historically continuous with those chosen by the Savior when among men), are in a class by themselves.

The *second stage* of Paul's apologia (1, 18–20) notes contact with Peter (identified by his name in Aramaic form, Cephas), but after a period of three years. Presumably this interval is to be counted from the time of Paul's inaugural experience, which is the logical point of reference for this whole series of "alibis" by which he indicates his apostolic independence from the Jerusalem community. Paul admits that he not only went "to visit" Cephas *(RSV),* but that he went "to get information from" *('istorēsai)* Cephas. The acquisition of various data, including even formulations of the kerygma or *(didachē)* material like eucharistic formulas and other words ascribed to the Lord,

54

would not conflict with Paul's understanding of his reception of the gospel in a kind of mystical experience unique in character and scope. What he would get from Peter, even material of the nature just indicated, would not "add" to his gospel, though it would indeed help him either in formulating his own preaching, as, for example, in the passage beginning with 1 Corinthians 15, 3, or in guiding the liturgical life of the communities he would found (cf. 1 Corinthians 11, 23 ff.). Even this visit to acquire information from Peter was of short duration, about two weeks. By adding this detail, Paul feels that he can make it quite clear that he was not a disciple of Peter; formal instruction of a disciple would have taken much longer. Paul goes on to deny contact with any of the other apostles except James, the brother of the Lord—a figure best identified with the James of 1 Corinthians 15, 7 and Acts 15, 13 ff., sometimes referred to by commentators as the "Bishop of Jerusalem." (Though an "apostle" in the sense that he, too, had seen the risen Lord and received authority from him, this James was not one of the Twelve.) Paul's gospel cannot be regarded as derived from human instruction, though it should be equally obvious from the contacts indicated that it was not at variance with the teaching of the other apostles.

Paul is quite emphatic, to the point of taking an oath, that this is the sum and substance of his first or first major contact with the church in Jerusalem after his investiture in the apostolate with a revelation of Jesus Christ. Acts does not seem to mention this visit at all, unless it perhaps again telescopes events in conjunction with Paul's conversion when it refers to his complementary vision in the temple on a return to Jerusalem (cf. Acts 22, 17). The year would seem to be 39 A.D.

In the *third stage* of Paul's apologia (1, 21–24), we find reference to his activity in Syria and Cilicia, probably in conjunction with a stay at Antioch (cf. Acts 11, 25 ff.). But Paul's point is that he was not even personally known in the churches of Judaea. He was known only by report as a former persecutor who now preached the faith he had tried to destroy. He was not

55

at odds with the churches in Judaea, but his mission lay elsewhere in accord with his apostolic call. Here again there is an apparent discrepancy with data in Acts, but one that can be resolved by a judicious consideration of the respective points to be made by Paul and Luke. Acts speaks of a visit of Paul in the company of Barnabas to bring famine relief to the Jerusalem church. This is mentioned in two different places in Acts (Acts 11, 30; 12, 25), though it is probably the same visit. In Acts 11, 30, Luke rounds out the story of the response of the church at Antioch to the prophetic prediction of the famine in Judaea and anticipates mention of the visit noted again in Acts 12, 25 (reading *eis,* "to" rather than, as in the *RSV, ek,* "from") when the visit actually took place. This would have been about 44–46 A.D., when the apostles had been dispersed from Jerusalem by the persecution of Herod Agrippa I. For Luke, a form of almsgiving like famine relief for Jerusalem was an important detail in showing the ties of the new church in Antioch to the mother church—and Paul's own role in expressing this charitable concern—prior to the Council of Jerusalem. For Paul, the famine visit would not require special mention, especially if in the previous five years he had not been known in the growing churches of Judaea. Paul mentions here only what was the case during the time he spent in Syria and Cilicia, that is, prior to the time at which Luke would place both the famine visit and what is known of Paul's first missionary journey, which was not in the area of Syria and Cilicia.

The *fourth stage* of Paul's apologia (2, 1–10) may be aligned with the Council of Jerusalem, though, as we shall see, not precisely with the Council as Luke represents it in Acts 15. Paul judges this to be the second (important) visit to Jerusalem which he made in the course of fourteen years. Again, the point of reference for the fourteen years is the origin of his apostleship. If this visit to Jerusalem corresponds in substance to participation in the Council in about the year 49 A.D., we can thus reckon Paul's conversion as occurring about the year 36 A.D. Paul makes it clear that on this occasion he was not *summoned* to

Jerusalem. He went up as the result of a vision, though he went in the company of Barnabas and took along Titus, which probably shows that the visit had a more formal character than the previous visit to seek information from Peter. The purpose of this visit was not to seek authorization for his gospel, but recognition of its legitimacy. Had Paul not received this recognition, which, moreover, he obtained privately—for there was no need for a public defense—his work might have been in vain. That is, it might have been considered to be at odds with that of the Church as a whole and might have led to schism. One can hardly suppose that Paul had wavered in his own conviction and had sought the reassurance of the Jerusalem community. The whole scope and tenor of his apologia militates against such a conjecture. Rather, Paul evinces his solicitude for the unity of the Church in common concerns like care for the poor and in furtherance of the one apostolate under God which was working out in different missions (1, 7–8).

Paul seems to feel a certain embarrassment, however, in recalling this meeting. He makes it clear that circumcision was not required, for even Titus, a Greek who was with him, was not to be circumcised. The next verses hint that he was none the less circumcised, but for other considerations. Apparently, a Pharisaic pressure group within the Church, whom Paul labels false brethren because they effectively repudiated the freedom from the law which had been realized in Christ, had disturbed the harmony of the meeting. Paul insists that he did not yield to them even for a moment, at least not by way of submission. He probably did yield to counsel from "those of repute" whom he had seen privately. When he mentions the latter a second time (2, 6), it is with perceptible irritation. Even in this case, he would have the Galatians know that human respect was not the motive for his action, but consideration for God's judgment, and he insists that their counsel really added nothing. In saying that they really added nothing to *him* ("me," 2, 6), Paul seems to be referring not only to his gospel but, more directly, to his apostolic integrity as one who was already fully authorized to do as he had been doing. The Apostle further affirms that the key decision of those of repute was to recognize how Paul's gospel was complementary to Peter's under the direction of the one God. Paul's distinctive grace was recognized and sealed openly with the sign of communion in the one faith (the *RSV* "fellowship" smacks too much of polite good will; the Greek *koinōnia,* "communion," more richly suggests oneness in sharing a common possession like faith).

The common bond was to be further attested by a work of charity, concern for the poor. This probably refers especially to contributions for the impoverished mother church in Jerusalem. But the Greek of Galatians 2, 10 is quite vague. It may mean that a particular collection was envisaged—either one which Paul had already made or one that he had set himself to gather together or one he had earnestly begun to plan. Or it may mean simply that there was agreement in principle concerning mutual assistance.

Luke's picture of the Council of Jerusalem agrees on the essential point, that circumcision was not required of gentile converts. Key figures like Cephas and James are also presented. The principle for recognizing the integrity of Paul's apostolate is similar. For it is in the spirit (Acts 15, 8. 28) that the work of the spirit (cf. Acts 13, 1–4. 9. 52) is recognized. This is roughly the Lucan equivalent of Paul's view that God was seen to be at work in different apostles and apostolates.

In other respects, there are notable differences, accounted for especially by Luke's composition of this pivotal scene in Acts. Titus does not appear at all in Acts, much less at this juncture, where he was a controversial figure. Luke does not label the agitators "false brethren" and seems to avoid placing them within the deliberations of the "Council" proper (cp. Acts 15, 1–5). Luke wants to represent in appropriately irenic tones the basic consensus which was reached at Jerusalem. This consensus was a further articulation of the principle already established by Peter in the conversion of the gentile, the centurion Cornelius (Acts 10, 1–11, 18). It would be necessary for Luke to show the continuity between the work of Peter and Paul, especially in view of the fact that Paul would occupy the center of the stage throughout the rest of Acts. The dominant theme of Acts is how the word of God went forth from Jerusalem, the heart of the Jewish world, to the heart of the gentile world through the action of the Holy Spirit and the instrumentality of men chosen by God to be his witnesses. In accordance with this theme and with his theological thesis of the one, catholic, apostolic Church, Luke has forged a strong link between the "Petrine" and "Pauline" sections of Acts by composing a scene dealing somewhat idealistically with the Council of Jerusalem.

Luke's additions and alterations to the scene are even more striking than his omissions of disturbing features. As he has done elsewhere (for example, in providing a composite picture of several visits to Nazareth by Jesus as though they formed a single visit, Luke 4, 16–30), Luke has gathered in one place events that actually occurred over a considerable period of time. Without entering into discussion that would lead us too far afield, we can note the following changes which help us to see how Luke and Paul can refer to the same episode but present it so differently. Luke has considerably reworked the scene. At least to some extent (v. 10), the speech of a certain Symeon, perhaps the successor of James as Bishop of Jerusalem (Eusebius, *Ecclesiastical History,* III, 11. 22, 32. 35; IV, 5. 22), has been ascribed to Peter (Acts 15, 14. 7). Peter was also known as "Simon," but "Simon" is not really the same as "Symeon"—though Luke seems to intend us to take the speech attributed to Symeon as a speech of "Simon" Peter. Luke probably did not want to invent a speech if he had one or two statements that could reasonably be thought to represent Peter's position as Luke understood it, so he placed one or more elements from "Symeon's" speech in the mouth of (Simon) Peter.

What is more, Luke has attributed to James, the representative of the Jewish-Christian group (and one who probably argued from the scriptures in Hebrew or in an Aramaic translation), an argument based on the LXX where the LXX as *contrasted* with the Hebrew is essential to the point of the argument. As historical fact, especially concerning a meeting in Jerusalem attended by "apostles and elders," it is most unlikely that James used the Greek text of the Bible to make his point where the Greek differs from the Hebrew. Luke's hand is in evidence here. In turn, the new context (complementary arguments) which Luke creates modifies the rather apodictic "I judge (Acts 15, 19) of James' speech. James' apodictic "I judge" does not seem to fit well with his giving a complementary argument. Nor does it fit well with this specific occasion, where the question is rather the need for circumcision on the part of gentile converts. James' "I judge," which is echoed in the "decree" accepted by all (Acts 15, 19–20. 23–29), does not really speak to the specific problem here. James' "judgment," then, was more likely given on a later occasion, when the question itself was different (not circumcision but common procedures in mixed communities), and when his was the deciding voice (that is, when Peter and other apostles were not present). Such an occasion is suggested also by the fact that Paul seems to find out about items in James' decision when he returns to Jerusalem some ten years later, at the end of Mission III (Acts 21, 17–26).

In other words, Luke has transposed to the "Council" from the ecclesiastical politics of a later period a decision made by James alone. Luke has made use of this "decision" to make his own point, namely, that the Council represented an explicit consensus that the mission to the gentiles was quite compatible with the existence of mixed communities and with respect for the sensitivities of Jewish Christians, but that circumcision was not required. By prefacing James' "I judge" with an argument from the LXX and a reference to a prior opinion (one attributed to Peter), Luke has muted the apodictic force of James' decision.

Luke has also provided a new context for the "decree"—a context of theological consensus in recognition of the Spirit's work among the gentiles, rather than a context of ecclesiastical politics under other circumstances. The "decree" itself has been transposed to this situation. It looks to abstention from things sacrificed to idols, from the eating of blood or of things strangled, and from marriage within forbidden degrees (*porneia*; not the *RSV* "unchastity"). In its present context, the decree appears in a somewhat new and more irenic light. It represents positive consideration for Jewish Christians without any compromise whatsoever on the score of the main question, the matter of circumcision. In another context, it would not imply a compromise on the question of circumcision, but it might look like an ecclesiastico-political ploy to establish the dominance of Jewish Christians in mixed communities. In the context that Luke has given the decree, it serves rather to spell out a policy of practical consideration for the sensitivities of what would become a minority group.

Lastly, Luke has represented Paul and Barnabas as implementing the decrees of the Council not only at Antioch but in the area previously covered on Mission I (Acts 15, 36–16, 5; cp. 13, 18–14, 23). To some extent, as we have seen in 1 Thessalonians 4, 1–8, Paul did seem to maintain certain Jewish practices even beyond the area covered in Mission I. The veiling of women is another such practice (1 Corinthians 11, 2–16). Thus Luke would have had some grounds for representing Paul's conformity to views characteristic of the Jerusalem church (especially in the case of marriage regulations, namely, regarding degrees of kinship). But he probably has greatly exaggerated factual conformity for his own overriding theological ends in presenting the work of Paul as being fully in accord with the faith and sensitivity of the Jerusalem church. From the point of view proper to the inspired author, this procedure is legitimate. Discerning this point of view and its implementations frees us from accepting hopeless contradictions. In particular, it enables us to see that, whether Paul is writing the Galatians in the northern or even in the southern area of "Galatia," the practices that he may have expected his converts to adopt are not to be judged by what we ourselves read

61

on the surface of the text in Acts. In following the subsequent argument of Galatians, therefore, we must purge from our imagination the thought that Paul had committed himself or the Galatians to the "decrees of the Council of Jerusalem." The only points of accord—and these are central—are that circumcision was not required of gentile converts and that Paul's gospel as it had been preached thus far needed no further authorization or additions, but was recognized in the spirit as being fully in accord with the will of God.

B. *The Gospel Enunciated in an Altercation with Peter at Antioch (2, 11–21)*

In the second part of his apologia (2, 11–21), Paul speaks of an altercation at Antioch. Luke is silent on this, for many of the same reasons he had in presenting the Council in an irenic light. In turn, the occasion for the altercation at Antioch as Paul presents it confirms the view that the Council had not settled by any decree the dietary practices of mixed communities, but had settled only the question of the need for circumcision.

Peter's vacillation in his conduct with the gentile community at Antioch, segregating himself from the gentiles' meals when some of those from James' circle arrived, nevertheless threatened to compromise an established principle. Paul represents Peter's example as having virtually the force of law ("you compel," *anagkazeis,* 2, 14b). Paul's position on this occasion, which (as we may presume from his forthright tone) proved to be successful, directly bears on the whole subsequent argumentation of Galatians. Indeed, it has come to be recognized as a kind of epitome of his gospel, or at least of his teaching on the central point of justification in Christ. The argument in 2, 14–21 has three principal stages (2, 14; 2, 15–17; 2, 18–21).

Paul begins with an argument *ad hominem* (2, 14), which is valid and telling in view of the force of Peter's inconsistent

62

example. Paul then ironically takes the "Jewish-Christian view-point" (2, 15) and proceeds to give a *reductio ad absurdum* (2, 15–17). There can be nothing wrong with living the way they have been living—as unsegregated Jewish Christians. For, if converted Jews like themselves, who were not sinners by definition, like the gentiles (a certain irony is perceptible here) had become sinners by this form of conduct as Christians (as Peter's segregation implies), then they would be such only because of Christ, on whom they rely in a new bond, that of faith. Thus Christ would be the cause of sin in the community, not really the sole basis for justification, as they had believed. But this is totally absurd! In other words, Jewish Christians like themselves had believed in Christ in order to be justified precisely on the principle of a bond of faith in Christ, which lay beyond the reach of mere human effort, and not on the principle of what man himself does according to a set of external norms, even those given by God. *A fortiori,* Paul could have added, one who is not a Jew to begin with has no need to go back to an insufficient principle. But he keeps his focus on the converted Jew. Jewish Christians themselves were in a privileged position to begin with (as those who had God's law and were not totally alienated from him, that is, were not "sinners" like the gentiles). Thus, if these privileged "non-sinners" were to be judged sinners because they ate with the gentile members of the community in Christ, then the instrument of this sinfulness would be the one who had brought them together in the faith. Christ himself would be the radical cause or occasion of sin. This would obviously contradict the whole supposition of justification in Christ. Accordingly, there can be no sin in the practice of common meals, a sign of that oneness in faith which is the keystone of Christian life for any Christian whomsoever.

Paul then takes the offensive in the third stage (2, 18–21). He points out in several ways where sin *really* lies. In compromising the definitive break with the order which has died in Christ, in whose death the Christian himself dies to live a new life in faith, one proves himself a transgressor. Paul uses the gnomic "I" in this passage, referring to the Christian, not simply to Paul as an individual. But, even so, it puzzles us to read "If *I* build up again what *I* tore down." By "tearing down," Paul refers to the dissociation from the law effected in Christ. Since the Christian is totally identified with Christ, Paul can speak of the Christian himself as the one who has "torn down" the bridge linking him to the law. If one tries to restore what he has demolished through Christ, then he is a transgressor. How so? The law itself is conceived as having a role in achieving this demolition. Through law itself, ironically conceived as Christ's executioner (v. 19a)—a point rendered more explicit in Galatians 3, 13—the break has occurred. The two unqualified, juxtaposed uses of "law" in verse 19 most probably present "law" in the same basic sense. Thus Paul is not opposing the law of the Spirit to the Mosaic law. Rather, he is comparing the Mosaic law conceived as an executioner (the cause of death) with the same law conceived as an authority (a set of norms spelling out transgressions). We shall have more to say about Paul's dim view of the law when we treat Romans 1–8, where Paul's polemic is less heated and his considerations of law are situated in a more adequate theological context. For the present, it must suffice to point out the personification of law as a domineering force or historical entity which, perhaps in spite of itself (for Paul does not regard the law as satanic or malevolent in itself), he has disowned the man who has verified one of its curses. Accordingly, the law itself may imaginatively be depicted as something which stands against the rescinding of the curse which is part of itself.

This highly charged, apocalyptic personification of law is alien to modern thought, and few will find it convincing. Paul himself does not rest his case on this literary conceit, however, but goes on to consider sin as the rejection of the grace of God and the negation of the value of Christ's death. Moreover, in justice to Paul, one must recall that he is taking the viewpoint of one with a similar cultural background whom he wishes not so much to refute as to persuade. The law itself must somehow figure in an argument intended to move one with a Jewish respect for the law's firm decrees. Furthermore, the intensely personal concept of justification, focused on Jesus Christ who is Paul's whole life and the life of any Christian, has repercussions on the imagery used for related concepts. It is almost inevitable, then, that in this vivid context the law be personified as "outlawing" those bound to one who has verified its clearcut malediction. As life is correlative to death, and "my" life to Christ's life, "my" death to his death, so "my" life for God in Christ is correlative to my death in his death to the law by the law.

Paradoxically, the life that the Christian enjoys is attributable to the union achieved with the one who was crucified. The mystery of the interior shaping of the Christian's life through the form of Christ's death and the sacramental mediation of baptism will be plumbed in Romans 6. In Galatians 2, 20, Paul intensely affirms the personal union with the crucified Lord that is at once the doctrinal and mystical heart of Christian existence, and thus the norm for discerning where sin really lies. The juridical image of justification (vv. 15–17) has yielded to the deeper, more ontological and personalist image of living union with Christ (vv. 18–21). The life now lived by the Christian is one that is not yet transformed by the resurrection; it is a life of weak terrestrial existence, a life "in the flesh." But it is nevertheless centered on the Son of God; it is interiorly structured by the bond of faith in one who has not been appropriated so much as he has given himself. This self-giving of Christ is concretely the grace of God, which one dare not set aside. Paul places his doctrine of justification squarely in its properly theological, that is, God-centered, perspective. Christ's death is not to be judged gratuitous in the sense that it might be regarded as being to no purpose. On the contrary, its value is that of the unmerited and sovereign personal favor of God.

Thus far (Galatians 1–2), Paul has affirmed the integrity

65

of his gospel by reaffirming its inextricable correlative, the integrity of his apostolic office. His distinctive apostleship was constituted by the revelation of the risen Lord. It was acknowledged in Jerusalem, but not received from men. It was necessarily and effectively exercised at Antioch in a confrontation with no less a figure than Cephas. Paul's apologia has concluded with a concrete illustration of the kind of situation involving the basic principles of the law and Christian existence. He has restated his argument apropos of this situation to apprise the Galatians of the basic contrast between two economies, that of the law and that of living faith in Christ. He can now address himself to the Galatians more directly, taking up the point of Christian faith and the liberty of sons that is consequent upon faith.

II. FAITH, LAW, AND THE FREEDOM OF GOD'S SONS (3, 1—5, 1)

In the second part of his letter (3, 1–5, 1), Paul first appeals to the lived Christian experience of the Galatians themselves (3, 1–5). We may be struck first by the Apostle's exasperation. He calls them "witless" and again suggests that they have been the victims of others' machinations. Here, some baleful superhuman agency is ironically suggested as the cause for their defection in faith in the face of the clear proclamation of Christ crucified. Their reception of the kerygma was equivalently their eyewitness to the crucifixion. Exasperation there is, but also an astute pastoral confrontation. For Paul is appealing to what his hearers already know. He is not trying to re-establish the gospel from the outside as if it were something that had been imposed and could be reimposed. He tries to reawaken faith from within, from their past personal experience of the kerygma centered on Christ, from their experience of the Spirit, and from their recognition of the one who has supplied the spirit and has worked miracles among them, that is, the Father. Their own

66

Christian experience, with a clear suggestion of its Trinitarian basis, grounds his reproach and his implicit appeal for a return to their Christian senses.

The basic question that Paul has just proposed is whether the rich Christian experience they had had derived from "works of law," that is, from what they did of themselves in following an external norm of conduct given through Moses, or from "the hearing of faith," that is, from what they had received through the operative word of God which involved a new bond in Christ. A merely "subjective" faith is not in question here, even though there is indeed question of the vivid confidence in God's power that is to figure as part of healthy Christian experience. For reasons that will appear especially in the discussion of Romans 3, 21–4, 25, Paul's understanding of justification must be judged to entail the notion of a restructuring of one's whole existence through a sacrificial bond in Christ. The most attractive features of this bond are those that are intensely personal, but the bond is also an ontological one that is "objective" to the point of admitting a juridical formulation. The fact that faith is opposed to law should not lead one naïvely to assume that there is no analogous basis on which these two can be compared, contrasted, even positively associated. Paul himself will call faith a law (Romans 3, 27) and regard it as the law *par excellence*. For he sees that faith, while being contrasted with law in basic respects, is by no means foreign to the notion of a juridical bond. With this in mind, the following dialectical passage contrasting the economies of the law and of faith can be much more readily grasped.

The implicit answer to the preceding question (Galatians 3, 5) is, of course, "through the hearing of faith." But Paul supplies the answer himself in terms of a dialectical contrast in the history of salvation. He is not attempting to give an exegesis of the Old Testament as such, but to provide in terms of the word of God and his own reasoning an "explanation" for the way in which they have indeed received the Spirit. The dichot-

67

omy stated in the question in Galatians 3, 5 governs the dialectical structure of the answer. The latter is given in three blocks; the argument is more "patterned" than "logical."

In the first block, Galatians 3, 6–9, Paul presents the pattern of justification (a blessing pure and simple) through the faith of Abraham. Paul does not regard the "reckoning" with Abraham as reward for a good work, but as a reward gratuitously bestowed, that is, a gift or blessing, on the simple condition that it is taken for what it is, that is, received as a gift. A needed paraphrase of the Greek text used as Paul reads it would be: "Abraham believed God and there was a reckoning for him [which consisted in putting him] into a state of justice [a *juridical* relationship that involves *personal rapport* with God as judge]." Paul sees "justice" not as the impersonal decision rendered according to an objective law, but in the Old Testament terms of "good standing with the honest judge who is now on my side and will defend me." He goes on to conclude, somewhat hastily to the modern reader who is not as ready to assume the corporate perspective that Paul takes for granted, that those "who are [men] of faith" are the sons of Abraham. That is, those who are in this new juridical arrangement which is like that of a "trust," namely, faith, are the true heirs of Abraham. What characterizes Abraham's fatherhood as a "just" man is faith. Hence, what characterizes those who belong to Abraham for what he is before God, a justified man, is also faith.

Paul, however, does not consider the association between son and father merely in terms of likeness. He considers it in terms of the concrete effect, inheritance of a blessing. Accordingly, he proceeds to quote scripture a second time (3, 8) to the effect that God, intending to justify the nations by faith, had announced to Abraham, the father of the faithful (their paradigm and source of blessing), that all the nations would be blessed in him. Thus the justification of Abraham is seen as an unmerited blessing, shared by those who follow him in faith, who, as God's plan will work out, are destined to be all nations.

68

The preliminary conclusion is stated in verse 9: "So then, those who are men of faith [that is, those who belong to this "trust" or distinctive, totally beneficial juridical arrangement not based on human merit] are blessed with Abraham the man of faith." The conclusion is only preliminary, because Paul must yet show how the benefit is communicated in no other way, and that it is communicated in the fulfillment of its messianic context, fulfilled in Christ.

The second block of his argument *begins* with the corresponding preliminary conclusion (3, 10). It goes on to cite scripture as illustrative proof, as did the first block of the argument. But the reasoning that is added, unlike that in the first block, is mainly in the form of *negative* statements. The preliminary conclusion is somewhat frightening and apparently exaggerated beyond credibility: "All those who are of works of law are under a curse." The *RSV* "all who rely on" is not really in error, but it does not accurately bring out the sharp rhetorical contrast between the juxtaposed preliminary conclusions. Nor does it suggest, as Paul does, that there is not simply question of "personal reliance" but of a juridical arrangement. The expression "those of (*'oi ek*) something" indicates a party, a group of affiliates, and so forth. Paul is contrasting to the party that enjoys the trust that is the blessing of God's unmerited justice the party that takes its stand precisely on its own achievements according to an external norm of conduct. His deliberately shocking statement that such people are under a curse is not meant to indicate that the law contains nothing but curses (for after all, the blessing of Abraham is, in a sense, in the "law"). It is a rhetorical contrast meant to jolt the reader into an awareness of the fact that law is not an unmitigated blessing but—even if only in part—is essentially characterized by sanctions, penalties. Thus, in the providence of God, the economy of law is radically distinguishable and distinguished from the economy of faith, and those who take their stand on law or faith are distinguished accordingly.

Backing up this preliminary conclusion, Paul appeals to a

text which verifies the curse. One under the law is bound to abide by all the prescriptions of the law precisely in executing them. Paul does not say here that this full compliance is impossible, though one may well suspect he thinks so. He goes on immediately to argue that by law itself (as is evident from the contrast implied in "before God"), no one is justified, that is, enjoys a rapport with God which is fully juridical, but not claim-based, as in "measurable accomplishments," "works of law." Paul could have added explicitly that it is not a thing, however holy and sublime, that of itself achieves a personal rapport with God, but God's own action. He encapsulates this view in the next quotation from scripture: "The man who through faith is just shall live." The "trust" in which he has placed himself by simple openness to God's gift is the basis for his life and hope of life. But, Paul argues again, "the law does not rest on faith," or, more exactly, "the law is not from faith." That is, the law is of another order altogether. As the final scriptural passage tells us, its own promise of life is based on what one himself does, that is, it is the norm of life only by being first a norm of judgment for what one has done. Eventually, Paul will give us the key for understanding how the law can even dare speak of life on the basis of works. The law's own fulfillment rests with what the law itself cannot give: a juridical relationship based on the personal favor of the wise and powerful judge. Given faith and the interior dynamism of the spirit, the law itself, in its abiding spiritual prescriptions, can indeed be fulfilled and serve as the guide to life. But Paul's present focus is on the radical difference between two economies of salvation.

That there is no third position he takes for granted. For all practical purposes, this is the case in the Galatian situation with which he is dealing. Even from a speculative point of view, for one who reads the Pentateuch not according to genera, strata, and traditions, as do modern scholars, but as a continuous account of personal contacts between God and his people, as Paul and his contemporaries did, there seems to be no third possibility. For the people of God is stamped by the law God gave through Moses, though this people appears first, prior to the law, in the person of the personally chosen patriarchs, especially Abraham.

The preliminary conclusions juxtaposed in verses 9–10 have already indicated a radical dissociation between faith and law. In the third block of his argument (vv. 13–14) Paul now shows how the dissociation was historically and definitively effected. The actual dissociation of the two arrangements is effected by Christ's own dissociation from law. The evangelists, notably John and Matthew, see the death of Christ ironically in the light of the Old Testament. The travesty of justice in the passion of Jesus is not attributed to the law itself, but to the perversity of those who represent narrow self-interest. This more "historical" view of the passion is itself susceptible to misinterpretation, though misinterpretation can be obviated by grasping the theological point through its literary mode of expression. For instance, one may fall into the mistake of failing to recognize that the Pharisees and high priests, while being actual men who did share responsibility for the death of Jesus, are presented as types of the false Israel. There is a deliberate exaggeration of their role, especially in Matthew, which may in part be dictated by polemical considerations of the time, but which finds its ultimate and adequate theological justification on other grounds. Those grounds are the somewhat apocalyptic presentation of a supra-political struggle, an engagement between God and forces that have a representative character that transcends the responsibility or the character of mere individual men of a given generation in calendar time. To present the death of Jesus for the *significant* event it was, the evangelists found it necessary to present it as disengaged from the level of secular history and events which are viewed simply as phenomena for which a human explanation is sufficient. Thus, one who grasps the typological viewpoint of the evangelists will not misjudge their characterization of the Pharisees or Jews as "anti-Semitic."

Paul's more "prophetic" view of the passion takes another turn, one that entails the same apocalyptic perspective, though more boldly and rhetorically presented. He casts the law itself in a hostile role. He sees in the text from Deuteronomy 21, 23, not without some justification according to the exegetical modes of thought of his day, a reference to the crucifixion. Hence he presents Christ as falling victim to the law as his judge or executioner. Yet he in no way impugns the law of God as God's law. He represents its catalytic role in working out the drama of salvation by rhetorically "typing" it as a hostile agent.

What is more, the law is really a foil for a more positive thesis. Paul does not focus on the role of law "in itself." He hastens to point out the personal love which really explains this revolting picture and converts it into a blessing: "for us" (v. 13). Christ endured dissociation from the law for us, rescuing us from its curse so that the blessing of Abraham might come to the nations in Jesus Christ himself, and, what amounts to the same thing, that we might receive the promise of the Spirit through faith, through the trust that is existentially realized in Christ.

The abiding validity of the promise is then supported by comparing it with a man's will (3, 15–18). Once a will is ratified, no one can set it aside or add to it. The "will or testament" as Paul conceives it is God's promises to Abraham and his heir. Arguing unconvincingly (to non-rabbinical ears) from the singular, "offspring," not "offsprings," Paul tries to bring out the point that Abraham's legacy was destined not directly for many but for one. Since he views the whole Old Testament in the light of messianic fulfillment known to him by faith, this "one" is Christ himself. The cogency of Paul's argument is not the basis for the validity of what he affirms, as it would be were he a philosopher presenting an argument meant to stand on its own merits. Rather, Paul is a pastoral theologian trying to bring his hearers to a more penetrating understanding and renewed appreciation of the blessing they have received in Christ. His resources in argumentation are the communications media of his own day and, primarily, his own authoritative insights into the mystery he has grasped in faith and would have his hearers grasp accordingly. What his arguments reveal above all is the mystery of messianic fulfillment for all men in one person, Christ. The law, which came later in the course of salvation history, cannot annul this definitive promise graciously bestowed on Abraham.

What, then, is the role of law (3, 19)? Paul must face this question, but he does so with an eye to the precise point at issue in this context, not with a view to giving a complete evaluation of the law itself. His treatment of law is dialectically contrasted to his understanding of the promise the Galatians had received through Christ. The law is being treated in a polemic, intensely pastoral context. It will appear to be simply distorted if one removes it from this genre. The genre itself renders a certain caricaturing of the law inevitable; on the other hand, the circumstances under which Paul writes render the caricature legitimate and not altogether ill-advised.

Paul's answer to the question about the role of law goes through several stages and a good number of verses. First of all, he points out a highly negative role, building on the human example of a testament that he has just given. The law was added "because of transgressions." That is, the law, containing so many negative sanctions that it may be characterized as a forbidding figure, said in effect that until the heir had arrived for whom the promise was made: "Hands off God's gift!" (3, 19a). Furthermore, the law did not mediate the promise, but was instead itself mediated. Paul repeats a common Jewish supposition of the time which was regarded as enhancing the dignity of the law but which Paul mentions to argue for its inferior, second-hand character: it was ordained by angels through an intermediary (by which Paul understands not so much a point of contact with the divine, a "Mediator," as a merely human "middle man"). In other words, there was a multitude of Israelites on one side, a multitude of angels on the other, and Moses, a middle man, in between. Thus, the transmission of the law

73

did not involve a direct transmission from God to his people. God is one (3, 20), not only in himself, but in his very divine action. That which is most truly God's attests to this oneness. By implication, this is the case with the promise, where oneness is seen in the intended heir (3, 16) and in the directness of transmission (3, 19), both unaffected by an intervening human agent.

The argument here strikes us as being somewhat contrived and perhaps even weird, but it remains profoundly theological. In effect, Paul evaluates the law in terms of God himself, whose oneness he sees not just statically as the numerical attribute of a unique being, but as dynamically operative by directly and personally intervening in human history through the conferral of a blessing. The law of Moses cannot supersede the promise because the law is not up to the same standard of God's oneness in act. In effect, the law is "secondary" to the promise on theological grounds, its secondary character being enunciated in terms of sharp rhetorical contrast with the operative oneness of God.

In the second stage of his argument (3, 21–29), Paul tries to present the law in a more positive light. It does not contradict the promises—Paul now speaks of them in the plural, probably to bring out the richness of the one promise which he has been discussing, or simply to treat "law" and "promise" more generically. Law cannot contradict the promises, for it is simply not in competition with them. If a law had been given that had the power to give life, then justification, which is life now and to come, would have come from law. But scripture discloses another role for law, that of bringing out the universal need for forgiveness and, therefore, for justification, through "consigning all things to sin." That is to say, the law articulated man's dissociation from God and thus provided the negative background for positively appreciating the promise. For the promise would be given on the basis of a bond of faith in Christ, a juridical (but not claim-based) "trust" of sorts, to those who accepted it accordingly, that is, by accepting it in

74

faith. A fuller explanation will be considered in the discussion of Romans 4.

Before faith came, before the trust came along as a reality in the drama of messianic fulfillment, men were kept under guard by law. The law's function was thus ordered to termination and therefore to a kind of fulfillment in the revelation of a new order, that of faith. The law became a *paidagōgos* for men—a term that Paul probably uses in the more general sense of "custodian" *(RSV)* rather than simply in the sense of the kind of servant who watched over the child in bringing him to school. The dominant metaphor here, at any rate, is the economico-political notion of a trust (cf. Greer Taylor). It was by this arrangement that justification was to come. By speaking in the first person plural in 3, 24, Paul shows that he regards the law as "our custodian" not only insofar as it affected the Jews, but as an historical entity significant for understanding the stages in the economy of salvation for all men. Thus, even though the "law" is the Mosaic law, it is taken as being representative of universal human history prior to the messianic fulfillment in Christ. Paul goes on to point out that, with the advent of faith, the custodian no longer governs our conduct. We have attained the maturity of sons. This maturity is seen in terms of its effective realization in the juridical (but not narrowly "legal") order; sonship has come effectively through the trust, the bond of faith, in Christ Jesus. We have been invested with Christ by baptism. The oneness of the promise is so realized in Christ that all other, discriminatory distinctions are of no account.

As the first stage of his explanation of the role of law vis-à-vis the promise had closed on the note of God's oneness, effectively realized through the directness of the promise, the second stage has closed on the further note of a oneness personally realized in Christ. Being the singular "offspring" of Abraham for whom the promise is intended involves incorporation into Christ through baptism for participation in the unique blessing. In a sense, this is "mediation," but of a kind quite different from that which Paul sees effected by Moses. For, in Christ, a new corporate entity of an order transcending the strictly human or "fleshly" distinctions of economic and social status, of sex itself, and implicitly of any like distinction of race or nationality, has come into being. The coming of "faith" is not just the transmission of a teaching or the individual's conversion to God, but the advent of a new bond among men in Christ himself. A juridical and ontological—because historical —order, which is nevertheless not really that of law, has come about in Christ.

The third stage of Paul's explanation (4, 1–11) pursues the distinction between the two orders in terms of the benefit now received, the status of sonship attested by the presence of the Spirit. The topic of inheritance dominates Paul's comparison of the status of the child under the temporarily effective decree of the trust received from his father. Paul probably adjusts the juridical metaphor, as he so often does violence to other metaphors, to make it conform with the all-important theological insight that he wants to communicate. It is the Father (by implication, God himself) who has determined the time for our inheritance in Christ.

Reference to the appointed time of fulfillment prompts Paul to describe in the apocalyptic imagery of cosmic history the status of the child who is effectively no more than a slave. He is regarded as subjected not immediately to the beneficent power of God but to the elemental spirits of the universe. Whether these "elements" *(stoicheia)* are actually to be regarded as spirits, as it seems they are to be, whether these elemental spirits actually exist, and even whether Paul was under the impression that they did exist are questions that are somewhat beside the point so far as Paul's central affirmation is concerned. He is intent only on affirming that the sonship of God is realized solely in Christ, through whom the promised spirit has been given by the Father—the same point that has governed this whole part of the epistle from the outset (3, 1–5). The apoca-

76

lyptic imagery enables him to depict the previous condition in vivid and dynamic terms (slavery to worldly elements) instead of in the static and more philosophical terms of alienation from God. The law itself seems to be personified as a figure allied with these elemental forces, though Paul does not seem to identify it with them. But he regards it as a figure under God that does not of itself achieve contact with God.

To achieve this personal contact that would make the slave a son, God sent his own son to deliver men from their condition. Paul's reference to the "incarnation" is subordinated to that of apocalyptic and eschatological fulfillment. Christ was born of a woman, thus sharing fully the human condition, and born under the law, the economy that governed the existence of men whose total condition was not yet that of effective sonship. Paul does not supply many of the distinctions called for to show how Christ's status even under the law is not altogether that of those with whom he identifies himself. But it should be clear enough that the redeemer himself is not redeemed from sin except in being redeemed from its concrete effects like death. Moreover, though the sonship we receive is qualified as "adoptive" and is consequent on redemption, Christ is designated as Son even when he is sent into the world. His own sonship must therefore be conceived in the unique terms of heavenly pre-existence and personal uniqueness. By being under the law, and by dying to the whole order in which it figured as a dominating force, Christ paid the price for our deliverance. The point here is that of costly effort resulting in deliverance, not that of involved transactions—especially not as implying one to whom a price was paid. The whole purpose of the "incarnation" is the acquisition of men as God's sons, achieved through Christ's own dissociation from law in death and his new existence as risen. The *fact that* we are sons (not the *RSV* "because you are sons") is attested by the address characteristic of Christian prayer, "Father!" (in the Aramaic form "Abba," which seems to have been familiar from the liturgy of the early church. The personal familiarity with God that this form of address implies is reflected, as Joachim Jeremias has often shown, in the formula itself. Its importance to Paul, however, lies in the unique reality to which it attests; the liturgical expression is a witness to the interior reality of sonship, and a pledge of the inheritance yet to be fully realized.

Paul closes his appeal to Christian experience with a further apocalyptic consideration of the Galatians' previous state (4, 8–11). In paganism, they were in bondage to beings who were not divine, but of the "physical" order of earthly creation, even though they may be regarded as "spiritual" beings. Now the Galatians have come to acknowledge God or, rather, in a beautiful turn of phrase that underscores the divine initiative of grace, to be known by God, that is, to be made his sons by personal acknowledgment. Relapse, then, is unthinkable. How is it possible that the Galatians have returned to a lower level of existence through the observances that they have adopted at the prompting of the Judaizers among them?

The Apostle adds that his personal work is at stake in this tragedy. Accordingly, he turns to a personal exhortation (4, 12–20). He argues from the heart, appealing to the loyalty they showed to a man they once esteemed, in spite of a repulsive ailment. When he had preached the gospel to them on his earlier visit (*to proteron,* v. 13, not the *RSV* "at first"), he had fallen ill—probably with a chronic ailment the nature of which remains unknown. They had not scorned him (by the apotropaic gesture of spitting, as if he had been afflicted or possessed by an evil spirit), but received him as an angel of God, as God's messenger, Christ Jesus himself. "What has become of the blessing [you were answered with]?" (v. 15, not as in the *RSV*). The blessing was none other than the gospel they had received. Paul attests their complete, self-sacrificing generosity, and asks how he could have become their adversary by having lived and

78

spoken the truth of the gospel for their benefit. Alluding to the self-interest of those who seem to have supplanted him in the affections of the Galatians, Paul plays on the word *zēloō,* which in different voices (active or middle) can mean "be interested in" or "be interested in for one's own benefit." The Judaizers, he says, are showing a personal interest in the Galatians in a way that is not noble; they really intend to shut them out (from the access to God made possible through the gospel) so that the Galatians will show a personal interest in them by becoming their adherents. Paul affirms that it is noble to show a noble (altruistic) personal interest at all times, and hastens to remind them of the fact that this means the present time as well, when he is not physically present among them (v. 18). He has a mother's intense love for them, but has to bring them to birth in the faith once more, that is, to see Christ formed in them. As he had once come to them as an angel of God, he would like now to come among them and change his voice (not the *RSV* "change his tone") in order to communicate effectively with them in super-language, angelic speech. For he is at a loss (not the *RSV* "perplexed") to find any other way to break through to them.

Abruptly, he finds yet another argument (4, 21—5, 1). Perhaps a midrashic homily to those who would place themselves under the law will bring them to realize that the freedom of God's sons is at stake, together with the ultimate inheritance which only the full-fledged son and not the slave will receive. As has been the case all along, Paul is trying to give not an exegesis of the Old Testament text, but rather appreciative insights into the Christian experience of personal contact with God, entailing supernatural existence, that is, sonship, freedom attested by the Spirit, and an eschatological inheritance (which he supposes they will rightly construe as fully realized in the resurrection). Since this passage often confuses even the sym-

79

pathetic reader, it may prove helpful to read first a schematically arranged translation and then follow a kind of running commentary on the text.

4, 21a   Tell me, you who want to be subject to the law,
   21b   do you not hear [what] the law [says]?

   22a   For it is written that Abraham had two sons,
   22b   one from the slave-girl
   22c   and one from the freeborn woman
   23a   But the one from the slave-girl
   23b   had been begotten according to the flesh,
   23c   whereas the one from the freeborn
   23d   [was begotten] through the promise.

   24a   These facts are representative [*allēgoroumena*]:
   24b   For these women are [that is, represent] two covenants,
   24c   one from Mount Sinai,
   24d   bringing forth [children] for slavery,
   24e   and this one is Hagar—
   25a   Sinai [Hagar] is a mountain in Arabia
   25b   connected with [or aligned with] the *present* Jerusalem,
   25c   for she is in slavery with her children.

   26a   But the Jerusalem on *high*
   26b   is freeborn,
   26c   and it is this one who is *our* mother.
   27a   Indeed, it is written [of our mother]:
   27b   "Rejoice, you barren one who bring forth no children;
   27c   Break forth in jubilant song you who have not undergone
                                           labor!
   27d   For many are the children of the deserted wife,
   27e   More than of her who has a husband."

   28a   Now you, my brothers,
   28b   are children of the promise, in the manner of Isaac.
   29a   But just as in those days
   29b   the one begotten according to the flesh
   29c   persecuted the one [begotten] according to the spirit,
   29d   so it is now.

   30a   But what does scripture say?
   30b   "Cast out the slave-girl and her son;
   30c   For the son of the slave-girl will never inherit
   30d   with the son of the freeborn."

31a And so, my brothers,
31b   we are not children of a slave-girl,
31c   but of the freeborn.

5, 1a Christ freed us for freedom;
  1b stand firm, then,
  1c and do not once more put yourselves in the yoke of slavery.

Paul's homily (4, 21 ff.) opens on to the exhortation in the last part of this letter (5, 1 ff.) and brings to a further focus the insistence on sonship and inheritance which figured so largely in the second part. It is haggadic midrash, that is, a story-like, imaginative retelling of some Old Testament passages in view of a new situation, aimed to edify or exhort rather than (as in halakic midrash) to instruct one in the ways of the law. As New Testament midrash, its main point of reference is not the understanding of the Old Testament but the understanding of an aspect of the mystery of Christian existence. In a way, Paul is giving here a kind of extended and objectified parable. But the illustrative material is drawn from a written source, the Old Testament, rather than immediately from human experience. It is further complicated by an apocalyptic perspective on the heavenly city, and by somewhat elliptical comparisons and abrupt transitions.

In verses 21–23, Paul appeals to what the law itself says— as interpreted in the light of Christian experience through Paul's imaginative presentation of it. He recounts the basic data, in which two main features are to be noted: the mothers (Hagar and Sarah) and the manner of birth of each son (Ishmael, according to the flesh, that is, the natural, "human" process of conception; Isaac, thanks to God's promise of life to Abraham against human hope).

Paul then develops chiefly the first of these main features, relying largely on an imaginative association of ideas. Ishmael, the son of Hagar, was father of the Arabs. Sinai, in "Arabia," is on the same earthly plane as Jerusalem, the Jerusalem of the present age (in the apocalyptic sense of merely terrestrial existence). Thus, Paul sees in a compositely representative picture

81

the earthly covenant of Sinai, the people alienated from the promise of Abraham, and the Jerusalem of the "present" age, the inferior age of salvation history, the age of merely human existence. Slavery is the destiny of the children. For slavery, explained by alignment with the "present," earthbound order of existence, is the status of the mother. The one mother thus stands for a whole juridical arrangement, an earthbound way of life known as the Mosaic covenant. But there is another mother, that juridical order on a higher plane, typified by the heavenly city. A hallmark of this mother is her freeborn status, and it is she whom Christians hail as their own mother. What is more, this mother is seen as having been endowed with amazing power and joy. In verse 27, Paul presents the mother of Christians as enjoying the unexpected grace of God. He does so by drawing on a text from Isaiah 54, 1, which depicts unexpected fertility for a spouse who had never had children, but who now has them in abundance without recourse to the natural process of childbearing. The "deserted wife," the one who had not been regarded as capable of bearing a son, has miraculously become the more prolific mother.

Given this presentation of the two mothers in terms of two orders of existence, with accompanying traits of slavery on the one hand and of freedom, power, and joy on the other, Paul turns to apply the lesson more directly. In verse 28, he points out that the Galatian Christians are children after the manner of Isaac; they are freeborn sons. But there is more to the notion of genuine sonship than meets the eye. For Paul, sonship means inheritance; it is to be judged in terms of a realization of function, not simply in terms of legal title nor precisely in terms of metaphysical status, though both are implied in Paul's understanding of sonship. What is more, the perspective of the passion and resurrection, as we shall have occasion to see repeatedly in his letters, dominates his whole consideration of Christian existence and, therefore, of the notion of sonship. Hence he first speaks of the negative conditions for the full realization of sonship, the endurance of trials. In verse 29, he

82

indicates that the persecution typified by the hostility which Ishmael was considered to have shown towards Isaac is now the lot of the genuine son, that is, of the Galatians. Neither scripture nor rabbinic and targumic elaborations of the relationships between Ishmael and Isaac adequately explain Paul's reference to Ishmael's "persecution" of Isaac, though the rabbinic and targumic explanations may prepare us to grasp it more readily, since they point up the basis (diverse morality) or scope (debate over inheritance) of the antipathy between these two sons. Paul himself qualifies the acknowledged hostility between the two sons in terms of the Christian experience in Galatia. The disturbing influence of the Judaizers on the faith of the communities in Galatia is equivalently "persecution," and this characterization is read back into the biblical account in Paul's homily. The present situation is also seen in the advance from the "flesh-promise" contrast of verse 23 to the "flesh-spirit" contrast in verse 29. The promise has been realized to some extent precisely in the possession of the spirit, the principle of sonship in the one who is now persecuted.

The theme of inheritance is implicit in verse 29, but it is not voiced. For, in the light of his previous presentation of the mother as the heavenly city, Paul will consider the inheritance of the son in a still further dimension, that of its absolutely final realization, of which the spirit's action is an advance indication but not the sole effect. Appealing again to scripture to show that the ultimate resolution of trials is in accord with the will of God, Paul declares in verse 30 that it is *only* the son of the freeborn who will receive the inheritance. A necessary caution in reading this passage is to avoid assuming that Paul is exhorting the Galatians to oust the Judaizers, especially by taking some course of action that amounts to persecution. This supposition cannot be supported by the sense of the context. There is no exhortation, but rather an appeal to scripture as an oracular source for understanding the action of God, as in verse 17. What is more, the following verse (31) must be taken as a conclusion (*dio,* "accordingly," "and so") to verse

30, and it cannot be taken in this way if one supposes that Paul is counseling the Galatians to a course of action in verse 30. The scope of verse 31 is to remind the Galatians by way of conclusion that they are indeed sons of the freeborn woman, and, by implication, that their lot is persecution now (v. 29) but the sole inheritance in the framework of God's eventual judgment (v. 30).

III. EXHORTATION TO LIVE ACCORDING TO THE SPIRIT (5, 1—6, 10)

The pastoral exhortation which naturally flows from the doctrinal exposition in this homily begins forthrightly in 5, 1. The "imperative" is immediately consequent on the "indicative" (cf. pp. 17 ff.): what one must do in the moral sphere is immediately consequent on what one is as a Christian, and what one "must" do as a Christian is what he is free to do as God's son. The salient point of the exhortation, then, like the salient point of the preceding exposition, is freedom through Christ. It is for freedom, understood as the liberty of God's sons, that Christ has freed us. In Paul's view, freedom is not an absolute good simply as human freedom. Freedom to "do as one pleases" makes no real sense to Paul unless it is viewed in closely personal relationship to God's will and God's own freedom. Hence the intrinsic value of freedom given to man stems from the spontaneous initiative of God in placing us with his own Son. It rests on this faith relationship by which merely human persons are fully constituted as persons, as free sons. The Galatians are therefore to stand firm in faith. To opt for the old order is not freedom but a relapse into slavery. How is this freedom to be understood and pursued in the concrete?

To answer this, Paul strikes at the heart of the present difficulty in Galatia by excluding the practice of circumcision, which, as it was understood, committed the Galatians to a norm of salvation other than Christ (5, 2–6). The Christian

84

looks for his hope of justification from faith, on the level of the spirit (5, 5). The "hope of justification" seems to have a twofold reference. First, there is a contrast in the here and now between seeking one's own justification on the basis of a simply external principle like law (v. 4); this is opposed to receiving hope on the basis of an interior principle flowing from the faith relationship which God has set up in Christ. Second, the "hope of justification" and therefore justification itself seems to involve a future point of reference. Justification or "righteousness," that is, standing in a favorable personal rapport with God the judge, is not fully or definitively achieved until the term of Christian life in faith. The suggestion of a life process in realizing the hope of justification already emerges in the dynamic word "spirit" in verse 5, and is brought out more clearly by reference in verse 6 to faith "working out" through love. Circumcision and uncircumcision are of no avail in Christ Jesus; in the context of the faith relationship, these external practices cannot be considered to empower man for achieving a present and ultimate, intrinsically personal rapport with God. What does avail is the faith relationship itself as actively working out through love.

Before showing how love is operative, Paul pauses to comment derisively on the way the Galatians have been victimized (5, 7–12). Who had crippled them to keep them from continuing to believe in the truth of the gospel? This persuasion is not from the one who has called them, not from God himself. Again Paul tries to bring them to see their plight in the light of the vocation which they have experienced. He implies, too, that it is not the whole community that is radically at fault, but a little leaven that has "contaminated" the whole batch (5, 9). He has confidence that they will regard the situation in no other way. As for the one who is responsible for disturbing them, he will bear the onus of God's judgment. Paul does not seem to know who this person is, and the previous use of the term "disturber" in the plural (Galatians 1, 7) as well as the present context (5, 12) suggests more than one. But Paul is considering

85

the figure generically, in such a way as to contrast him with the One who has given clear direction to their lives by his call (v. 8). Paul does not demand that the "disturber" be ousted, but, as he did with the "Seizer" *(katechōn)* of 2 Thessalonians 2, 7, he implicitly consigns him to the judgment of God. As for Paul himself, who has apparently been represented as preaching circumcision (perhaps without the necessary distinction between what he did before and after his conversion, as in the case of the charge about his "pleasing men," Galatians 1, 10), why is he attacked if the allegation is true? The stumbling block of the cross, which lies at the heart of his preaching, would then be no effective stumbling block at all. This sharp reference to the false representation of his own doctrine is followed by a sarcastic reference to those who incite the Galatians. It plays on the notion of circumcision and on the crippling effect that the Judaizers have had on the Galatians (v. 7). Though somewhat tasteless, the remark does reveal the intensity of Paul's feeling, and also shows that he considered the disturbance tantamount to an incitement to revolt *(anastatountes)*.

In Galatians 5, 13–26, Paul returns to the theme of freedom by developing the law of love (5, 13–15, with a brief admonition concerning strife in the community), and principles of conducting oneself ("walking") in the spirit (5, 16–26).

The freedom for which they have been called implies existence on what we would call the "supernatural level," the level of the spirit, which is the principle of existence as God's sons. Accordingly, one is not to use freedom as an opportunity for acting on merely human principles, on the level of "the flesh." Paul does not regard the "flesh" specifically under the aspect of what is material; it stands for the whole man. By the same token, he does not regard it as some shadowy part of the whole man which must be purged out. Rather, "flesh" characterizes the as yet untransformed aspect of man's whole being. One who is in Christ may still be "in the flesh" (1, 20), but he does not live "according to the flesh." One who is not alive in Christ lives "according to the flesh" as well as "in the flesh." The initial

86

stage of transformation comes with reception of a new principle of activity, which enables man, though still "in the flesh," to live "according to the spirit." The final stage comes with the resurrection, when man's being is liberated from the perils of defection from a life on the level of the spirit. Being "in the flesh" connotes weakness and, in men other than Christ, liability to personal sin. But "flesh" itself is not bad. As is so often the case, the term must be judged in a dialectical context, that is, in relation to that with which it is contrasted in a specific context. The "flesh" becomes "bad" when it marks the ceiling of man's activity and implies the repudiation or ignorance of the higher level of activity and being that God intends and makes possible for him. In this sense, being "in the flesh" can be regarded as being radically at odds with being "in the spirit" (Romans 8, 8–9). The principle of this higher level of activity is not precisely another "part" of man, but suffuses his whole being when he is alive in Christ.

On the level of the spirit, which is thus contrasted with the level of the flesh, one's freedom is a form of service in love. On this level, the whole law itself can be and is fulfilled; its plethora of commands are effectively synthesized in action flowing from a principle that lies beyond it, the spirit. Conversely, the thrust of the flesh is not fulfilled (5, 16; *versus* the *RSV* "gratified"). In speaking of the alternative to love, "biting and devouring one another" so as to be "consumed by one another" (5, 15), Paul is thinking of more than the social ills resulting from such conduct. He has in mind moral disintegration as reflecting the whole order of decay to which merely "fleshly life" is doomed. Hence it is that he can explain himself in verse 16: "What I mean is this . . ." He places the whole discussion of moral conduct on the theological plane of flesh/spirit opposition, that is, in the framework of the transformation of man's nature from imperfect to perfect.

Flesh and spirit, as principles of activity, do not thrust in the same direction and are therefore at cross purposes. The result is that one does not do the things he might want to do.

87

His voluntary acts are not fully integrated or successful. The conjunction that Paul uses in verse 17, however, (*'ina,* "in order to" [prevent]) suggests more than unfruitful results. It suggests that this uncoordination has a purpose in bringing man to awareness of his own insufficiency. But this awareness of insufficiency in moral achievement has two radically different contexts. If one is simply "under law," then he is doomed to failure, for, in fact, he does not then have the spirit. If one's whole existence is basically determined by healthy faith and thus involves the action of the spirit, he is not under law, and his efforts are not doomed to failure, even though he still experiences a certain tension and awareness of his own insufficiency. The fruit of the flesh is sin, and its price is the inheritance of God's kingdom, risen life. The "fruit" of the spirit (not so much its "works," the multiple things that it does, but the rich, single yet manifold blessing it brings) is all sorts of contrary dispositions. The negative aspect so characteristic of law is not verified here (5, 23). That is to say, the fruit of the spirit indicates the level of genuine freedom and the integration of one's acts. The new structure of life in Christ has made possible this integration: "If we live by the Spirit, let us also walk by the Spirit" (5, 25). Picking up the point he had made in 5, 15, Paul once more spells out some practical consequences (5, 26).

The Apostle expects the community itself, however, to take charge of correcting its own ills. Those who are "spiritual," those who can judge what is to be done according to discernment in the spirit which they have as healthy Christians, are to restore one who has fallen in some way. Paul is equally concerned to remind the man who gives the correction that he is not immune from danger himself (6, 1). The law of Christ is fulfilled in a corporate effort of mutual assistance, not in placing oneself haughtily in a position of superiority. Such pride is self-deception. However, one's boast, his confident rejoicing in something he has achieved, is to be based on whether or not he has found his own work to be commendable. For his helping to carry the burdens of another does not mean that he is not to carry his own (6, 5). But he who has received the word should share in all good things with the one who has transmitted it (6, 6).

This last verse is particularly obscure, but it seems to fit into the pattern of the dialectical contrasts in 6, 1 ff. Perhaps the man who had fallen in some way was himself a teacher in the community. This might more easily explain Paul's use of the image of carrying burdens; he seems to associate burdens with the exercise of authority or with some more responsible function in the Church rather than with "burdens of life in general" or with commands imposed by others. It would also help explain his repeated insistence on humility and the danger of self-exaltation for one who is "nobody" (in comparison). The warning against deception given in verses 7–10, concluding on the note of doing good to all (cf. v. 6), especially to those of the household of the faith, seems to fit with the same picture. It places the danger of deception in the more theological and doctrinal context of God's own judgment. God is not mocked; he is not deceived or thwarted by men's actions. For men's actions will have their effect according to what he has ordained as productive or disastrous. What is productive of salvation (under the image of eternal life) is action based on the spirit; what leads to judgment (under the image of corruption) is action based on the flesh, such as pursuing one's own self-interest. In this perspective of the final assizes, Paul encourages the community not to grow weary in their noble work, but to use the season given them (6, 9–10). If "charity begins at home," it is because faith, the bond in Christ for the whole community, is the basic framework for the exercise of love in the spirit.

CLOSING ADMONITIONS: SIGNS OF APOSTLESHIP (6, 11–18)

Taking pen in hand at the close of his dictation, Paul boldly adds the final lines (6, 11–18). He has more in mind than the prevention of forgeries or the addition of a personal touch. He is giving the indications of an authentic apostle: not only his own signature, but equivalently the sign of the cross which is his central boast and an indication of the sufferings (the beatings he has received) which are the marks (*stigmata,* v. 17) that this commitment has left on him.

The conduct of the Judaizers and of Paul himself is placed in the light of the opposition between flesh and spirit considered both Christologically and theocentrically. A self-interested, "fleshly" concern for the Galatians, which Paul regards as the sign of his adversaries, is reflected in their own unwillingness to suffer for the cross of Christ. The exact meaning of this, probably something like a refusal to undergo missionary hardships in preaching their doctrine which is opposed to the cross, we have no sure way of knowing. In any event, Paul sees in the Judaizers' doctrine an attempt to exult in the achievement of inflicting on others some mark of allegiance to themselves. On the other hand, Paul's own boast is in the cross of Christ which has dissociated him from the "world," from the whole order of existence on the level of the flesh. He pursues this thought by contrasting with fleshly criteria (circumcision or non-circumcision) the presence of a new creature—the concrete expression of a new creation. This "new creature" is surely that which is effected by the cross of Christ through which Paul has been crucified to the world, namely, the new man who lives for God, the man whose life is that of a bond of faith in Christ animated with the spirit and working itself out in self-sacrificing love. Thus, the new creature is a kind of law, a law of personal fulfillment. The union with the crucified Christ of which it is the positive expression is a norm for conduct (v. 16). The messianic blessing of peace and the covenant blessing of mercy *(eleos, ḥesed)* is on those who follow this norm, that is, on the Israel which is not that of men but of God.

The marks of the beatings which testify to the Apostle's identification with Christ (and thus to his participation in the new creation and the peace of God) ground his demand not to be troubled in the future. It is not just that he has suffered enough. Rather, he is in a sense alienated from the whole level of existence where toil is the order of the day; by his identification with Christ's death even in his daily apostolic trials he is no longer "of the world." Obviously, the Apostle is not an escapist from reality. But his concrete injunction is really intelligible only in the light of his understanding of the mystery into which he has been taken up. This mystical understanding, radically the faith insight into the mystery of the risen Christ who was crucified, is the light which radiates even into the most practical and particular details of the Apostle's life. "I want to see no trouble in the future," becomes for him the occasion for being a living sign of the mystery of faith and of his own complete immersion in it.

CHAPTER 4

PHILIPPIANS

THE SITUATION: A LETTER FROM PRISON

As he writes this letter, Paul is in prison, probably about A.D. 56, sometime during his three-year stay at Ephesus, the greatest urban center in Asia Minor. There is no certain evidence, to be sure, that the Apostle was ever imprisoned at Ephesus, even during his relatively long sojourn in that city. But there is nothing in Paul's letters or in the data provided by Luke's Acts which would militate against reasonably assuming a brief captivity at Ephesus. The other "captivity letters" (Colossians, Ephesians, and Philemon) clearly suppose a Roman captivity and date from the following decade. A few details in Philippians which at one time suggested that this letter, too, be dated from a Roman captivity in the early sixties of the first century may be explained equally well in terms of an Ephesian captivity some six or seven years previously. It is quite possible, for instance, that the *praetorium* mentioned in Philippians 1, 13 could have been located in cities other than Rome, and that even the "household of Caesar" (Philippians 4, 22) could be found in a metropolitan center like Ephesus.

Moreover, the letter supposes relatively close contacts (the goings and comings of Timothy, 2, 19–24, and of Epaphroditus, 2, 25–30 and 4, 18). The assistance that the community rendered Paul likewise favors assuming close contacts. Philippi was only seven days from Ephesus by the transportation then in use. Also, Philippians 4, 10. 16 suppose that Paul had received nothing from the Philippians since Mission II (circa A.D. 50–51), when he had converted them. This would not fit if he wrote from Rome, for by that time (A.D. 61–63) he would have passed through Philippi a second or third time (both visits occurring at the end of Mission III, *circa* A.D. 57–58; cf. Acts 20, 1–12).

The theology of the letter, too, seems to be earlier than that of Ephesians and Colossians, since it centers markedly on the parousia theme and contains a good number of expressions that are more like those of 1 and 2 Thessalonians and Galatians than like those of Colossians and Ephesians. Accordingly, increasing numbers of scholars date Philippians about eight years before the first Roman captivity. The opening references to "bishops [overseers] and deacons" (1, 1) is then a specially noteworthy indication of organization of a hierarchical nature in at least one of Paul's communities.

The letter is probably a composite of two or more of Paul's letters to the Philippians which have been edited and regrouped as a single letter. The tone changes abruptly at Philippians 3, 2, and the problems of the community which can be inferred from the text after 3, 2 seem to be more acute and of a somewhat different nature from those alluded to in 1, 1–3, 1. In the first two chapters of Philippians, Paul seems to know of no difficulties at Philippi other than a rather general opposition from adversaries who seem to stand outside the community itself (2, 28). Difficulties within seem to be equally generic, namely, vying for positions of importance rather than putting the common good and the service of others in first place (2, 3–4). Serious enmity on the part of other selfishly motivated Christians, with the notable exception of Timothy's attitude (2, 21), is rather Paul's own lot at this time. The remarks about Epaphroditus (2, 25–30), which would normally stand towards the very end of a letter, suggest that no further concerns about the Philippians weigh on Paul's heart. His final word, one that is repeated because it seems that there is nothing further to say, is solely one of encouragement to rejoice (3, 1).

In the last two chapters, however, there are incisive warnings against a certain species of Judaizer (3, 2 ff.). The Judaizers at Philippi seem to have presented circumcision and observance of the law as a kind of "special way of knowledge," more perfect than that which Paul would ascribe to the gospel. Sharp conflicts between specific persons in the community (the two women, Euodia and Syntyche) are now known to Paul. There seems to be a special co-worker of Paul on the scene, perhaps Timothy (4, 3), who is expected to reconcile them. Epaphroditus seems to have returned to Paul in good spirits with a contribution from the Philippians (4, 10–20), and it is probably from him that Paul has received more details concerning the community in advance of personal contact with Timothy (cf. 2, 9 ff.). For clarity of exposition, we shall have to advert to the composite structure of the letter as we discuss it.

Nevertheless, the warmth of Paul's thanks—from the thought of the Philippians in his own trials (1, 3) to the joyful acknowledgment of material favors from them—gives coherence to the letter as a whole. The key themes of *joy, solidarity* in Christ, and the hope of the *parousia* (or anticipations of this in triumph of the Christian life in faith over the trials that beset it) reappear in various combinations again and again in the course of the epistle. Throughout the letter, too, Paul's mood is basically one of buoyant happiness, notwithstanding some sarcasm and irony in 3, 22 ff. Except for these blunt and caustic admonitions, aimed at what he obviously regards as a minority, Paul's words of correction for others in the community are quite discreetly urged and are tied to the theme of rejoicing (cf. 4, 4).

95

OPENING ADDRESS AND THEMATIC THANKSGIVING (1, 1–11)

In opening his letter, Paul's address and greeting to "the holy ones at Philippi with their bishops and deacons," is equivalently an address to the Church as such, seen concretely in a given assembled community. As a sanctified body assembled together with those in charge of it, and not simply as a collection of individual Christians, the community represents the image of the Church as a whole. That Paul speaks of its members as "saints" [holy ones] does not, of course, reflect a naïve assumption that all can presume that they will be saved or that all are already perfect. It reflects, rather, the basic health of the community in Paul's eyes, and more particularly, his understanding of the Church in an eschatological, even apocalyptic setting. The "saints" are those who will receive the kingdom (cf. Daniel 7, 18). Their destiny is to triumph with Christ at the parousia through the pattern of life that was his and has been verified or ratified for them in the life of his Apostle.

The greeting which is so characteristic of Paul's letters, "grace and peace . . . ," is not just an adaptation of the Greek and especially of the Palestinian form of epistolary salutation, but a reflection of Paul's whole theological grasp of the eschaton, or final stage of salvation history. God's grace, shown in Christ, so one with him that it can be predicated of Christ as its source as well as of the Father, governs the eschaton from the beginning. "Peace" is a term that covers the sum total of messianic benefits realized by grace, and that looks especially to the final consummation that we are called to enjoy. Thus, even a simple personal communication like Philippians, far as it is from a theological tract, betrays from its opening lines a dominant theological and eschatolagial perspective.

In this perspective, the thanksgiving and prayer (1, 3–11) beautifully state the principal themes of the letter. Joy *(chara)* is an obvious theme, easily recognized throughout even when

96

it is not always mentioned in so many words. It is part of the
fruit of the spirit (cf. Galatians 5, 22) and therefore stands as
the sign of life in the spirit. Solidarity or "communion" *(koinōnia,* the *RSV* "partnership") is likewise more than a human
emotional response or a disposition of "fellowship" with others.
Its roots are sunk in the faith that has made the faithful one in
Christ, and it will appear in varied forms as sharing the consequences of life shaped by faith. Paul places the origin of
koinōnia on the day of the Philippians' conversion, and sees it
as perduring to the present. As faith is the basis for the activity
of the spirit, so *koinōnia* is the basis and framework for the joy
that Paul feels in his prayer for the Philippians. But past and
present communion enjoy still a further dimension, the consummation brought about by the Father, the one who has inaugurated among them a truly good work—their very life of faith.
That further dimension is the coming "Day of Jesus Christ," the
parousia. Thus, thanksgiving looks not only to benefits past and
present but to benefits yet to come, and thanksgiving can form
one voice with prayerful petition.

In the tenor of these dominant and joyful sentiments, Paul
speaks more fully of his own personal right to show his regard
for them in this way. Affection is backed by a deeper reality.
They are at the same time co-sharers with him in his defense
and consolidation of the gospel, for they are co-sharers in God's
grace, the whole order of life in Christ based on faith. Thus, he
is justified in personally thanking God for what he knows of
them. Their "good work" (which is the basis for his "right")
is his own by God's making it one and the same. For the good
work is none other than the life of faith from its reception to
its consummation, a triumphal advance to the parousia. Under
another aspect, the correlative aspect of the trials, the life of
faith becomes the defense and consolidation of the gospel, God's
grace in Christ, which is theirs as well as his. Hence, in giving
personal thanks, Paul must thank God for that which is also
theirs in himself.

His additional prayer (1, 9–11) requests of God the growth

of their love in knowledge and full perception. For faith works itself out through love, and love is thus ordered to sound moral judgment and a wholesome life for the Day of Christ. On that Day, it is Paul's hope that they will be filled with the harvest of justification. Again, the Christological focus of justification is further centered on the eschatological theme of God's glory and praise.

PERSONAL REFLECTIONS ON PROSPECTS FOR THE GOSPEL AND FOR PAUL (1, 12–26)

Paul then turns to speak of his own situation (1, 12–26) as having turned to the advantage of the gospel. It is as though the chains which bind him have become for Christ an open revelation, not only to those in the *praetorium* but to everybody else. Playing again on the notion of imprisonment as an occasion for revelation, Paul states the second way in which the gospel has forged ahead. Most of his brothers in the service of the Lord have taken confidence to speak the word of God, a confidence that may be construed as a form of hope based on the "revelation" effective in the witness of Paul's chains, or as an encouragement, now that Paul is somewhat out of the way, to assert themselves in preaching the gospel (1, 14). Their motives are not always commendable (1, 15). But, whether they act out of love in solidarity with the apostolic commitment for which Paul is in bonds, or from rivalry, maliciously intending to aggravate his plight, Paul can only rejoice. The essential point is that Christ is proclaimed (1, 18). The correlative of this proclamation is the triumph of the parousia. Paul views his joy in the light of this consummation as well as in the light of the present manifestation of Christ in the proclamation of the kerygma.

Therefore, he immediately speaks of his future joy (1, 19). He sees for himself in the future, thanks to their prayers and the help of the spirit of Jesus ("solidarity theme"), his own

98

deliverance from prison. He speaks of this deliverance, "salvation," in words borrowed from Job 13, 16 (LXX), and seems to understand them to typify his deliverance from prison in the light of the eschatological mystery of the resurrection, much as he seems to have understood the attempt to aggravate his plight as an attempt to subject him to the climax of eschatological trials. The dynamic power that will bring about his "salvation" is that of prayer, which is itself the voice of the spirit (cf. Romans 8, 15–16; Galatians 4, 6) and the support of the Spirit that is ours from Jesus Christ. Salvation by such means is in line with Paul's eager expectation and hope of judgment in his favor. The judgment will not, therefore, cause him to blush, but will enable him to manifest for Christ's glory in his own body that apostolic courage in declaring mysteries (*parrhēsia,* the *RSV* "full courage") which has always been his hallmark.

Since Paul views his coming appearance in an earthly court (with possible sentence of death in the offing) under the theological light of the mystery of God's judgment at the resurrection, he can add that life or death makes no difference as far as his hope of genuine acquittal is concerned (1, 20). It is not his own deliverance precisely as his own that is the focus of his hope, but the honor which, with his whole being ("body" in the sense of the whole man), he will render Christ. Life under any condition can be summed up in one word: Christ. For even death cannot separate him from the one with whom he is united. To die physically would itself be a gain, for it would mean full security in Christ. If he is to live on in the human existence now known to us, he has the opportunity for fruitful labor. For human achievements are possible only on the level of existence which is not yet fully transformed and itself achieved by God.

Paul cannot bring himself to choose between his own yearning and the Philippians' need. But he is convinced that (not the *RSV* "Convinced of this") he will remain, not alone, but with them for their forging ahead in faith and for their joy in doing so. Once again, the themes of joy and solidarity are sounded, this time with an even clearer allusion to the Christian mystery which is reflected in Paul's deliverance from prison, the parousia. Paul will remain alive so that their "boast" or confident rejoicing in the achievement of Paul's deliverance from prison will redound to Christ's glory in "Paul's second coming" (*dia tēs emēs parousias palin*) to them.

Thus, Paul's account of his own situation in prison, the attitudes of his confreres in Christ, and the prospects for his sentence in a coming trial are all recounted in the light of the mystery he preaches. His personal news in a given concrete situation is the good news itself. Accordingly, it is a consummate form of pastoral theology, a most personal communication of the mystery of salvation in Christ. The man himself is his message.

EXHORTATIONS TO CHRISTIAN TRIUMPH THROUGH SELFLESS SERVICE (1, 27—2, 18)

The second major stage of his letter (1, 27–2, 18) is hortatory in character. Before Paul's triumphal "parousia" (second coming) among them, there will be an "apousia" or period of absence in which they are to work out their salvation by God's power (cf. 2, 12). For this period he lays down guidelines which are centered on an effective understanding of the mystery of Christ's glory for God the Father's glory. This understanding in turn is to arise from what the community already knows— the mystery of the glorified servant which was probably hymned in the liturgy of the church at Philippi (2, 6–11).

He begins (1, 27–30) with the salient point that they are to conduct themselves as citizens (*politeuesthe*) of the gospel of Christ. The pedestrian phrase in the *RSV*, "manner of life" (v. 27), obscures the reference to the Christian's true city. Adapting himself to the Philippians' esteem for their Roman citizenship, somewhat as he had adapted himself to the Gala-

100

tians' esteem for the law (Galatians 4, 21 ff.)—though obviously without any sarcasm in this case—Paul speaks of the gospel, the faith he preached, as a kind of city on a heavenly plane. The reference to a juridical order on the heavenly plane will become explicit in the course of Paul's answer to the Judaizers at Philippi (Philippians 3, 20). But, given the eschatological and even apocalyptic tenor of Paul's remarks previously (1, 3–26) and within this paragraph (1, 27–30, especially v. 28), the implied image seems to figure here as well.

The super-citizenship of the gospel is to be exercised even in Paul's absence by steadfastness in the power of the spirit which effectively unites and directs them. Turning to the image of an athletic contest or struggle, which he transposes to the level of a cosmic battle ending in destruction or salvation, Paul urges the Philippians to strive with one mind and heart. They are to show supernatural unity of the spirit concretely in singleness of energetic purpose for the faith of the gospel. They are not to be frightened in any respect by adversaries, by those who actively oppose the furtherance of the gospel.

Paul views this present situation, the two-sided contest between those furthering the faith and their adversaries, in the light of its ultimate resolution in terms of God's judgment. For the adversaries, their very opposition is a clear, advance indication (*endeixis,* cf. *endeigma,* 2 Thessalonians 1, 5) of destruction to come; for the proponents of the gospel, it is an indication of the contrary, namely, salvation. He hastens to add that the achievement of salvation is not as such their own doing, but God's (1, 28). How so? It is an instance of God's grace to them (*'ymin echaristhē;* the *RSV* is weaker: "it has been granted to you") that they not only believe in Christ but suffer on his behalf (v. 29). Paul will later make it clearer that this grace goes beyond simple intention or service and represents the very inner structure of Christian existence in solidarity with the Lord who was crucified. At the present time, it suffices for him to show their solidarity with his own struggle past and present. The Apostle again presents effective and immediate

101

witness to Christian existence in terms of his own life as they have known it when he was at Philippi and as they now hear of it in his letter from Ephesus.

The second part of his exhortation (2, 1–11) begins with a correlative aspect of solidarity in Christ. Paul's own struggle is a kind of *paraklēsis* (the *RSV*, "encouragement"), a confirmatory proof and at the same time an exemplification of Christian existence which is intended to help them live out the faith. He would now find *paraklēsis* in their own conduct. The basis for this mutual *paraklēsis* is, of course, "in Christ." It resides in their very oneness in the bond of faith realized in him. In parallel phrases, Paul depicts more vividly further aspects of this *paraklēsis*: the solace afforded by love, not as mere assuaging of pain, but as an incentive to love itself; the sharing (*koinōnia*) of the Spirit, through whom that love is operative in our hearts (cf. Romans 5, 5); and the human emotions of affection and sympathy, which find their own further value and richness in this supernatural context.

He appeals to this solidarity both personally and in the light of a kind of eschatological realization: "fulfill my joy" (2, 2). This they will do by an intensification of their oneness in Christ, shown in one and the same mind, one and the same love, the same unity of purpose. Insisting on oneness of mind (*to 'en phronountes*, v. 2), he shows that he is not thinking about mere conformity of judgment, but rather a singleness of outlook befitting their oneness in Christ. Put negatively, this means doing nothing in line with strident self-interest (*eritheia*, the same term used earlier of Paul's rivals, 1, 17) or conceit (2, 3a). Positively, it means esteeming others as superior to themselves (2, 3b). This, in turn, requires explanation, for it is not to be construed as self-effacing make-believe; what is meant is a thoroughgoing willingness to serve others, humility in selfless action. Thus, negatively again, Paul says "not with each one looking out for his own interests," and then, positively: "but with each [looking out] for the others' interests" (2, 4).

102

Yet a third time in this paragraph he insists on the oneness of mind that he would see realized in them: "Have this mind among you which [was] also in Christ Jesus," and there follows the hymn of the servant acclaimed to the glory of God. What the Philippians are to keep in mind is what occurred in Christ himself, in the whole mystery of his life as focused on the passion and resurrection. But this "Christ event" is also a revelation of Christ's own mind, his completely selfless attitude which ultimately redounds to God the Father's glory. Key verbs in the hymn bring out Jesus Christ's own line of choices. Thus, the pastoral exhortation to unity of mind in their outlook towards one another is based not only on what occurred in Christ, whose existence shapes their own, but on the whole conscious outlook of the one who is adored as Lord of the universe.

The hymn itself has yielded all kinds of interpretation, especially when it has been disengaged from its context. But it will interest us mainly as it stands in Paul's own exhortation. We shall also try to interpret it in accord with the additions that are more apparently his own, namely, the phrases: "even death on a cross" (v. 8), and "to the glory of God the Father" (v. 11). We shall further seek to interpret the Pauline version of the hymn according to the apocalyptic framework of Paul's thought. The translation of the hymn is itself a problem. For consistency and clarity of exposition, we provide here a rather literal version of our own:

2, 5b . . . Christ Jesus,

2, 6a Who, really being in God's form,
   6b Did not regard being equal to God as something to be snatched
                                             at [or, clung to],
   7a But emptied himself,
   7b Taking a slave's form.

   7c Becoming just like men,
   7d And in manner of acting found as a man,
   8a He humbled himself,
   8b Becoming obedient to death—
   8c Death on a cross.

9a   Accordingly, God raised him on high
9b   And graciously bestowed on him the name
9c   Which stands above every name,
10a That in the name of Jesus
10b Every knee would bend,
10c   In heaven and on earth and under earth,
11a And every tongue would publicly confess:
11b   "Jesus Christ is LORD"—
11c To God the Father's glory!

What we shall find perhaps most helpful in grasping the thought of this hymn as Paul presents it is a point already suggested by his own context for the hymn. Paul does not think in the abstract, philosophical categories of "nature" and "person," but in more existentially concrete categories of manifestation in act and of outlook, judgment, personal response. Thus, he has presented "the virtue of humility" in terms of thinking others to be one's superiors, and he has explained this concretely as not seeking one's own things, but those (the interests) of others. Unless we are prepared to understand Paul in terms of his imagery, with its reference to the concrete, rather than in terms of abstract concepts, we shall almost inevitably misread him. On the other hand, if we do try to grasp the images in terms of concrete events, notably in the existential reference of a drama in salvation history, we will even be prepared to probe more deeply on a speculative plane the mystery which he presents. For we shall have first understood the data of revelation on their own terms, and shall then be more assured of preserving them as a whole, especially with their direct reference to Christian life. We will not have regarded Paul's citation from the outset as imaginative speculation which does not quite reach the stratosphere of refined theological distinctions, and therefore as a somewhat impoverished and embarrassing approximation of the truth which we need really to supply from elsewhere.

The Apostle's viewpoint is that of salvation history, a kind of supercharged perspective which goes notably beyond the "actual course of events" to depict God's sovereign intervention. Paul even regularly accentuates this perspective by speaking in the language of apocalyptic. He considerably mutes the bizarre imagery associated with this style of theological exposition, but nevertheless indulges a certain vivid, bold descriptiveness that is foreign to modern taste. Thus, as Paul sees being in terms of concrete function, he sees essential transcendence in terms of a special "glow," "glory." Like Mark among the evangelists, he shows no hesitation about jolting his readers into a rude awareness of mystery, with all the apparent rawness of its paradox.

The first stanza (2, 6a–7b) bluntly speaks of Christ's "emptying himself." This central affirmation in the first stanza is the positive aspect of "not regarding being equal to God as something to be snatched at [or: clung to]," and explains the "transition" from God's form to a slave's form. Being in God's form was already his possession, and implies divine equality. To be equal with God is therefore not something he aspired to have, but something that he rightly did not think was a prize to be snatched at or clung to, much less something undeservedly seized. If the Philippians are to regard (*'ēgeomai,* 2, 3) others as superior to themselves, they are to have in mind as normative for their own conduct what was verified in Christ who did not regard (*'ēgeomai,* 2, 6) equality with God as something to be snatched. In neither case is there question of real lack of equality; in each case the point is an attitude equivalent to a willingness to serve. The "form" that Christ enjoyed was God's glory, the external appearance befitting the dignity of the one he was. Most commentators think of it as pre-existent glory. But we may prefer to take it as that heavenly glory (conceived atemporally) which belongs to Christ by personal title as God's equal. In either event, the status implied by "being in God's form" is not exercised. We may even say that the form is "gone," if we understand the "form" not conceptually, as the divine nature in itself, but phenomenologically, as that effulgent state of existence permanently befitting one who really is equal to God. What has taken place according to this astounding imagery of selfless service is a kind of transfiguration in reverse. Whether seen in terms of actual pre-existence or simply on the

105

symbolic atemporal plane or one who could be expected to reveal himself only in glory, the heavenly being has not stood on his rights. Similarly, we can say that the "taking of a slave's form" refers to the incarnation if we understand not the incarnation as such but its concrete form, the status of a servant—and if we understand even this as being only an initial stage of the humanity fully to be realized in the risen Christ.

The second stanza (2, 7c–8c) contains as its main thought a further act in line with Christ's self-emptying: humbling himself by becoming obedient to death. Once more, the hymn underscores not the fact of the incarnation but its manner: complete identification with men (v. 7c), an identification spelled out in the parallel clause (v. 7d) as Christ's being found in the daily way of life as man. His "humbling himself" (complexive aorist) may be taken as including this ordinary manner of life and thus as restating in terms of daily activity the other two complexive aorists in verses 6b–7a, which highlight his fundamental option for service rather than the enjoyment of existence due to one of his divine standing. But it also marks a progression. "He humbled himself" gravitates towards the ultimate act of Christ's existence as an ordinary man, his death. His "obedience," seen in the total context of his status as a slave, was up to (*mechri*) death. It was not obedience to a command to die, but obedience to a command which was fulfilled in a whole life's work, even at the cost of death. Paul himself (adding to the stanzas which are so well balanced structurally to this point) proceeds to underscore the manner of this death and thus bring out the "scandal" of the mystery: death on a cross.

The last stanza (vv. 9a–11c) is arrayed in sharp contrast with the first two and yet forms their conclusion. Exaltation by the Father for acclaim by all creation is the salient theme. The use of the term God in verse 9a (it has the article in Greek) denotes the Father. In verse 6ab the term was *anarthrous* in Greek as befitting generic reference to a "divine" state or condition. Paul underscores the Father's role in verses 9 ff. by adding at the close (v. 11c) that the acclaim given Christ further redounds to God the Father's glory. The exaltation or raising of Christ on high refers, of course, to his resurrection and ascension.

Parallel to this and explaining it in more explicit terms of enthronement is the bestowal of the name. The "name" is not "Jesus" but "Lord (*Kyrios*)," as is indicated by the "public confession" which consists in acclamation (v. 11ab). The divine title of universal sovereign is not seen here directly as something acquired by Christ but as something graciously bestowed by the Father (*echarisato,* v. 9b). For this mode of expression sets in sharper relief the specifically divine action as contrasted with that proper to the slave's own condition. The bestowal of the name, moreover, does not imply that Jesus "became divine" at this point, any more than his becoming a servant implied that he lost his divine being in becoming man. The perspective is that of fulfillment of a role in the history of salvation. The hymn depicts Christ's sovereignty in terms of rewarded, thoroughly obedient service, as elsewhere early New Testament Christology presents his divine sovereignty or dignity in terms of a mission accomplished or an effect produced (see, for example, Romans 1, 3–4; Acts 2, 36; Hebrews 8, 1–6). According to this hymn in Philippians, one who completely set aside the prospect of a glorified life from the outset with enjoyment of his prerogatives and became fully obedient in his entire human conduct is now to be hailed in act and word by all the universe as sovereign Lord.

Most modern New Testament scholars have paid special attention to the form and scope of the hymn studied in itself. This legitimate but narrower focus has led a good number of them to try to explain the image of the "one in God's form" as an instance of Adam typology—the presentation of Christ in terms of a new Adam who, unlike the Old Testament archetypal figure of mankind, did not prove disobedient. The suggestion is an attractive one, but it does not seem to be precisely to the point as an explanation of the hymn as Paul employs it and as he himself would have us understand it. The exegete should above all try to determine the theological relevance of this hymn in the light of the pastoral context in which Paul himself recalls the hymn and evokes its lesson for the Philippians. No doubt the hymn has had its own history and may admit a somewhat different or supplementary interpretation according to the strata of its earlier contexts (which, in any event, remain even more problematical). But the exegete, for all his interests in reconstructing the life and worship of the early Church, should primarily attend to the meaning of the hymn for the author himself, especially in the context in which he uses it. Both on the score of the context and on the score of Paul's own views elsewhere, however, we see no reason to assert that we should understand verse 6 as Adam typology.

The context suggests that Paul himself is not speculating here on a reversal of Adam's role. It suggests, rather, that what is significant for the Apostle is the mystery of a personal renunciation of privileged status which bears on Christians' practically implemented understanding of existence in Christ. There are differences, to be sure. In the case of Christ, the *kenōsis* or "emptying" of verse 7, though resulting in Christ's own exaltation and redounding to the Father's glory (*doxa,* 11c), is not a renunciation of "empty glorying" (*kenodoxia,* Philippians 2, 3; the *RSV,* "conceit"), but the setting aside of an exercise of divine equality in manner of being. For Paul's Christians, the humbling of themselves (*tapeinophrosynē*) shown concretely in regarding (*'ēgeomai*) others as being their superiors is opposed not to a right to glory but to "empty glorying" (*kenodoxia*).

However, in "setting up" the hymn by describing what the Philippians are to do on the basis of a fundamental outlook proper to their life in Christ, Paul has drawn attention not to Adam-speculation but to the features of Christ's own choices and their consequence. He has brought the "example" of Christ to bear on their own lives, for all the differences which must be acknowledged. He has done this largely by speaking in words that will figure prominently in related form in the hymn that he

108

is about to cite (cf. *'ēgeomai,* "regard," vv. 3 and 6b; *tapeino-phrosynē,* "humility," v. 3, and *tapeinoō,* "humble," v. 8a; *kenodoxia,* "empty glory," v. 3, and *kenoō,* "empty," v. 7a, with *doxa,* "glory," v. 11c). He has also focused attention on what the Philippians' own outlook is to be, perhaps playing on words in the process (*tapeinophrosynē,* v. 3, "humility" in the sense of "humble outlook or mind"; along with the repeated use of *phroneō* in vv. 2, 3, and 5, translated with its objects as "being of the same mind," "being of one mind," "have this mind" [better: "have in mind this, which was (verified) in Christ Jesus"]).

The force of Paul's presentation of this mystery, for all its acknowledged differences, somewhat resembles that in 2 Corinthians 8, 9, when he presents the mystery of generosity which should govern Christian contributions: "one who, being rich, made himself poor for our sake." The use of the hymn in Philippians 2 is surely more akin to the mystery of Christ as Paul presents it in 2 Corinthians 8, 9 than to his own speculation on Adam. For Paul, Adam seems never to have been in "glory." Nor does Paul, for all his attention to Adam's disobedience, present him as attempting to achieve equality with God. Most important of all, it is as risen, not either as a pre-existing being or as a living man prior to the resurrection, that Christ is the "new" or "last" Adam (cf. 1 Corinthians 15, 45–49).

The pastoral context that precedes the hymn and that we think should govern its interpretation as an assimilated part of Paul's theology is borne out in the pastoral exhortation which follows the hymn (2, 12–18). Paul spells out as a consequence the continuance of their Christian obedience (*'ypakouō,* v. 12; cf. *'ypēkoos* in v. 8b of the hymn). The appeal to "fear and trembling" in working out their salvation (v. 12) is a biblical reference to the disposition of the slave or servant of the Lord (cf. especially Psalms 2, 11). No more to be taken in a fundamentalistic, "shaker" sense than the preceding exhortation to humility is to be taken as advocating hand-wringing servility, this idiom does suggest the awesome role of God's power in their lives. The achievement of God's "good pleasure," his grace under the aspect of a sovereign and salvific design, is the work of God himself in them. God himself is intimately active not only in the performing of their works, but in the very prompting of the will to achieve something in regard to this salvific plan in the service of the Lord hailed by the faithful.

But the concluding exhortation also moves beyond the scope of the hymn. As in the first paragraph of this exhortation (1, 27–30), where Paul spoke apocalyptically of what was to be done his absence, the reference to his absence or *apousia* in 2, 12 suggests the framework of the final consummation in the parousia of Christ, of which Paul's hoped-for *parousia* ("coming," "presence") among the Philippians is a kind of advance realization (cf. 1, 26) or typological preview. "Parousia" as used in 2, 12 of Paul's "presence" among the Philippians has a pregnant sense. He employs it not only in reference to his own past contact with them and to the second contact to which he has looked forward, but with an implicit reference to the "presence" of the Lord and the conditions under which this presence is to be realized. Paul's own "presence" is really an advance type of the "presence" or parousia of the Lord. The typological scope of the terms begins to emerge with Paul's reference to what is to be done in the "absence" (*apousia*) of the Apostle. The Philippians are to work out their salvation, an awesome task, since God himself is at work in their actions for the achievement of his salvific purpose. The framework for Paul's request that they work out their salvation in his absence is really his apocalyptic understanding of the whole course of Christian life as a divine work ordered to the triumph of God's salvific plan in the parousia.

Similarly, Paul's moral exhortations in verses 14 ff. are to be understood in the framework of an apocalyptic understanding of the new exodus. The Philippians' avoidance of "grumbling and questioning" in their service of the Lord is more than the avoidance of specific sins. It is the avoidance of those sins

110

typical of God's people in the exodus, sins which represented their rejection not only of the leaders appointed for them but of God himself. The imagery of the new exodus is escalated in the apocalyptic dimension of a cosmic event. The Philippian Christians are to be blameless and perfectly pure (the image is that of rays of the sun rather than the negative one suggested by the *RSV* "innocent") in the midst of an alien environment, typified by those who of their own accord are on the way to perdition. The Philippians themselves are to be luminaries in the world, not just of themselves, but as holding fast to the faith, the word of life. The note of the final triumph which is the goal of this cosmic exodus rings out twofold in the phrases: "for a boast [confident rejoicing in achievement] for me," "for the Day of Christ." The consummation of their course of life will be the consummation of Paul's own race and labor; their "exodus" is ordered to the Day of Christ as his own race, and their success can be hailed as his own.

The richness of Paul's exhortation here is dizzying. A simple admonition to the Philippians to avoid strife among themselves in the service of the Lord is charged with layer upon layer of allusions. The pedestrian facts of the Philippians' daily existence in Paul's absence are seen in the light of mystery past (the Old Testament allusions to the exodus), present (the divine activity in those who are obedient to the Lord Jesus), and to come (the cosmic image of a triumphal consummation as the climax of a present struggle). Even in this temporal framework, there is overlapping or, rather, interpenetration. Nor does the temporal framework of progressive realization of salvation history in an apocalyptic dimension stand as the richest level of understanding. In and through this there is the interpenetration of personal activity, that of God's working among the Lord's servants, that of a march by the Father's children whose glory is not an empty effect of Paul's own work in the race. Lastly, there is the liturgical theme of God's holy people (cf. v. 15) whose faith is Paul's own apostolic offering and priestly service. Here, too, his joy is one with theirs, and theirs with his. What-

111

ever befalls him, even the sacrifice of his life, will be his joy.
For his service of them in the sphere of faith is his service of
God, and this can mean only the joy which comes from achiev-
ing a divine work.

PERSONAL MESSENGERS FOR JOY
IN THE LORD (2, 19—3, 1)

The Apostle wants to provide in his absence more than these
words of exhortation (2, 19–24). He plans to send to Philippi
his closest associate, Timothy. To be cheered by their progress,
Paul will have to dispatch a man who can thoroughly be trusted
to show genuine concern for them, which equivalently means
concern for the things of Christ. Paul feels himself surrounded
by people who, though Christians, are really seeking their own
interests. Timothy's role promises to be even more significant
if something should happen to Paul, so there will be a slight
delay until Paul discerns the outcome of his own present imprisonment. But, as he hoped for the Lord's service to send
Timothy (v. 19), he trusts for the same end that he himself
will be able to come to them quickly.

The sending of Epaphroditus (2, 25–30), who is probably
the bearer of the letter we have as Philippians 1–2, seems to be
more immediately necessary. He appears to have become se-
verely homesick (not simply distressed because the Philippians
had heard he was ill, as in the *RSV*), which led to the report
that he was ill. Indeed, he had been seriously ill, but had recovered. These items of personal information from Paul are
once more suffused with the spiritual outlook and joy that
make the man himself his message of pastoral concern. Solidarity with Paul in his struggle has been shown by Epaphroditus,
especially as his "fellow soldier." On behalf of the Philippians,
this has amounted to their apostolic, religious ministry to Paul
himself. Epaphroditus' recovery is seen as God's mercy both to
Epaphroditus and to Paul, and his return to Philippi should be

112

an occasion for that full joy connoted by divine deliverance from trials in apostolic service, a supernatural joy based on solidarity in work for the Lord. Paul's appreciation of Epaphroditus' total self-giving to the work of Christ is his appreciation of the Philippians themselves, and hence a tacit, appreciative appeal for continued loyalty.

Nothing remains but to insist on joy in the service of the Lord (3, 1). To speak of "joy in the Lord," however, means for Paul to speak of the whole work of revelation in apostolic toil. This "toil" is not bothersome for him, for he says that writing repeatedly about rejoicing in the Lord is not "irksome." For the Philippians, Paul's advice to rejoice in the Lord's service is "safe," that is, a proved way of progress in Christian life. The contrast between the two words "not irksome" and "safe" seems to reflect also the contrast between the conditions under which this service is exercised: Paul's imprisonment and the Philippians' relative security from persecution. Characteristically, however, the focus remains on the disposition of joy in the common effort to be pursued in and for the Lord.

APOSTOLIC CHRISTIAN PERFECTION
(3, 2—4, 1)

Philippians 3, 2 abruptly puts us into the middle of another letter to the Philippians, probably later than the first. Paul seems to be refuting a false perfectionism proposed by Judaizers at Philippi. He does this in a personalized pastoral admonition which presents an apologia for his own ideals judged as formative for the ideals and conduct of his converts.

He bluntly states an introductory warning (3, 2–4a): those who urge circumcision are not the genuine people of God. The latter are those who serve God in the Spirit and rejoice confidently ("boast") in Christ instead of relying on the flesh. The contrast is formulated partly on the level of principles of worship, the divine action of the spirit and the specifically human

113

action of flesh as contrasted with spirit. It is formulated also in the light of actual conduct, with an implicit appeal to lived Christian experience. To this appeal Paul will return explicitly (3, 16).

But he begins to answer his rivals' theology in terms of his own lived experience as an apostle (3, 4b–11). Paul himself can "rest his confidence on flesh" if there is need to do so. The "flesh" or specifically human level of existence is not to be belittled or despised in itself, but is to be disavowed only when it represents or comes to be taken as the ceiling of life in the service of God. Hence Paul can and does appeal to a sevenfold criterion for boasting, centered on his being a Hebrew in the superlative degree. He is not boasting of his being a persecutor, of course, but of his zeal for the law (cf. Galatians 1, 13–14). His "justice" or righteousness by the standard of the law was such that no man could find fault with it. But, according to the superior form of knowledge in Christ the risen Lord, per- haps alluding by "my" Lord to his own conversion-experience (v. 8), he has regarded this and all other things as loss. "Jus- tice" or righteousness implies an "action" by which one "gains" an advantage. There are two dimensions in which these terms can be understood. What Paul has repudiated in his own ex- perience is that "justice" which stems from his own action precisely as being in a greater or less degree attributable solely to himself. He has repudiated this form of justice precisely by looking for his own "gain" in another. By the new bond of faith achieved in Christ, the "justice" in question is a standing which has its proper and sole origin in God himself. The question of perspective here is all-important. Reliance on God cannot be tempered by a "percentage" point of view in which human agency even in some little degree rests independent of God in the achievement of God-given norms of action.

More concretely, what is it that Paul has now gained on the basis of his identification with Christ in the faith relationship? First of all, the gain must be explained "passively": not in terms of Paul's own achievement, but in terms of "being found" by God (3, 9). Paul's gain thus means "being known by God" (cf.

114

Galatians 4, 9) as well as knowing Christ. The intimate personal union with Christ in the bond of faith is formulated in the language of experiential knowledge. We may say that it is formulated in the language of mystical experience if we do not consider mystical experience mainly in terms of spectacular actions or states foreign to the general run of Christians but as that mature understanding of the faith expected of all adult Christians. "Knowing him" is further clarified (3, 10) in the context of the paschal mystery as it bears on the life to be realized in the individual Christian, for whom Paul implicitly presents himself as a type (cf. v. 17). "Knowing him" means, above all, being made to experience the power of his resurrection, which is now operative in the life of the Christian but is yet to be realized in his own future transformation on the Day of the Lord. Accordingly, "knowing him" means a share in his sufferings. For the very form of Christian life, its essence, as it were, and its structure for future realization, is the shape of the death of Christ. Personal gain or fulfillment is placed squarely in the mystical context of faith knowledge in Christ and at the same time in the historical context of a mystery to be fulfilled in time.

The temporal perspective suggests the image of a race (3, 12–16), but the mystical image of "perfection" (with a play, perhaps, on the idea of "initiation," for the "perfect"—*teleioi*—could in some circles be considered "initiates") seems to govern it. The image of the race is surely forced, in any event, by more sovereign, theological considerations. For all his gains in Christ, Paul has not yet received the prize; he runs in the hope of taking it at the goal. But this he does on the basis of having been himself taken by Christ Jesus. He does not attribute his hoped-for success to himself, but, basing his hope on what Christ has already won in him, he does not pause to look back. He is ever intent on what lies ahead—and here the race takes a vertical dimension—the prize of a calling to move on high, God's call in Christ Jesus. The "call" implies the vocation that has governed the course from the beginning. But just as the means to win the race has been anticipated by Christ himself in his making Paul his own, so the call upwards is yet to be realized.

The application to those who are "perfect" (*teleioi,* a word with more connotations than the *RSV* "mature") is clear enough. Their mind, that is, their whole outlook in Christian life, is to be governed by the picture which Paul has presented of his own "perfection" *in fieri.* The image has the force of God's revealed word. If they have in some respect another outlook (perhaps there is irony here, though Paul does not rigorously present his own view as the only charismatic representation of the mystery), God will himself confirm this vision that Paul has presented. The one point that he could have them keep in mind in any outlook is that the direction of their progress is to be in line with what they have already attained. Thus it is clear that the gain in Christ becomes the standard for future conduct (*stoichein,* "holding true" in the sense of walking ahead steadily by some norm). In effect, perfection cannot be obtained by losing what one has, but solely by progressing in that which has marked the advance thus far.

Explicitly, with hard words for his adversaries—and theirs —Paul contrasts his own example to that of those who are enemies of the cross of Christ (3, 17–21). Again, as he did earlier (1, 28; cf. 1 Thessalonians 2, 16; 2 Thessalonians 1, 5–10), he views adversaries to the faith in the light of an apocalyptic picture of the future. Their "end" (*telos,* still playing, perhaps, on the idea of "perfection" or final goal) is destruction. Alluding to dietary practices and the rite of circumcision, he derides the whole earthbound outlook which he sees as the fundamental distortion: "their god is their belly and their glory is in their shame."

While Paul himself has the Judaizers in mind, his perspective should not be limited to them. What he said apropos of the particular situation at Philippi is relevant proportionately to any earthbound set of values. And any set of values remains earthbound as long as it attributes some salvific good, independently of God's immediate action in Christ, to what man does of himself. The cross is the focal point of the opposition between these

116

two sets of values and those who stand for them. Not only was the cross of Christ historically the moment of redemption and a central theme of Paul's preaching, but it now effectively represents the whole mystery of God's power in human weakness.

In contrast to the earthbound level of existence represented by the Judaizers in the situation to which Paul addressed himself (3, 17–19), the Christian level of existence is seen as a heavenly commonwealth (*politeuma*) (3, 20 f.). The "negative" imagery of the cross, important as it is, yields here to the "positive" image of the advent of the risen Lord, the savior, who will transform us into the existence fully conformed with the status that is really ours on the heavenly plane or, as we would say today, supernaturally. As the Christian has been conformed to his death, that is, shaped to the image of Christ crucified (3, 10), he is destined to be conformed to the body of his glory (3, 21) in the resurrection. But the latter implies a transformation that goes beyond the interior. Paul therefore speaks in 3, 21 of a contrast entailing a whole external form of life. Accordingly, he speaks of the whole man under the aspect of the "body." It is this second, joyful aspect of the apocalyptic process towards which Paul gravitates. His sorrow at opposition to the cross is more than balanced by his thought of the dynamic achievement of Christ's power on a cosmic scale (3, 21). Therefore, he concludes the appeal to be "imitators" of himself with an appeal for the Philippians to stand firm in the Lord's service. They are his joy and crown, and are to stand firm "thus" in the Lord's service, not only as those whom he yearns to see and who are his own reward, but as those who are God's "well beloved."

CLOSING SENTIMENTS OF PEACE AND JOY (4, 2–23)

The themes of solidarity in Christ, Christian joy, and hope for the parousia have been woven together repeatedly in many-hued strands and different patterns throughout Paul's correspondence with the Philippians. All three themes are woven on the warp and woof of the Christian "mind" or "outlook," which is simply the conscious awareness in faith of one's existential relationships in faith. In dealing briefly and somewhat enigmatically with the quarrel between two women (4, 2–3), Paul appeals to agreement in the Lord, that is, to the "same mind or outlook in the service of the Lord." This should be the governing principle of reconciliation between them. The "yokefellow" of Paul is to help them in achieving this, with the special fact in mind that they had shared Paul's struggle in union with those whose destiny at the Lord's final reckoning is to be life.

In widening his consideration to all those who have worked with him, Paul widens his basic injunction to encompass the attitude of all: "Rejoice in the Lord always; again I will say it, rejoice." Forbearance (*to epieikes,* "modest, inoffensive bearing in dealing with others") is to be the hallmark of the community before all men, not to mention the faithful themselves. This forbearance is the practical corollary of their joy in the Lord's service. "The Lord is near" (v. 5b) does not affirm the clock-and-calendar imminence of the parousia, but reaffirms the grounds of Christian joy in a phrase borrowed from the liturgy of the time: the Lord's coming will be the goal and consummation of their lives. The coming is already under way, for the "last days," already inaugurated by the death and resurrection of Christ are those in which the Christians live. In view of these facts and the confident expectation that, for Christians true to their faith, the day will be one of triumph, not of wrath, the rays of the parousia are already to warm the lives of those in Christ. For the same reason, their outlook is to be free from "anxiety," that is, from the care which springs from double-mindedness, from even partial preoccupation with the things that will not abide. This eschatological singleness of outlook finds its expression in every prayer and petition with thanksgiving, in which their requests are gratefully laid open before God. And it can hope to receive that eschatological blessing, the peace of God which lies above any human understanding.

118

While single-minded awareness of the Lord's coming as the goal that already lights the Philippians' lives is all-important, a multiplicity of good things is not to be regarded as foreign to them (4, 8–9). But the value of these things must accord with the single-mindedness of the eschatological outlook. If there is anything reputedly of value, the Philippians are to "think about these things" (the *RSV* for *tauta logizesthe*). That is, they are to reckon their value in the light of God's judgment. Or, more simply, whatever is already recognized in the light of the final consummation as being of real value is to be "chalked up" as a present gain. More concretely and practically, what is to be done is what they have learned and received and heard and seen in Paul himself. Thus, not only will God's peace keep safe their minds and hearts when they make their requests of him (v. 7), but the God of peace himself will be with them in their undertakings.

Concluding these practical remarks on outlook and concerns that he expects of the Philippians, Paul thanks them for the concern he himself has been shown (4, 10–20). Their mindfulness of him has been a cause of his own expansive joy. He speaks of their concern for him in terms of the coming of spring (*anethalete,* v. 10), an image which is continued in the rest of the verse and which makes it somewhat easier to understand the conjunction: "because you were indeed concerned all along, though you did not find the season." Their concern for him, which was always present, had been able to grow up or bloom only in the present circumstances. His joy in response to their practical concern is not occasioned so much by the sustenance that has been provided him, as by the affection it attests on the part of the Philippians. As for himself, an apostolic self-sufficiency under all conditions is the order of his daily life. The present trial and the present consolation are judged in the context of the whole pattern of the Apostle's life. In turn, the vital force at work for becoming self-sufficient under any circumstances is the apostolic energy that is God's own power in Christ. Paul's own life stands once more as the personal mes-

119

sage he preaches. Even in thanking the Philippians, he can instruct them.

The instruction becomes commendation for their share in his trial ("trouble") (4, 14–20). This eschatological term, which refers, of course, to Paul's present imprisonment, evokes the whole perspective of his struggle and the final reward. Hence he immediately recalls the service the Philippians had rendered him "at the beginning of the gospel," the moment when the new world of faith had begun for them. He recalls their complete share in his apostolate by being as generous to him in their own way (through needed contributions) as he had been to them (in preaching the gospel without asking a fee). Thus he can look forward to their own reward, the "harvest of justice" from their generous dealings with him. His thankfulness therefore turns to encouragement for their own hope of reward from God, and he can end with a prayer for the fulfillment of their own needs in Christ's glory.

CHAPTER FIVE

1 CORINTHIANS

COMPOSITION AND GENERAL BACK-GROUND: A LETTER TO "GNOSTICS"

Certain passages in 1 Corinthians (for example, 5, 9) indicate that our present 1 Corinthians was not Paul's first written communication to the Church at Corinth. It may well be that 1 Corinthians 15 itself, which is easily detached from the whole, formed part of this earlier correspondence. Theologically, this chapter seems to lie somewhat closer to 1 and 2 Thessalonians than do other parts of 1 Corinthians; its apocalyptic imagery, for instance, is somewhat more vivid and concrete. The pastoral tone and scope of this chapter do not seem to fit with the rest of what we have in this letter. For 1 Corinthians 15 seems to suppose doctrinal misconceptions rather than moral problems. Yet, in spite of the seriousness of its topic, the understanding of the resurrection, the chapter does not contain the somewhat heated admonitions characteristic of much of the rest of the letter. What is more, it contains a remark about the law (15, 56) that seems alien to the scope of 1 Corinthians and which is enigmatic even in its present, limited context. If Paul had written a previous letter to the Corinthians that dealt not only with the resurrection but also with freedom from the law, the statement in 15, 56 would be more intelligible. That statement, which is not necessarily formulated as a kind of aside, should not gratuitously be judged a gloss. The manuscript evidence in its favor, moreover, is completely solid, which means that any addition would have to have been made extremely early in the tradition. But it is hard to see what would have motivated the supposed glossator at this necessarily early stage—certainly not the integration of this chapter into the rest of what has come down to us as 1 Corinthians.

If 1 Corinthians 15 had existed in an earlier letter written along the lines indicated above, the pastoral situation of the rest of 1 Corinthians could more readily be explained. The misunderstanding of Paul's views concerning Christian freedom, which must be presumed in the light of his admonitions throughout 1 Corinthians 1–14, can more easily be grasped in the context of a previous polemic against the law. Likewise, the admonitions of an earlier letter which Paul does recall (5, 9) would have been more in accord with the method he used in corresponding with the Thessalonians. He would have expected the Corinthians to have understood somewhat indirectly phrased norms regarding sexual ethics and to have handled the matter themselves (5, 9–13). As it is, they seemed to have conducted themselves quite immaturely. Accordingly, what we now have as 1 Corinthians 1–14 and 16 contains some of Paul's clearest and strongest admonitions.

The basic problem underlying the fifteenth chapter was a misconception of the importance of the kerygma concerning the resurrection. Some at Corinth had apparently failed to see the importance of this in the message of the whole apostolic Church as well as in the preaching of Paul. A number had even denied the reality of the resurrection, perhaps because they regarded it too materialistically, for example, as a reconstitution of the kind of body that men possessed here and now, or perhaps because they simply could not imagine how the event

122

would take place. Christ's own heavenly existence in a risen body may not have been denied, but the Corinthians who denied the resurrection failed to see that the reason for Christ's resurrection lay not only in his own glorification after suffering, but in the divine plan for men's redemption, namely, the re-creation of men in the image of God's Son. Christ's resurrection makes full theological sense not as his own personal resurrection alone, but as the first fruits of a new order of creation, the kingdom, which is yet to be realized fully.

With regard to the rest of the letter, the picture becomes more complicated. Paul himself seems to have had to construe the various problems from at least two principal sources. We, in turn, must construe everything from his replies. One of Paul's sources was clearly information brought by word of mouth through employees of Chloe (1, 11); other information, no doubt, came from Stephanus and his companions (16, 17; cf. 1, 16; 16, 15). Perhaps the information brought by the latter reached Paul together with his second main source, a letter from the Corinthians themselves. Paul explicitly refers to such a letter in 7, 1, and he seems to have its other topics or statements before him when writing chapters 5 and 7–14. This letter from Corinth was at least partially in answer to one which Paul himself had written (and which was concerned at least in part with a marriage situation at Corinth that was out of keeping with Christian principles, 1 Corinthians 5). The Corinthians' letter to Paul might well be characterized as a letter of "self-commendation" in which the Corinthians expressed their own satisfaction with the solutions they had found for a number of problems. But they clearly had misunderstood Paul's previous communications in at least one respect (5, 9) and probably had misunderstood his teaching about a number of other points. Paul gives the impression at times either that he is answering a quotation of his own misunderstood principles or that he is trying to correct a false conception of Christian freedom which found expression in certain ambiguous slogans. The expression "all things are lawful" is a case in point (6, 12; 10, 23).

One of the more basic problems at Corinth was factionalism based on human considerations. One may perhaps sense the beginnings of this problem from cautions in chapter 15, where Paul appeals to the basic message of the kerygma as being independent of the dignity of the one who preached it (15, 1–11). The situation reflected in the opening chapter, however, is more clearly virulent and destructive of the community as a whole. The Corinthians judged their faith in accordance with the relative importance of the one who had baptized them or whose preaching they favored. Their factionalism showed itself, too, in a kind of "club spirit" at liturgical functions. Christians were in danger of confusing the Church with a philosophical or political club like those common among the pagans. The Corinthians seem to have tended to look on their new association as a means for social advancement or at least personal satisfaction in various cliques. The spirit manifested in these offenses against unity and charity likewise appeared in a disdainful disregard of the scandal caused to weaker members of the community in the matter of eating food that had been sacrificed to idols.

Charismatic abuses in the Church at Corinth further involved open disorder in the liturgical community, a lack of reverence (especially on the part of certain women), and a lack of consideration for the contributions of others both in liturgical functions and in the general life of the Church as one body. This open lack of concord and discipline showed itself, too, in the litigation between one Christian and another. Sexual moral offenses ranged from toleration of flagrant laxity and fornication to a kind of scrupulosity, seeing sin where there was none. An instance of incestuous marriage was at least tolerated, as were other more common sexual offenses like extra-marital relationships. Marriage seems to have been looked upon by some simply as an expeditious remedy for concupiscence, not as a state entailing mutual obligations while offering the opportunity for spiritual growth through the practice of continence. Problems of broken marriages involving a non-Christian partner called for Paul's guidance. Some who practiced virginity were also

124

disturbed. In particular, the practice of a virginal marriage which excessively tested the virtue of one of the spouses required counsel on the licitness of converting the virginal marriage into one calling for sexual relations.

Underlying the destructive disunity and lack of charity, and touching in particular on the sexual ethics of the community was a misconception of Christian freedom and obligation. It is perhaps the apparent incompatibility between freedom and obligation in the minds of the Corinthians, along with their failure to grasp the total eschatological perspective which was basic to Paul's teaching, that makes this letter especially relevant to modern Christians.

The much discussed gnostic tendencies at Corinth must be treated reservedly. Reconstructions must be worked out by the exegete, but in line with his professed concern, he should work them out and use them only to the extent to which they are really helpful for interpreting the text. All too often one has the impression that the critic who reconstructs gnosticism at Corinth has become more interested in gnosticism itself or in features of early Church history than specifically in an integral and solid interpretation of the text. The latter is decidedly normative for the reconstruction used by an exegete. Gnostic tendencies at Corinth do not seem to have involved doctrinal elaborations, but to have enjoyed the aura of a kind of religious sophistication. Certain terms, ideas, and ways of looking at things were "in the air," much like existential terminology and ideas of the present day among those *au courant* who have never studied or read Kierkegaard, Sartre, or Heidegger. Fanciers of the intellectual life and of the passing lecturer would no doubt have figured or posed as "those in the know" among the members of the community. Most serious, it seems, was a tendency to think in terms of separability: to place the earthly in opposition to the heavenly in a way that brought one to disdain the flesh and belittle the value of required modes of conduct; to see the theoretical at the expense of the practical; to pit freedom pure and simple against obligation. A catholic

125

state of mind, which tries to see things as a whole and in a perspective admitting varying degrees of importance, maintaining a balanced perspective even at the expense of clear-cut, simple solutions, was in danger of being lost to a good number. It was in the Corinthians' faulty perspective and attitudes more than in any specific doctrine that the real danger lay. It is to restoring the proper perspective among self-styled religious intellectuals that Paul repeatedly devotes his efforts in this letter.

The letter as a whole was written from Ephesus (16, 8) about Easter of A.D. 57, during the last year of Paul's stay in Ephesus on Mission III. The best date for chapter 15 would be no more than two years previous to this; if it formed part of the letter referred to in 1 Corinthians 5, 9, it was probably written only a few months before chapters 1–14, and 16.

OPENING APPEALS FOR UNITY (1, 1–17)

In the address (1, 1–2), Paul already hints at a theme that will pervade the letter. He hails the "Church of God at Corinth" as one with "all who call upon the name of the Lord Jesus Christ in every place, theirs and ours." The basic unity of the Church in any one area is seen as an instance of the unity of the Church everywhere, for it is a unity of the faithful in Christ.

The customary greeting (1, 3) is followed by a thanksgiving (1, 4–9) in which Paul shows that he does not regard the Corinthians as being radically deficient in faith. But he does place their own richness in speech and knowledge in proper faith perspective, the grace of God in Christ (v. 5a) and Christ's testimony among them—a reference to Paul's own preaching. In addition to this foundation in Christ which they have received, they lack no concrete manifestation of grace (charism) as they look hopefully for the consummation of their faith and the grace of Christ in his second coming. The foundation that is Christ's testimony among them finds a correlative, more dynamic aspect in God's action which is ordered to this happy consummation. Paul repeats the same word (*bebaioō*) in two

126

tenses, past and future, when speaking of Christ's testimony ("confirmed," v. 6) and of God's action in "sustaining" them to the end. Once again, as in other letters (for example 2 Thessalonians 1, 3–10; Philippians 1, 5–6. 27–28), Paul's thanks for the faith of his community reveals the dynamic thrust of his apocalyptic thought: the consummation in the second coming is the fulfillment of a life of faith in Christ. The divine action which pervades this span of faith is God's own fidelity to the call he has given them, a call that finds its unity not just in its source in the Father, but in his Son's communion (*koinōnia*), that is, in a oneness shared in Christ.

Paul immediately pursues this thanksgiving with an exhortation (1, 10–17) to unity, criticizing specifically the factionalism at Corinth. The name of the Lord Jesus Christ, as representing the basis of the unity they profess, forms the basis of Paul's own appeal for unity in understanding and judgment. Underlying this appeal to a conscious unity is Paul's awareness of a more radical unity in their very existence. Christ himself is not "divided" in being "shared" (cf. *koinōnia* in 1 Corinthians 1, 9). The Corinthians' union with Christ consists radically in the effective oneness he achieved on the cross and in their baptismal consecration. Paul's own name figures in the factional acclaim at Corinth, and he quickly dissociates himself from this partisan misunderstanding of his apostolate. He can do so by showing that his work was not to baptize but to preach, and that even in preaching he presented the word in a manner that brought out not his own power of eloquent understanding but the power of God in Christ.

I. GENUINE WISDOM AND JUDGMENT VERSUS FACTIONALISM (1, 18—4, 21)

What we may call the first part of the letter that we have as 1 Corinthians runs from 1, 18 to 4, 21. In these chapters, Paul strikes directly at the sophistication of the Corinthians, the fact that they pride themselves on a derived wisdom (as followers of a given teacher) rather than on the things of God, whose servants in the apostolate are men like Apollos and Paul.

In 1, 18–3, 4 Paul takes up the theme of God's power and wisdom. He discusses the scope of his catechesis in terms of the recognition of what its very paradox reveals, the wisdom and power of God (1, 18–25). In view of the situation he confronts with the pastoral purpose of restoring the proper understanding of the Corinthians' unity in Christ, it would be unfair to judge Paul to be anti-intellectual. He certainly did not pursue the arts for their own sake, for his call to be an apostle required a total and energetic immersion in the toil of the ordinary man. But he could use well the literary forms of his time, as chapter 13, written in the style of the Stoic-cynic diatribe, attests. That he did so at least on occasion should caution one against taking his remarks here as an assault against human wisdom and eloquence as such. What is more, all human values were in Paul's eyes to be judged ultimately in another perspective altogether, that of supreme values, seen dynamically as God's power and efficacious wisdom. The Corinthians had set their sights much lower. Paul feels that he can jolt them into an awareness of the wisdom that really matters.

The context for understanding real wisdom is the context of mystery. The apocalyptic approach was a theological method of the time especially suited to highlighting the element of mystery; it was able to convey a sense of the awesome power of God's judgment. That salvation itself began to take place in the shocking events of the crucifixion was reason enough, even aside from the probable background and tastes of a converted, fiercely zealous Pharisee like Paul, to commend to the Apostle an apocalyptic cast for the kerygma. Characteristic of the apocalyptic cast of thought is a negative emphasis on destruction and desolation serving as the necessary correlative for the positive stress on creative power in righting the cosmic course of religious history. The negative stress makes sense and is meant to make sense only in the framework of this dialectical correlation with the positive image of triumph. The pattern of apoca-

128

lyptic thought becomes more cohesive through the Christian message itself and through the images and categories of thought proper to the writer who uses it to convey his message. In the case of Paul, whose gospel derived from the jolting experience of his own conversion by God's grace, together with the revelation of the crucified Jesus of Nazareth as the Lord, the pattern is perhaps more sharply defined than in any other writer of the New Testament. The mystery of God's power in transforming Paul's whole outlook by the negation of his past values and the revelation of wisdom in Jesus Christ shaped the message by shaping the man himself who was to bear it. The apocalyptic of Paul's thought is rooted in the *apokalypsis* (revelation) to him of the mystery of Christ crucified and risen (Galatians 1, 12. 16).

His message, then, is "the word of the cross" which is unintelligible on the level of "this [present] age" from which we have been delivered (cf. Galatians 1, 4). A new order is in the making, and it commences, in apocalyptic fashion, with the destruction of the old. In developing his contrasts between foolishness and power, foolishness and wisdom, signs and wisdom, and so forth, Paul manifestly understands wisdom in line with the Old Testament sense of a practical, *operative* wisdom, a wisdom that "works" and connotes a certain vital level of creation itself. Similarly, he regards God's power not as a kind of brute force distinguished from the order associated with intellect, but as creative wisdom at work with undisputed efficacy. Along with these ways of understanding wisdom and power, the concept of a twofold age characterized by two levels of activity, one representatively human (that of the flesh), the other representatively divine (that of the spirit), underlies Paul's contrast in 1, 18–25 between what is of men and what is of God.

The level of the "flesh" becomes explicit in 1, 26–31. Paul here moves to discuss the change effected in the Corinthians themselves by their Christian vocation. In effect, they themselves were "nobodys," so that God's choice of them was a sign

129

of confounding the humanly strong and powerful. Thus, any confident rejoicing in their own achievements as the work of human sufficiency is ruled out before God. Their conversion is not their own "achievement." For it is from God that they are in Christ. It is he, then, who has become their wisdom, their justice and sanctification, their redemption. In this threefold phrase, Paul reminds them that in Christ is realized the creative plan of God, their own present standing with God which is yet to be realized fully, and God's final acquisition of his people at the resurrection, when the Lord's own achievement will reach its complete goal. Accordingly, the one who confidently rejoices in this achievement is to do so in the Lord.

Thirdly, Paul shows that his own manner of preaching reflected the standard of values it proclaimed (2, 1–5). Whatever may have been the nature of Paul's physical state on his arrival at Corinth—the situation may have been deliberately edited (v. 3b) in order to bring out the awesome task of preaching the mystery—Paul was anything but reliant on human oratorical skills to win his audience. The proportionate signs for a spiritual message were, instead, of a miraculous nature. It is, of course, not the prodigies themselves to which Paul calls attention. Whatever the actual nature of these events may have been, they were signs for those who were shown them, meant to bring them to an awareness of God's power. The preaching of the gospel in a given cultural situation where wonders were "expected," its preaching in a strongly apocalyptic form, and the absence at the time of other concrete testimonials (like the sign of a universally established Church with its works of sanctification and charity), probably called for signs of power other than those that might be judged necessary or sufficient for an audience of our own day. Whether or not these signs were "beyond a natural explanation" in themselves is really rather irrelevant. They were meant to be effective signs that would not force faith, but that would lead one to recognize in faith the power of God. Since the gospel itself was conceived as God's power (cf. Romans 1, 16), it was fitting that its proclamation be attested in works of power.

Thus far, Paul has presented in predominantly negative fashion the wisdom and power of God in three interrelated areas of pastoral activity: the kerygma itself (1, 18–25), the ones to whom it was preached (1, 26–31), and the manner of the Apostle's own preaching (2, 1–5). He now defends more positively the wisdom of God, which is the wisdom of his own preaching to the "perfect" Christian, the one mature in the faith (2, 6–16).

Employing apocalyptic imagery to depict the power figures of the "present age," which is doomed to disappear and is already rendered ineffective for those in Christ, Paul speaks of God's wisdom as one that is unseen. That is, God's wisdom pertains to an order different from "phenomenal" creation— including such "spiritual" figures as angelic or quasi-angelic "rulers of this age." That God's wisdom is unknowable short of God's own manifestation of it in the Spirit can be seen from the fact of the crucifixion. This event, in Paul's eyes, is one that engaged the whole order of creation, including angelic powers, and he imaginatively attributes the event to their instrumentality because of what they represent, namely, the reality of sin. Had they known God's wisdom, they would not have crucified the one who was the Lord of glory; they would have been overwhelmed by the powerfully effulgent wisdom of God in Christ. It was there in the man who was to be crucified (cf. Philippians 2, 6), but it was not seen. The glory was hidden in Christ to be revealed not for their benefit, but "to our glory" (2, 7). Its very revelation, moreover, was not on the basis of what could be physically perceived, but on the basis of faith (v. 9). "What eye has not seen or heard" refers directly to the mystery of God's power shown in Christ as received in faith. More accurately still, it refers to the revelation received in faith as effected through the Spirit. Thus, the activity of the Spirit, whose reality cannot be questioned, is brought into view by the counterweight of an apocalyptic representation of sin in mythological terms of angelic powers. The rulers of the age have not experienced even a faint perception of wisdom in the event they brought about. The Spirit, on the other hand, is one who reveals

131

to those who have received the love of God by believing in the crucified one the very depths of this mystery.

The focal point of wisdom, then, is still the cross of Christ. But it holds a hidden wisdom which the Spirit of God alone can probe, not the malign spirits of this age which stand for sin or a knowledge marred by a kind of native incapacity for spiritual perception. Keeping to the cosmic plane, but focusing his attention on the contrast between God and man (vv. 11 f.) rather than on the contrast between angelic powers and the Spirit (vv. 8–10), Paul speaks of the Spirit as the unique means of communicating the things that pertain to God. "The spirit of the world" (v. 12) designates the way of thinking proper to "this present age," and defines what fails to be the principle of Christian understanding. For Christians, the principle of understanding is more than a way of thinking. It is the Spirit who is from God, the one who understands by "connatural existence" the things of God, in whom he exists. Accordingly, this Spirit brings to the awareness of Christians the knowledge of what is most intimately the action of God in our regard, the "gracious gifts" bestowed on us by God. It is these gifts that Paul reveals in words not calculated by human wisdom but taught by the Spirit himself. He blends spiritual things for spiritual-minded people. That is, his utterances concerning supernatural realities are intended to be assimilated by people who have a connatural principle of understanding. "Connatural understanding" of something like love is had by a man in love; similarly, the understanding of the things of the spirit is had by a man in the spirit.

Paul goes on (vv. 14–16) to contrast the attitude of the "unspiritual man" (*psychikos,* the one whose highest level of perception is still distinctively earthbound though not simply "material"), and that of one who operates on the level of the spirit (*pneumatikos,* the one whose level of activity is not determined, as it were, by a downward thrust into matter, but by an upward thrust to God himself). The "unspiritual man" is by definition unreceptive to what pertains to the spirit of God.

132

"Connatural" knowledge of these things becomes impossible for him; like one who has never been in love, he cannot really understand it, but judges it to be utter foolishness.

Paul's own comparison, however, is soberly juridical. The unspiritual man cannot come to know what is spiritual, because the latter is "judged" or discerned spiritually. Things on the level of the Spirit cannot be evaluated by the norm of what lies below them or by an inferior mode of perception. On the other hand, the spiritual man is able to discern the value of all things in his judgment and is himself not liable to judgment by anyone else. By this latter statement, Paul seems to have in mind the spiritual man's status as one with that of the final judge and risen Lord of creation, Christ himself, from whom one receives the Spirit. Accordingly, Paul continues with a reference to Isaiah 40, 13, which speaks of the judgment ("mind," *nous*) of the Lord, the creator, and he proceeds immediately to affirm that we have the mind (*nous*) of Christ. Thus, as the cross of Christ is the focal point of wisdom, so the mind of Christ, at work in us through the Spirit which we have received from God, is the principle for understanding this mystery and, indeed, all the things graciously bestowed on us by God.

After sketching the wisdom that he does utter among the spiritually mature, and noting the principle by which it is grasped (2, 6–16), Paul reproaches the Corinthians for being unable to receive it (3, 1–17). They are still on a "fleshly" level of existence, conducting themselves much as any other men. Moral defects of self-centeredness solidly indicate this. Paul sees the specifically human concretely in terms of "fleshly" limitations. Here again, he judges specifically "human" existence not in itself, after the manner of the philosopher or the humanist, but in relation to a transformed human existence that is not "angelic" (a facile and misleading opposition), but "spiritual."

The guiding principle for the Apostle's contrast and for the pastoral rebuke that he launches from it is his understanding of the mystery of transformation in Christ who, now risen, is most truly man by being the "spiritual" man (cf. 1 Corinthians 15). The modern Christian who often pits the "incarnational" against the "eschatological" will be at a loss to understand Paul, much less accept him, unless he is willing to see the "incarnational" in its adequate dimension, eschatological transformation. It is not simply Christ's becoming man that is the center of the Christian mystery, but his transformation by death and resurrection into the new, "spiritual" man who brings us and all things under the sovereign power of a loving Father. Christ is most fully human precisely as the "spiritual man," the new Adam.

In the present context, Paul is more immediately concerned about showing how the factionalism at Corinth reflects not only the Corinthians' spiritual immaturity but, more concretely, a misunderstanding of the role of those to whom they would attach themselves in such a limited, divisive way. People like Apollos and Paul are simply instruments of God in transmitting the faith. These ideas are spelled out in two illustrations. The first illustration is that of God's plantation (3, 6–9). The second (3, 9b–17), closely joined with the image of the plantation (end of v. 9), is that of God's building, the temple (cf. v. 16). In both instances, there is one work, and God himself is the one who determines its value. The first illustration stresses the vital activity of God as well as his giving the final reward. The second underscores the divine initiative in the work of the apostle (v. 10a), the unique foundation, which is Christ himself (v. 11), and the holiness of the community as the abode of the Spirit (v. 16). The image of the building is further escalated into the picture of a temple that is to undergo an eschatological conflagration by which the value of the worker's contributions will be proved in God's eyes. Paul wants to bring the Corinthians to an awareness of the fact that they are not men's work, but God's. His answer to their problem of factionalism lies in evoking an awareness of that to which God's co-workers, their co-operating ministers, are subject.

Against this background concerning God's powerful word

134

(1, 18–2, 5), God's spiritually discerned wisdom in Christ (2, 6–16), and God's use of various preachers to achieve a work that he himself furthers and judges (3, 1–17), Paul directly admonishes the Corinthians concerning self-deception (3, 18–4, 21). No one is to boast in men or in human wisdom as such. Again, we can discern the apocalyptic framework in Paul's reference to "this age" (v. 18), equivalent to "this world" (v. 19), as expressing the level of an imperfect, earthbound existence alien to that which represents the divine. But Paul does not mean to imply by this apocalyptic reference that the world itself is evil or that there are surd elements in creation that cannot be brought under the sway of God. He is intent precisely on restoring the proper theological perspective, which will preclude self-deception. Positively, this is an upward view, the recognition that all things are shared by those who are Christ's, who is God's (3, 21–22).

Thus, the Corinthians are to judge even preachers like Paul and Apollos and Cephas as dispensers of God's mysteries, not as the ultimate source of these gifts (4, 1 ff.). These ministers must demonstrate their own fidelity to God. But the criterion for this demonstration is not to be set by the Corinthians; it is the Lord alone who renders judgment (4, 1–5) in this decisive way, for he alone can really judge men's hearts according to what he has given. What Paul has applied to himself and to Apollos comprises a lesson to the Corinthians not to think that they have achieved their life aim of attaining God's kingdom, for the apostles themselves are at present like the men at the end of a triumphal procession—captives doomed to die in the arena (4, 6–13). The Corinthians "have not yet made it" to the kingdom. If they had done so, then the apostles would have attained it too, since the glory of resurrection for the one group is the same crown for the other. But, in the present stage of the eschaton, the apostles themselves are outstanding only for their trials. At this point, Paul employs irony to show the Corinthians how false is their own complacent self-assurance: if the apostles are outstanding only for their trials, for this is the way to the

135

kingdom, then how can the Corinthians realistically judge their own course differently? "We are fools for Christ's sake, but you are wise . . ."

The irony, however, has a constructive purpose. Paul goes on to deny (4, 14–21) that he is berating them, and solicitously insists that he is only trying to correct his own dear sons, for he is the father who has brought them into existence in Christ through the gospel. In his concluding exhortation, then, the Apostle urges that they take his life as a pattern for their own. He has sent Timothy to recall to their minds his universal teaching; Paul demands no more of the Corinthians than he expects of Christians in general. But he prefers not to come in person. Such a course of action might require unwelcome harshness under the circumstances, a full-scale proof of apostolic power versus hollow self-assurance. He pointedly notes that the choice of treatment remains theirs, while at the same time he indicates that he himself prefers the milder course of action.

II. VARIOUS PROBLEMS APROPOS OF CORRESPONDENCE (5, 1—14, 40)

A. *Undiscerning Toleration of Immorality (5, 1–13)*

With 1 Corinthians 5, we begin what may be called the second part of the letter, in which Paul more directly refers to specific problems in the light of previous correspondence or discusses points closely related to this correspondence. In the first part of the letter, the main point at issue had been the report of factionalism and Paul's correction of this in the light of what his preaching and that of others really stood for. The specific abuse mentioned at the outset of chapter 5 is one that Paul has heard persists in spite of his previous letter (cf. 5, 9). What most irks him now is not the instance of incest itself, but the state of the community. It is puffed up with pseudo-knowledge (5, 2; cf. 8, 1) and has failed both in the sense of judgment

136

expected of it and in the actual handling of this case. Paul has to take strong measures himself. He excommunicates the man concerned (5, 3–5), gives a homily to the Corinthians explaining the necessity of such a course of action (5, 6–8), and points out with perceptible irritation how they misunderstood the obvious aim of admonitions in his previous letter (5, 9–13).

The basis for the exercise of his excommunication, a juridical act, is the common bond of the Spirit which both possess in a kind of assembly where the power is seen as that of the Lord Jesus himself (v. 3). The exclusion of the culprit is tantamount to placing him once again in that "aeon" or age from which the Christian has been delivered by Christ; he is under a curse, on the apocalyptically conceived road to destruction. Even so, the judgment of Paul which is to be executed by the community is not God's final judgment, but a medicinal corrective. For it is done with the intention that this chastisement will somehow result in the man's salvation on the day of judgment. The status of the culprit is now radically ambiguous; he does not enjoy that confident assurance in the power of the Lord which is the hallmark of the Christian. The ambiguity of his status is reflected in the "flesh-spirit" antithesis, each element looking not to a separable "part" of the man, but to the whole man under two opposed aspects, that which is distinctively human and perishable and that which is divine (hence, Paul says "the spirit" in v. 5 rather than, as in the *RSV*, "his spirit").

The Corinthians themselves should realize that their grounds for boasting, their handling of the situation as a basis for confidence regarding their future salvation, is not good. In his homily (5, 6–8), Paul explains this by appealing to their knowledge of the pervasive action of a little leaven. The image of "leaven" in a paschal context is one of an element that must be purged out. It obviously refers to the evil conduct of the man just excommunicated, but it stands, too, as a more general moral and doctrinal principle. Paul urges the Corinthians to purge out the old leaven of sin in their own lives. He grounds this "imperative" in the "indicative," that is, on what they really

137

are in Christ by his paschal sacrifice, the "unleavened bread" of the paschal feast. Therefore, they are to celebrate by being "perfectly pure" (like the unadulterated rays of the sun, rather than "sincere," as according to the *RSV*).

How this purity was to have been understood even before Paul's drastic action and admonishing homily leads him to remind them of what he had written. He had not unrealistically asked them to dissociate themselves physically from life on this earth. He was tactfully endeavoring to get them to dissociate themselves from anyone in the community whose whole mode of life was simply not compatible with his profession to be a Christian. Paul's jurisdiction, and hence his previous admonition, concerns those within the Christian community, not those outside it. What is more, the community itself should have taken care of exercising jurisdiction in its own area. As for those outside, God is the sole judge. Paul concludes by citing the Deuteronomic injunction that marks the people of God as a holy people.

B. *Unwarranted Litigation (6, 1–11)*

Another topic flows naturally from the preceding one. The community's powers of judgment are not a license for litigation before pagans (here viewed apocalyptically as the "unjust" in contrast to the "saints," that is, to members of God's holy people). Basing his argument on the resurrection as marking the moment of God's judgment shared by those who receive the kingdom in Christ, Paul tries to get the Corinthians to see the here and now. The holy community should certainly be able to handle lesser matters among themselves (6, 1–6). It is bad enough, virtually a being worsted in judgment, that they have lawsuits among themselves at all. For this testifies to the sorry state of charity among them according to the ideal of the gospel (6, 7–8). Their own injustice is itself placed in the light of the kingdom at the resurrection: people who commit injustices will not inherit it (6, 9–10). As Christians, they have been

138

changed from this state of sinful injustice to that of men at once justified by their profession of faith in Christ and by the Spirit of God.

As in the preceding passage (5, 1–13), Paul combines the juridical theme of judgment and the liturgical theme of sanctification; he views action taken in the present as governed mainly by the divine judgment to come; he exhorts the Corinthians to practical conduct in the light of the mystery of their existence. Thus, even in these most forthright reproofs, he remains true to the principles we saw exemplified in his letters to the Thessalonians and Philippians. He does not attempt to solve problems by legislating solutions. Even when he has to take juridical action himself, he does so on the principle of the Spirit, connoting God's dynamic power in judgment and in holiness. At all times he endeavors to bring the community itself to grasp the mystery of which they are a part, for only in an awareness of this mystery is genuine self-direction possible. Self-direction on the basis of divine power, without self-assertion, repeatedly appears as a cardinal principle of the Apostle's pastoral theology. To grasp this principle, however, one must enter into the Apostle's own modes of thought, suffused as these are with the mystery of God's achievement in Christ on the level of the Spirit. One may not confidently assert superficial views or simply quote slogans.

C. *Extramarital Sex Versus God's Sacred Rights (6, 12–20)*

The next topic (6, 12–20) begins with a kind of slogan which needs to be understood. The topic itself is not so abruptly introduced as may appear at first reading. Sex and ownership ("being mine" or "being yours") were, if anything, more closely associated in first-century Jewish or Pauline thought than they are today. What is more, previous references to holiness and judgment serve to introduce both sex and personal rights into the theological context of Paul's discussion of problems at

139

Corinth. As we have noticed, too, what Paul has been striving to do is to communicate to the Corinthians a way of thinking about their own Christian existence. His repeated "Do you not know . . .?" (5, 6; 6, 3; 6, 9) does more than recall his previous instructions; it challengingly urges understanding in the present through a presumed understanding of the goal implied by future realization of Christian existence. But before Paul again indicates the solution with insistent repetition of "Do you not know" (6, 15. 16. 19), he states the fundamental problem. The problem is not the verbalized principle or slogan but how to understand it. Thus, it is not really necessary to determine whether the principle is one that Paul would not use because of its ambiguity, or one that he may have used and that has been misconstrued. It does not seem that he rejects it outright, but that he is trying to give the perspective in which he expects it rightly to be grasped.

The text presents difficulties of translation and punctuation that we cannot hope here to justify in detail. Perhaps translation and punctuation can never be justified on merely critical grounds, if, as we have reason to assume from Paul's argumentation thus far, he is intent on communicating a perspective rather than on formulating a principle that will stand of itself. But the difficulties are such that our own translation and punctuation are called for. In providing this, however, certain options will be indicated which will disengage the over-all interpretation from interpretations of a secondary nature.

One thing that should be noted in any interpretation proposed via translation is that Paul apparently plays on words and ideas throughout this section, notably on those in verse 12: "is permissible," "authorized" (*exestin,* connoting *exousia,* "authority," "power over"), and "be under the authority of," "be enslaved by" (*exousiazomai,* "be under authority"—with either a favorable or a pejorative connotation). The notion of "possession," or "belonging to," which reappears constantly in the rest of this section, is obviously related thematically to the words in the principles or slogans of verse 12.

140

A second feature to be noted is that the original text gave none of the convenient indications of punctuation that the reader of modern languages takes for granted as signposts for turns of thought. Instead, we have abrupt changes like those in the Stoic-cynic diatribes, notably those of Epictetus. Fortunately, however, the parallelism of structure which is more characteristic of the Old Testament and Jewish thought and which reappears in Paul, helps articulate contrasts and comparisons, whether in whole or in part.

6, 12a   "All things are lawful [*exestin*] for me,
      but not all things are helpful [*sympherei*]."
  12b   All things are lawful [*exestin*] for me,
      but am I not to be under the authority of anybody?
      [*all' ouk egō exousiasthēsomai 'ypo tinos*]
      [or: but I for one will not be under the control of anything!]
  13a   "Food is for the stomach
      and the stomach for food."
  13b   God, though, will put an end to the activity
      of both one and the other.
  13c   The body, on the other hand, is not for immorality, but for the
                                Lord,
      and the Lord for the body.
  14   God, you see [*de*], raised the Lord
      and will raise us through his power!
  15a   Do you not know that your bodies are members of Christ?

Verses 12a and 13a do not necessarily represent false principles. They even seem to reflect Paul's own principles. Nevertheless, in the dialectical context of his statements here, they represent a limited and therefore imperfect or false perspective. We shall see another example of this dialectical progression in the Apostle's discussion of eating food sacrificed to idols, where he insists that the basic principle is not *my* freedom but what is for the good of another:

"All things are lawful [*exestin*] for me,
  but not all things are helpful [*sympherei*, 'expedient']."
All things are lawful [*exestin*] for me,
  but not all things build up!
Let no one seek his own [*interest*] but that of the other! (1 Cor. 10, 23–24)

141

Still another similar progression of thought will appear at the outset of chapter 7, in Paul's discussion of sex in marriage. All these passages have in common the question of a principle of Christian conduct, the theme of authority or *exousia,* and consequently the question of Christian freedom and obligation under God. In all three cases, the basic solution lies in a proper perspective rather than in any principle itself. Dominating the whole perspective is God himself as known in the mystery of Christian existence. The dialectical statement of principles serves not to annihilate one principle in favor of another, but to lift the mind to a higher plane of understanding. In this case, the focus on self yields to a focus on God, the focus on the negative aspects of transformation yields to a focus on the positive aspects.

The statement in 1 Corinthians 6, 12a is balanced by that in verse 12b even more than the first part of verse 12a is balanced by the second part of verse 12a. What is lawful (or permissible), so that I am free to act, is indeed balanced by what is "helpful" (*symphoron*). But the latter alternative is ambiguous; it can mean that what I am free to do is governed by what is merely "expedient," *symphoron* in a self-centered sense. Whether what is "helpful," that is, "expedient," is in accord with freedom as *my* freedom to act (that is, with what is permissible for me and therefore in "my authority") is not the whole picture. Verse 12b adds another dimension, qualifying the whole of verse 12a, especially the notion of "what is helpful." The phraseology of the second part of verse 12b strongly suggests that it be taken interrogatively. The use of the indefinite pronoun after the preposition *'ypo* favors the view that it be taken of personal agency, especially since there is question of authority or power. The thrust of the whole passage (cf. 6, 17. 19) further suggests that neither Paul's personal freedom nor that of the Christian is the main point at issue, but one's being not one's own. Understood in this way, verse 12b qualifies verse 12a by saying in effect: My freedom to act is to be judged in the light not simply of what is helpful to me but of another's right. Who this other is becomes evident in the further course of the dialectic: it is the Lord himself. At this point in his attempt to get the Corinthians to see the mystery that is operative, Paul decides that it suffices to pose a question; in effect, he asks: "But is my freedom *absolute* freedom?"

In verse 13a, Paul quotes another slogan or principle only to add in verse 13b that physical functions like alimentation must be judged in the light of the resurrection, when God will put an end to them. The perspective of a physical function is governed by the perspective of God's transforming action in its negative aspect of putting an end to the function, somewhat as the perspective of one's own conduct (v. 12a) is governed by the perspective of a limitation of one's authority (v. 12b). Somebody *else* ultimately determines the limits of my activity and establishes certain positive norms of conduct by the very fact of his active personal relationship to me. In turn, verse 13ab is balanced against the whole of verses 13c–14. A function of man in the flesh (v. 13a) yields to the perspective of the whole man ("the body") as destined for the Lord and in no way for a sinful activity on the level of the flesh (v. 13c). The "negative" perspective of God's activity in putting an end to specifically fleshly functions (v. 13b) yields to the "positive" perspective of God's activity, the mystery of transformation at the resurrection, which has already been achieved in the One to whom we belong totally and which is to be realized in us through divine power.

In the light of this dialectical progression, Paul in effect strives to redirect the Corinthians. That is, he tries to turn them away from judging on the level of their own rights, their own advantage, and perhaps from regarding themselves as liberated from any norms regarding sexual morality on the grounds that the sex urge, after all, is as irrelevant as is the temporal satisfaction of the fleshly appetite for food. The position from which Paul endeavors to avert them appears to have been this: As a Christian, I am free to use sex for my own benefit, just as I can use food, but it is not always helpful (expedient) to do so.

143

When it is expedient for me, I can go ahead. A code of "freedom" or "self-fulfillment" which admits of sexual excesses precisely on the basis of a wrongly conceived "spiritual" or "personalist" outlook has not been a rare phenomenon in the history of the Church. It seems to be the case here.

In any event, Paul's argument gravitates towards bringing the Corinthians to see that they belong to Christ. By the mystery of the resurrection, their bodies are one body with Christ's. Hence, extra-marital sexual relationships, which in effect substitute another kind of bodily solidarity for that which is compatible with Christian existence, are altogether to be shunned. For Christian existence implies a truly personal ("bodily") union on the plane of spirit, not on the plane of flesh. Immorality in the area of sexual misbehavior is not the greatest sin, even in Paul's eyes, but Paul judges that it possesses a special malice. For, by immoral conduct in sexual matters, a man strikes at his very consecration as a Christian; he profanes himself, God's temple. Indeed, the malice really lies in acting as though he were his own, whereas he is a precious sanctuary that belongs totally to God. For he has been acquired by Christ at great cost. Rather than blaspheme what is God's and commit injustice by appropriating what is God's, the Corinthians are to glorify God in their bodies. In effect, what is "helpful" or "advantageous" or "beneficial" (*symphoron*) for them is to be judged in the further perspective of their belonging to God for his glory (cf. the same general line of argumentation in 10, 23–11, 1; and cp. 7, 35).

D. *Sexual Marital Relationships and Virginal Relationships (7, 1–40)*

Paul now refers explicitly to the Corinthians' letter (7,1). He embarks on a frequently rough and quite eschatologically oriented discussion of some perennially vital problems of Christian life: marital sex, various sexual marital bonds, virgins and

144

problems of virginal marriages. This lengthy chapter, which
embraces a number of interrelated problems and repeatedly
evokes a somewhat vexing eschatological perspective, merits
fuller discussion than we can normally allow in these pages.
What may at first reading appear to be a forbiddingly negative
perspective can yield place to a more attractive perspective of
liberating hope based on God's gracious call only if we take
the trouble to re-examine more attentively the line of Paul's
thought throughout this chapter.

1. OPENING REMARKS: CORRECT PERSPECTIVE
ON MARITAL SEX (7, 1–7)

It seems quite probable from the general formulation of the
introductory phrase (v. 1a), "Concerning what you wrote," that
a quotation follows immediately upon Paul's reference to the
Corinthians' letter. Otherwise, the introduction becomes un-
necessarily elliptical, as if Paul were saying, "Concerning what
you wrote," and forthwith proceeded to quote only himself or
to give only his own observations. If the reader supposes that
the very next words contain Paul's unannounced reference to a
specific principle affecting marriage or adult Christian life in
general, he may not read these words (v. 1b) in an emphatic
tone of approval, for example: "It *is* good for a man not to
have sexual relationships with a woman." For the Greek will
simply not bear this emphasis. The reader's alternative, then,
may be to assume that Paul makes a very generic reference to
the Corinthians' letter and proceeds directly to state a principle
(not necessarily with reference to marriage) that covers sexual
relationships in general.

In this event, Paul's argument must be construed roughly as
follows: It is good (or better) for a man not to have sexual
relationships with a woman. But because of current abuses, each
person should be married. In the married state, each owes
marriage rights to the other, and the partners are not to deny

themselves the exercise of these rights except under restricted circumstances. This is what I allow (or advise); I do not command it. I would rather have all men be as I am (unmarried), but each has his own particular charism from God. Thus, Paul would be encouraging marriage as a remedy for what proves to be (at Corinth) an unworkable ideal, at least as a general rule. He would then insist (quite elliptically) on the sexual rights and duties of each of the partners concerned, allowing or advising temporary abstinence as a more spiritually motivated course of action. His closing remarks would then have to be taken as another formulation of the ideal of celibacy (v. 7a), followed by a somewhat belated recognition that marriage itself, after all, is a gift of God.

This interpretation of Paul's line of thought is open to serious questioning. The following lengthy discussion should reveal its principal weaknesses, especially on the scores of general coherence and more clearly defined Pauline modes of argumentation. A more solid and attractive interpretation should emerge from this discussion.

We can begin with the reasonable assumption that, when Paul writes in verse 1a "Concerning what you wrote," he is about to refer precisely to what they did write. The Corinthians apparently wrote on a *number* of topics: those which Paul later treats in turn (for example, the topic of virgins or celibates, 7, 25; the question of pagan sacrificial food, 8, 1; matters concerning charismatics, 12, 1), or those that he treats at this juncture as specific cases of sexual marital unions (widows and widowers, 7, 8; married Christians, 7, 10; marriages in which one partner is not a Christian, 7, 12). Does it seem likely that, at the very outset of a point-by-point discussion of various topics, Paul would refer to the Corinthians' letter in only a general way, to plunge immediately into a discussion of his own general views? He usually indicates rather clearly that he himself addresses the situation, or notes who does address the situation (cf. 7, 8. 10. 12. 25). When he does not do so, he seems to be *quoting* something, such as a slogan which he is

146

about to correct or refocus (cf. 6, 12a; 10, 23a). At times, he may include himself in quoting somewhat acidly a principle that needs to be understood rightly (such as at 8, 1b: "We know 'we all have knowledge' "). It seems reasonable to suppose that, when Paul refers explicitly in 7, 1 to what the Corinthians wrote, and proceeds somewhat abruptly to state a position, he is *quoting* that position. It seems unnecessary and unwise to suppose that he is flagrantly elliptical when we can assume that he simply cites what the Corinthians actually wrote him as soon as he has finished saying "Concerning what you wrote." Let us see where this reasonable option for coherence leads us.

If we have assumed that what immediately follows "Concerning what you wrote" comprises a citation of one of the written statements in the Corinthians' letter, we must now determine how far the quoted statement extends. In conjunction with this task, we shall have to discern whether Paul's response is approving or disapproving, whether or not it entails some qualifications and, if so, how.

When we try to delimit the length of the quotation, we meet two possibilities. The first, which other scholars have already suggested, confines the quotation to verse 1b, and attributes quite clearly to Paul himself the rest of this paragraph (v. 2 as well as vv. 3–7). The second possibility, which we ourselves would propose, extends the quotation to include verse 2 as well, and finds that Paul's response to a more fully stated position begins with a countering set of statements in verses 3 f. Thus, the passage would read:

7, 1a Concerning what you wrote:
   1b "It is better for a man not to have sexual relations with a woman,
   2a but because of [*dia de*] fornications [actual abuses (plural), not just
                                danger of fornication]
   2b each man must have [imperative, *echetō*] his own wife
   2c and each woman must have her own husband."
   3a The husband must render his obligation to his wife
   3b and, correspondingly, the wife to her husband.
   4a The woman does not have authority [*ouk exousiazei*] over her own
                                    body,
       but her *husband* [does],

147

4b   and, correspondingly, the husband does not have authority [*ouk exousiazei*] over his own body,

      but his *wife* [does].

5a   Do not deprive one another,

5b   except by agreement, for a time,

5c   in order that you may have occasion for prayer

5d   and again be together

5e   in order that Satan may not test you

5f   on the score of [*dia*] incontinence.

6   This, though, I say by way of advice [*syggnōmē*, "counsel" or "permission"],

      not by way of command.

7a   You see [either *de* or *gar*], I wish all men were as I myself;

7b   but each one has his own charism from God—

7c   one in one way, one in another.

The length of this quotation in verses 1b–2 may at first strike us as somewhat unusual. But Paul's dialectical response seems to suppose here a dialectical and somewhat full statement of the view on which he will straightway comment by juxtaposing his own. Certain grammatical and stylistic features will weigh in favor of the interpretation that we shall offer on the basis of the foregoing options. Above all, the whole of Paul's response will appear more coherent and more in keeping with his line of argumentation elsewhere in this letter.

We may start by noting the difficulties if we were to limit the quoted position to verse 1b. We would then have to assume that in verse 2 Paul virtually endorses the Corinthians' position as a matter of basic principle but adds a reason for qualifying that principle. Is it likely that Paul would endorse such a principle as a point of departure, proceed to insist on the necessity of marriage (apparently because he conceded that the "ideal principle" of v. 1b was generally unworkable), and mention only at the end of the passage (v. 7), apropos of an exception to the general rule of marital obligations, what he would wish if it were not for the way God gives his graces? If he endorses the view in verse 1b by urging marriage in verse 2, he would apparently be relegating to a second-level norm of conduct the "grace each one has from God" (v. 7b). His basic consideration would be not what one has received from God or what one

148

partner owes the other, but what each one must have for himself or herself in view of an unworkable ideal. To a disturbing extent, Paul would seem to advocate "practical expediency" as the immediate response to a difficult and even supposedly unworkable ideal. But this line of reasoning is akin to the very attitude he has just opposed in chapter 5 and in 6, 12 ff., and which he will reject again (1 Corinthians 10, 23–24).

In effect, verses 1b–2 present the better course as not engaging in sexual relationships, but allow these because of the dangers of immorality for a man or woman considered as an individual ("each one"). Each one is to "have" what he or she needs for his or her own good. Each, by implication, is free to seek the practical good he or she needs. This line of thought accords quite well with that of the Corinthians elsewhere. A given Pauline guideline (not associating with sinners, 1 Corinthians 5) or dictum (the Christian is free to do all things, 1 Corinthians 6, 12; 10, 23) has been misjudged by the Corinthian community. It is considered as an ideal that needs to be tempered or compromised by practical considerations of *self-satisfaction* or *self-interest* instead of being implemented by self-discipline and selfless interest. On the other hand, verses 3–4 say in effect that each partner in a marriage "owes" conjugal relationships to the other. Each one does not belong to himself so as to "exercise authority over" his own body (the *RSV* "rule over" obscures the fact that the same verb, *exousiazein,* has just been used in 1 Corinthians 6, 12). He or she is under the *exousia* of the other partner and, equivalently, does not belong to himself or herself.

This Pauline line of thought here is evidently quite similar to that which we have observed in the immediately preceding passage (6, 12–20), which deals with sexual relationships outside of marriage. As elsewhere, Paul puts "what one has" under the light of the one to whom one belongs (for example, 1 Corinthians 3, 21–22; Galatians 3, 26 ff.), one's own good under the light of what others have claim to (1 Corinthians 10, 23 ff.; Romans 14). Paul takes his basic stand on a question of

149

justice: "Do not refuse [*mē apostereite*] one another." The conduct he "allows" and even seems to "counsel"—though the Greek text of verse 6 is somewhat obscure—is that, given mutual consent, the partners abstain from the exercise of their rights in order to devote themselves to "prayer." By "prayer" Paul probably has in mind "eschatological practices" like nightly vigils and/or that converse with God which fittingly supposes centering personal interest on him alone.

But the normal married state of sexual relationships on the basis of the other's right is itself the remedy to temptation. This line of thought is not that of verse 2, where marriage is viewed as the remedy to the temptation of those who are not necessarily married but who find it necessary to have a wife or husband in order to avoid immorality. For it is one thing to see another person as the remedy for one's own temptation (in the face of an unrealizable ideal); it is quite another thing to see consideration for the other's marital rights (in an already stable state) as the basis for avoiding temptation to either partner. In the former case, one "has" or "gets" what supposed Christian frailty requires. In the latter, one "owes" or "gives" what the other deserves or needs, and does so in the exercise of his or her own charism (cf. v. 7b). Paul would have all men in the more clearly eschatological state, a state which he himself enjoys. But each one has his own charism from God, his own gift in the Spirit. As in the concluding remarks of 6, 12–20, the final note here stresses the spiritual gift of God. What one "has" is to be seen as that which one has received from God, not simply as that which ones takes for one's personal satisfaction or for one's own individual need.

Now, can we avoid ascribing to Paul in 7, 1–7 the unattractive and uncharacteristically compromising line of thought that seems to follow if we must confine the quoted position to verse 1b (or even if we were to try to dodge the issue by taking v. 1b, too, as part of Paul's opening statement)? Unfortunately, no. For the opening words of verse 2 [*dia de*] cannot easily be construed as introducing a mild concession, especially if they introduce Paul's response in juxtaposition to a statement assigned to others. For, at least as abruptly introducing *another's* response to a bald statement, these words would amount to a *rebuttal formula*. The only way in which this unavoidable tone of rebuttal can be preserved in an interpretation is to take verse 2 as *insisting* on a qualifiation of the principle or "ideal." The qualification therefore amounts to a *compromise* of the principle itself; as an ideal, the principle will simply not work. Paul would be urging "each man . . . each woman" to get or have a partner for himself or herself. Only by a considerable jump to verse 7b, moreover, could this "having" be construed as a grace of God.

In addition, it would be necessary to assume that between verse 2 and verse 3 Paul leaps from the question of acquiring a partner to the responsibilities of married life itself. We would mentally have to supply something between these second and third verses, for example, "Then, once each one has married to avoid sins, . . ." On the other hand, the asyndetical contact between verses 2 and 3 proves to be much easier to follow if we construe verse 3 as enunciating a Pauline perspective on marriage which Paul then dialectically contrasts to the whole state of the question implied by the Corinthians in verses 1b–2. No mental interpolation between verses 2 and 3 is required. Paul simply states the *Corinthians'* position and proceeds to correct the state of the question by posing his *own* practical (and more personally considerate) view.

We may accordingly discern in the very next brief section (vv. 8–9), where Paul deals with widowers and widows, a genuinely Pauline line of thought. Other commentators generally appeal to this "parallel" to support the explanation that attributes to Paul himself either the norms in verses 2 ff. or the whole paragraph beginning with verse 1. But the "parallel" better serves to articulate a theological perspective which we feel is perceptibly at variance with that which appears in verses 1b–2, though in accord with that in verses 3–7, as the reader can see for himself.

In verses 8–9, Paul first indicates the precise case under discussion (the "unmarried," here paired with "widows," are to be understood as "widowers"). He then states the ideal personally, in terms of his own apostolic life: "It is good [ideally better] for them if they remain as I am." When he qualifies this ideal, he does so not demandingly, but conditionally: "But if [*ei de*] they do not practice continence, let them get married, for it is better to marry than to burn [with passion, or, probably, 'at the judgment']." Paul clearly admits remarriage as a remedy for "being on fire." Presumably, this means that he admits remarriage as a remedy for concupiscence, though his formulation, considered in the light of other texts (for example, 7, 25b. 28b. 32; 7, 5ef) might suggest rather that he wants to spare them specifically eschatological (superhuman) temptations, which may prove too trying and entail judgment (cf. 1 Corinthians 3, 13–15; 2 Thessalonians 1, 8; Romans 12, 20).

As we shall see later, the Apostle presents his own way of life as a special grace of God which expedites rather than impedes one's eschatological existence (life in Christ during these last days of special trials and coming tribulation with the governing hope of full transformation at the parousia). He cannot predict whether or not God will bestow this better, specifically prophetic grace on a given individual, but he esteems it as something desirable for others as God grants it (cf. pp. 168–174). He habitually propounds the ideal of sexual abstinence personally, in terms of his own example (for instance, 7, 7. 8. 25; cf. 9, 5) and in terms of God's call (for example, 7, 7; 7, 25 and 2 Corinthians, 4, 1; 7, 20. 26 ff.), not, as is the case with verse 2, simply in terms of a general principle stated independently of any reference to his own apostolic life or to a kind of divine vocation.

Furthermore, he does not suppose here or elsewhere—apart from the problematical verses 1–2—that a given group of Christians cannot as a general rule be expected to control their sexual appetite. He recognizes certain serious dangers, but he does not suppose them as a general rule or appeal to necessity (cf. v. 2) instead of to freedom of choice (cp. 7, 36) when he discusses them. Furthermore, he expressly adduces the alternative as a good thing (*kreitton,* "better," v. 9; cp. 7, 38), even as a means of avoiding temptation, whereas verse 2 is silent on this point and seems to suggest that a kind of "lesser evil" is necessary for those who cannot actually live up to the commandments, much less to a (somewhat impersonal) ideal of sexual abstinence. Lastly, Paul regularly considers the personal ties of both parties whom he advises (cf. vv. 3–5; vv. 8–9; vv. 10–11; vv. 12 ff.; vv. 27 ff.). He does not speak somewhat "divisively" (as does v. 2) of what each is to have for himself or for herself. When he does advise or admonish "each one," he communicates the basic perspective of personal selflessness or generosity (for example, Galatians 6, 5; 2 Corinthians 9, 7) or of personal response to God's action (for example, 1 Corinthians 3, 5–13; 7, 7; 7, 17. 20. 24; Romans 12, 3; 14, 5; cf. 10, 24) and frowns on acquisitive self-interest under any guise (for example, 1 Corinthians 1, 12; 11, 21). Never—except for the problematical verse 2—does he initially urge a less ideal course of action as a matter of moral choice that is practically "forced" on Christians by the circumstances. We doubt that he does so here in verse 2.

2. WIDOWERS AND WIDOWS (7, 8–9)

The next short section (7, 8–9) deals with widowers and widows. The term "unmarried" (*agamoi,* v. 8) is best taken in the admissible, specific sense of "widowers." For one thing, it is paired with "widows." Furthermore, this short section (7, 8–9) stands in contrast to those immediately preceding and following it. The former section deals with basic perspectives concerning marriage. The latter (7, 10–11) deals with those who are already married but who seem to be contemplating divorce. The ones whom Paul designates in verse 8 as "unmarried" are therefore best taken as men who have already been married but are not now married. The supposition in all three sections, however, is that all the persons concerned are Christians. For "the rest" in verse 12 will introduce the case of a Christian partner and an unbeliever (7, 12–24).

In the case of Christian widowers and widows, Paul first indicates that the better course is that they remain unmarried, like Paul himself. It is the celibate state of Christians, with or without previous marriage, that Paul regards as better. For his dominant viewpoint is echatological; he considers Christian life primarily from the standpoint of the resurrection. The married state of Christians is a union of two in one flesh; the "moral person" that results falls under the word, command, or name of the Lord, as we shall see, but at its heart is something transient, not *fully* eschatological, namely, the union in flesh.

Even though Christian marriage represents a further union in Christ, it is distinct from that immediate personal union with Christ of the baptized believer, and inferior to it in point of eschatological permanence. One who is married is by no means a "second rate" Christian in Paul's view, for the married person is just as much baptized as any other Christian, with the radical transformation of flesh which baptism implies. But his charism operates in the secular area of the flesh. There is an objectively higher charism, more clearly grasped as a kind of prophetic charism, manifested concretely in the Apostle himself, which operates more on the level of the spirit. Paul does not preach egalitarianism in God's gifts. One whose marriage bond has been dissolved by the partner's death seems to be open once again to the more high-powered charism, which is "freer" (because less "limited" by the level of fleshly existence). Hence, Paul judges it preferable for the widower or widow to remain unmarried. His judgment is rooted not in some abstract principle (as seems to be the case in 7, 1b) but in the apostolic charism as he himself enjoys it (7, 7a; cf. 7, 25).

Nevertheless, he recognizes the legitimacy of an appeal even to something other than one's own charism from God. If one cannot exercise self-control, he or she is in a perilous state, and the more secure course is to marry rather than burn. No

154

doubt there are other, more positive values (like giving one's children a complete home) which we might expect to have been proposed. But Paul is not trying to give a detailed treatment of the subject, especially not in the perspective of the socio-logical concerns of later millenniums. He is trying to indicate a solution to practical problems in the immediate Corinthian context of what one is free to do and/or needs to do, and in the context of his own eschatological concern for the better, less limiting or constricting course of action. He does provide in very few words the whole spectrum in which other motives can be situated. Here, again, his main solution lies in giving most concretely and practically the wide theological perspective in which cases can be properly judged by the Corinthians them-selves.

3. MARRIED CHRISTIAN COUPLES AND DIVORCE (7, 10–11)

The next case that Paul discusses is by no means as simple as it appears, if only because Paul surprisingly distinguishes at this point between the Lord's word and his own, and even *contrasts* them, which he has never done heretofore. We find it almost unavoidable in this case to suggest a more satisfactory explana-tion for this puzzling contrast and to develop some of its im-plications concerning Paul's views on divorce.

For those who are already married (7, 10–11), Paul appeals to the word of the Lord himself. He is not simply counseling a course of action. For two married Christians, divorce with re-marriage is forbidden, though, as we shall see, it may not ab-solutely be ruled out. For Paul does not seem to be appealing to the Lord's authority as formulated law regarded as an ab-solute. The basic problem here is to understand what Paul means by saying "I give charge (*paraggellō*), not I but the Lord" (v. 10), and by opposed or similar distinctions elsewhere in this chapter, such as: "To the rest, I say, not the Lord" (v. 12); "Concerning the unmarried [celibates and those in

155

virginal marriages], I have no command of the Lord, but I give my opinion as one who by the Lord's mercy is trustworthy," (v. 25).

We may begin by excluding some interpretations that do not square with Paul's concept or exercise of his apostolic authority. He is not saying in any of these cases that he has or lacks special documentation (like *logia,* "sayings" of the Lord) to prove his position or supply better direction. He who insisted that he had the whole gospel from the outset of his apostolic activity and had it by his being invested as an Apostle through a revelation of Jesus Christ (Galatians 1, 11 ff.), and who in this very letter has claimed to have the mind of Christ (1 Corinthians 2, 16) is not about to admit pastoral embarrassment on the score of adequate documentation or full authorization.

Nor, obviously, in appealing to the word or command of the Lord is he legislating a solution even mediately, as a rabbi might work out a further application of the law.

Nor is he administering a law after the manner of one who adduces a formula for conduct about which he himself is not free to do anything but apply or enforce. For, if he were, it is hard to explain the sense of the twofold opposition between himself and the Lord: "not I but the Lord" (v. 10), and "I, not the Lord" (v. 12). The two formulas seem to require basically the same principle of solution, for the problem is basically the same in each case, namely: why the reversed contrast between identical elements? The formula in verse 10 might more easily admit of the explanation that Paul is not free to alter the command of the Lord. But would this line of thought fit with repeated affirmation of his identity with the Lord and his plenipotentiary apostolic power? Would he not rather conceive this opposition in less personal terms: "not *man,* but the Lord," rather than "not *I,* but the Lord"? Furthermore, this solution for verse 10 (that he is not free to alter the command of the Lord) would seem almost to be negated in the second case (v. 12), unless one reverts to supposing that Paul does not really regard himself as a plenipotentiary. For, in verse 12, he would seem to set aside

156

the Lord's authoritative word. But can he be saying in verse 12 that his own word and not the Lord's authority is to govern the case of mixed marriages (in which only one partner is a Christian)? How could this view be squared with his appeal to God's call (vv. 15, 17) and to what the Lord has assigned each (Christian) (v. 17; cf. also vv. 22 ff.), not to mention his reference to keeping the precepts of God (v. 19)?

Lastly, it does not seem that either case (the contrast in v. 10 or that in v. 12) can be neatly explained by distinguishing between commands and counsels, as though the word or law of Christ were the former and the word of Paul were the latter. Paul shares with other New Testament writers the conception of Christ's law as both a realizable ideal and a norm of action that is governed by grace, and hence one that is not in every detail binding under sin. There is a minimum, represented by what one *cannot* do and still enter the kingdom, but the perspective is governed by the maximum, which always remains an ideal that is only proportionately realized even though it is indeed thus realized or realizable. But the law of Christ is not just "part" of this picture of God's gracious will; it is not "commands" as perfectly distinct from "counsels." The Lord's word is both command and counsel, necessary norm and ideal, though with differing emphasis. The emphasis must be discerned in proportion to the degree or kind of freedom and grace which both aspects of the Lord's word imply. The distinction between commands and counsels may be implied by the statements in verses 6 and 25—provided that the two are not dissociated by being opposed in terms of different individuals or classes, such as: the Lord (source of command) and Paul (source of counsel) Christians generally (object of command) and a class of the "perfect" or "religious" as a distinct and different kind of Christian (object of counsel).

What is more, the "parallel" statements in verses 6 and 25 must be used with discernment in explaining the contrasts ("I" —"the Lord") of verses 10 and 12. For verse 6 speaks of the manner of Paul's word; it does not contrast Paul's word with the Lord's, as do verses 10 and 12. Verse 25, in turn, speaks of Paul's giving an opinion in accord with the Lord's mercy shown to him (in his being constituted an apostle). The contrast with *"I do not have* a command of the Lord" does not dissociate the Lord's invoked word from his own; rather, it explains his reliance on the judgment he has received as one who, inasmuch as he has been shown mercy by the Lord, is fully trustworthy (not just that one makes no mistake in following him, but that the positive guidance he gives fully agrees with the mind of the Lord). As we argued before, verse 25 cannot suggest apostolic insufficiency in this pastoral situation. What, then, does it suggest?

We submit that "I do not have a command of the Lord" suggests that "command" or "precept" is not the necessary, useful, or proper perspective for treating the matter discussed. The case of "virgins" (celibates or those in a virginal marriage) is one in which no juridical order as such—beyond that implied in the bond of faith and baptism—is entailed. There is no "law" or "precept" or "command"—all of which seem to have a "negative" cast for Paul—to be used. "I do not have a command" as said by the *Apostle* means equivalently that there is none to be had, for the situation (in direct reference to which he makes this statement) is not one that calls for it in any way. The situation in this case (virginity) is that of the baptized individual as one simply united with Christ.

Now, our understanding of verse 25 can shed light on all three of the other cases that we have mentioned in this discussion. In 1 Corinthians 7, 6, Paul has just given as a principle of Christian conduct for Christian married couples something that is not proper to their state as such. They are two in one flesh (cf. Ephesians 5, 31; 1 Corinthians 6, 16), though their union is a Christian union and therefore one that is under the Lord. From a union of two Christians in one *flesh,* however, there arise specific fleshly obligations of each to the other. This situation in which fleshly obligations are incurred is specific to the area of precept or command, even though it is a situation

158

under the Lord. For the situation is not *fully* eschatological. The fleshly union will not perdure as such at the resurrection. Thus, when a specifically eschatological consideration is introduced (namely, "prayer"), which is basically different from physical "togetherness" (*epi to auto einai,* v. 5), Paul's manner of handling the situation is to give prophetic counsel, not to invoke a precept. The concrete situation (a union of two Christian persons in the flesh, constituting a "third thing," a "moral person"—but a "fleshly one"—in Christ) is governed by what one "owes" the other. This situation calls for precept. But a more fully eschatological modification of the situation does not fall under precept or command; it concerns the individual's personal, charismatically spontaneous rapport with God ("prayer"). Not that prayer is purely an individualistic thing! But in this context "prayer" represents something other than what is specific to the union of two in one flesh, even though those forming the union be Christians. It represents the transcendent commitment of the baptized individual as a baptized Christian, not as a married Christian, and it represents something that will endure at the resurrection. Hence, Paul founds his statement in 7, 5b ff. on his own charismatic, prophetic judgment, not on the charism proper to that of married Christians.

In the second case, in 1 Corinthians 7, 10, the situation is again that of married couples, both of whom are Christians. Paul does not invoke his *own* word, which would be that according to his prophetic, apostolic charism, for the situation is not that of the *basic* Christian union with the Lord (that of the believer who is as an individual person one with Christ), which is that of Paul himself. He invokes the *Lord's* word, for this covers all Christian situations, even those distinctively other than his own (because involving a fleshly union with another person in Christ). Thus, he is not in the least compromising his apostolic authority. He is simply not invoking his *personal* charism as an Apostle in dealing with this situation. His apostolic authority to deal with the situation remains intact, for he authoritatively invokes the *Lord's* word (whether or not a specific *logion* is involved). The Lord speaks to them somewhat as the law speaks to those "under the law" (Romans 3, 19); a special bond in the Lord is implied by appealing to the Lord's word in this case. But the situation is not one in which Paul can appeal to his personal charism—or his being an object for imitation. Those of whom he speaks were already married and are still married. Hence, Paul indicates a specific basis for his remarks, a relationship in the Lord in terms of the one who speaks to this situation. In verse 8 he can and does appeal to his personal status because the widowers are once again as Paul is.

On the other hand, in 1 Corinthians 7, 12, the third case, the situation is that of a marriage that is not a further union in Christ (in modern Catholic terminology, it is not properly "sacramental") because one of the partners is an unbeliever. Accordingly, it is not the Lord who speaks to *these couples*. The Lord does not speak to these couples as couples because the union here of the two in one flesh is not as such a union in the Lord. It is Paul, the Apostle to the gentiles, who can and does speak to them. He speaks, however, *directly* of the Christian partner. Therefore, notwithstanding the initial distinction between his word and that of the Lord (when *these* couples as *couples* are addressed), Paul can go on to invoke God's call, the Lord's apportionment, God's command, the call in the Lord. For he is then dealing with the Christian partner or with other Christians simply as Christians in a given temporal situation.

Let us return now to examine further Paul's pastoral admonition in verses 10–11. It is still his own pastoral admonition, even though he does not invoke his own word, that is, his own prophetic charism (which, concretely, is the example of his single status in the Lord). For he is presenting the norm for Christians' conduct in view of their distinct, "married" union in Christ. The union of two married Christians cannot be dissolved (v. 10a). But the next clause shows that Paul is not adducing a law of the Medes and the Persians, which admits no change whatsoever (Esther 1, 19). The next phrase supposes the legitimacy of an exception—even in the union treated on the basis of the Lord's word. Could further exceptions be allowed? The over-all answer is hypothetical. If the union of two Christians in a fleshly bond in Christ (which not only supposes baptism but which is distinct from it and not as eschatologically important or permanent as baptism) can be judged to impede the baptismal commitment and eschatological fulfillment—and *if* remarriage could be judged in the Spirit to serve these ends, then it seems that the divorce of two Christians with remarriage for one or other partner or both could be allowed.

Reasons for this may be indicated briefly. Christian marriage, like any other marriage, is dissolved by death, for it is radically a union in flesh, even though it is obviously also a personal union in higher aspects of love. But, as non-virginal marriage, it is radically a union in flesh (by which, of course, we are still to understand a human and not an animal union, and a noble human union at that). Paul notes that this union can also be somewhat dissolved by physical separation. He has further shown that he does not insist on the highest motives even when he proposes them; in the case of remarriage by widow or widower, he admits of a motive tantamount to survival as a Christian (vv. 8–9). He does this even where the basic state (that of one who was married but is *now* single again) might call for more insistence on the higher motive. His arguments in verses 8–9, moreover, do not exclude more positive considerations like spiritual welfare of the widow and/or her children from a previous marriage. His position would welcome further motives provided the basic perspective that he supplies is kept. Formulations by Paul or the lack of them are not the final court of appeal. Most important of all, he repeatedly bases pastoral considerations not on physical facts as such but on demands of specifically Christian existence. For him, no formulated law can substitute for profound and authoritative wisdom in the spirit. True, the law of Christ may be comprised in the pregnant formulation of a precept, as is the law of love, but it cannot be conceived simply in terms of sterile formulation.

Suppose, then, that Paul had been confronted with a case in

which one of the Christian partners had not only been seriously offended by the other, but had suffered and would probably suffer real detriment to the life of faith if he or she lived alone instead of remarrying. No doubt Paul would not immediately have admitted the lowest possible legitimate motive, but would have tried to bring either or both persons to an awareness of the better course in view of the Lord's service and the salvation of others—as we shall see him do especially in 1 Corinthians 7, 12 ff. But would Paul have insisted rigorously on the heroic ideal? In particular, would he have regarded what is tantamount to the physical existence of the other baptized partner as a sole, sufficing criterion for prohibiting the remarriage of the Christian partner who otherwise was or would be in spiritually dire straits?

Obviously, the biblical theologian cannot answer these questions with the apostolic authority of Paul, though there are those whose derived apostolic authority enables them adequately to meet a need to answer the question (should it arise) according to the mind of the Apostle. But the biblical theologian must speak the mind of the Apostle as he sees it. As this writer sees it, the answer to the questions proposed at the end of the preceding paragraph lies in the negative. What is more, the really wise answer, whoever has full authority to bless it for the use of the faithful in general, seems to this writer to arise more from a grasp of Paul's thought and mind (as he himself appealed to the mind of Christ, 1 Corinthians 2, 16) than in an adherence to his formulations—or to the lack of them. The Apostle's mind is always one with his basic catechesis and previous instructions, but it is never static. He does not always appeal to the past. He meets new problems in his churches as these problems arise, for his authority is more prophetic than legislative. Even when he invokes the Lord's word, as we have seen, he invokes it in virtue of the specific situation with which he deals. In invoking it, he does not confess apostolic inadequacy but rather illustrates his apostolic authority to deal with situations not covered by his personal charism.

As in our own day, members of the Church, especially in the

big city with its cultural crosscurrents and strong secular under-
tow, were formulating their own solutions. They did not do so
rebelliously, but they did so without real wisdom. Where the
formulations were improper or misleading, Paul reformulated
them. But he pursued the problem and gave positive guidance as
the need arose—not legislating solutions beyond what was called
for on occasion, nor legislating even in these cases by way of
simply imposing a regulation. He seems to have tried above all
to instill the proper theological perspective, to exercise not personal control through law, but pastoral leadership through wisdom.

4. UNIONS BETWEEN CHRISTIANS AND UNBELIEVERS (7, 12–24)

Turning now to 1 Corinthians 7, 12–24, we can follow a good
example of Paul's wisdom at work. Paul's own word has to be
invoked at the outset, not merely or mainly because he has
no statement from the Lord, but because the couples addressed
are not as couples a unit in the Lord. His basic principle favors
the union that exists, and the reason for this is that the non-
Christian partner is sanctified in the Christian partner (v. 14).
Whatever this means, it means that the non-Christian partner
is helped spiritually, and therefore in the direction of salvation.
Paul seems to take it for granted that the children of such
marriages are holy. What he has specifically in mind by this we
will not guess. But he does take the children's being holy as an
indication that the cause of sanctification for the non-Christian
partner lies in the Christian partner. "Holiness" is not seen in
terms of the marriage union as such but in terms of the Christian partner's role. Out of consideration for the good that the
Christian partner can do, Paul has enjoined the Christian partner
not to divorce the other.

On the other hand, if the unbeliever separates, let him do so.
The Christian partner is not bound in these circumstances. Once
more, however, Paul indicates the alternative: "But [*de*, not the
RSV "for"] God has called us for peace." His point of view is

163

that of eschatological reconciliation, "peace" in the sense of a reconciliation with God that governs all Christian hope and action. He is definitely not saying in effect "let the other partner go to have the *peace of mind* which God intends for you." The bonded service of the Christian partner (*douloō,* v. 15) is considered in the light of the spiritual good that the Christian partner can do for the non-Christian partner. In a "mixed" marriage of this type, this good depends on the personal willingness of the other to live with the Christian partner. When this condition is shown to be absent on the part of the other, the Christian is no longer bound. But the ideal of reconciliation remains, not directly in the light of the bond with the other partner (as in the case in v. 11), but directly in the light of the "call" of the Christian partner (concretely, faith and baptism).

In following this call, discernment is necessary. Paul proposes its need by way of a question. A number of scholars like J. Jeremias and J. Dupont have already interpreted this question positively, not in the sense: How do you know whether you will save your husband? (You do not know, therefore go ahead and let him separate), but in this sense: How do you know whether you might not save your husband (by reconciliation in line with your call by God)? (Therefore, try to be reconciled.) This more positive view is a definite improvement, but it seems to read a bit too much into the Greek of verse 16 itself, and cuts short Paul's argument, which continues through verses 17–24. The question appeals to discernment in the light of one's call, but is then followed by a conditional clause that gives a Pauline principle or maxim on the basis of which the question can be answered. Thus, the passage should read (not as in the *RSV* but as follows):

7, 15c   But God has called us for peace [final reconciliation in Christ].
  16a   Wife, how do you know whether you will save your husband [that
                      is, help him to share this eschatological peace];
  16b   husband, how do you know whether you will save your wife,
  17a   unless: "To each as the Lord has assigned him,
  17b   each one as God has called him,
  17c   this is the way he is to conduct himself"?
  17d   And this is the way I give instructions in all the churches. . . .

164

What Paul then states in verses 18–24 explicates the general principle of verse 17 and includes restatements of it in verses 20 and 24, such as: "So, brethren, in whatever state each was called, there let him remain with God." In other words, Paul indicates the answer to the question concerning salvation of the other partner; he indicates the answer by supplying a principle common to his teaching in all the churches and goes on to exemplify the principle. He does not himself tell the Christian partner what the answer will be—in the sense that he simply "lays down the law" and leaves no room for personal discernment. It is precisely personal discernment that he expects, though he gives guidelines for it. What the believer is to do is to follow his call as a Christian. The general principle given one suggests that one is to make the most of the situation in which one finds oneself at the decisive moment of that call, which marks the beginning of eschatological existence. Though one is not "bound" to the other partner, but only to Christ, it would be "better" (from the standpoint of eschatological existence in Christ) to seek reconciliation.

The clarifications of this general principle, which are given by way of further examples in verses 18 ff., all suppose as fundamental the notion of Christian existence and therefore of Christian opportunity for a kind of apostolic action. A man is not to look to his own condition as such but to God's manner of calling him. The point here again is one of over-all perspective, expressed in terms of sharp contrasts. If the reader takes Paul literally, supposing that his statements would not admit qualification or further attention to the detailed situation, he does him an injustice. For he then misconstrues Paul's whole effort, namely, to provide the perspective for judgment according to God's will.

It is easy for many to grasp Paul's point in verses 18–20, where he speaks of the physical condition of circumcision or non-circumcision. But the same people are often scandalized by his parallel statements in verses 21 ff., where he speaks of slavery. The text of the *RSV* translation reflects at least embarrassment on this topic. To be true to Paul, one should read verse 21 as follows: "Were you a slave when called? Never mind [that is, let it not be your earnest concern to change your condition]! But even if you can gain your freedom, make use [of your present condition] instead." Paul does not justify slavery in itself. He will later indicate, in his letter to Philemon, that he thinks the Christian slave should be freed. The Christian mystery of love, however, and not social reform as such will dictate Paul's considerations.

The Apostle might be faulted for his lack of "social concern" in the matter of slavery in general if we were to judge him by the conditions and insights of a later age. Had he attempted to lay down principles that would not stand up for an age later than his own, we still might legitimately fault him. But his theological perspective is itself the basic principle that he is trying to communicate for solving moral problems that arise in the lives of Christians. This principle holds as long as Christian existence is governed by the service of the Lord and what this implies: the call of God, the definitive transformation of the human condition not by man's effort as such but by God's raising him from the dead. Paul's eschatological perspective has room for what modern theologians call the "incarnational," because the "incarnational" itself makes theological sense only in terms of the call for final transformation in Christ. Thus, Paul does give a comprehensive and basically sufficient perspective for Christian moral conduct even today. The cardinal consideration is one's service of the Lord on the basis of the Lord's transcendent action which is seen concretely (as in the beatitudes) in the circumstances of one's call.

Before passing on to Paul's treatment of virgins, one may reflect on the consequences of a basic similiarity in his pastoral remarks to Christian and "mixed" married couples. Similarity rather than difference alone should be noted here. It is not that his remarks to Christian married couples (vv. 10–11) represent a law "which no power on earth can change," but that his remarks to the "mixed" married couples (vv. 12 ff.) represent a "Pauline privilege," which is a kind of exception to the general

166

law. This distinction in one form or another seems to rest on a misconception of the dicta "not I, but the Lord," "I, not the Lord."

The Church has recognized that Paul's statements in verses 12 ff. rest on his apostolic authority, and she has more readily extended them in the matter of what is permitted by apostolic authority derived from him. She has interpreted the basis for "separation" more widely, in terms not of the initiative of the non-Christian partner but of the good for the faith of the Christian partner. And she has allowed the remarriage of the Christian partner—though Paul himself certainly does not go so far in what he says or positively suggests. The Church has also recognized (though not apparently for the reasons that we ourselves find exegetically sound and necessary) that the bond with which Paul is dealing in verses 12 ff. is not as such a bond in Christ like that with which Paul deals in verses 10–11, where he enjoins no remarriage. But, given the fact that the bond in the two cases is not the same, does this justify regarding the bond in the first case (vv. 10–11) as unchangeable by apostolic authority—as an unalterable law, even in view of a more fundamental, permanently eschatological bond in Christ?

There is a remarkable similarity that should also be weighed. In both cases, the general line of Paul's command and counsel is the same—given his awareness of the further bond in the first case, which is shown in invoking the Lord's word. He states the case negatively (by way of a prohibition, with attention to certain concrete, circumstantial conditions); he appeals for reconciliation even in the light of conditions that affect his fundamental statement; at all times, he considers the problem in terms of Christian existence in the Lord, and does not stop short with juridical formulations. Thus, it seems to us that the Church can extend her interpretation of the first case—though with proportionately greater discernment as a further though subsidiary bond in Christ is involved—along the most solid line she has followed (practical consideration for the "faith" of the Christian partner) in the second case.

5. VIRGINAL DEDICATION AND VIRGINAL
MARRIAGE (7, 25–40)

In the further case of those of either sex who have not been married and who do not intend to marry, Paul has no word or command of the Lord to invoke. For this case involves no further union in Christ of two in one flesh, but simply the union of the Christian believer as a believer. Paul invokes his own judgment not as the private judgment of a mere theologian, but as the judgment of one who enjoys the Lord's mercy, the grace of an apostolic call with all that this implies in Paul's own view of the Lord's mercy shown him (cf. 2 Corinthians 4, 1).

His apostolic viewpoint is again a markedly eschatological viewpoint. It covers the whole "end-time." Also, it is an apocalyptic viewpoint which stresses certain negative aspects of the present in view of the transcendent glory to come. Its positive aspects usually come out towards the end, and they may not always be stressed too clearly, but the positive aspects dominate the picture in the last analysis. Here, the positive aspects are brought out in verse 35: Paul's norms are intended to promote their advantage (*symphoron*, not the *RSV* "good order")— understood as a spiritual advantage for the whole man. His norms are not intended to restrict their freedom, but to secure their undivided devotion to the Lord. By this, he has in mind not just a present single-mindedness, but readiness for the Lord at the parousia.

The negative aspects of Paul's apocalyptico-eschatological viewpoint appear more clearly at the outset, as when he speaks of the better state of being in terms of the "present necessity" (rather than the *RSV* "impending distress"), verse 26. The "present necessity" (*enestōsa anagkē*) seems to be the advance stage of the "distress" or "tribulation" (*thlipsis*) that represents the climax of the eschatological struggle by which one comes before the Lord in judgment to obtain final glory. Both are "negative aspects" of the eschatological condition, but serve to represent it quite accurately as an arduous period to be crowned with deliverance by the Lord rather than by one's own efforts.

The perspective is, as always, one of God's grace entailing trials by which his glory and ours with Christ is realized.

In view of the "present necessity," then, it is better for one to remain as he is, "thus"—and Paul gives examples. In effect, one is not to change his married or single state. No sin is implied for either a man or a woman simply in marrying. But Paul sees this further involvement in the flesh as being of one piece with the trials of "earthly" existence. The "present necessity" is bad enough. Those who marry (and, more basically, those who "seek" something other than the state in which the Lord has called them) will have "tribulation in the flesh" (not the *RSV* "worldly troubles"). Paul is not thinking here solely of marrying or not marrying, but of marriage as a way of changing one's state according to what one "seeks." One is free to "seek" in this area; there is no sin in so doing, for the presumption is that one's seeking is related to the Lord and his coming. But those who seek what involves a further union in the flesh will have "tribulation in the flesh." By this phrase, Paul is not thinking of the woes of daily married life simply as physical woes which the celibate does not have. For such a view is basically non-theological; it judges things as they are or as they appear by themselves, not precisely in relation to the coming of God's glory. Paul is thinking not in terms of physical phenomena but in the apocalyptic idiom of the final, climactic affliction. What is more, he is thinking of events so described precisely in their relation to the coming of the Lord, not in relation to what is implied by one's "seeking" (a somewhat earthbound though not distorted view of one's own needs). The further voluntary involvement in flesh, even though it is a holy involvement (the corollary of its not being sinful or at least guilt-laden) makes one more vulnerable to that which is represented by "tribulation." One becomes more committed to what will pass away rather than simply more committed to the one who transforms everything. Paul would save them the "anguish" of the ultimate losses they incur by their own "seeking" of that which will not abide forever.

The Apostle's view is not that of the Stoics, though it bears a superficial resemblance to it. He does not want to kill or neutralize desire but to direct it to more ultimate concerns. These ultimate concerns are formulated somewhat negatively, in terms of physical events or prodigious trials to be avoided. It is characteristic of apocalyptic to depict a principle like "detachment" in concrete images like "not going back for one's cloak" (cf. Matthew 24, 17; Mark 13, 15–16). It is likewise characteristic of apocalyptic to present urgent demands on mankind in arresting and somewhat operatic terms, like the plight of women with children in time of war (cf. Matthew 24, 19 f.; Mark 13, 17 f.). It is also characteristic of apocalyptic to underscore ultimate concerns for transcendent values by starkly depicting the necessary loss of everything that belongs typically to "this-worldly" existence; God's earthly temple is itself no exception (cf. Matthew 24, 15; Mark 13, 14).

Christian apocalyptic takes this cast not only because apocalyptic was a prevalent theological idiom of New Testament times, but because Christians were vividly aware of the central mystery by which Christ came to exercise universal dominion, namely, the cross, death, and burial as the way to the resurrection. This mystery is not palatable, but it is a consummate achievement of God's power. The way in which the mystery could be fittingly expressed and applied was the language of apocalyptic. Its translation into this theological idiom cannot be expected to be more palatable than the mystery itself. No doubt the mode of expressing the mystery could have taken a more winning rhetorical form than that of apocalyptic, even though the first century was not a golden age of literature for any culture in the Mediterranean area. But we should try to recognize the mystery in the form, however unappealing, in which it is given. What we shall then discern, among other things, is Paul's prophetic keenness of vision in focusing on ultimate concerns basic to Christian life in the service of the risen Lord.

He proceeds to explain himself in imagery of detachment from this-worldly preoccupations (v. 29). If one does not

170

impose on him a clock-and-calendar perspective, or regard him as a somewhat latent gnostic who looks on matter simply as contamination, or take his negative view as his final view, he is really not hard to follow. In explaining himself he is actually communicating a total point of view that is quite positive.

He begins with a reference to the "shortening of the appointed time." The "last days" are seen in an image that suggests the furling of the sail as the ship heads into port. What is one's fundamental, total outlook to be in view of the journey's end, the presence of the end-time?

7, 29b	For the time remaining, let	
29c	even those having wives	be as not having,
30a	and those weeping	as not weeping,
30b	and those rejoicing	as not rejoicing,
30c	and those buying and selling	as not possessing,
31a	and those using the world	as not using it to the utmost.
31b	For this world's manner of acting is passing away.	
32a	But I want you to be unpreoccupied.	

Paul's paralleled contrasts help progressively to clarify themselves and Paul's whole point of view. He is discountenancing a preoccupation with what is passing. His is not the somewhat secular view of an Ecclesiastes, "a time for laughing and a time for weeping," and so forth. His is a view of a time above time. Daily concerns, legitimate and needful as they are—and as a number of those mentioned here were for Paul himself (v. 30a–c)—are not to delimit the horizon of one's thoughts and actions.

Which way of life incarnates, as it were, this eschatological view? His own, of course. For Paul, a truly theological viewpoint, the one he had really experienced himself, was no merely speculative consideration, even though it was a vision. For it was a vision of the Lord, at once his whole gospel and his whole vocation as an apostle. His pastoral advice, therefore, is none other than the viewpoint which means a life like his own. The "mercy" shown to him (v. 25) is reflected in his own "sparing" the Corinthians (v. 29). His sparing them is one with his desire that his brothers be unpreoccupied. His eschato-

171

logical viewpoint, then, is incarnated in a way of life that is patterned on the viewpoint and vision of the Apostle himself and which he would have them share.

The eschatological viewpoint of the Apostle is an "undivided" one, which is such as to channel one's total energy of body and spirit to effective consecration for the Lord's service. "Pleasing" someone supposes for Paul a whole complexus of practical concerns but, fundamentally, a kind of intense personal dedication. When one "pleases men" (Galatians 1, 10), one by definition does not look to God's interests. "Pleasing one's wife" is *not* for Paul the same as "pleasing men" in contrast to "pleasing God." "Pleasing one's wife" is compatible with service of the Lord and may, concretely, be one's own charism in the Lord. But "pleasing one's wife" nevertheless introduces a further personal consideration which renders the basic viewpoint less prophetically "single-minded." Paul does not argue that "pleasing one's wife" saps human energy, much less that in every case or in most cases it will render one effectively less a Christian. Rather, he sees "single-mindedness" in terms of a realizable ideal for all Christians, according to their call, in *effective* consecration to the Lord. By "effective consecration" is implied the really freer life of the whole human being and his highest modes of operation (v. 34a) as experienced by the Apostle himself, who is as free as any man (1 Corinthians 9).

Paul's presentation of the "undivided" view is theory. He supposes the theory can work, and it has worked in himself. Whether the theory *will* work in others is not his point. But it can, given the Lord's call of the single person and his seeking nothing else but the Lord himself. Whether the theory will even appeal is yet another question. If "pleasing another human being" finds its ultimate appeal in the mystery of personal human love, one can only find the ultimate appeal of "pleasing the Lord" in the mystery of the personal divine love with which Paul himself was blessed.

The last passage in this chapter (1 Corinthians 7, 36–40) deals, as H. Schlier has shown, with a virginal marriage. The translation should read: "If anyone thinks he is not behaving properly *towards his virgin,* if his passions are strong, even thus should it be: let him do what he wants; he does not sin; let them get married. But whoever is firmly set in his heart, being under no necessity but having his desire under control, and has determined in his own heart to *keep* [treat] *her who is his* [as] *a virgin,* will do well, so that he who has his virgin marry does well and he who does not cause her to marry does better." Apparently, the "husband" in this situation enjoyed a certain priority in determining the nature of the relationship—which is not surprising, given the domination of males in households of Paul's day.

The inference that Paul is dealing with a virginal marriage also helps make better sense out of what follows in verses 39–40. The "wife" in this context is the "wife" of the once virginal marriage. After her husband has died, she is free to marry again, though she is to do so "in the Lord," that is, for his service, which is generally taken to mean that she should marry a Christian. Paul concludes by saying that she will be "more blessed" (not the *RSV* "happier," which connotes an emotional disposition rather than a spiritual state) if she remains as she is, a widow. Once again, perhaps with a little irony suggested more by what he is about to say than by what he has said in this chapter, Paul appeals to his own possession of the spirit. For the case is one in which his personal charism is properly invoked as the principle for judging the mode of conduct to be followed.

Virginal marriages should not surprise one in view of the social circumstances of the time. A woman required more protection then than she did in a predominantly Christian society of later centuries. The most practical form of what we know as a "religious community," especially for women, would in Paul's day have been a kind of "family situation." Apparently, one or more cases of this mode of virginity were not working out. The practice may have disappeared soon afterwards (though *virgines subintroductae* were known in the third century), but the lack

173

of evidence for the practice in the earlier centuries, apart from what we find in 1 Corinthians 7, does not stand as a sufficient reason for denying its existence in Paul's day.

E. *Christian Freedom and Sacrificial Foods* *(8, 1—11, 1)*

The matter of eating food sacrificed to idols (8, 1–11, 1) seems at first sight to be somewhat irrelevant to modern Christianity. But the principles underlying the practical question of giving scandal to some of the more sensitive and less solidly grounded members of the community remains perennially relevant. The practical question radically engages Christian "knowledge" under complementary aspects of freedom and obligation and, above all, under the aspect of love.

Meat sold in the markets of Corinth had often been sacrificed to idols, and its connection with the pagan sacrificial cults may well have been more or less explicitly advertized. The principle for Christian conduct in this matter, however, is not simply "what *I know*," but what may help or hurt another who is equally Christ's possession (8, 1–13). Arguing along lines familiar from our interpretation of 1 Corinthians 6, 12 ff., Paul refers (here by a sarcastic allusion) to the outlook of the Corinthians that "all have knowledge." He then dialectically contrasts "knowledge" (as it is regarded in the Corinthians' self-centered perspective) and love. For Paul, knowledge must be outgoing, shown in practical acknowledgment of others in relation to God. As true wisdom is the wisdom of God, so genuine knowledge is being known or acknowledged by God, the sign of which is one's concrete love of God (8, 1–3). Given this over-all theological perspective concerning knowledge, Paul can quickly draw his conclusion about the food of pagan sacrifices. The fact that a man acknowledges only one God and one Lord is the root of his freedom to eat anything in creation that is in line with his being directed towards God through Christ (8, 4–6). Those

174

who do not have this knowledge in the proper degree, but who still think that there is something wrong with the thing itself should not be victims of the knowing Christian's freedom. Paul's recognition of the inner basis of freedom in faith finds its corollary in his insistence on consideration for the conscience of another. "Freedom of conscience" for oneself is not an absolute, except as the ultimate freedom which one has in Christ —and this means concern for others who belong to Christ.

Paul himself is as free as anyone, and his apostolic authority (a testimony to that freedom) is not exercised for his own benefit, but for gaining others for Christ (9, 1–23). Mention of his apostleship apparently causes him to digress. But the digression is not simply a distraction; it takes account of the factionalism treated in the first part of the letter. Some factions at Corinth had no doubt belittled Paul's authority on the basis of an external manner of life different from that of other Apostles (like Cephas) who had visited them. Without placing himself above these others, Paul turns the charge into an occasion for showing how freedom in Christ has been used for their benefit. He whose apostolic example is especially formative for the community that he founded has exercised his freedom by service and has looked for his reward in giving the gospel free of charge, so as to share it with others.

Once again, Paul's line of thought speeds ahead to the consummation, the final reward of his apostolic endeavors (9, 24–27). He exhorts the Corinthians even as he reveals his own motivation, the imperishable crown of the resurrection. But the prize is not to be taken for granted; it demands spiritual conditioning like that of participants in the Isthmian games at Corinth.

In 1 Corinthians 10, 1–13, Paul is still dealing with the practical problem of sacrificial meats and idol worship, strange as this may seem to the reader who simply looks at the pericope in itself. In fact, one might say that Paul is at the heart of his solution to this problem. For, as ever, his principal solution to a practical pastoral problem lies in arousing a vivid awareness of one's whole new relationship to God in Christ. The passage has been called "rabbinic," though it is doubtful that a rabbi would acknowledge it as such. For the perspective that really governs the argumentation is specifically Christian. Nevertheless, the passage can be called rabbinic or midrashic in an analogous sense, for it makes use of Old Testament texts and themes with certain traditional amplifications in order to illuminate the present situation. By a kind of midrash, then, Paul tries to make the Corinthians aware of the implications of their being in Christ through baptism and their nourishment from Christ in the eucharist. Their relationship to the whole question of idol worship will be solved practically in the light of their understanding of how they stand in Christ. How they stand in Christ, in turn, will be seen through the tinted lens of God's word, the Old Testament in traditional understanding.

By way of reading Christian baptismal and eucharistic terminology and ideas back into Old Testament salvation history, Paul points out that one cannot presume that his liberation and sustenance in Christ has gained him the kingdom. His life is to be lived according to God's commands; he is not to tempt God by his self-interest. What temptations he himself does experience can be overcome by God's grace.

The opening verses (10, 1–5) allude to God's protective presence in the cloud, to the people's dedication to follow Moses, and to the nourishment provided them during the exodus. Actually, the Old Testament does not speak of "baptism into Moses." The expression makes sense, however, as Paul's reading back into the events of the exodus the Christian understanding of complete dedication to Christ achieved through the climactic act of deliverance made operative in baptism. Similarly, the Old Testament does not speak of "spiritual" food or drink. But the expression makes sense as Paul's reading back into the events of the exodus the Christian awareness of spiritual sustenance in the eucharist, Christ himself. Where Jewish legend spoke of the rock that Moses struck as something that was ever present to them (harmonizing various instances in which

176

a rock figured by supposing that a given rock "followed" them), Paul takes the story in a Christian dimension.

As we have seen before, it is really irrelevant to ask whether or not he believed the story was factually (and in this sense "historically") true. It is likewise irrelevant to ask whether or not this or related events are the meaning of the Old Testament text taken in itself. The text is read in the double context of what it says and how it was interpreted relevant to the life of Israel, and at the same time in the further context of an understanding of Christian existence which it serves to illuminate. The "literal sense" of God's word is realized fully only in grasping it as relevant to the event and implications of Christian existence. In his pastoral advice, therefore, Paul is not trying simply to convey a "truth" (considered according to the content of a message) but a way of thinking: a consideration of one mystery in the light of another mystery, the mystery of the event of God's people in Christ bespoken in the mystery of the events of the exodus.

The last of the opening verses (v. 5) recalls the outcome of these events as pregnant with warning for the descendants of this generation. How did they stand with God? Most never reached their destination. Paul then indicates clearly that the typology here is one bearing on Christian existence, concretely, on the life of those to whom he is speaking (v. 6). The outcome of this event is not to be verified in their lives. The general point (v. 6b), specified in four illustrations (vv. 7, 8, 9, and 10), is that of self-centered "desire" (*epithymia*). The word connotes for Paul what one wants for himself short-sightedly or greedily. This appears especially in the first illustration. The last three illustrations stress the penalty, but the first stresses the basic sin itself, "idolatry," presenting it under the aspect of self-satisfaction in a meal. Repeating the theme of typological relevance of the events spoken of in the Old Testament, Paul appeals directly to the eschatological understanding of the Christian community. All "ages" or "aeons," including that of the historical experience of the generation in the wilderness,

177

have come to bear on the Christians themselves. Not that these experiences automatically follow, as though history repeated itself, but that they bear on Christian existence as it is to be understood in relation to God. Accordingly, one is not to feel cocksure of himself. Paul may have in mind a greater trial to come, one of satanic dimensions, when he says (v. 13) that no temptation has overtaken them except a "human" one. The danger of their self-reliance would thus be seen more clearly in the light of the final consummation, suggested by mention of the ends of the ages (v. 11). In any event, however, God's fidelity is the answer to the problem of temptation; the Christian is able to pass through it, though he will do so by God's power.

The temptation that Paul has had in mind is equivalently the radically human temptation to "idolatry," which he sees as really the desire for self-satisfaction at the expense of God's interests. Accordingly, when he tells the Corinthians to flee idolatrous cults (10, 14 ff.), he immediately appeals to the outlook they are expected to have on the basis of their liturgical life. The eucharist is a "sharing" in Christ himself. The oneness of Christians, therefore, is not an individualistic oneness but a corporate oneness in Christ. Comparing this sacrifice with the sacrifices of Israel, which were still being offered in the temple, Paul underscores the aspect of communion or sharing in the sacrifice on the part of those engaged in it.

His comparison does not seem to be altogether favorable, for he sees oneness (deriving from that which is shared) in terms of an impersonal thing, the altar. What he is *saying* (substantially the same phrase occurs in vv. 15 and 19) is what he is *implying* in the light of these two revelatory religious practices (one as perfect, the other as imperfect but still revelatory). The *sharing* has to be judged not in terms of a sacrificial *practice* but in terms of the one with whom one is united by the sacrificial sharing. In effect, one cannot compromise one's belonging to the Lord by associating in worship that is not directed to him. In verse 19, while drawing attention to what he *is* saying, Paul mentions what he is *not* saying. He does not imply that there really is anything in idol meat to unite one to an idol (whereas the bread and the cup are indeed the body and blood of Christ), or that the idol itself is a reality to be reckoned with (whereas even in the case of the altar of Israel there was a holy reality on a fleshly level). Rather, he means that what matters in the sacrifices is the beings with whom they put one into contact. Paul's polemic against idolatrous sacrifices is not based on *things* but on the *personal communion* that is implied. In saying that pagans sacrifice to demons, he is not imputing motives to pagans. He is simply considering what they do for what it represents, and states his case in the polemic language reminiscent of Deuteronomy 32, 17. He does seem to assume that demons themselves (unlike the idol) are a reality. But one need not agree with his personal and cultural assumption. His point is not to affirm the existence of demons but to bring his readers to see the worship of God as excluding any compromise.

The worship of idols is, therefore, a practice to be shunned, not as a "thing which is taboo" but as a contradiction of the Christian outlook and Christian existence, as seen in the light of the sacrifice by which all show their oneness in Christ. Once again as he concludes his treatment of the topic in 10, 23–11, 1, Paul strikes at the basic difficulty: the outlook of the Corinthians who are wise in their own eyes, quite reliant on their own concept of freedom or "personal authority" (*exousia*). "All things are permissible" is something to which Paul himself could subscribe, if it were *understood* properly. Even "all things are not helpful" is a statement which Paul could endorse, if it were *understood* properly. There is no formula that substitutes for understanding. In Paul's pastoral exhortations, the same is true again and again. So he endeavors once more to bring the Corinthians really to understand by giving them a kind of dialectical ladder, in which one phrase or statement has to be seen in conjunction with a second, and thus as determined by the

179

second. If punctuation is needed, it seems better to punctuate the first statement (v. 23a) as attributed to the Corinthians and the second (v. 23b) as Paul's rejoinder, thus:

10, 23a "All things are lawful, but not all things are helpful [*sympherei*, 'are expedient']."
10, 23b All things are lawful, but not all things build up!

This dialectic is immediately given an explicitly pastoral focus: "Let no one seek what is his own [that is, his own good], but what is the other's [that is, the good of the other]." What is within my power to do (v. 25, eating anything without raising problems on the score of conscience) is based on what belongs to the Lord (v. 26, the whole of creation). What I can buy to eat (v. 25) I can eat in the company of unbelievers (v. 27). But here I must consider the conscience of the other as well as my own. My own liberty is not thereby compromised (v. 30), but the good of the other must be considered (v. 29; cf. v. 24).

In brief, what I am free to do and what I should do are resolved in the perspective not simply of what *I* am free to do or of *what* I do but of God's glory, that is, of what belongs to him and pertains (like conscience) to the acknowledgment of him. The concrete norm can be seen in the life of the Apostle himself, whose "pleasing men" means looking to their interests rather than seeking his own, and understanding their interests in terms of salvation. What is "helpful" (*symphoron*), then, has been clarified in a theological perspective here (v. 33 vis-à-vis v. 23) much as it has been in 1 Corinthians 7 (1 Corinthians 7, 35 vis-à-vis the point of view in 1 Corinthians 6, 12).

F. *Liturgical Practices (11, 2—14, 40)*

1. VEILING OF WOMEN'S HEADS (11, 2–16)

Recalling his own example leads Paul to recall his own teaching concerning another topic, that of liturgical discipline. In conformity with practices in other churches—and for reasons that

180

Paul himself seems to be aware are not convincing—women are to veil their heads in the assembly (11, 2–16). He seems to be dealing not simply with what we would call the "attendance of women in church" but with the exercise of a function in the church, for he speaks of "praying [aloud] and prophesying" (v. 5). One may suspect in Paul's appeal to "nature" in verse 14 that he is referring to what one can judge even apart from a theological argument, and that implied in this is the everyday situation at Corinth. An unveiled woman at that time and in a city as proverbial for its vice as Corinth was, would be considered a "free" woman in a quite pejorative sense. Such grounds of reproach would also ill befit the dignity of the Christian assembly, where angels were present in adoration (cf. v. 10). The discipline, then, is not so unreasonable, though it is obviously not on the level of an unchangeable practice. Even if Paul regards this practice as a kind of tradition, it is a disciplinary tradition that is basic neither to the kerygma nor to Paul's gospel.

Nevertheless, even his discussion of an alterable practice like the veiling of women in the liturgical assembly brings out Paul's habitual mode of pastoral exhortation. He at least endeavors to justify his viewpoint theologically; he never simply legislates a solution. Even when he recognizes no other practice, he does so in view of a general custom in all the churches—with recognition of their unity under God—and in opposition not to respectful revision but to a kind of self-willed spirit of contention (v. 16). His theological view entails a kind of eschatological hierarchy, not one of ecclesiastical function but one of glory under God. Thus, one might well argue according to the mind of Paul himself that if a woman's function in the Church can be so conducted as to reflect the glory of God and not draw attention to herself at the expense of God (cf. v. 15), it can be recognized as a contribution to the worship of God. It is this that is the central principle of Paul's argument: God's glory, not that of any human being considered apart from it.

2. CONDUCT AT THE LORD'S SUPPER (11, 17–34)

What most disturbs Paul with regard to adherence to his teaching, and calls for an outright rebuke to the whole community (vv. 17 and 22), is the way in which the Lord's Supper is celebrated—to the Corinthians' disadvantage instead of to their total benefit (11, 17–34). They do not assemble in a spirit of unity but in one of factiousness, inevitable as this is for proving those of genuine worth. The Lord's Supper at the time seems to have involved two stages: the community banquet (*agapē*) at which all would share table fellowship, not simply in a secular way, but as *preparatory* to the partaking of the Lord's body and blood, and the partaking of the table of the Lord (the consecrated bread and wine) itself. But the meeting for the Lord's Supper was really one meeting, notwithstanding its two stages. An abuse in the first carried over into the second, especially if it involved drunkenness, as Paul indicates is the case here (v. 21). The *agapē* was debased by the fact that each one cared only for himself and did not share with the others. He faults the whole spirit of the liturgical gathering at Corinth.

Returning explicitly to his reproof (v. 22), he confronts their conduct with the tradition he had given them. This tradition points out that the Lord's Supper is an anticipation of the coming of the Lord, a real presence before the time of definitive judgment or salvation. "Proclaiming the death of the Lord until he comes" does not mean simply re-enacting the Lord's Supper until a point in history arrives at which the Lord comes and the practice ceases. The formulation and especially the theological notion of "remembrance" imply an operative presence of the covenant in the Lord's own body and blood. Community action here anticipates the Lord's physically manifest coming (11, 23–26). It is no wonder, then, in the context of such abuses, that many are suffering in advance adverse effects of the Lord's coming as judge (v. 30). The reality of these effects itself attests to the reality of the Lord's presence in the food consumed (vv. 27 ff.).

Paul does not naïvely regard physical ailments as the effects of sin. He sees physical transformation in terms of the resurrection and judgment. Hence, when he judges a physical affliction here as the penalty for sin, it can only be in the light of his understanding the eucharist as a real presence of the Lord who will come visibly at the parousia. Nevertheless, the physical afflictions that Paul ascribes to unworthy reception of the eucharist are medicinal chastisements rather than the definitive judgment to come on the world (vv. 31–32). Again, the present is seen in the light of the future, with the understanding that the present is eminently the time for grace and repentance. Paul's conclusion is straightforward and clear (vv. 33–34). Had he not had to deal with an abuse, he would no doubt have been able to bring out more positive aspects of the Lord's Supper, such as the anticipation of the health and joy of the parousia. For the theme of "condemnation" is the reverse of the theme of salvation.

3. EXERCISE OF CHARISMATIC GIFTS (12, 1—14, 40)

The following three chapters (1 Corinthians 12–14) treat of the exercise of charismatic gifts in the community, and, at their center (chapter 13), the more excellent way of service which is that of love. Charismatic activity had also been open to abuses at Corinth, probably because of vestigial paganism, in which ecstatic cults were common. Before their conversion, the Corinthians had been led astray as impulse directed them (12, 2; the *RSV* is a bit too awkward). The activity of the Spirit in the community is not impulse in any direction. It is in strict accord with the profession of faith ("Jesus is Lord"), so that no impulse that is at variance with this is a work of the Spirit. On the contrary, the Spirit is that by which one professes his faith in Christ (12, 2–3). Diversity in unity is beautifully brought out through a trinitarian reference (12, 4–6) to the same Spirit, the same Lord (Jesus), the same God (*'o theos,* the Father). The spiritual gift to each one is ordered towards the advantage (*to symphoron,* in the *RSV*, "common good") of the community, for it is the same Spirit which is always operative, though in full freedom (12, 7–11). Having described the oneness of the community in terms of the oneness of faith and of the Spirit, Paul looks at its oneness in terms of the body of Christ (12, 12–27) and of God (the Father's) design (12, 28 ff.).

Paul's treatment of the "body of Christ" has many aspects, all of which reveal and rest on a fundamental understanding of the mystery of union with God and each other in Christ. The image of the body itself should not be treated as some third thing like a "corporation," a "body politic," or some other merely moral person, even though it is analogous to these. Wherever Paul derived the image, it is his own understanding of it that reveals to us its nature; that understanding is properly mystical, and likewise the body is mystical. Fundamentally, the body of Christ is himself as risen from the dead, the man who is now above every limitation of flesh (and therefore of race or nationality) and who is the universal source of the spirit through baptism (12, 12–13). Christ's "spiritual body" is a source of spiritual union of those who are incorporated into him by faith and baptism even though they are not yet transformed into his own "spiritual body." In the present, they have functions in the spirit which they derive from their being in him. Paul goes on to stress the interdependence of function of those who are in Christ, and the way in which every part must be seen and presented in terms of the whole (12, 14–27).

The assembly of the faithful, the "Church," those "called by God," seem even in the transition between verses 27 and 28 to be identified with the "body of Christ." Speaking of God's action, Paul indicates a certain hierarchy of function which means that some gifts are better than others. One should desire the higher gifts (v. 31), but not in a self-seeking way. To show the way superior to these gifts themselves which is the abiding bond of those in the body of Christ, Paul speaks of love (*agapē*) (1 Corinthians 13, 1–13).

The "higher way" is really threefold, that of faith and hope as well as love. For, in comparison with the exercise of various functions within the community, all three "abide." For Paul, faith itself implies not mainly a lack of evidence in truths accepted on God's authority, but a new bond of existence in Christ. Whatever may befall one's exercise of charismatic functions, this bond abides. Its eschatological permanence is the sign of its special character. Hope, too, abides, for it is not simply the desire to possess in the face of obstacles what one does not yet have. It is a yearning to possess ever more fully what one has already been given, the union with Christ in the Spirit. But love is the greatest of the three "theological virtues" which abide, for love most perfectly describes God's own action which makes faith and hope possible. Of all these three, love is the most characteristically divine.

Without love, one really communicates nothing (v. 1), is nothing (v. 2), and gains nothing (v. 3). Love's beauty and power are revealed in what it does and does not do (vv. 4–7). Its superiority to the charisms is viewed in the eschatological perspective of what abides and becomes perfect (vv. 8–12). Paul's praise of *agapē* is voiced in the style of the Stoic-cynic diatribe, but one has only to compare it with the following passage from Maximus of Tyre on the topic of *erōs* (passionate love, especially in the sublimated sense of philosophic love) to appreciate the difference of theme and perspective which marks the Apostle's words:

Passionate love [*erōs*] does battle with no one so much as necessity and
                                             fear;
it is a treasure proud and frightfully free,
yes, freer than Sparta herself—
even if one regards in the human dimension alone [this] passionate love.
But when one meets it in its pure state,
    it is not wild-eyed at wealth,
    it has no fear of the tyrant,
    it is not struck with panic fear at kingly state,
    it does not cautiously regard the court,
    it does not flee from death.
      No beast is terrifying to it,

nor fire,
nor beetling cliff,
nor sea
nor sword,
nor hangman's noose.
 But impasses it finds easily traversed,
 and forbidding things easily won,
 and frightening prospects easily surmounted,
 and rough ways easily borne.
  Every river becomes navigable,
  and winter weather the best for sailing;
  mountains are easily scaled;
 At every turn it acts boldly,
 it looks beyond every difficulty,
 and over everything asserts firm control.

Returning to the spiritual gifts, which are to be desired when pursuing the high road of love, Paul stresses the gift of prophecy (14, 1–40). He does not have in mind specifically predictions of the future, but the gift of declaring God's ways in the light of the consummation to come. The gift of tongues seems to be a form of ecstatic prayer which required the complementary gift of interpretation. Paul does not belittle it, but he sees it as mainly a sign for unbelievers. His paramount consideration is "edification," a play on the notion of "building up" the body of Christ. The Corinthians, not unlike a growing number of Christians in our own day, seem to have been overmuch impressed with the spectacular. Paul scores them for immaturity (14, 20). He insists on good order for the benefit of all, seeing the present situation in the light of God's being a God of peace, implying their eschatological calling to peace (v. 33).

In stressing good order at Corinth, he keeps in mind the practice in all the churches (14, 33b–36). He does not want uniformity for the sake of uniformity, but judges the situation according to the word of God. The subordination of women was according to the law, and Paul deems that it should obtain here because the Corinthian community was not the only one to which the Lord's word (in the gospel) had come. There were Jewish-Christian communities as well which had to be kept in mind. No doubt the restriction on the function of women in the

186

Church has somewhat outlived the force of Paul's own reasons. What is really at issue here, however, is a principle that still holds, in spite of the cultural changes which suggest considerable modifications of the actual practice Paul sanctioned. Innovations should not be made in disregard of the religious sensibilities of the people of God as a whole; they are to further the attitude of worship of all in the community, and the local community itself is part of a greater whole.

Concluding his treatment of charisms and charismatics (14, 37–40), Paul points out that what he writes is not written simply on the basis of a prophetic function in the Church. He is not just another prophet whose word is no more normative than that of anyone else who thinks himself (wrongly or even rightly) to be a charismatic. What Paul himself writes is to be judged as enjoying plenipotentiary power; it is the Lord's command. It should be noted that Paul is not distinguishing here between his word and the Lord's; rather, he affirms their identity. He implicitly distinguishes between the view which an ordinary charismatic might propose and that which he himself has prophetic authority to propose. The distinction, then, does not alter what was said earlier about the distinction between Paul's word and the Lord's or between Paul's word and the Lord's command (1 Corinthians 7, 10. 12. 25, and so forth). For, in all instances (here as well as in chapter 7), the basis for the distinction employed is in the situation itself with which Paul deals. The distinction is not directly in the concept of the word or command of the Lord or in the *concept* of Paul's role, as though he always had to refer to the Lord's word or command or to his own authority in the same way (that is, univocally). His understanding of his authority is always basically the same, but the situation in which it is invoked calls for various distinctions which affect the way in which that authority is presented. The way it is presented, in turn, sheds light on the kind of situation with which Paul is dealing. In this case, he has to distinguish between his authority and that of any other charismatic in the community. In so distinguishing, he shows that the situation is

187

one which arises in accord with the very basic level of communal existence in Christ, community worship. The Lord's command has to be invoked here, for there is question of what must be done under such communal circumstances. Good order among members of the community is essential. In 1 Corinthians 7, 25, on the other hand, the Lord's command is not there to be invoked, for there is question of a fuller exercise of freedom simply in one's personal relationship with Christ.

III. RESURRECTION AND PAROUSIA AS THE GOVERNING PERSPECTIVE OF CHRISTIAN FAITH AND HOPE (15, 1–58)

This lengthy chapter (1 Corinthians 15) has two main sections. Verses 1–34 deal with the fact of the resurrection as a doctrine to be accepted in faith; verses 35–58 (beginning with an anticipated objection), present the way in which the resurrection is to be understood. These, of course, are only general lines, but they should help one to follow the main thrust of Paul's thought. How the resurrection is to be understood is really the sense of matters to be accepted in faith; the word that is accepted in faith is the solid basis for the attempt to understand what is implied as the consummation of faith.

The first main section opens with a reminder of the efficacious word of the gospel. The preferable translation is one which brings out the efficacy of the word that Paul preached. It is not only that which they received and that which will save them, but that by which they hold fast (read in v. 2, "if by it you hold fast"). For the word is conceived dynamically at all times. Faith is not merely a status, but a relationship with God in which God acts to bring men fully to himself. The Christian's salvation is conditioned on initial faith and on holding fast not only to faith but in faith; his holding fast is by God's power at work through the word received.

Although the dynamic aspect of the word is primary in Paul's

188

thought, the word can be formulated in credal fashion. He provides such a formulation in verses 3–11, incorporating himself into a list of witnesses, and closing with an appeal to a factor that transcends the human witnesses, whoever they are. In the kerygmatic formula itself, "according to the scriptures" serves to situate the central events of Christ's death and resurrection in their adequate context: not that of secular history as such but that of salvation history. The "Christ event" must therefore be interpreted in the light of God's word. What is received in faith makes sense as God speaks of it and therefore as God understands and intends it. The appearance to witnesses further situates the events of salvation history in the area of immediate personal communication of the same message by all of them, whether they themselves are alive or dead. The human worth of the witnesses chosen, like their physical condition, is beside the point. Paul speaks of himself as the least of the apostles, repulsive as one untimely born. What matters in the witness is the operative grace of God. Hence, the message which the Corinthians have received stands, as it were, *"ex opere operato."* The word of God itself is really what they have received, and with it, the knowledge of God (cf. v. 34).

The reason Paul stresses this word is that everything else in Christian life depends upon it. He begins to explore the consequences somewhat negatively, showing up contradictions in the whole existential situation of the Corinthians. How is it that some of them can say anything but what is preached (v. 12)? A denial of (our) resurrection is necessarily a denial of Christ's, for, as Paul will make clear in the lines ahead, Christ's resurrection makes sense only as the advance realization of a whole new creation under God through him. What seem to be illogical temporal connections (vv. 13 and 16) are really logical existential connections in the perspective of salvation history. The one event (Christ's resurrection) is inextricably ordered to the other (our resurrection); a denial of the one is a denial of the other. What is true of the twofold event is reflected in the word which makes it known. Christ's resurrection (as the prin-

189

ciple of ours) determined the value of Paul's preaching and of
the Corinthian's faith. If Christ is not risen and the dead do not
rise, then Paul would be a false witness before God and the
Corinthians would still be in their sins for having listened to
him (vv. 14–17). Dead Christians would simply have perished
and living Christians would be the most miserable men on
earth (vv. 18–19).

In verses 20–28, Paul develops the consequences of the resurrection more positively, with a view to the new order under the
new Adam and the Father. The mystery of human solidarity
in death is realized in the mystery of men's life in Christ. But
the stages of this realization are schematized in a kind of
"apocalyptic chronology" which is not simply that of clock-
and-calendar time. Christ's resurrection means our own, but at
the time of his coming. That coming marks the end, the point
of consummation for his work as the new Adam, God's "Son"
in a messianic sense which highlights his *role* (not his "nature")
as concretely realized. Only then will Christ's victory be complete—a victory not only over sin in all who are now united
with him, but over death itself in those who will be united with
him at the parousia. The sovereignty of God (the Father) is
conceived in terms of the wholeness of a new creation. The
kingdom will be fully realized.

Concluding the first part of this chapter are a number of
practical consequences (vv. 29–34) for the life of the Church
here and now. The main practical consequence, of course, is the
futility of the faith and of the whole notion of Christian existence (vv. 12–19). But there are other practical consequences
related to this which Paul can adduce to show the Corinthians
how wide the implications are. First (v. 29), he appeals to
"baptism for the dead." The practice is not really known to us,
but may refer to a rite by which one prayed for departed pagan
ancestors. If so, it was a primitive way of recognizing the universal scope of Christ's death and resurrection, and attested to
the value of Christians' supplication for the departed. Second,
Paul's own perils, notably in dealing with his adversaries in the

apostolate (v. 32a), would make no sense. One might as well take the popular Epicurean advice of those the Bible calls fools (cf. Wisdom 2, 1–9. 21; 3, 1). He seems to imply that the Corinthians should be on their guard against corrupting elements within the community.

The anticipated objection (vv. 35 f.) is more than an answer to some people at Corinth. It is a somewhat stylized device (as is the reproach "You foolish man!" in v. 36), used to develop the argument as a whole. A main difficulty in accepting the resurrection lies, as Paul sees it, in a kind of materialistic conception of the risen body. He answers this difficulty by providing a quite different perspective, one involving the spiritual body (vv. 36–44), the heavenly man (vv. 45–49), and the mystery of transformation in the victorious coming of God's kingdom (vv. 50–57).

In verses 36–44, the agricultural image (vv. 36–38) is employed to bring out the decisive element of God's efficacious choice; the illustration supposing the cosmology of the time (vv. 39–41) is intended to bring the reader to see "bodies" and "glory" in an analogous sense, not a univocal sense. Then, in verses 42–44, Paul moves to apply to the risen body the perspective generated by the preceding examples. It is simply a different kind of body, one that is incorruptible and glorious, brought about by God's power. It does not exist on the level of the merely human creation (*psychikon,* in the *RSV,* "physical") but on the level of the new creation, that of the spirit of God.

One feels quite frustrated in trying to find a translation for the term *psychikon* that will convey Paul's notion in a satisfying way. The reason for the translator's agony in handling this term is that Paul himself conveys his thought not so much in single terms or phrases as in contrasted or parallel terms and statements. He thinks both dialectically and "analogously," endeavoring to bring his reader not only to accept a "truth" but to reach a way of thinking truly. His own progressions of thought are really dominated by the grasp he has of the "princi-

191

pal correlative" or "prime analogate" towards which he moves in his exposition; he does not simply "reason through" to a conclusion. The prime analogate which he already understands is what governs the sense of the other terms that he uses to lead others to his own act of true understanding. Thus, in verse 44, he says: "If there is a physical body [*sōma psychikon*], there is a spiritual body [*sōma pneumatikon*]." He does not mean simply that there are two kinds of bodies. He sees the imperfect as arguing for the perfect—not in the Platonic context of ideas, of course, but in the dynamic biblical and apocalyptic context of salvation history. The existence of the one kind of body now or previously makes sense in the light of the other kind of body to come.

The sense of this verse as we have interpreted it rests not just on the course of the argument in verses 36 ff., which rises to statements on the spiritual body (vv. 42 ff.), but on the scriptural example immediately conjoined with it ("So, too, is it written:" v. 45). The line of thought is the same in both cases. The first is seen dynamically in the light of the second, the physical (*psychikon*) in terms of the spiritual (*pneumatikon*). The "spiritual" is on a "heavenly" plane, but it is really defined existentially in terms of the risen Christ, not in terms of some abstract idea. For Paul's mention of Adam regularly is determined by his understanding of Christ himself (1 Corinthians 15, 20 ff.; Romans 5, 11 ff.).

With verse 50, Paul moves on to speak of the "spiritual" realization of the kingdom, showing as he does so that he views the specifically human, "flesh and blood," as the perishable which must become imperishable. The "mystery" which he describes in apocalyptic language is not simply a "truth hidden in God which man could not have known without revelation," but a dynamic transformation as well. It is not strictly an evolutionary concept, for it is not a notion of progressive change in the course of natural historical events; it implies "progression" of another order, that of God's transforming action at the moment of judgment.

192

Paul does not say that death is necessary for this transformation, but that transformation of earthly existence is necessary for the realization of the kingdom at the Lord's coming. As the New Testament attests elsewhere, Christ will come to judge "the living and the dead" (Acts 10, 42; 1 Peter 4, 5; 2 Timothy 4, 1). Paul probably hopes to be among those Christians who are alive at the time (cf. "we," v. 52). Since it is a merely personal impression, however, his hopeful supposition no more affects Paul's basic affirmation than does a contrary supposition on our own part. The transformation in the resurrection of those who have died and the transformation into the risen body of those who are still alive will mark victory according to the perspective of salvation history. Death itself will be undone. It will have no more force, no "sting." Paul views "death" not just as physical death, but in a complexive way, as a power-figure that represents what can in certain ways separate men from the living God. Its force is really in sin, and the venom of sin "really works" when the individual confronted with God's law fails to realize its command. Thus, the law can be said to be the "power" of sin. *De facto*, it furthers the realization of sin. The victory over death is already won for us by Christ, and in him we already enjoy it in some measure. But our own final transformation in Christ will mark the end of death itself and thus of all the forces which it uses. The new reign which will be realized will be equivalently a "spiritual" kingdom, achieved by the Father through Christ.

Like the reference to sin and law in verse 56, the concluding remarks in verse 58 do not fit well as part of the rest of the letter. With the implications of verses 33–34, they would stand better in earlier correspondence, and probably look to more than what remains of it in chapter 15. Firmness in faith seems to be the scope of this conclusion, the Corinthians' life in faith being viewed as "the work of the Lord." Nevertheless, the death and resurrection of Jesus Christ and a proper understanding of it is central to the life of faith which is expected of the Corinthians.

IV. THE COLLECTION, A WORK OF LOVE
(16, 1–24)

The fourth part of the letter (16, 1–24) is introduced by the topical formula familiar from much of the third part ("Concerning . . .": 7, 1. 25; 8, 1; 12, 1). What seems to be a somewhat mundane matter, the taking up of a collection, means much more to Paul. It was a concrete sign of the solidarity in the faith between the churches in which he had worked (the four major areas of Galatia, the Province of Asia, Macedonia, and Achaea) and the mother church in Jerusalem.

His own plans for travel are dominated mainly by considerations of the good he can do (which he sees militantly, v. 9) in various areas. As usual, it is Timothy who is Paul's principal legate at this time (vv. 10–11), though his coming to Corinth does not seem definitely planned. Paul's urging of Apollos to go to Corinth with those who were bringing his letter back to the community there probably reflects his desire to show that the two really work closely together (cf. 1 Corinthians 3, 4–9). But Apollos apparently had to consider his own work, and Paul did not force the issue. He simply adds an exhortation to faith and love (vv. 13–14). The community is not without some structure to secure good order, but their service depends on the cooperation of others (vv. 15–18).

Final greetings from the community (vv. 19–20) are followed with Paul's own (vv. 21–24). If the reader has not been jolted by Pauline paradoxes before, he will be jolted now. Paul's greeting begins as a curse! A personal love of the Lord is all important, but it is couched in a formula that suggests the negative aspect of judgment. Corresponding to it, however, is the liturgical cry *Marana tha* "O Lord, come!" and the wish for the Lord Jesus' blessing on them (vv. 22–23). If Paul's personal greeting is paradoxical, it is because his personally apostolic and pastoral outlook is so vividly governed by the "end of the end," the judgment and salvation to be fully brought about at the Lord's coming.

CHAPTER SIX

2 CORINTHIANS

COMPOSITE LETTER TO A PROUD BUT REPENTANT COMMUNITY

Within about a year after the correspondence which we have in most of 1 Corinthians Paul had to make an "interim visit" to Corinth to settle problems there. After returning eastward across the Aegean, he wrote at least three more letters to the Corinthians. We have in 2 Corinthians a collection of portions of at least three different letters which Paul wrote subsequent to the interim visit he made shortly after Pentecost, A.D. 57. The interim visit was not the one that Paul had planned to make according to 1 Corinthians 16, 1–9, but required a return to Ephesus during Mission III and further changes of plans. Only around the winter of A.D. 57–58 was Paul able to stay for some months in Corinth. Following the interim visit, he was busy in Ephesus, Troas, and Macedonia.

Our present 2 Corinthians represents his correspondence from one or more of these areas across the Aegean. Paul moved from Ephesus to Troas (2 Corinthians 2, 12–13). Not finding Titus there with news about the church at Corinth, he proceeded to Macedonia, to reach Corinth from the north. The first part of the letter (chapters 1–7) was written once Paul had reached Macedonia. The third part (chapters 10–13) was written on another occasion, though whether this was earlier or later is a matter of debate. The second part of the letter (chapters 8–9) deals with the collection that Paul was gathering at the time (cf. 1 Corinthians 16); chapter 8 seems to go with 2 Corinthians 1–7, but chapter 9 seems to represent part of a third letter (written after 2 Corinthians 1–8). In order to follow Paul's thought more easily, at least the first and third parts of the letter must be distinguished in view of two different situations at Corinth which are tied in with Paul's travels in A.D. 57–58.

Some attention, therefore, must be devoted to two major hypotheses regarding in particular the writing of the third part (2 Corinthians 10–13), which is the most troublesome to place. Each of these hypotheses concerning the composition of the letter entails further hypotheses regarding the situation to which Paul addresses himself. The reader may prescind from a number of details in these hypotheses when interpreting the letter, but if he adverts to the main lines of the problem, he will at least be spared considerable confusion. Whichever hypothesis he follows, he should then be able to appreciate Paul's attempt to defend himself as identified with his attempts to draw the Corinthians to a keener appreciation of his gospel in any situation he confronts.

The first hypothesis, basically that of Hausrath (1870), is rather simple: 2 Corinthians 10–13 equals "the letter written in tears," which Paul mentions a number of times in 2 Corinthians 1–7 (for example, 2, 3. 4. 9; 7, 8. 9. 12). This means that chapters 10–13 were written from Ephesus on Paul's third missionary journey (before he went to Macedonia), after a second, "interim" visit to Corinth across the Aegean, a visit which Paul would have made in the spring of A.D. 57 and before writing our present 2 Corinthians 1–7 (or 1–9). Two serious difficulties may be leveled against this position, though they do not seem to be insuperable, and the theory still finds adherents.

196

The first difficulty is that the tone of chapters 10–13 is one of anger, indignation, even sarcasm—and thus does not seem to qualifiy as a "letter written in tears." It is not clear, however, that Paul could not have regarded a harsh letter to those he loved (cf. 2 Corinthians 11, 11) as a letter written in tears—especially when he so characterizes it *later* (2 Corinthians 2 and 7) in a letter which aims at reconciliation.

The second difficulty is more serious. In 2 Corinthians 2, 5–10 and 7, 12, there is question of "an offender" and "one offended." To avoid any misunderstanding (whichever theory one adopts for 2 Corinthians 10–13), it should be noted that this is not a reference to the incestuous man of 1 Corinthians 5. It is an allusion to someone who challenged the authority of Paul or of one of Paul's representatives. But 2 Corinthians 10–13 makes no mention of this "offender" who seems to have figured so large in the "letter written in tears" which Paul recalls in 2 Corinthians 2 and 7. Hence, 2 Corinthians 10–13 cannot very well be the "letter written in tears" which Paul must have sent before he composed the reconciliation in 2 Corinthians 1–7 (9). In assessing this difficulty, however, one should note that 2 Corinthians 10–13 is not a complete letter; we may simply lack the passage that treated of this individual. Or, and this is not unlikely, Paul may have avoided a direct reference to an individual even while he knew who would be directly affected by his remarks in what we have as 2 Corinthians 10–13.

The second hypothesis, that of scholars like Krenkel (1890) and Windisch (1924), states in effect that 2 Corinthians 10–13 was written *after* 2 Corinthians 1–7 (and hence likewise after the "letter written in tears," which we must accordingly presume was lost). Supposedly, Titus encountered difficulties in taking up the collection (cf. 2 Corinthians 8–9) and Paul's adversaries renewed their charges. Paul then wrote an angry letter which mentions a projected third visit to put matters in order. This theory seems to give too much weight to pure speculation concerning the matter of the collection, and does not adequately explain the Apostle's delicate apologia for his authority in 2 Corinthians 1–7.

197

Now, whichever theory is adopted, it seems better to read chapters 10–13 first. For the charges which Paul answers in chapters 1–7 are substantially the same as those that he encounters in 2 Corinthians 10–13. But we can much more easily understand from the shorter and more pointed chapters at the close of this collection what these charges were. Hence, we first offer some summary comments on 2 Corinthians 10–13 and will then turn to the beginning of the letter.

FORTHRIGHT REFUTATION OF CHARGES
(10—13)

We can readily sense irony and even sarcasm in Paul's opening barrage (10, 1–11). Paul rejects the accusations of personal weakness, of acting from natural motives (*kata sarka,* "according to flesh"; the *RSV,* "in worldly fashion"), and of asserting his own authority by way of self-centered boasting. He will be bold enough when he comes, not weak! His boldness stands in line with the campaign he is waging for Christ, not a campaign for his own selfish interests. His authority derives from the Lord, and he wields it to build up (the temple or body of Christ), not to destroy. The man he is in his letters is the same as the man he is when present among them, for the Apostle's power is ever the same, the power of God's word.

He then takes up the charge that he has really nothing to boast about, that he simply asserts himself or commends himself (10, 12–18). The Greek text in this passage contains a considerable amount of word play on terms like "measure" and "norm" which are obscured in any translation. In effect, the measure of Paul's boast is not to be taken with regard to the accomplishments of others (although it could be, at least with regard to work among the Corinthians, for he himself founded the church at Corinth). That is, the measure of his apostolate covers even Corinth. The measure of his boast is a divine norm; that is, he can confidently rejoice according to the apportion-

198

ment of God's gift to him, which is at one and the same time his gospel and his being an Apostle (for the gentiles). He hopes that the increase of their faith will help his apostolate so that he will have no other basis for his boast than the measure of that which God has allotted to him. For the increase of the Corinthians' faith is brought about by God in accord with a divinely intended norm for the scope of Paul's apostleship. "Boasting" means confident rejoicing in hope of the full harvest to be expected. The extent of this boast is the extent of the work to be done, and the Corinthians themselves form part of the field which has been measured out by God for Paul. In short, Paul's boast is to be understood on the principle of a boast in God. What he has to boast about is one and the same as what God has apportioned. Hence, the only commendation to which the Apostle appeals is God's commendation.

With this largely defensive introduction behind him, Paul turns to show concern for the fidelity of his converts (11, 1–12, 18), specifically, their fidelity to his preaching, by which they were betrothed to Christ, the new Adam (11, 1 ff.). Paul's pastoral approach in this case, where the Corinthians have succumbed not only to factionalism but to heeding "superlative" apostles who are no apostles at all, calls for an approach like that which he felt compelled to use with the Galatians. But, in proportion as his Corinthian audience is more complacently wise in its own esteem, Paul draws on sharper words to deflate them. The false methods and claims of false apostles are implicitly contrasted with the full wisdom and selflessness of the Apostle himself (11, 4–11). The contrast closes with an eschatological perspective of the present masquerade (11, 12–15): the end will be according to their deeds, not according to appearances.

In the following passage (11, 16–12, 10), where Paul boasts in his weaknesses as triumphs of endurance which prove God's power, the irony grows suddenly dense as a thicket of thorny paradox within thorny paradox. Even the parenthesis in 11, 17 seems to be ironical. Paul recognizes as most properly his own his very deficiencies. In speaking of his deficiencies, then, he does not speak "according to the Lord." His very way of boasting "according to the flesh," on the other hand, is aimed at deflating esteem for one who speaks of merely human accomplishments. Thus, his foolishness is really wisdom according to the Lord. From the outset, however, a boast in merely human accomplishments is the boast of a fool, like that of the false teachers whom the Corinthians would hail. A genuine boast depends thoroughly on God's power, which is made perfect in the weaknesses of his Apostle. The Apostle's limitations serve as the background to bring out the *éclat* of Christ's power in him. He is a true apostle after all, and the Corinthians should recognize it in proportion as they have benefited from the self-lessness of his apostolate shown personally or through others whom he sent to them (12, 11–18).

Paul continues (12, 19–21) by averring that his apologia is not really an appeal to the Corinthians—as though he were compromising his authority—but rather an admonition for their benefit. He warns them against specific sins of self-interest. The topic would seem to have changed from that of false teachers, but in Paul's mind false teaching received with self-adulation germinates immorality of all kinds. Healthy moral conduct is secured only when faith itself is healthy.

Paul mentions once again (13, 1; cf. 12, 14) that this is the third time he will visit them. Actually it seems that, in either of the two hypotheses given earlier, Paul did not visit them as he had *planned,* though he did make a third visit. The second visit (mentioned in 2 Corinthians 13, 2) was probably the interim visit which Paul made from Ephesus in A.D. 57. He regards this projected third visit as a kind of "third witness" against them. Alluding to the mystery of the passion and resurrection, Paul declares that his own weakness and power is that of Christ. It is equally as selfless, too, because all he looks for is their own benefit. He thus ends (13, 10) on the note which he struck towards the beginning of this whole apologia (10, 8).

Final admonitions and salutations (13, 11–13) and a trinitarian blessing, which amplifies the usual greeting (13, 14), bring the letter to a close.

A number of the most characteristic features of Paul's pastoral approach appear throughout this section, even though its irony and sarcasm are much more intense than usual and do not reflect his habitual or preferred pastoral approach to a community.

In the opening major section (10, 1–18) of this part, Paul still appeals in some measure to the Corinthians' fidelity in the past. For in saying that he is ready to punish every disobedience, he supposes first of all that the Corinthians' obedience has been complete in the past (10, 6). The complete obedience of which he speaks, in the context of 10, 5, is radically the obedience of faith, viewed not as a blind leap, but as the knowledge of God. Complete initial obedience in faith puts one totally under God's guidance. Disobedience to apostolic authority is tantamount to rebellion against the knowledge of God and submission to Christ, which Paul supposes to be the foundation of their Christian lives.

Besides denouncing present rebellion with an implicit appeal to past fidelity, Paul tries to prompt the Corinthians to acquire a proper perspective. In 10, 7 he says (according to the *RSV*): "Look at what is before your eyes"; or, according to the translation that we prefer: "You see things according to appearances [*ta kata prosōpon blepete*]." In either case, Paul is speaking of a way of looking at things. According to the *RSV* translation, he wants the Corinthians to grasp the meaning of apostolic authority so as to understand in the light of what this means how Paul is acting. According to the other translation, which seems to do more justice to the idiom in verse 7a and to the coherence of Paul's thought in this context, Paul is reproving a false perspective. The Corinthians do not see that belonging to Christ is not something that concerns the individual alone, but is to be reckoned along with the role of the Apostle. The

201

Apostle's authority in Christ is essentially constructive, aimed at building up the community. Hence, the point at issue is not something on the level of appearances, the way men see things (namely, as Paul's individual attempt to assert himself over another individual Christian, as if he wanted to frighten them). Nor is the point at issue Paul's individual conduct or ability, but his exercise of God's word and work. In short, the proper perspective must be not that of one's own individual existence in Christ but one which includes recognition of Paul's place in Christ and thus of the function which he is to exercise.

A further attempt to bring the Corinthians to proper perspective occurs in 10, 17–18. The principle of boasting in the Lord and of receiving commendation as the Lord's commendation sheds light on the way any concrete action is to be judged. The alternative perspective is to compare oneself with others, and thus implicitly make oneself the norm (cf. 10, 12). Such judgment is short-sighted because it really does not rise above the level of human standards. It is in view of the Lord's service (*en kyriō*, boasting "in the Lord" [10, 17]; not the *RSV*, "of the Lord") and therefore in view of the standards which the Lord has set that one's work measures up or not.

Thirdly, Paul identifies himself with his audience in his entire outlook and basic affection. The whole understanding of his apostolic work requires that he be judged as one with them in Christ (10, 7). They are part of the apostolic field which God has measured out for him (10, 14). His genuine affection for the Corinthians comes out most strikingly during the height of his apologia in the second section (11, 1–12, 18) of this part of the letter. His anger is a jealous anger to preserve the Corinthians' marriage with Christ (11, 2). God knows how he loves them (11, 11)! His "foolishness" in boasting (11, 16 ff.) is the foolishness of one whose total, apostolic love is unrequited (12, 11 ff.).

Lastly, and perhaps most profoundly, the Apostle's pastoral effort must be judged in the light of his pastoral message, and, indeed, reveals that message in accord with the pastoral situation. His pastoral effort consists in striving with all his energy to shake the Corinthians into a vivid awareness of the mystery lived by the genuine Apostle. Had his gospel not been so firmly welded with his own apostleship, he might have been able to take a less intensely personal stand. Accordingly, he might have been able to deal with false teachers and with the Corinthians' errors without such fiery personal engagement. But his gospel was thoroughly one with this apostolic commission in the vision of the risen Lord who had been crucified. The passion and resurrection, then, as a mystery lived by Christ who, living, had transformed Paul's life, cannot fail to form Paul's pastoral message. The pastoral situation that Paul faces provokes his pastoral effort and therefore evokes the aspect of the mystery revealed in the Apostle's own life.

Thus, the charges leveled against Paul represent him as a "weak," that is, mediocre, apostle who really overextends in self-assertive action what authority he has. These charges really serve to establish others in Paul's stead, and entail a perversion of his gospel if only by turning allegiance to Christ into what is primarily a personal following. Specifically doctrinal differences do not seem to have appeared, or at least to have become prominent. Nevertheless, the faith itself is affected when loyalty to Christ, represented fully by loyalty to his plenipotentiary, the Apostle, has been turned into the personal following of one or more men who have come within the community.

The Corinthians' sophistication in willingly accepting a false notion of apostolic teacher forms part of the same situation. Unjustified pride is their charge, but unjustified pride is really their offense. Paul's response to the situation is therefore to puncture the Corinthians' pride and to demonstrate at the same time that his own boast lies solely in God. To bring out God's power in his own apostolic accomplishments is to boast mainly in his own weaknesses. The theme of "weakness" reappears repeatedly in the main section (11, 1–12, 18; for instance, 11, 5. 21. 29. 30; 12, 7–10). His service of Christ is a kind of recapitulation of the passion (11, 23 ff.), an apostolic passion

203

entailing solidarity in all that adversely affects his churches (11, 28 f.). The principle which the Lord gives him to strengthen him is that the Lord's grace is sufficient for him, for the Lord's power is brought to perfection in and through Paul's weakness (12, 9). This principle expresses radically nothing but the mystery of Christ's own passion, in which God's power worked through human weakness. Paul's whole conception of his own apostolic power is an articulated insight and awareness of God's power in Christ and Christ's in Paul for the fulfillment of the service expected of him.

CONCILIATORY MANIFESTO (1—7)

A. *Heartfelt Hope for Reconciliation (1—2)*

The first part of the letter (2 Corinthians 1–7) deals with a new situation. Paul has just recovered from a grave illness, which he refers to as a death sentence (2 Corinthians 1, 9). Perhaps it was a severe recurrence of some chronic ailment, and perhaps this in turn is what he apocalyptically alludes to in 12, 7 as an "angel of Satan." The nature of the ailment has defied speculation and will probably continue to do so. Whatever its nature, Paul employs it as an occasion to heal the hurt feelings which followed the "letter written in tears." At this time, he sees no real threat to the Corinthians' faith— either because the difficulties to faith implied by 2 Corinthians 10–13 had not yet arisen or, as we think is more likely, because the Corinthians were brought to repentance by the way he handled the situation. He apparently had not made a visit which he had firmly indicated he would make. This gave grounds for some to repeat or echo in muted tones the charge of weakness, pointing to the Apostle's vacillation. Paul tactfully guards them against this assumption and against the more basic misinterpretation of his apostolic exuberance as empty self-commendation.

Instead of beginning with his own thanksgiving for the addressees, as he customarily does, the Apostle opens with a tactful appeal for the Corinthians' thanksgiving for what God has done for Paul, who is completely devoted to them (1, 3–11). Paul combines several points in these verses:

1. Thanksgiving to God—a motif which "frames" this section, by appearing in verses 3–4 as the blessing rendered to God by Paul himself, and in verse 11 as the thanksgiving hoped for from the Corinthians.
2. An allusion to his illness and its lesson, reliance on God rather than on oneself (vv. 8–10).
3. A theological treatment (mainly in vv. 5–7) of the interrelationships among God and Christ, Paul, and the Corinthians. The basis for this treatment is communion or sharing (*koinōnia*) both in sufferings and tribulations (*pathēmata, thlipseis*) and in consoling assistance (*paraklēsis;* in the *RSV,* "comfort").

Prayerful thanksgiving, personal news, and theological understanding of solidarity in Christ are beautifully blended into a discreet pastoral greeting.

In verses 3–4, Paul blesses God and speaks of the way in which the *paraklēsis* (strengthening of faith in its affective and effective aspects), which has been shown himself in every tribulation, comes from God for the benefit of the Corinthians. In verses 5–7, he indicates as the theological reason for this Christ's own sufferings and consolation (*paraklēsis*) which overflow into Paul. Both these sufferings and these consolations which he experiences are for the benefit of the Corinthians, since they, too, share in the same sufferings which Paul experiences. How so? Not that the Corinthians have been physically sick and physically healed like Paul. Rather, a particular illness of one member of Christ—the suffering peculiar to Paul—is viewed in the larger and adequate context of tribulations as an inseparable part of the pattern of existence in Christ. It is on the basis of

205

his theological perspective that Paul can say that the Corinthians endure the *same* sufferings (v. 6). His pastoral tact and
prayer are thus permeated with theological understanding of the
action of God in Christ.

The themes of tribulation and salvation (v. 6), of patient
endurance and hope (vv. 6–7), of death and resurrection (v.
9), of deliverance now and in the future (v. 10) are all eschatological themes connoting the final triumph in Christ which ever
governs Paul's thinking. The triumph itself suggests a "boast,"
confident rejoicing in what God achieves on our behalf for his
own glory. Hence the apparently abrupt transition in 1, 12 is
a quite logical one from Paul's eschatological viewpoint. He
sees that boast here, however, in terms of a personal triumph
involving his work among the Corinthians, and he views it
further in terms of its interior, personal basis in God's eyes.
That is why he speaks of it as the testimony of his conscience,
especially regarding his work among them, made possible by
God's grace. This eschatological boast, an anticipation of the
final triumph at the judgment, is a testimony in the present.
Where is it given? In Paul's conscience. But the Corinthians can
read him clearly in what he writes (v. 13a).

At this point, Paul puts even their reading him into its eschatological perspective. They can read him truly, but they are also
to read him fully (*'eōs telous,* "to the end," v. 13b)—which
suggests the final manifestation at God's judgment. For, concretely, Paul's boast is not his own, but theirs, as theirs is his,
on the Day of the Lord (v. 14). Thus, while giving his own
boast, he includes theirs as well—and gives both concretely
in the eschatological dimension of Christ's own final triumph,
the Day of the Lord.

As he has delicately explained his own boasting in terms of
his apostolic work among them and of their own grounds for
boasting—and all this in an eschatological perspective—so he
proceeds to explain his own travels. What makes Paul so dif-

206

ficult to follow is the fact that he is not simply talking about his travels or giving valid reasons for a change in his plans. He is formulating this information, a) in the light of his understanding of his and the Corinthians' common bond in Christ and b) in the perspective of the final judgment. In short, apologia for a change in missionary travels is given in the light of the mystery of union in Christ finalized by Christ's parousia. A mystical explanation for a change of itinerary!

Paul's pastoral method does not consist simply in trying to soothe ruffled feelings or to ruffle complacent attitudes, but in endeavoring to get his converts to see things through God's eyes—as the Apostle himself sees them. Thus, in 1, 15, he begins by grounding his whole explanation on "what he was sure of," that is, on his confidence of the Corinthians' ultimate understanding to be attained on the Day of the Lord, when Paul's boast would be fully understood to be their benefit as well.

His planned, "earlier" coming (rather than the *RSV* "first") was simply to have anticipated his coming again to them after a temporary round-trip from Corinth to Macedonia prior to their sending him on to Judaea. There may well be an allusion here to the first and second comings of Christ, the second being the "second grace" (*deuteran charin;* not the *RSV deuteran charan,* "double pleasure"—though the allusion could be the same). This interpretation, though it accords with the terminology and with the foregoing context, by no means imposes itself. Nevertheless, it would fit well with Paul's presentation elsewhere (for example, Philippians 1, 26) of his comings and goings as apostolic reflections of the presence and absence of the Lord.

Similarly, as he goes on (1, 17) to show that his plans were not whimsical but were in line with what God wanted of him (or with what God wanted to give through Christ—which for Paul amounts to the same thing), he soars into a liturgical representation of his affirmed apostolic word with strong eschatological connotations. First of all, he distinguishes his mode

207

of acting as that of one who plans on the level of the spirit (negatively, "not according to flesh," that is, by this-worldly standards, v. 17). On this level, the fidelity in question is fidelity to God, expressed in terms of the faith which Paul, Silvanus, and Timothy had affirmed among them. The affirmation that was preached is none other than the realization of God's promises in Christ; the apostolic preaching is God's "yes" to what he has promised. The Christians' "Amen," a liturgical response to the covenant realized in Christ, echoes the "Yes" of God's answer to his own promises, and enunciates the glory of God. This presentation of faith in terms of "affirmation" enables Paul to go on to speak of its corporate aspect in terms of "God's establishing" the missionaries and the Corinthians together. In turn, the liturgical presentation of the affirmation is mirrored in the notion of God's anointing (the *RSV* "has commissioned") them all. With a probable allusion to baptism as that which marks them as God's own possession, mention is also made of God's gift of the spirit in our hearts. The eschatological connotations emerge in the whole picture of the realization of God's promises, in the mention of "glory," and in the expression "guarantee" (*arrabōn*) of the Spirit. The "guarantee" is God's "down payment" on that which he intends to give us fully in due time. Thus Paul has tried to alert the Corinthians to see his original plans as those which were quite in accord with the whole affirmative nature of his apostolic preaching and which entailed mutual benefits in Christ according to the eschatological situation.

Firm as this projected plan was, Paul did not execute it, for he wanted to spare them pain (1, 23 ff.). In mentioning his projected plan, he appealed to God's fidelity. In mentioning his change of plan, he appeals to God's testimony (v. 23a). Both in the case of his projected plan and in the case of his changed course of action he likewise introduces the perspective of faith. Since he does not lord it over their faith, however, and since their faith is firm (probably in view of a positive response to hi projected visit), he could act as he did. This line of reasoning implies that Paul's pastorally motivated journeys are guided by the faith which he preaches. His missions are his faith in steadfast act. His projected journey was not according to an arbitrary decision, nor was his change of plans. In both cases, his considerate understanding of the faith of the community, for which he was responsible, decisively governed his actions.

In 1, 23–2, 11, he adduces a further consequence of faith, joy which he wanted to foster by not forcing a confrontation by coming to them personally. His own joy is implied in theirs. If he caused them pain by the lines he wrote, it was only with grief to himself at the time, and, above all, to exercise his love for them. He hoped that the letter would really make a more painful course of action (his visit) unnecessary. Turning from an explanation of his own causing them pain (2, 2) to the pain caused by the offender (2, 5), Paul appeals to the community to show the offender love at this time, lest the offender himself be pained further. For the aim of Paul's letter has been achieved. Forgiveness (the word used is the same as that for "showing grace or favor") on their part amounts to Paul's own forgiveness, and this, in turn, is forgiveness in the presence of Christ. Paul concludes by suggesting that such forgiveness is exercised in Christ's tribunal so as to protect the community from the divisive action of Satan, who would acquire the community for himself.

Thus far, Paul has given the Corinthians to understand his original plans (1, 15–22) and his change of plans in not coming to Corinth personally, as he had indicated in a strong letter that he would do (1, 23–2, 11). His reasons have been given fundamentally in terms of faith and love involving a threefold personal context: God and Christ, Paul (and his companions), and the Corinthians. In continuing to indicate the reason for a change of plans, he introduces once more the perspective of faith, this time apropos of his missionary opportunity in Troas. When he arrived in Troas (whence he would have set out for

209

Corinth as planned, and from Corinth would have made a round-trip to Macedonia), he felt it was necessary to see Titus. Practical reasons for this contact can be inferred from 7, 5–7. Titus had been sent to effect a reconciliation, and Paul had to find out the state of affairs at Corinth before journeying on to that city. Hence, Paul proceeded to Macedonia first in order to meet Titus there and so to receive news of the Corinthian community. The news was good, and Paul dispatched Titus from Macedonia to Corinth with the passages we have as 2 Corinthians 1–7. Though practical considerations underlay Paul's change of plans, the dominant consideration was his whole missionary enterprise for Christ.

It is this perspective which appears in 2, 12–17. At Troas, Paul discovered an opportunity for the Lord's service, though an opportunity which was probably not restricted to that immediate area. He felt charismatically guided ("found no rest for my spirit," v. 13) to contact Titus, so he went on to Macedonia. This move proved to be a triumph in Christ. Without offering any details about what actually happened in Macedonia, Paul abruptly introduces an acclamation of God's grace in his own missionary triumph in Christ when preaching the gospel wherever he goes (v. 14). He describes himself as the incense burned in Christ's triumphal procession. The fragrance has salutary or suffocating effect depending on the differently disposed people who inhale it. As he moves from describing a particular journey to depict every journey, he escalates the imagery into an apocalyptic perspective. For some, Paul's preaching the knowledge of Christ simply brings death leading to further death; for others, life leading to further life. The death principle and the life principle are thus expressed dynamically, that is, in terms of a total process: from beginning to end (cf. Romans 1, 17).

With this passage, Paul also shows that his triumph in preaching the faith is not to be reckoned as a merely human triumph, hence, not as one motivated by self-interest. He simply utters the unadulterated word of God (2, 17). The passage thus marks a transition from the question of Paul's change of plans to a more explicit consideration of his apostolic authority and his alleged self-commendation.

B. *Prophetic Ministry of the New Covenant (3—7)*

Is Paul not commending himself (3, 1) by describing himself in such a potent role—as an occasion of death or of life? He answers (3, 1–18) by exposing the mystery of the new covenant as he and they and, above all, Christ himself figure in it. He begins by saying that he looks for no letters of commendation but the Corinthians themselves; they are both his letter and Christ's. The metaphor breaks down hopelessly under the weight of the meanings that Paul sees implied in this apostolic letter of commendation. They are his own letter in that they are written in his heart (v. 2) and also inasmuch as he has been the inspired amanuensis through whom the spirit writes on their hearts (v. 3). By way of alluding to the passages in Jeremiah 31 (LXX 38), 31 ff. and Ezekiel 36, 26 at the end of 2 Corinthians 3, 3, Paul makes it clear that the Corinthians themselves are, as Christ's, the new covenant. The fully and definitively personal covenant of the living God resides in the hearts of his people, and therefore resides in them through their being Christ's via Paul's service.

His sufficiency, then, in such a potent role (cp. 2, 16 and 3, 5) and the "confidence" that springs from it, are not his own as his own, but that which he has through Christ in relation to the Father. To account completely for the qualifications ("sufficiency") provided by God (the Father), Paul goes on to speak of his ministry as a ministry of the Spirit, not of the letter. In one stroke, he places his ministry in a trinitarian perspective and in contrast to the service of the law (3, 4–6).

He advances this contrast between the two covenants in 3, 7–18. Paul's pejorative remarks about the old covenant, however, must be taken in terms of the dialectical contrast by which he formulates his views. He is not attempting to evaluate the old covenant in a limited historical context or even in itself alone; he is striving to bring out the surpassing glory of the new covenant, *in comparison with which* the old covenant represents no real glory at all, but death and lack of knowledge. To accept what Paul says, and even to understand him, we must realize how for him the revelation in Christ had put everything else in shadow. His negative view of the law is simply the corollary of his positive understanding of the mystery in Christ. A dialectical habit of thought, a penchant for sharp rhetorical contrasts, personal struggles with Judaizers in a number of his churches—all these factors and more, certainly help account for his negative presentation of the law. But the principal factor seems to consist in the intensely personal revelation in Christ by which for Paul all else was cast into shadow and was inevitably viewed negatively. The closest human analogue to Paul's view is that of one who is so intensely in love that his love (as *his* love and as *whom* he loves) becomes both the principle of understanding by which he begins to comprehend his love and at the same time the principle for disparaging everything else in proportion as it calls for contrasts with outstandingly attractive features of that which he loves. The viewpoint of one in love with God, especially when it comprises the understanding of God's revelation, and therefore of mysteries, and most especially when it springs from a personal communication from the Lord, as in Paul's case, becomes a genuinely mystical viewpoint. We cannot properly judge that contrast between the two covenants which Paul voices in 2 Corinthians 3, 1–18 unless we try sympathetically to recognize Paul's mystical viewpoint and the way in which he understandably expresses it in apparently foolhardy dialectic.

The service of the old covenant he calls a dispensation or ministry of death (3, 7), for of itself the "letter" kills and does not bring life (cf. 3, 6); only the spirit of the living God (cf.

3, 3) really brings life (cf. 3, 6). Yet it had its splendor ("glory"), seen as a physical glow on Moses' face. Paul contrasts with the passing glory of the old covenant the glory of the new covenant which is yet to be realized (at the parousia) (vv. 7–8). This contrast in point of glory, stressing that of the ministry of the spirit, he pursues with a parallel (v. 9). In verses 7–8 he contrasts the two ministries in terms of the final end and the principle at work in them; in verse 9 he contrasts them in terms of their more immediate effect, but he focuses both contrasts on the theme of glory. Then, in verses 10–11, he affirms the surpassing, permanent splendor of the new covenant. The glory of the old is only partial in comparison with its surpassing fulfillment, and it is therefore (with the logic of a mystical dialectic) no glory at all.

Paul's confidence rests not on self-commendation but on the covenant of God, written in the power of the spirit, and characterized by surpassing glory that will abide (3, 1–11). In a new key (3, 12), he repeats the theme of "confidence" as his "hope," for the basic perspective is eschatological, that of fulfilled glory now in the light of fuller glory still to come. He regards the whole definitive revelation as the removing of a veil.

Before trying to follow the course of his argument in 3, 12–18, a few words of comment are in order apropos of the "veil." Paul's image of the veil defies imaginative or diagrammatic presentation. Like so many other images he employs, it must be understood in function of his theological argument as a whole. The veil represents an obstacle to direct personal knowledge of God for the people concerned, as God intends to give that (eschatological) knowledge. Furthermore, Paul makes some changes from the Old Testament and even from targumic interpretations concerning the veil to bring out the relative inferiority of the Mosaic revelation. Paul declares, for instance, that Moses put the veil over his face not in order to hide the glory of the Lord which would have been too much for the Israelites, but rather to conceal the fact that the glory which radiated from

213

his face was a fading glory (3, 13). Lastly, the Apostle considers the veil in the context of several sets of relationships, which we may sketch as follows:

Paul (with regard to those to whom he preaches) and
Moses (with regard to the Israelites), verse 12;
The Israelites (even today, with regard to God's word in
scripture)
                               and
Converts (with regard to the fulfillment of God's word in
Christ), verses 14–16;
Paul together with all other Christians (with regard to the Lord,
Christ, who is the revealer), verses 17–18.

Now, Paul's argument is that his outspokenness (*parrhēsia*, the *RSV* "boldness") is to be understood in terms of his role in the covenant revelation. This understanding is quite complexive, entailing all the contrasts just indicated apropos of the "veil," which is conceived as an obstacle to revelation. The Apostle's outspokenness admits no attempt to hide the truth before those whom he addresses in his ministry of glory, unlike Moses, who veiled his face (vv. 12–13). Not that Paul really blames Moses for the lack of full perception on the part of the Israelites! There was something wrong in them (v. 14a). Even to this day, what is wrong, he says equivalently, is that they do not see beyond the veiled Moses. The definitive revelation or glory is possessed only by one in Christ. The obstacle actually lies not in the revelation of the Old Testament, but in the minds of those who read it as God's last word. Paul does not accuse them of culpability in this. Rather, alluding to Moses' own setting aside the veil when he conversed directly with God (Exodus 34, 34; 2 Corinthians 3, 16), he shows that the remedy for their own deficient understanding and that of any man is the Lord himself. "The Lord is the Spirit" (v. 17a), that is, the Lord is the Revealer. (Cf. M. McNamara.) Paul does not identify the Lord as the Spirit in terms of "nature" or

214

"person" as used in later theological terminology, but in terms of function; the Lord himself, as risen, is both the revelation and the revealer of God.

Paul's outspokenness stands out as an instance of that freedom of access to mysteries which is given with the Spirit of the Lord. Paul does not regard himself, however, as the unique possessor of this revelation (even though his experience of it was unique). He places himself alongside the Corinthians (v. 18) as one who shares with them the revelation in Christ. Since the revelation is that of the risen Lord, the present glory that is seen in him by faith is but the beginning of the glory to be perceived at the resurrection. The change "from glory to glory" (v. 18) we may best construe in the over-all eschatological context of Paul's thought as a reference to the ultimate manifestation of Christ at the parousia, the realization of the new creation. Again (cf. 2, 16), the prepositional phrases seem to express dynamically a basic, all-inclusive principle. That is, the phrases express a principle in terms of functional theology. The glory which derives from Christ is that glory towards which we are changed; it is the principle of our transformation.

With 4, 1 ff., Paul's apologia for his way of acting becomes more forthright; he develops with greater intensity the theme of courage (4, 1—5, 10) and begins to speak more clearly of the differences between himself and false apostles. Alluding to their underhanded methods, he appeals for commendation only on the basis of the glory of God in the gospel, the faith which he preaches and shares with the Corinthians (4, 1–6). The theme of "glory" obviously depends on the preceding development, as does the image of the veil, which reappears here in a more apocalyptic context. In defending himself, Paul is really looking to what he stands for, the glory of God. Similarly, in speaking of the blindness of his adversaries, he is actually looking to what they stand for. He is not passing final judgment on them personally any more than he is offering an absolute commendation of himself. But he does see his opposition in terms of a supernatural, epic struggle of faith and anti-faith, of the god of this aeon (Satan) and the one in whom the new mankind and a new order of creation are realized.

As for his own personal role, Paul stresses only his weaknesses, much as he did in 2 Corinthians 11, 16—12, 10, namely, as the condition for manifesting the power of God (4, 7–11). The explanation for this attitude lies once again in his understanding of union with Christ who suffered and was raised, and in a corresponding understanding of solidarity with the rest of the faithful. He is ever being given over to death so that Jesus' life may appear in himself, even in this life (4, 11). His own trials serve as a result of his union with Christ to bring life to the Corinthians as well (v. 12). But the present stage of life in Christ for himself and for them is one in faith, dynamically oriented to the future. The present dynamism of faith serves to reveal that future. Hence it is that Paul says: "having the same spirit of faith according to what is written [rather than the RSV "according to him who wrote"], 'I believed, therefore I have spoken [a word of revelation]'." Paul speaks in faith of the future resurrection with the Corinthians to God's glory.

A second time Paul says he does not lose heart (4, 16; cf. 4, 1), this time appealing to the life of the "inner man" (the RSV "inner nature"), by which he means what we might call the level of life in the spirit which is not yet exteriorized in the visible glory of the risen body. The eschatological thrust of Paul's thought is once again evident; it gravitates toward the eternal glory of the resurrection, which is as yet unseen (4, 13–18).

His understanding of this future hope, which so characterizes his apostolic confidence in pastoral solidarity with the Corinthians, is hardly that of a man who concerns himself simply with the immortality of the soul. Here as elsewhere, Christ's own risen life as one for which Christians are destined decisively shapes Paul's conception of the future. In 5, 1–10, therefore,

216

Paul's courage is based on the hope of resurrection. The building from God, not made with hands, is primarily the risen body conceived typologically as that of Christ himself. Paul's image of the dwelling undergoes some puzzling mutations (building, dwelling, suit of clothes), but a basic contrast obtains between the permanent, heavenly dwelling and the "tent" of our present, earthly existence. The tension that he experiences (perhaps against the background of his recent illness) is a desire to gain the heavenly without being utterly dispossessed of the earthly by physical death. But how can one come to terms with this tension? Paul himself finds assurance in the fact that God has given us the Spirit as a "down payment" on the heavenly home intended for us. What is mortal will in any case not simply be lost; it will be transformed. Paul's courage rests, then, on his faith in the radical continuity of Christian life. Whatever happens, pleasing the Lord, that is, seeking his interests and not our own, remains the uppermost value in the Christian's mind. For the judgment of Christ at the resurrection will be based on actions performed during this earthly life.

The Apostle's apologia for confidence in terms of the glorious gospel he preaches in all his trials now approaches its close. Paul once again returns to the topic of self-commendation, with an appeal to the Corinthians that his whole way of acting and looking at things be fully manifest to them (5, 11—6, 13). When he defends himself, he really intends to supply the Corinthians with a defense against those who boast in externals (5, 12).

At this point, Paul seems to allude to a charge that he was "carried away" like a fool or ecstatic. He answers that if he was beside himself, it was for God's sake (v. 13a). Even with regard to his ecstasies, he will not boast in externals, to draw attention to himself, but only to glorify God. But Paul was not always carried away. Even in his spiritual enthusiasm he was reasonable, able to account for his every action—and his practicality was for their benefit, not his own (v. 13b). In either

217

case it was love for Christ (recalling the ecstatic element) that governed his actions and enabled him to judge (recalling his reasonable practicality) the solidarity of all in the mystery of Christ's death and resurrection.

The characteristically limited human point of view, of which Paul speaks in verse 16, is therefore a non-theological point of view, a view "according to flesh." Even if Paul had regarded Christ from a human point of view (the statement seems to be contrary to fact, rather than, as in the *RSV*, an historical reminiscence), such is not the perspective which must be had now. For Christ is now risen, existing fully on the level of the spirit. Consequently, man must exercise his judgment according to his existence in Christ, that is, on the level of the new creation. This whole order of things is from God, a work of reconciliation in Christ. Paul is Christ's ambassador, and his own appeal is thus God-centered, "theological."

An appeal for recognition of the God-centered manner of Paul's persuasion of men, which should be perfectly evident to the Corinthians and therefore show that he is not commending himself, has led Paul to recall the whole mystery of reconciliation which binds them together (5, 11–21). His own viewpoint, which lies at the heart of his pastoral appeal for reconciliation with the Corinthians, is justified in the perspective and content of their common faith in God's reconciliation of all in Christ. From the height of this mystery of one's standing aright with God in Christ (5, 21), Paul moves back through an exhortation (6, 1–12) to the interior recognition which he expects from the Corinthians (6, 13; cf. 5, 11b). Paul's service is an appeal for openness to receive the power of God's grace; he puts no obstacle in the way, and his self-commendation as God's minister lies accordingly only in that which he endures and gains through empowered endurance.

In tone and style, the passage in 2 Corinthians 6, 14—7, 1 interrupts the course of Paul's letters; it is probably a later

218

insertion from something else that Paul had written to the Corinthians. The insert is not altogether out of place when one considers that Paul's preceding and following appeals implicitly admonish the Corinthians to beware of false apostles. But it looks to a more virulent threat than does the rest of 2 Corinthians 1—7. The "mismatches" to which Paul refers in verse 14 are not mixed marriages, but associations with unbelievers which are not in accord with the word of the gospel. The incompatibility of the relationship is stated in terms of an allusion to Deuteronomy 22, 10 (not yoking an ox and an ass together) and apocalyptically conceived oppositions regarding the sanctity of the community.

In his concluding remarks (7, 2—16), Paul returns once more to the theme of his boast on the Corinthians' behalf and the *paraklēsis* which he has received, this time under the aspect of the news which Titus has reported concerning their change of heart. The insert in 6, 14—7, 1 may well have pertained to the painful letter which Paul had sent to Corinth. He had appealed for holy conduct (cf. 7, 1) and now recognizes that the Corinthians have proved themselves "holy" (7, 11, the *RSV* "guiltless") in the matter of the accusation which he had brought against them. Paul had probably misconstrued their personal guilt in the situation. In view of the salutary results, however, he grieves only that they were themselves grieved for a time. He now rejoices in his perfect confidence in them.

APPEALS FOR GENEROUS CONTRIBUTIONS
(8—9)

The second part of the letter (2 Corinthians 8–9) seems to comprise two major sections, which correspond to each of its two chapters. The first fits well with chapters 1–7. Paul has contacted Titus in Macedonia. He has also experienced the

219

generosity of the churches there, and decides that what Titus had begun in Macedonia (before Paul's own arrival in Macedonia), he should complete at Corinth (8, 1–7). Paul does not appeal to the Macedonians' generosity in a way that might shame the Corinthians into taking prompt action. His appeal is phrased more tactfully (8, 8–15). The genuineness of their love will be shown in solidarity with the earnestness already shown by others. The love shown to them by Christ will be reflected in fulfilling the work that they had desired to do a year previously —a desire proportioned to what they can actually share. The earnestness expected of their love motivates Titus himself, who is returning not just as Paul's envoy, but of his own accord. At least two further associates (vv. 18 and 22; cf. v. 23), apostolic representatives of all the churches, are sent along with Titus, so that it will be clear that the collection is not to Paul's personal advantage (8, 16–24).

The second section (2 Corinthians 9) is noticeably more straightforward. It seems to reflect some embarrassment on Paul's part at the lack of prompt action, especially in view of more immediate plans for his own coming to Corinth. Those whom he sends in this case (v. 3) are not necessarily the same ones referred to in chapter 8. A further delegation, sent specifically with Paul's own arrival in mind, seems to be mentioned. What really vexes Paul is that the whole character of the collection may be distorted if prompt action is not taken in his absence (9, 1–5). With this in mind, he offers further motivation for generosity on their part, not looking simply to the relative abundance of the gift, but to the grace of God, which will reward their spontaneous generosity.

CHAPTER SEVEN

ROMANS 12—16

BACKGROUND: A SPIRITUAL SERVICE IN ADVANCE OF PAUL'S COMING

Paul had not as yet visited Rome when he penned to the Christian community there what most of his discerning readers value as his greatest letter. At the time, probably the winter of A.D. 58, he was in Corinth waiting to return to Jerusalem with the collection gathered on Mission III. He had tried to reach Rome a number of times (Romans 1, 13) but was prevented from doing so. When he wrote the Romans, he had at least representatively completed the circle of nations in the Mediterranean as far as Illyricum (Romans 15, 19). He intended to go on to Spain after visiting Rome (Romans 15, 24. 28). His projected trip to Rome, however, was not to be just a stop on a journey farther to the West. Although he had not founded the community in Rome, he recognized it as a charismatic community with which he should share spiritual gifts for the universal harvest expected of him, in fulfillment of his worldwide obligations as an apostle (1, 11–15). The breadth of his pastoral concern was coextensive with the breadth of his whole concept of the gospel and his apostleship.

221

In writing to an audience that he had not yet contacted directly, Paul has bequeathed us perhaps the most comprehensive single presentation of his gospel, especially in the first of the letter's three parts, chapters 1–8. He also provides, notably in the second part, chapters 9–11, one of the best examples of his dialectical, theological argumentation apropos of a topic that profoundly affected him personally, the disbelief of his own people in the gospel that was intended for them in accord with the promises of God. Our treatment of these first two parts of Romans will be deferred to later chapters of this volume, where they will afford the basis for a more comprehensive view of Paul's gospel and of his theological line of reasoning. The third part of his letter to the Romans, chapters 12–16, can easily be treated here. It is a good example of his pastoral solicitude for a respected, charismatic community (cf. Romans 1, 8–13). While even in this part of his letter he is writing to a community that he has not contacted personally, he is not unaware of basic needs that require encouraging counsel. Nevertheless, although he seems to be aware of certain specific problems, he treats them in such a general pastoral perspective that it is more difficult than usual to reconstruct the situation. More than ever, the problems to which he alludes will have to be recognized and solved by the members of the community themselves in the light of Paul's pastoral, charismatic guidance.

The problems in the community seem to have arisen from its mixed nature. Undoubtedly, the church at Rome contained both converts from Judaism and converts from paganism, though it is difficult to assess the proportions of each group. Further distinctions, however, are supposed in the exhortation addressed to the community as a whole, especially in Romans 14, 1–15, 13. The distinction between the "strong" and the "weak" is not simply commensurate with the distinction between gentiles and Jews, but looks mainly to the relative maturity of faith on the part of the groups concerned. This maturity is shown in not attaching great significance to certain dietary and calendar-regulated practices that do not pertain to the marrow of faith.

The first major section comprises Romans 12, 1–13, 14, with a later insertion consisting of 13, 1–7. Paul begins with a general principle portraying all of Christian life as a liturgy, a spiritual sacrifice (12, 1–2). The transformation that this entails is theologically grounded both in God's will (12, 1–2) and in the varied graces actually shown to each one (13, 3–8). Specific exhortations are centered on the theme of love (12, 9–21). After the inserted admonition to defer to civil authorities out of obedience to God and, concretely, to pay one's taxes (13, 1–7), the exhortation centered on the theme of love is resumed, and concludes in the eschatological perspective of the coming day of salvation (13, 8–14).

The second major section in this part of the letter consists of 14, 1–15, 13 and deals with the problem of the relationships between the "strong" and the "weak" in the community. Paul insistently scores judging others, for he finds the example of forbearance classically represented in Christ's sacrificial endurance for each and all in fulfillment of God's fidelity and mercy.

Personal news (15, 14–33), final salutations (16, 21–23), and a doxology (16, 25–27) conclude the letter. A letter of commendation for Phoebe (16, 1–16) with its own final greeting (16, 20b) has been inserted, perhaps with some particular warnings against false teachers (16, 17–20a). The doxology, too, may have been added from another letter. The precise scope of the letter for Phoebe and particularly the warnings against false teachers remain a puzzle, but it is clear from their nature as appended fragments that they should not seriously affect one's interpretation of the whole. The only appended element that does not seem to have come from Paul himself, however, is the passage regarding good order under civil authorities (13, 1–7). Perhaps its insertion into the context of an ex-

223

hortation concerning Christian love (*agapē*) shows in any event that it was to be interpreted in the Pauline perspective of service that is fundamentally service of God in love, not fear.

CHARISMATIC WORSHIP IN FAITH AND LOVE (12, 1—13, 14)

In opening the first section of his exhortation (12, 1–13, 14), Paul focuses attention on what is pleasing to God, the "spiritual worship" which makes a liturgy of the whole of Christian life 12, 1–2). He places his exhortation in the context of God's grace, viewed as a special kind of consideration for others, the mercies of God. In the light of the mercy that God himself has displayed, the faithful are to respond by disposing themselves wholly to him in a kind of living sacrifice. The sacrifice is not primarily something negative. After all, it is "living" and consists primarily in "spiritual," that is, supernatural worship involving one's whole self ("your bodies"). At the same time, the sacrifice does entail a negative aspect, eschatological dissociation from "this world," the "present age" of imperfect existence. One is not to conform himself to this world's manner of acting, but to be renewed in his whole outlook, to discern God's will. The words "good, acceptable, and perfect" describe not three stages of progress but rather three aspects of the same sacrifice: what is *truly* good and not transiently so, what is focused on God's interests, not on one's own, and what is whole, not partial. The first thing Paul does, then, is to establish an eschatological and sacrificial perspective for his whole exhortation.

In this God-centered context, implying God's merciful initiative and stressing supernatural worship of God, Paul begins to specify his own charismatic words of encouragement (12, 3–8). Once more he places his exhortation in the context of God's grace (12, 3a), but this time as a grace given to Paul for every one of those to whom he writes. The Apostle seeks to encourage judgment based on the faith that God has bestowed

224

proportionately on each one. For Paul, faith is the basic structuring of one's life in God, but it is also a personal principle of understanding by which a man grasps his relationship to God and which thus formally shapes his whole outlook. The "measure of faith" is a principle of sober judgment. One should not conceive it as a kind of intense feeling or conviction, but primarily as a favor of God which is a principle for repeatedly exercised understanding, given in different ways to different Christians while remaining fundamentally the same. For Paul himself goes on to explain it in terms of the activity of various interdependent members in the body of Christ, each having different charisms (*charismata*) according to the grace (*charis*) given him. He does not equate the sanctifying favor of God with special gifts. But neither does he neatly separate the two as is customarily done in more speculative theology. In Paul's dynamic perspective, God's grace is ever operative, and it is so through the whole structure of faith, that is, on the level of what we may term the supernatural or, more biblically, the eschatological order. The charisms are the channels in which the grace of God in the adult Christian works for the building up of the whole community of the faithful. The charisms, therefore, are really instrumental in the work of sanctification. What best illustrates this instrumental function of the charisms is that which Paul himself is doing: he exercises his own charism (12, 3 ff.) in speaking for the benefit of others. He enables them to live more fully on the eschatological plane he has indicated (12, 1–2) by offering a profound understanding of the interdependence of all in Christ according to their functional share in faith.

The lineup of charisms which exemplifies both the diversity of the various gifts and their functional aspect is given in verses 6–8. The gift is indicated either by name or by characterizing the one who exercises it (for example, "if prophecy . . . one who teaches . . ."). In each case, the second part of the phrase brings out the way in which the gift is to be exercised. We may find a bit puzzling the fact that the second part of the

225

phrase sometimes clarifies the meaning of the first part with a different word (as in v. 8b), and at other times simply repeats in a different form the word already used (as in vv. 7 and 8a).

We will find even more puzzling the phrase (v. 6b): "if prophecy, in proportion to faith [*eite prophēteian, kata tēn analogian tēs pisteōs*]." But the list that follows verse 6b serves to clarify that line as well as the other problematic features of the list. Thus, the second part of the phrase stresses the exercise of the gift or the *activity* of the one who has it; the gift is one *to be used* for what it is (vv. 7 and 8a). At the same time, the exercise of the gift reveals its *distinctive character* and mode of exercise (v. 8b). Accordingly, the second part of the phrase shows that "having gifts" (v. 6a) means *using* them according to their *kind*. Now, with regard to verse 6b, the gift of prophecy (mentioned in the first part of the line) is explained in terms of the way it is to be used (the second part of the line). Prophecy is par excellence a measure of faith (cf. v. 3), and heads the list. It is a gift by which the Christian understands and declares his relationship to God in Christ (that is, the gift of understanding and declaring "the faith"). The very basis for its exercise is the agreement of one's understanding with the whole structure of the relationship (faith) involved. Prophecy, then, which is elsewhere presented as the knowledge of mysteries (1 Corinthians 13, 2; cf. 1 Corinthians 14, 6. 22), is here mounted to show a complementary facet: the declaring of one's understanding of the Christian's relationship to God in Christ according to the agreement of that understanding with the actual relationship (faith) itself. The charism of prophecy is the power to declare the very meaning of the faith relationship. Therefore, we might well call prophecy the charism of the Christian theologian. The relationship of men to God in Christ becomes the *focal point* of his exercise of understanding, and it becomes at the same time the *norm* for his understanding; he understands "the faith" in "the light of faith."

Having placed the charisms in the perspective of God's grace and of the exercise of faith, Paul now presents an exhortation focused on love (12, 9–13, 10). He proceeds in the somewhat lapidary fashion of wisdom literature, connecting various lines or blocks of material rather mechanically, by employing hook-words and inclusions. Nevertheless, two main thematic sections are discernible, interrupted somewhat by 13, 1–7. From 12, 9 to 12, 21, Paul stresses adherence to what is good, ending on the note of a victory over evil in doing what is good. To this picture of personal victory in love's often paradoxical services, he adds that of the fulfillment of the law in the continual payment of the debt of love (13, 8–10). Law is fulfilled not in the dimension of conduct according to an external norm, but in the personal dimension of a continuously selfless victory, love.

Blending the dispositions and conduct which they are to show towards one another with that which the faithful are to show even towards those outside the community and hostile to them, Paul closes with the perspective of God's judgment (12, 9–21). His ideals throughout the passage, including the final lines, which speak of heaping coals of fire on the head of one's enemy, are not inferior to those of the gospel. Krister Stendahl has suggested that, whereas the Qumran ethic required hatred of one's enemies and the gospels required love, Paul sets forth a kind of modified ideal, that of non-retaliation. But this interpretation of Paul is alien to the scope of the context as a whole and to the lesson that Paul explicitly draws in 12, 21. Balanced understanding of the passage is to be sought, rather, along another line which is, we think, a most valuable contribution of Stendahl's study. The fundamental perspective (as Stendahl has noted) is eschatological and apocalyptic, that of God's own judgment, traditionally represented under the image of fire. Paul establishes the perspective of God's judgment in verse 19: "Beloved, do not avenge yourselves, but yield [give] place to the Wrath [that is, to the final judgment of God against evil-doers]." Scriptural quotations are then adduced apropos of God's exclusive right to final, vindictive justice (v. 19b) and of that which the Christian is to do (v. 20). In the latter case, the quotation is borrowed from Proverbs 25, 21 and its sense

227

is modified substantially in the light of Paul's own eschatological concept of justice. In effect, he is saying: continue to do good to your enemy, for in doing this you bring about God's judgment on him (not your own).

Now, a further understanding of God's judgment is necessary if we are to grasp what is meant by "bringing about God's judgment on him." Paul does not look at God's judgment, even on God's adverse, retributive judgment against sinners, simply from the point of view of damnation. He does not regard it as a "bad thing"—because he does take the standpoint of the sinful man who has brought judgment's sanctions on himself. Rather, he sees the adverse judgment as the fulfillment of rejected mercy, truth, love shown by God. God's judgment is mysteriously identified with the ultimate victory of his own grace and mercy. It is one aspect of the end result of his own grace and love—the aspect of mercy definitely unrequited. The hell of the sinner is the sinner's own rejection of the mercy that God has repeatedly offered.

In presenting this rejection, however, Paul predicates of God himself the whole process towards judgment, since it is God who gives the grace that is being rejected and since it is he who determines the consequences. God's judgment is indeed at work—and by the very fact that this connotes a whole process towards judgment, God's judgment is not to be regarded conceptualistically, that is, as a perfectly distinct divine act seen in itself. Accordingly, it is not something intended vindictively, even though the justice in question may be labeled "vindictive [retributive] justice." It is "intended" only as one facet of the entire salvific process which is predicated on God's free gift and man's rightfully expected yet free acceptance of it. Thanks to the state of basic alienation from God in which man now enters the world, man must freely accept God's gift—as one who gladly reaches out for a life preserver. But God cannot be regarded according to Paul's theology as one who foresees that the life preserver will not be used and who therefore does not

228

provide it, or provides one that is less than adequate. His action in bringing to judgment those who put themselves outside the effect of his mercy is an inevitable aspect of the whole working-out of his mercy, which requires free and generous acceptance (cf. Romans 2, 1–6; 9, 19–29). In brief, Paul views God's ordering things towards judgment in terms of everything that this process supposes, notably, God's kindness, as well as in terms of the end result.

In the light of this *complexive* concept of God's judgment the ideal for the Christian's conduct as proposed in 12, 19–21 becomes easier to understand. Negatively, he is to yield place to God's judgment and not to impose his own. Positively, he is to act in the time now given him to act as God himself acts in the lifetime of the sinner. He is to do good to his enemy, and ("for") in doing this good he is bringing about God's judgment.

By saying "for," Paul does not imply that the Christian should *intend* the adverse judgment in itself—any more than he implies that God so intends it. Rather, he places the Christian's action in the context of the whole apocalyptic process towards divine judgment. The Christian's "intention" is to be completely aligned with God's own desire to complete the mystery of his mercy (cf. Romans 9–11). If the Christian were to requite evil with evil, he would really be conquered by evil (v. 21); he would succumb to the whole process of inhibiting or rejecting God's mercy, truth, love. On the other hand, by doing good he is winning out over evil in a way analogous to God's own manner of acting, which is ordered to his own final judgment.

Paul says elsewhere that the Christian will share in that judgment (cf. 1 Corinthians 6, 2–3). Here, however, he is concerned with what the Christian is to do in the present everyday situation, where he is to discern the will of God (12, 21) and show genuine love (12, 9). He is not to anticipate the end of the process in his own actions, for that point comes only by God's determination. Nevertheless, he is to share in the process

229

towards the ultimate stage of God's judgment by doing good in the present. In so doing, he participates in the whole process towards judgment and furthers what God himself does.

The inserted passage (13, 1–7) enjoins orderly conduct (*'ypotassesthai*, vv. 1, 5) under civil authorities in view of their role under God (and supposes that whatever authority they profess to have is compatible with allegiance to God). Although the civil authorities are to be thus "obeyed," they are not to be regarded with fear by one who does good. The reason for this rejection of fear is basically the same as the reason for their claim to cooperative deference: they are powers under God. To be subject "for the sake of conscience" (v. 5) is, then, to be subject because of one's awareness of God's authority.

In the concluding passage of his exhortation on love, (13, 8–10) Paul tells his hearers to "continue owing nothing to anyone except mutual love" (*opheilete,* present imperative). The debt of love is one that is never to be regarded as paid in full. The fulfillment of the whole law, even the key prohibitions of the decalogue, is comprised in the command to love one's neighbor as oneself. Paradoxically, Paul colors the law's fulfillment by speaking of it in a rather negative light; it is fulfilled in the fact that love does not do evil (v. 10; cf. v. 9a). The prohibitions of the law are all ways of spelling out evil, aptly represented as "don'ts"; the law's integral fulfillment is essentially positive and single: unselfish concern for good.

Paul does not leave even this complexive moral principle, however, without anchoring it in an eschatological perspective (13, 11–14). For "fulfillment" of the law implies not only the "whole" as opposed to the "part," but the spiritual existence of the last days as opposed to the non-eschatological works of the period of preparation. Whenever the time of the parousia may be, the moment of the resurrection, which is for Paul

230

"salvation" par excellence, is nearer now than when the life of faith began in us. For Paul, faith is the dawn in one's own life of the light of the resurrection. The wakefulness it demands in view of the Lord's coming is a militant wakefulness amid the practical details of daily life. The armor of light which one must put on (v. 12b) is really Christ himself (v. 14a). To "put on Christ" is not to live according to the "fleshly" outlook by which one's own urges take priority. The believer will eventually "put on Christ" in the sense of enjoying the state of his own risen body, but in preparation for this moment of salvation, the Christian is militantly to defend himself with "virtues," which are fundamentally the power of the Lord he serves.

THE "STRONG" AND THE "WEAK"
(14, 1—15, 13)

The second major section (14, 1–15, 13) urges "welcome acceptance" of the "weak in faith" by those who are "strong." The ultimate theological reason for "welcome acceptance" on the part of some members of the community is, of course, quite concrete: what God has done and what Christ himself has done for God's glory (cf. 14, 1; 14, 3; 15, 7). Thanks to this genuinely theological perspective, however, the particular problem that Paul treats in his pastoral exhortation is not of merely historical interest, but becomes relevant to the understanding of similar pastoral problems and their solution in the Church today. In Paul's day, the "weak" members of the Roman community were those who attached a certain importance to particular practices covering calendar observances (14, 5), abstinence from meat (14, 2), and perhaps abstinence from wine (14, 21). The principles of his solution for the problem apply equally, however, to present-day situations in which a number feel at least uncomfortable if not scandalized by the attitudes of their more "progressive minded" brothers towards practices which they themselves have long regarded as sacro-

231

sanct. Examples will readily come to mind and need not be offered here. Granting that the "progressive minded" really enjoy the "stronger" faith—the more vigorous understanding of what one's relationship to God in Christ really means—according to the mind of the Apostle himself, they are nevertheless so to act that the status of the weaker members before God is not jeopardized.

In the first subdivision of this section (14, 1–21), Paul concentrates on not despising or belittling another, which he scores as tantamount to unjust judgment (14, 3–4 and 14, 10–12). The other is a fellow servant of God (14, 4) and one's own brother (14, 10). Whether he stands or falls in God's eyes is a matter between him and God (14, 4), and we are all to stand before God to give an account of ourselves in judgment (14, 10). In the verses that lie between these progressively restated warnings against human judgment (5b–9), Paul develops the theme of divisive "disputes over opinions" (14, 1). Each one is to be primarily concerned not with refuting the other, but with the integrity of his own understanding. Each one's integral or coherent and full understanding will actually derive from his active service of the Lord, the directing of his actions to God. As he did in 1 Corinthians, Paul again bases Christian freedom of conscience on him to whom one belongs. Whatever be the human actions in question, even life and death, they are to be discerned in relationship to the universal lordship of Christ (vv. 8–9).

From concentrating on no longer judging one another, Paul goes on to inculcate avoidance of scandal (14, 13–23). One is to "judge" (the RSV "decide" obscures the transitional play on words) that one is not to put an obstacle in another's way. Paul's notion of "scandal" (namely, the "stumbling block") is rather broad, for it stands as the antithesis to his notion of "edification" or building up the whole Christian community. The correlative theme of edification is worked out in the central verses (vv. 16–19), probably with an allusion to the temple and the spiritual worship of the community. The Christian's prized good (the *RSV* "what is good to you"), that is, the valuable possession of God, equivalently the Christian community including one's fellow servants, is not to be "blasphemed" (the *RSV* "spoken of as evil"). Paul does not altogether identify this "good" as the kingdom, for the kingdom remains for him primarily the consummation of the whole eschatological age. But he considers this "good" in the light of God's kingdom. Things that pertain to the "peace" or reconciliation which is eminently realized in the kingdom are to be pursued now (vv. 17, 19). Service of Christ in the light of the kingdom renders one "pleasing" to God (the *RSV* "acceptable"), the aim of one's spiritual worship (cf. 12, 1–2), and justifies the praise of men (v. 18).

In the verses preceding and following verses 16–19, Paul says that there is nothing wrong with the thing itself, but that it becomes an occasion of sin for one who regards it as wrong (v. 14) or for one who moves another to act against his convictions (v. 20). A Christian does not act in love if he destroys by his own action the person for whom Christ died (v. 15). Therefore, he should not impose his faith (supernatural understanding) on another and thus dismantle God's work (vv. 20–23). Moral judgments concerning what is sinful do not rest on the thing as such, but on one's understanding of what his relationship to God entails. Paul thus inculcates the avoidance of scandal on the basis of one's whole relationship with others before God and, at the same time, on the grounds of a clear-cut understanding of this relationship.

Taking up the theme of "pleasing God" which lies at the heart of one's service of Christ (14, 18) and spiritual worship (12, 1–2), Paul embarks on a lengthy conclusion (15, 1–13), punctuated by two complementary prayers (15, 5–6 and 15, 13). The first prayer looks largely to patient endurance, regard for one another in Christlike fashion, and a shared glorification of the Father. The second looks to an abundance of hope in the power of the Holy Spirit as the desired outgrowth of the Romans' life in faith.

233

Somewhat as he did in Philippians 2, 1–11, Paul presents Christ's service of God as a norm of judgment or discerning outlook (not directly as an inspiring example which he expects to be copied externally). Paul's expression in verses 5, *to auto phronein eis allēlous kata Christon Iēsoun,* "to have the same mind towards one another according to Christ Jesus" remarkably approaches his advice to the Philippians (Philippians 2, 1 ff.). Here, too, the mind of Christ is given in terms of a hymn, not a specifically Christian hymn, however, but an Old Testament psalm of the Just Sufferer (Psalms 69 [LXX 68], 10). The line that Paul selects from this psalm indicates the precise point he has in mind. He might have quoted the preceding stichos of the verse from this psalm, "zeal for your house has devoured me," had he wanted simply to insist on the intention of serving God. But he seems to have passed over this line in order to bring out what Christ *endured* in the interests of pleasing God. In effect, Paul's argument is *a fortiori*: Christ did not just put up with other men's weaknesses (which is all that Paul has really asked the Romans to do), but underwent reproaches (blasphemous treatment) which dishonored God. The words of God in scripture are eminently realized in the central mystery of the passion and resurrection which they thematically announced in analogous terms. Paul brings God's word in the Old Testament to bear on the mystery of Christ's passion and, through this, to bear on the Christian's everyday share in that mystery. He wants the central revelation of Christ's passion and resurrection to motivate the faithful to exercise patient endurance (*'ypomonē*—a somewhat passive aspect of hope, grounding the positive hope [*elpis*] of the resurrection).

The verses preceding the second prayer (15, 7–12) elucidate the more positive aspects of Christ's service of God. Whatever be the particular divisions in the Roman community, the most radical distinction that Paul can conceive has been eliminated by Christ. Consequently, he places the distinction between "strong" and "weak" in the light of Christ's reconciliation of gentile with Jew in one people to God's glory. The covenant

234

virtues of "truthfulness" or "fidelity" (*'emet*) and "mercy" (*ḥesed*) are realized in Christ's coming to fulfill God's promises. The union of gentile with Jew is brought out through a distribution of the two "covenant virtues" which express one reality: "for God's truthfulness [or fidelity]" and "for God's mercy." But the union is a union in Christ entailing a dynamic progression from the glorified man, which Christ became, to the empowering of the gentiles to act now for God's glory. Christ's action in event and word is regarded as both past and present. The words of the psalmist (vv. 9–12) seem to be initially placed on the lips of Christ, balancing his confirmation of the promises to the Patriarchs. Christ's praise of the Father is heard publicly among the gentiles (v. 9); they are to rejoice in messianic blessings shared with his people Israel (v. 10); this praise is to be voiced on a universal scale, and is praise of the Lord (Jesus) himself (v. 11); under the Davidic king, the ruler of all men, the gentiles live in hope (v. 12).

Every pastoral exhortation which the Apostle delivers involves at least one or more of the following features, a good number of which are exemplified in Romans 15, 1–3. He is ever trying to bring his audience to a way of thinking, a spiritual or supernatural point of view, rather than to legislate a solution. Uppermost is God's glory achieved in and through the glorified Christ and thus achieved through intimate personal solidarity among all the faithful. The horizon of one's life in Christ can never be mere externals or what stops with self-concern. A God-centered view empowered by a genuine perception in the Spirit of God becomes indispensable. Accordingly, Christ is a "model" for action, as is, proportionately, the Apostle himself, insofar as he has not only effectively realized the service of God but actively shapes the whole spiritual outlook of those who profess faith in Christ. All this further involves a metahistorical perspective, that is, one which is "temporal" and anchored to factual events like the passion

235

and resurrection, the moment of conversion, and the parousia, but which rides above the phenomenological course of events and which is therefore not as such the perspective of clock-and-calendar time. In this metahistorical perspective, everything is dynamically ordered to the consummation, so that the word of scripture is seen in terms of its fulfillment in Christ and the Christian community, and the reality of life in Christ is seen as the beginning, though conditioned by trials and the need of fuller transformation, of the glory of God to be attained in full measure at the resurrection.

CLOSING SALUTATIONS AND DOXOLOGY
(15, 14—16, 27)

Romans 15, 14–33, with the concluding salutations of 16, 21–23 and perhaps the doxology of 16, 25–27, form the close of the letter as a whole. In explaining why he has written to the Romans (15, 14–21), Paul tactfully indicates his confidence in their healthy and mature Christianity and their ability to instruct one another, making it clear that he writes them rather boldly (v. 15) only to exercise his priestly grace of preaching to the gentiles, not to declare anything but the unadulterated substance of his apostolic message of divine power, "that which Christ has done through him" (vv. 18 ff.). He does not simply fear or forbear to build on another's foundation, but rather looks to fulfilling the universal commission entrusted to him. His priestly service in administering the gospel of God (v. 16) is one with his fulfillment of the gospel of Christ (v. 19). Both, in turn, amount to his boasting in Christ of his work for God (v. 17). Following this explanation of why he has written them, he passes on (15, 22–33) to indicate the further course of his intended apostolic journey and to ask for their militant prayers (vv. 20 ff.), ending with the blessing of the God of peace (v. 33).

Whether or not the doxology originally pertained to the

236

epistle to the Romans, it fittingly enunciates the prayerful glorification of God through Jesus Christ which Paul hopes to further through communicating to the Romans his gospel (as one with the general preaching of Jesus Christ). His prayer of adoration to God who can strengthen them through Paul's gospel is identified with a prayer that God will open their eyes to the hidden mystery revealed now and made known to all nations. No less than do his previous exhortations, this doxology epitomizes the Apostle's total pastoral concern. He has simply tried to raise their hearts to glorify God in their very understanding of a dynamic event of tremendous proportions, "what God has wrought." The understanding of the mystery revealed in Paul's own gospel should certainly have practical consequences in their everyday conduct, but these consequences in turn will follow from the strengthening power of God. The primary concern is glory to God according to Paul's gospel, that is, according to an understanding of the mystery now disclosed and effectively manifested to all nations.

PART TWO

CHAPTER ONE

PAUL'S APOSTOLIC CONSCIOUSNESS

PAUL'S OWN AWARENESS
OF HIS MISSION

Paul's awareness of his call to preach the gospel pulses at the heart of his missionary work. He regards himself as being under a certain constraint to preach the gospel (1 Corinthians 9, 16). He had not volunteered; his previous role as a persecutor had only set in relief how totally unmerited was the change effected in him. Thus, he felt that his only real opportunity to serve the Lord with full freedom or active cooperation lay in exercising his apostolate in an especially selfless manner, for example, by supporting himself when he could have claimed support from his communities, and by living a celibate life (1 Corinthians 9, 4 ff.). This distinctive missionary selflessness forms part of the Apostle's theology in practice, an implemented understanding of the transforming grace of God in his personal call to witness to the gospel.

The theme recurs frequently in his early letters. In the impassioned defense of his apostleship subsequently written to the Corinthians, Paul adduces the fact that he does not burden

241

them as proof of his apostolic love for them (2 Corinthians 11, 7–11); his boast in ministering to them freely further serves to undermine the claims of false apostles (2 Corinthians 11, 12–15). When thanking the Philippians for their timely gift, he tactfully suggests that he does not require it from them (Philippians 4, 10–20) and deftly turns the occasion of their kindness to indicate that decisive sustenance in his apostolic trials comes by way of God's power. Again, in writing to the Thessalonians, Paul's manner of life helps distinguish Paul and his companions from itinerant pagan lecturers of the day; it reveals the personal pastoral concerns which look ultimately to God's kingdom and glory, not to self-enrichment in the present (1 Thessalonians 2, 1–12). Thus, his apostolic awareness of God's grace is theologically concretized in the missionary witness of his apostolic style of life.

Paul's missionary dedication, traceable ultimately to his call to be an apostle, unfolds in still other ways which show that the theological scope of his work is quite concretized in meeting various situations as they arise. Crises of factionalism are resolved in terms of one message of salvation and complementary functions in the implementation of God's activity (1 Corinthians 1, 18–4, 13). Even Paul's journeys, as Johannes Munck has shown, are responses to various theological problems concretized in situations to be faced at Jerusalem or Rome or wherever else lies a task to which Christ has called him.

Nevertheless, certain authors like Munck have too readily assumed on the basis of Paul's missionary orientation a lack of any unifying theme or principle in the Apostle's understanding of salvation in Christ. Munck would call Paul's "theology" "the practical solutions according to which the Christians can regulate their lives." But it should be clear from what Paul states at various junctures that a knowledge and awareness of the mystery of salvation in Christ underlies and governs the practical solutions that Paul proposes. He is a man with a vision, not a problem solver. In Galatians, for instance, the practical insistence on revitalizing the faith that he preached is governed by

242

Paul's own understanding of the integrity of his gospel, the sole gospel. This gospel, in turn, is one with the Apostle's understanding of his life's work: to preach Christ among the gentiles is to serve to reveal God's Son in fulfillment of the prophetic office with which Paul was graced.

But, if one cannot regard Paul's theology simply or mainly from the standpoint of pastoral problem solving, one must beware of disengaging it from his thoroughgoing apostolic consciousness. The root problem here seems to be the way in which one understands the revelation that Paul received. If one considers that revelation, namely, the gospel that Paul received at his conversion, mainly from the standpoint of factual or conceptual content, then one has already in principle academically disengaged Paul's theology from his missionary activity and apostolic consciousness. The Apostle becomes a preacher of doctrines. Such a conception of his work then stands at odds with the apparently unsystematic presentation of his thought. What is more, it does scant justice to Paul's own protestations concerning the personal nature of his gospel and no more justice to his intensely personal manner of proposing it, as when he insists on his pattern of life and on imitation of himself, or when he presents himself in terms of Moses or even in terms of the instrument of the Spirit (2 Corinthians 3).

As A.-M. Denis has shown, there is an inseparable unity between Paul's call, and therefore his apostolic consciousness or sense of mission, and the revelation by which he was "invested" as an apostle. He does not present his conversion as an enlightenment followed by a commission, much less as a commission that required further substantial instruction in the message he was to preach. Gospel and commission were given as one. What is more, the communication by which he was made an apostle came in the form of a transforming grace in the personal revelation of God's Son. For all that we know from Paul's own account of his conversion, the communication which he received may have taken place without any formulation in words or distinct concepts. What was central to the communi-

243

cation, however, and gave it full substance was the personal mystery of Jesus, the Lord.

Before we attempt to describe further what seems to have been implicit in the insight into the personal mystery of God's grace in Jesus Christ crucified and risen which was Paul's inaugural experience, we should exclude two misconceptions of his gospel. The first misconception is that represented by E.-B. Allo's position. Allo went so far as to affirm that the Apostle's whole doctrine was "in act" from the day of his conversion. Allo's professed intention in formulating this view was to counteract a view of the development of Pauline theology that supposed a kind of transformist evolution entailing a genetic mutation of the gospel message. We would not fault Allo's intention, but we must fault his conceptualistic approach. The integrity of the gospel that Paul himself affirmed may be open to a kind of development in formulation which by no means entails an altered gospel. But, at the very least, the gospel should not be regarded *a priori* as adequately and explicitly contained in a given formulated act of understanding. Such a supposition tends to dissolve the mystery that is the heart of the gospel message. One gets the impression from Allo that Paul learned certain "truths" or one basic truth from which his later statements were derived as conclusions from premises; the truth was somewhat statically or conceptualistically possessed from the outset. Allo's study was generally ignored or discountenanced; it seemed most unrealistic to those who wrestled with the Apostle's unsystematic dialectic. Had Allo looked rather to the element of personal communication, however, in which the whole is grasped while remaining a transcendent mystery open to a wide spectrum of formulations and requiring ever renewed insights and new situations occasioning those insights, the adverse judgment of his position might have been less harsh and less deserved.

A second misconception is more current. Recent authors, like D. E. H. Whiteley, for example, tend to regard Paul's gospel from the standpoint of kerygmatic formulations, a gospel in the

244

sense of a collection of facts or data to be preached. Undoubtedly, Paul acknowledges traditions which he "received," and at least one of these may be regarded as containing the substance of the gospel message (1 Corinthians 15, 3–8). But the fact that Paul himself insists on his having the one gospel by direct revelation of the Lord antecedently to contacts with other apostles requires that we grasp his gospel more radically in terms of a distinctive, totally formative personal communication at the time of his conversion. We cannot rest content with regarding his gospel from the standpoint of formulated data in the nature of creeds.

If this be the case, one may well object that what we call "Paul's gospel" is altogether uncontrollable. For it remains cloaked in a unique mystical experience which Paul does not describe in any detail. How can we come to grips with what Paul can be said to have "learned" in this inaugural experience? The answer seems to lie in viewing a number of other factors in connection with Paul's brief description of his own conversion. We have already seen that the revelation imparted to him is closely bound up with his awareness of having a selfless apostolic mission. If we find in his writings a certain constant and central theme or principle that is intimately bound up both with his gospel and with his personal apostolic outlook, we may feel sure that we have at least in large measure acquired an insight into Paul's formative inaugural experience.

We may begin by reviewing what Paul says in a number of those situations in which he feels his apostolic role is being sorely tested. Writing the Philippians from prison, he shows us that he considers his situation a struggle for the defense of the gospel. Rival preachers more than his imprisonment constitute the trials he endures (Philippians 1, 12–17). Paul's motivation in these circumstances reveals the basic thrust of his apostolic consciousness: the desire to be with Christ, provided this be to the benefit of the faithful (Philippians 1, 18–26). The needs of the faithful themselves are dominated by the theme of a struggle consummated in the Lord's own triumph and that of

245

all Christians with him (cf. also 1, 5–6. 9–11). Undergirding Paul's hope for the successful outcome of his own present affliction and his exhortation for unity of mind and heart among the Philippians themselves stands a solid appreciation of the way the lives of all in Christ are shaped by the mystery of his service unto death and his resurrection to the Father's glory (2, 1–11; cf. 1, 29–30). In turning to more specific problems in Philippians 3, 2 ff., Paul reveals quite clearly that his own apostolic motivation—which is none other than that supposed for others in the community who would be brought to perfection —is the desire to achieve the calling from on high through the power of Christ's resurrection and a share in his sufferings (Philippians 3, 8–15). All his options have been staked on the personal knowledge of Jesus, the bond through faith by which he is set right with God. Even the key theme of "justification" is rooted in the mystery of knowing Christ, concretely, the mystery of the power of his resurrection and the share in his sufferings ordered to the Apostle's final assimilation to Christ in the resurrection from the dead.

When he judges that his apostolic role has been quite seriously challenged, as in 2 Corinthians 10 ff., Paul words his appeal in language which evokes both the mildness and sovereign power of Christ (2 Corinthians 10, 1–6). The paradox of this twofold appeal makes sense ultimately in terms of the existence of the risen Lord whose power is exercised in the fullness of the spirit (cf. Romans 1, 4; 5, 5; 8, 2. 9. 11; 15, 19; 1 Corinthians 12, 13; 15, 45; 2 Corinthians 3, 17); one of the characteristics of activity in the spirit is mildness shown in dealing with others (Galatians 5, 23; 6, 1; 1 Corinthians 4, 21). Paul associates his own exercise of authority with the power of the risen Lord; he does not really act "according to flesh" but in the power of the spirit. The power he exercises, which is to be understood mainly as a constructive power (2 Corinthians 10, 8), is a power from the Lord, accounted for by Paul's identification with Christ (2 Corinthians 10, 7), and bestowed on Paul in full measure (2 Corinthians 10, 12–18).

246

Thus, his apostolic boast rests squarely on what the risen Lord has done in and through him.

The way in which this power of the Lord has been exercised reveals, in turn, the central mystery of the passion and resurrection. Paul's very trials witness to God's power; in his weakness is his strength (2 Corinthians 12, 10), for that strength is the power of Christ (12, 9). Thus, the Apostle's boast, for all its apparent foolishness, is as triumphant and solidly grounded in God's grace as is the folly of the cross. Paul can speak as he does in answer to his critics only because his awareness of an apostolic mission is permeated by an awareness of the grace of God in Christ operative in and through the pattern of the paschal triumph. That pattern was the shape of all Paul's apostolic endeavors from the outset of his apostolic career. Even in 2 Corinthians 11, leading up to his statement in 2 Corinthians 12, 10, he mentions in the recital of trials his very early experience in Damascus at the hands of King Aretas. Whether or not he had clearly perceived the pattern of triumph through weakness at the moment of his conversion cannot be immediately inferred from what Paul says. But his recital of past events seems to find its ultimate unity in an understanding of his work as that of the Lord's prophetic apostle whose message and life were shaped by the knowledge of one who suffered and rose to live in the power of the spirit.

The Apostle perceived in the pattern of his own life a pattern proportionately verified in the lives of those whom he had formed by the gospel (for example, Philippians 1, 29–30; 1 Corinthians 1, 26–31; 1 Thessalonians 3, 4; Galatians 3, 13–14) and he would learn to formulate it more explicitly and profoundly in writing to the Romans (Romans 6, 1–10). The shape of the life of every Christian is none other than the shape of Christ's own mysterious transformation, the dynamism of passion and resurrection by which one's whole existence has been radically changed.

We have endeavored to indicate that at the core of Paul's understanding of trials and triumphs, whether in the warp and woof of his own daily apostolic life or in the lives of his converts and fellow Christians beats a constant awareness of the mystery of the passion and resurrection. This awareness is so rooted in the Apostle's personal outlook that it seems to be radicated in the basic thrust of his life given at his conversion. What Paul "learned" in his conversion experience was, above all, Christ himself, the concrete expression and summation of God's grace. Eloquent confirmation of this in Paul's own words may be found in his arguments to Peter at Antioch (Galatians 2, 11–21), which Paul himself seems to relate in connection with his conversion partly to epitomize that understanding of the gospel that he derived from his decisive inaugural experience and that he feels is basic to solving doctrinal and pastoral problems among the Galatians.

Paul "learned Christ himself, the concrete expression and summation of God's grace." That could perhaps be said of all the apostles. In Paul's case, however, there occurred a sudden transformation which was accountable only in terms of the exceptional *power* of God's grace and which concentrated, as it were, in a single perception the successive events of the passion and resurrection. This exceptional mode of Paul's conversion—quite apart from any factual or fanciful details about his being knocked from a horse—must also be judged to have been formative in what he learned and was made permanently aware of in that inaugural experience. He gives no indication that he had ever wavered in his zeal for the law or had been tortured by doubts concerning the possibility of observing it (Galatians 1, 13–14; Philippians 3, 5–6; 2 Corinthians 11, 22; for Romans 7, 7–25, see below, p. 383). His life was altered unexpectedly, suddenly, decisively. It is not unlikely that this abrupt change in the life of the zealous Pharisee had as much to do with a certain revolutionary cast of Paul's thought, as did features of his environmental background or personal temperament. His emphasis on the new creation theme, on a decisive break with the old order of the law, on the enlightening and transforming power of the spirit, and on the personal

248

efficacy of the apostolic word becomes more intelligible in the light of Paul's own vivid personal awareness of what his conversion entailed (cf. 2 Corinthians 5, 14–21).

PAUL'S CONVERSION ACCORDING TO THE ACTS OF THE APOSTLES

In the foregoing attempt to appreciate the unity between Paul's conception of his gospel and his apostolic consciousness, we have deliberately avoided appealing to anything besides his own writings, notably the earlier ones. Paul is his own best commentator; there is really no need to have recourse to Acts in order to form an adequate judgment of what Paul received at his conversion. What is more, we should beware of reading into what Paul himself says one or more of the three accounts of his conversion as given in Acts (chapters 9, 22, and 26). For these accounts, even granting that they convey certain factual information which we may critically distill from them, were composed from a different theological standpoint. What we have already seen relative to the Lucan and Pauline presentation of Paul's contacts with the Jerusalem church can be expected to obtain, *mutatis mutandis,* in the accounts of Paul's conversion. Luke has evidently overpainted the actual situation. Nevertheless, the accounts in Acts should not be ignored altogether. For, on the one hand, they will set in relief Paul's own distinctive presentation of his conversion. On the other, they may confirm the view founded on Paul's own account that he received at his conversion a prophetic understanding which thoroughly shaped both his personal vocation and his apostolic understanding of the gospel.

Each of the accounts of Paul's conversions given in Acts is told in function of a given situation and in function of the development of the theme of the whole book. Each of these distinct accounts further contains a particular emphasis, discernible from the way in which certain details are repeated in slightly different form, or from the way in which others are added or dropped. The over-all emphasis proper to each account also gives the most satisfactory solution to certain obvious discrepancies among the accounts that are not explained adequately, if explained at all, by merely grammatical considerations.

The first account (Acts 9, 1–19) shows how Paul, after having been confronted by Jesus, was brought into the Church through the instrumentality of Ananias. The role of Ananias in healing Paul and in baptizing him is relatively more prominent here than it is in the other accounts. The subsequent instrumentality of Paul himself is indicated in the Lord's words to Ananias that Paul is to be a "vessel of election" (Acts 9, 15). In the sequel to this account, Paul departs from Damascus and is introduced to the apostles in Jerusalem through the instrumentality of Barnabas (Acts 9, 27).

Besides stressing the theme of human instrumentality, the first account brings out the reality and uniqueness of Paul's contact with Jesus. Those standing about hear the voice, but they do not see anyone (9, 7). Paul alone receives the blinding illumination. The objectivity of this event—though full participation in the event is uniquely Paul's—is attested by the fact that his companions are said to have perceived part of it (they hear the voice). This objectivity of Paul's encounter with Jesus is further brought out by the fact that other "visions" are mentioned in the same account, but are clearly "visions" of another, lesser order: 'oramata. Ananias receives an auditory vision in his sleep telling him to seek out Saul (Acts 9, 10–11); Paul himself is said to have received an ocular vision (9, 12) concerning one who would restore his sight. Lastly, with a distinctively Lucan touch, Paul's personal dispositions in preparation for what will prove to be his reception into the Church are singled out: a probable allusion to fasting in Acts 9, 9b, and a clear reference to prayer in Acts 9, 11b.

The second account, which occurs in a speech attributed to Paul himself (Acts 22, 1–22), sets in relief Paul's role as a witness to all men, especially to the gentiles. It is particularly as a hearer of the Lord's word that Paul is depicted here, and as one who, in a subsequent mystical experience in the temple, has been personally entrusted by the Lord with a mission (cf. especially 22, 14 ff.). It should be noted that Paul's companions are said to have seen the light, but not to have heard the voice of the one speaking to Paul (Acts 22, 9). Again, these companions get only *part* of the experience, and that part is not the element of personal communication.

The apparent contradiction with the first account has been explained by an appeal to grammar: "hear [the voice]" takes the genitive in Acts 9, 7; "did not hear [the voice]" takes the accusative in Acts 22, 9. D. M. Stanley has tried to reconcile the two by arguing that "hear" with the accusative means "hear with understanding." Thus there would be no contradiction: the bystanders could indeed have heard the voice (Acts 9, 7), but they would not have heard it with understanding (Acts 22, 9). This solution, however, is not convincing, even on the basis of Lucan usage. What is more, a sense grammatically opposite to that which Stanley defends can be found in John. In John 19, 8, Pilate "hears this word" (accusative), namely, "he made himself Son of God"—but does *not* seem to understand; rather, he fears. But in John 19, 13, Pilate, "hearing these words" (genitive), namely, ". . . anyone who makes himself king speaks out against Caesar," seems to understand quite well; he takes immediate action. Thus the grammatical solution proposed by Stanley seems highly questionable, to say the least.

Perhaps another kind of solution is possible pending a more acceptable grammatical study or simply in place of any plausibly contrived grammatical solution. The kind of solution we suggest seems to save all that really needs to be saved, that is, not the consistency of physical details but the theological significance of the event so paradoxically described.

With regard to the first and second accounts, there are discrepancies concerning both what was seen by whom and what was heard by whom. Note, however, that Luke does not say in Acts 9: "they heard the voice but did not see the light" and in

251

Acts 22: "they saw the light but did not hear the voice." Rather, he says in Acts 9: ". . . they heard the voice but saw *no one*," and in Acts 22: ". . . they saw the light but did not hear the voice *of the one speaking to me*." In short, it is the *element of personal communication* that Paul's companions do not perceive. The physical details of the account are subordinated to a point of theological importance: it is Paul's personal contact with Jesus that is the key element, not the physical phenomena as such. Moreover, the companions of Paul seem to be said to have experienced that aspect of the phenomenon that is relatively less important to the account as a whole. The first account seems to stress the blinding of Paul (by the glory of the one whom he saw). The message heard on this occasion is somewhat subordinated; it is to be supplemented by instructions given through Ananias. Paul's companions simply stand dumbstruck, then lead him by the hand into Damascus (Acts 9, 7 ff.). They saw no one and are not even said to have perceived the blinding light. The second account, however, which places proportionately more stress on Paul's role as a witness and on his hearing the Lord, is also the one which excludes an auditory experience on the part of Paul's companions.

With regard to the first and third accounts, there are further discrepancies that may be handled in a similar way. They concern the position (standing, Acts 9, 7; fallen to the earth, Acts 26, 14) that is predicated of Paul's companions. The "contradiction" in physical details can be explained in function of the scope of each account as a whole and in function of other details as theologically significant details. In the first account, stupefaction is the point. Paul's companions did not know what to make of what they heard, since they had not seen anyone. In the third account, what is stressed is the overpowering action of God. There is a fuller description of the light (cp. 26, 13 with 9, 3 and 22, 6). Significant words, "It is difficult for you to kick against the goad (26, 14b)," are added to the dialogue (cp. 9, 4–5; 22, 7–8). The idiom "kick against the goad" seems to refer to resisting divine power. It is attested in this sense in Euripides' *Bacchae,* 794: "I would rather sacrifice to him than arrogantly kick against the goad, since I am mortal and he divine." What is more, Saul is then told, in words borrowed from the call of the seer Ezekiel (Ezekiel 2, 1 ff.), to "stand on his feet." Fittingly, then, both Saul and his companions have been earlier presented as felled. Saul is singled out to stand; he is to be a seer to illuminate others. Accordingly, too, his blindness is not even mentioned in the third account. In the first account, on the other hand, Luke intended to show how Paul himself was blinded by the Lord to be illumined through the instrumentality of one of those whom Paul would have persecuted. Paul himself is smitten to the ground, rises unseeing, and receives through Ananias his sight and the Holy Spirit.

The third account, as we have already seen in part, underscores Paul's prophetic mission as a seer destined to illuminate others. In addition to points just discussed, one may note the imagery, drawn from the prophets (Acts 26, 17 f.; cf. Jeremiah 1, 7; Isaiah 35, 5; 42, 7. 16; 61, 1), concerning Paul's role in opening men's eyes, turning men from darkness to light. The encounter is referred to in the more properly apocalyptic terms of "heavenly vision" (*tę ouraniǭ optasią*, 26, 19). Similarly, Paul is represented before this transformation not only as a persecutor but as an irreligious fanatic, one who tried to make men blaspheme (26, 11), one who was a kind of false ecstatic prophet (*emmainomenos,* 26, 11b). His "mania" now (cf. the accusation in 26, 24: "Paul, you are mad!" *mainę, Paule*), is presented as an inspired prophetic utterance, like that on Pentecost (26, 25; cp. the Greek of Acts 2, 4. 14b).

From even this cursory study of the three accounts in Acts dealing with Paul's conversion, it should be clear that Luke wanted to bring out various aspects of the role of Paul: his being introduced into the Church; his becoming a witness, especially to the gentiles; and his being constituted a prophetic seer to open the eyes of others. The context of each account dictates in large measure what Luke will underscore, a context which further analysis discloses to be the dominant theme of Acts

253

(*see* p. 59). In Acts 9, Saul intends to bring those of the "Way" captive to Jerusalem; he himself is brought into the Church and goes to Jerusalem. The narrative of his conversion forms part of the narrative about the Church as it existed in close relationship to Jerusalem. Subsequent accounts occur in Paul's own speeches, and in the second half of Acts. When Paul gives his testimony to the Jerusalemites in their own language (Acts 22, 1 ff.), he at first makes a concerted effort to present himself as a witness acceptable to them. The theme of "witness" is underscored at almost every turn. The high priest and the whole priesthood bear him witness regarding his previous devotion to the law (22, 3–5), a dedication demonstrated notably in connection with Jerusalem (vv. 3, 5). Ananias is represented as a religious man according to the law; he is witnessed to by all the Jews dwelling in Damascus (22, 12). Ananias has told Paul that he is to be a witness to the Lord before all men (22, 15). But Paul's testimony will not be received in Jerusalem (22, 18) any more than was that of Jesus' witness, Stephen (22, 20), so he is sent to nations far away. Paul's testimony to the witness that he must give forms part of the testimony of Acts to the Church's dissociation from Judaism largely at the hands of those who would not accept a universal witness (cf. 22, 22). Lastly, before Agrippa, Paul's self-presentation as a prophet is placed against the background of Agrippa's reputed respect for the prophets (cf. 26, 26 ff.). In shrewdly apologetic fashion, Luke conveys the impression that the prophetic word poses no threat to civil rulers (26, 28–32).

If these successive accounts complement and in general build upon one another, it seems that the dominant understanding of Paul's conversion is that given in the third account. If so, Luke's principal representation of Paul's conversion may be judged to approximate the main point that Paul himself makes, that he received an apocalypse which constituted him an apostle as a kind of prophetic servant.

In conclusion, we may advert to what recurs as really the only constant element in Luke's three accounts of Paul's con-

254

version (besides the fact of Paul's prior activity as a persecutor), namely, the Lord's word to Saul: "I am Jesus . . . whom you are persecuting" (Acts 9, 5; 22, 8; 26, 15). One may argue that at least this constant element in the accounts of Paul's conversion is a matter of fact which Paul had communicated to Luke or to others from whom Luke obtained it. On the other hand, Paul himself apparently felt no need to quote any actual utterance in recounting the personal communication that took place at his conversion. Even this bare formulation of the Lord's identity may be a theologically motivated construct on Luke's part to express a truth which for Paul himself would have required no verbal communication (though Paul does allow for this at other times, such as in the revelation he recounts in 2 Corinthians 12, 6–9).

In any event, Luke probably discerned particular significance in this exchange. He underscores Paul's direct confrontation with the Jesus of history (especially in 22, 8, where "of Nazareth" is solidly attested) as precisely an encounter with the Lord, who is now, even in glory, identified with the persecuted community. Quite apart from the question of factual accuracy, the logion can be taken to confirm the theological understanding of Paul's conversion which he himself provides. The career of the persecutor was radically altered by a personal confrontation with the risen Lord, one and the same person as the historical Jesus himself (whom Paul sees as the crucified one). Furthermore, while it would be somewhat gratuitous and unnecessary to discern in this confrontation the genesis of Paul's image of the Mystical Body (as expressed in 1 Corinthians 12, Romans 12, Ephesians and Colossians), which is neither a uniformly developed image nor one which seems to be present in his earliest writings, the confrontation did entail an awareness of the union in Christ of all who belonged to him. Paul surely did not regard his experience in a strictly individual dimension. The difference between the Lucan and Pauline understandings of Paul's inaugural experience is not that between a communitarian scope and an individualistic scope. The difference occurs rather in this, that Luke stresses Paul's relationship to the existing, persecuted community, whereas Paul himself looks to the nations to whom he is to preach. Accordingly, in Luke's accounts of the conversion, further attention is devoted to what Paul must yet learn, often from others within the community. Paul himself sees in his inaugural experience a more strikingly prophetic impulse to preach Christ in gentile lands with no need to consult "flesh and blood."

Eventually, the Apostle's prophetic outlook led him to send his word ahead of him to places that he had not yet visited. His apostolic concerns could not be contained even by the communities with which he was already burdened. New foundations were not necessarily in question. But Paul felt that the urgent grace of his apostolic office demanded that he generously communicate a richer charismatic understanding of the faith (Romans 1, 11–15) to all within the horizon of his world (Romans 15, 18 ff.). We shall now turn our attention to the Apostle's theological line of reasoning and to formulated expressions of his gospel, both of which we can best study in his greatest spiritual legacy, the epistle to the Romans.

CHAPTER TWO

PAUL'S THEOLOGICAL PERSPECTIVES

What is it that makes "Pauline theology" really theology and yet really distinctively "Pauline"? Our purpose in this chapter will be to provide some answer to this question by way of offering some insights into Paul's argumentation, mainly as exemplified in Romans 9–11. We can perhaps more solidly set forth what one should understand by "theology" and by "Pauline" theology by presenting some major examples of it rather than by discussing it in the light of a general definition. Our approach in answering the question proposed above will therefore be largely inductive.

SYNTHESIS OF PRECEDING OBSERVATIONS

We may begin by synthesizing some of the observations already made in the course of reading through a representative selection of Paul's epistles. Paul repeatedly surveys a concrete problem in terms of God's action or dynamic being. The concrete problem or situation that the Apostle treats is always some aspect of Christian existence and frequently entails reference to life ac-

257

cording to the spirit. Even when he speaks of other kinds of human existence, Paul refers by way of comparison or contrast to the meaning of being in Christ. It should be clear, then, that he is not simply addressing himself to the "human condition." His focus is Christological, not humanistic. The Christological focus, in turn, is but a more immediate aspect of an ultimate focus on the action or dynamic being of the Father, 'o theos. It is this ultimate focus on the Godhead ('o theos) that makes Paul's treatment of any problem or situation theological in the strictest sense.

This theological focus is shared, of course, by all other New Testament writers. But there are a number of features of Paul's works that give his theology a distinctive ring. In faith, of course, he is of one mind and heart with the other authors of the New Testament. He himself recognized only one gospel (Galatians 1, 6–7). But the characteristic difference of his own understanding of the faith is revealed in an interlocking pattern of certain themes which are more vigorously emphasized in Paul than in other New Testament writers.

In the first place, Paul conceives the goal of Christian life in the imagery of an apocalyptic transformation by which God's power and wisdom fully triumph among men. The new creation is already underway, to be climaxed by an ultimate victory over death at the parousia. More strikingly than other New Testament authors, Paul regularly stresses the final transformation of the faithful in the likeness of God's Son at the resurrection. Characteristically, he portrays this transformation in terms of a triumph, a victory achieved through conflict.

Secondly, he relentlessly judges the present stage of Christian life in the light of its future consummation. As W. Thüsing puts it so well: "Paul thinks from fulfillment back to the present [Paulus denkt von der Vollendung her]." Present conflicts are anticipations of the final conflict; present joys in the spirit are a foretaste of union with Christ at the parousia; present possession of the spirit itself is valued as the "down payment" or advance from God on what is fully to be given us at the resur-

258

rection. Both present and future stages of Christian existence combine to form what we may call the "eschaton," the final stage of salvation history as a whole.

For Paul, the eschaton is defined as a kind of bond of faith in Christ. We may consider this bond both objectively and subjectively—though personally in each case—to discover the whole truth emerging from these two complementary aspects. Objectively, the eschaton is defined in terms of the Lord's own twofold personal triumph, that of the passion and resurrection and that of the parousia. Subjectively, the eschaton is defined in terms of personal faith at the time of conversion and lived faith fulfilled in the coming of the Lord.

While Paul's Christological perspective is delineated by strongly futuristic strokes, it is filled out in a markedly down-to-earth, missionary style. For all practical purposes, the eschaton begins with incorporation into the risen Lord through faith at the time of conversion and baptism. By faith a man is effectively transposed to another level of existence, a bond in Christ, life for God, new activity and understanding on the plane of the Spirit. This new existence for men in general is made feasible by the new existence of the risen Lord, which is literally the felicitous beginning of the end. The present stage of Christian life is really an anticipation of the end, that is, of the life of the resurrection. By Christ's own resurrection as apprehended in faith men are transposed into the state of eschatological existence.

With regard both to the objective and subjective aspects of the eschaton, Paul's theology recognizably differs from that of other New Testament authors, notably from that of the evangelists. Paul says practically nothing about the life of Christ prior to the passion and resurrection, and does not handle the central mystery of the passion and resurrection itself on a narrative basis. While the evangelists certainly do not give a biography of Christ in the modern sense, they do present the gospel somewhat more complexively and concretely in a story of Christ's life. They illuminate the central mystery by editing the words

259

and deeds of the Lord himself rather than, as Paul does, by rhetorically elaborating eschatological themes. They depict the whole end time by seeing it comprised in the life experience of Jesus himself among the men of his generation. It is not that they convert the eschatological perspective into an incarnational perspective; they maintain a dominantly eschatological perspective. But they tend towards historical, descriptive verification of the revelation in Christ. They view the objective revelation more richly in the schematically arranged, systematized words and deeds of the Lord himself, and they articulate apostolic proclamation in actually or interpretatively dominical statements and actions. In a sense, the evangelists try to allow the Lord to explain himself; they regard the apostolic testimony more concretely and radically as Jesus' own utterance and his own total life.

Accordingly, the evangelists' presentation of the eschaton differs in its subjective aspect as well. The eschaton begins with faith, but the focus is not so directly on the faith of the convert himself, as it is in Paul. Rather, the focus centers on the response of men and women of faith who lived before the reader of the gospels and "typify" the faith of later believers. Faith itself is more historically concretized. It is even "typified" more directly with reference to Jesus himself; it is not Abraham (Paul's favorite model, apart from himself) as much as Mary or the disciples associated with Jesus of Nazareth among men whom the gospels present as the paradigms of faith.

A third feature of Paul's theology may be described as its pronouncedly dialectical cast. The future realization of the eschaton involves a kind of present dialectic in existence itself: the existence of unbelievers and that of the faithful; the existence of Christians living at one and the same time "in the flesh" but "according to the spirit." The faithful are regarded as those destined for salvation (in hope, however, for salvation cannot be taken for granted); unbelievers are viewed apocalyptically as those destined for destruction (presuming that they do not respond to God's mercy and truth in the gospel). This opposition

260

corresponds to that between the Lord and the Man of Rebellion, Christ and Beliar, and so forth, which is resolved in the victory at the parousia. The evangelists give evidence of similar apocalyptic contrasts, but they couch these in language describing events of Christ's own life on earth or in predictions attributed to him rather than phrase them quite directly in terms of the life experience of the contemporary community or in terms of the Apostle's rhetorical imagery and dialectical argumentation.

The dialectical cast of Christian existence itself is not without parallel in other New Testament authors. John, for instance, will speak of being "in the world but not of the world" (John 17, 11–17). Perhaps the closest parallel, however, to Paul's dialectical presentation of life "in the flesh" but "according to the spirit" and not "according to the flesh" is that which Matthew and Mark give us (Matthew 26, 41; Mark 14, 38): "The spirit is willing but the flesh is weak." Nevertheless, even in this most striking parallel to the characteristically Pauline antithesis of flesh and spirit, there are differences of nuance, largely attributable to differences in mode of presentation. In this text from the synoptics, "the spirit" is regarded less as a life principle and more as a moral disposition. It represents a willingness to be vigilant with Christ in the hour of struggle and thus to be secure from temptation. What is surely noteworthy both in Paul and in the synoptics is that there is question of an eschatological struggle. But where Paul looks on the spirit as that principle of life and fulfillment of the law that is derived from the risen Christ, the synoptics see the spirit in terms of a disposition for association with Jesus in his passion. The synoptics concretize the eschatological struggle in narrating the passion of the Lord himself; the personal relevance of the spirit/flesh antithesis is mediated by the picture of the Lord with his disciples in Gethsemani. Paul, on the other hand, views the dynamics of the eschatological struggle in the Christians whom he addresses directly (cf. Rom. 8, 5–13) or in a dramatic monologue evoking the image of Adam (Romans 7, 7–25).

A fourth feature of Paul's theology really accounts for many

261

of those already noted and may be taken as a quite characteristic feature. His presentation of revelation is always directly and intensely personal. His genre, for instance, repeatedly takes the form of a kerygmatic preaching or epistolary communication. While the evangelists, as individual, personal figures, stand somewhat outside or behind what they have written, Paul is always immediately and personally engaged at the heart of the revelation that he communicates. It really matters little to the interpretation of John's gospel whether or not one can identify the "beloved disciple" with the evangelist himself. The "beloved disciple" is a type of the really perceptive disciple, but he remains cloaked in individual, personal anonymity. While Paul may also be considered as a "type" of the genuine apostle, he intrudes more personally.

Some of the characteristic themes of his theology are good indications of this intensely personal factor, and help to distinguish his personal approach from that of the other New Testament writers even among the epistles. Paul frequently "boasts." The boast always focuses on what God himself has done, past, present, and future, and it embraces Paul's converts as well as Paul himself. While characteristically personal, then, it is by no means exclusive or self-assertive. But it is a personalistic mode of expressing the paradox which lies at the heart of Paul's gospel: that God's power is made perfect in weakness; that the dialectic of human existence is finalized in a stupendous triumph which Christians share with each other by being enabled through Christ to share it with God (Romans 5–8). Similarly, the characteristic theme of "imitation" most personally expresses living solidarity in Christ who died and was raised. Paul, by self-effacing service, brings his converts to the Christ-formed existence which he shares personally. For, as an apostle, who has been invested by God's grace (Galatians 1, 11 ff.; 2, 9; Romans 1, 5; 12, 3; 15, 15; 1 Corinthians 3, 10; 15, 10), he enjoys this existence in exceptionally full charismatic measure, and is pressed to impart it to others (cf. 2 Corinthians 5, 13–15).

If we seek an adequate explanation for this characteristically personal theology of "boasting," we will find it in the topic treated in our preceding chapter and in our discussion of Galatians 1–2. The distinctive mode in which Paul received the gospel explains his theological emphases in enunciating it. We cannot simply stop with the fact that Paul's vehicle of expression is epistolary correspondence. Nor can we rest content with conjectures concerning Paul's personal temperament and background. We must have recourse to the prophetic Apostle's inaugural experience. His whole life had been suddenly changed by the power of God's grace in the revelation of Jesus Christ, which was an illumination on the level of the spirit. His gospel was "infused" with the sudden and indelible experience of a personal transformation; it was "his" gospel as much as it was the only gospel, not in an exclusivistic sense, but in an intensely personal sense. Even if and when he later acquired narrative data concerning Jesus or logia attributed to him, it would have been both unnecessary and uncharacteristic for Paul to have made much use of these data—unnecessary, because he had received the whole gospel by way of a direct, personal vision; uncharacteristic, because his apostolate was to communicate by preaching that which he himself had directly and personally been given to understand. For an adequate explanation of characteristically Pauline themes of Paul's preferred genre, we must have recourse not just to his native temperament or background, but to the heart of his theological thinking: the vision of faith that had been personally communicated to him in the unmerited and transforming revelation of the risen Lord.

As Paul's conversion and theological themes are personal paradoxes, so is his characteristic line of reasoning. He delights in sharp, almost shocking contrasts, like those between God's wisdom and power versus human foolishness and weakness. In apocalyptic fashion, the mystery seems to become more elaborate and difficult to comprehend even as it is being "explained," and one mystery finds its explanation in the flowering of another of still richer beauty, to the astonishment of the beholder. We dare not cut Paul short if we want to grasp the total

263

evolution of his dialectically phrased argument. A good example of a passage where we must allow Paul to speak out his mind fully, in a series of affirmations and negations, is his development of the notion of his apostleship in 1 Corinthians 1, 14–17, where he speaks of his not having baptized anyone. To grasp his mind in other passages, too, we must regularly infer from comparisons and antitheses over a considerable amount of text the perspective that unifies them and the overriding theme that Paul is developing. One understands him not so much in terms of ideas or concepts as in terms of developing themes and an incessantly antithetical or dialectical way of thinking in which the *greater* power or *greater* good or glory is eventually made clear.

Even the terms that Paul employs are notably action oriented, so that we must be wary of taking them in a static sense. To "know" is usually to know experientially. Moreover, present knowledge is often related to a kind of future knowledge. To "have" is often not simply to be in possession of, but to have for use, for exercise of power. "Wisdom" is not a quiet contemplation of truth so much as a practical, creative implementation of power. "Sonship" is not so much a state of being as a coming into one's inheritance, and present sonship connotes the full realization of the inheritance yet to come. Even the oneness of God is conceived dynamically, not as merely static, numerical oneness, but as direct communication, such as of a blessing, or as effectively bringing about in the law of faith that which the Mosaic law stood for, but could not achieve, namely, the oneness of God over all.

GENERAL SURVEY OF THE ARGUMENT IN ROMANS 9—11

A number of features of Paul's theology discussed thus far can perhaps best be grasped by seeing them exemplified in Romans 9–11. This lengthy, well-integrated passage is especially valua-

264

ble for illustrating Paul's dialectical mode of argumentation in a matter which engaged him quite personally. The problem he treats is basically the non-conversion of those who are his own people according to the flesh. A personal attestation on Paul's part serves to indicate the three major stages in his development of the problem and its solution: Romans 9, 1–5; 10, 1; 11, 1. After we have sketched the over-all line of development, we shall provide the text along with further commentary.

Paul begins by averring his personal involvement in the problem of the non-conversion of his own people as a whole (9, 1–5). He first defends God's way of governing the course of human events (9, 6–18). Israel's infidelity is no reason to affirm that God's word has failed—the key proof being God's election in the case of the patriarchs. God is free to be faithful to the one he chooses (9, 6–13). Nor is it against God's justice to choose in this way—the proof being his words to Moses and to Pharao. He shows mercy according to his free choice. Paul supposes that God's justice is not legal but personal, and that it admits, therefore, of special consideration, which is not an injustice to one who cannot lay claim to it at all (especially since it is offered to everyone, a point that Paul supposes from Romans 1–8 but one which he will shortly repeat). Paul then overrules objections to what he takes for granted—on the basis of his reverential faith—as being a sovereignly powerful and wise divine way of acting (9, 19–24). He implies that the objector not only challenges God instead of seeking to understand him, but also misconstrues the whole nature of God's power, which is not (as the objector supposes) a brute force that "steamrollers" man's will. Paul tries to impart the proper perspective by presenting God's choice of the gentiles as a favor that does not deny a remnant to Israel (9, 25–26. 27–29). Given this defense of God's sovereign power, freedom, and mercy, Paul makes the transition to Israel's own infidelity (9, 30–35).

Continuing with another avowal of devotion to his own kindred (10, 1), Paul argues that Israel's infidelity is really a zeal

265

not guided by genuine knowledge (10, 2–3). Even the law, as understood properly, attests to a superior kind of justice, the kind leading to salvation and involving faith (10, 4–13). While this faith surely comes from hearing, Israel by now must indeed have heard (10, 14–18). But Israel has not recognized the message; others have done so (10, 19–21).

How, then, are we to understand Israel's culpable disbelief —and the frustration of the effectiveness of God's promises that it apparently entails? Beginning anew with an attestation of personal grace (11, 1), Paul prophesies that Israel's infidelity is partial (11, 2–10) and temporary, for the benefit of the gentiles (11, 11–24), who are to be wary of the self-reliance that caused the loss of the original branches. The ultimate "solution" for the present evil of disbelief is affirmed to lie in an understanding of the mystery of God's gracious mercy, his creatively salvific power to work a greater good out of present disobedience (11, 25–32). Paul fittingly concludes with a doxology to the power of God's wisdom (11, 33–36).

In brief, God has not failed or shown himself unjust, but is employing the infidelity of Israel to achieve a greater eschatological good. The answer to the problem of God's actual fulfillment of his promises is an understanding in faith of the mystery of his way of fulfilling them paradoxically and superabundantly.

TEXT AND COMMENTARY

A. *Romans 9*

9, 1a I am speaking the truth in Christ, I am not lying:
  1b my conscience bears me witness in the Holy Spirit
  2   that I have great grief and unceasing pain in my heart;
  3a   indeed, I could wish myself to be anathema from Christ
  3b   for the sake of my brethren,
  3c   my kinsmen according to the flesh.
  4a   They are the Israelites,
  4b   theirs are sonship

266

4c	and the glory,
4d	the covenants,
4e	the code of laws,
4f	the liturgy,
4g	and the promises;
5a	theirs are the patriarchs,
5b	and from them is descended Christ according to the flesh;
5c	he who is over and above all, God, is blest for all ages.
	Amen.

As he begins to state the problem, Paul protests that his own feelings and his own "conscience" are deeply involved. Not that he feels guilty for what has happened to his people, but that he is vividly conscious, "aware before God," of the scandalous situation in which the people so favored by God have not as a group accepted the fulfillment of the law and the promises. He attests in "conscience," that is, in the awareness of his relationship to God, his own grief, refracted from the disbelief of Israel. At the same time, he stands before God as one of his own people and experiences a frightful tension, like that of Moses (Exodus 32, 32), to perish with his kindred. The pull of the "flesh" on one who is in Christ was experienced most keenly by Paul (v. 3) in the area of faith itself. We can hardly construe his opening statement otherwise, for example, as being merely a literary device to introduce the problem of Israel's disbelief. We should accept the attestation of his grief, especially with the added remark in verse 3, as the admission of a kind of temptation (a trial, however, rather than an enticement to evil) which Paul attests not only in "consciousness" but in "conscience."

To resolve this crisis of faith, Paul will have to probe the mystery of God's gifts and God's way of acting. He will not airily dismiss the defection of those dear to him as being their own fault. For the word of God is an efficacious power. Thus, in order to understand Israel's defection, God's own action needs to be understood. But the only real answer to this problem, especially as one attested in Paul's own conscience, will lie in a humble and appreciative probing of the mystery of God's power in the word. The answer to any crisis of faith will have to

267

be deeper understanding in faith; Paul proves himself to be no exception.

The list of Israel's privileges includes a kind of sonship, even though it is not the eschatological sonship realized in Christ; the Israelites were recognized by God as his own people. The "glory" of God's dwelling among them in the desert and in the temple was also theirs, with the "covenants," the word given not only to Moses but to Abraham and David, the code of laws spelling out the will of God, the temple service, the many prophetic blessings and assurances of God's aid. All these benefits are placed in the total context of Israel's history by what Paul says in verse 5; that history commences with the lives of the Patriarchs. This pre-messianic history eventually reaches its climax in the coming of Christ according to the flesh. Paul concludes this list of the privileges of his kinsmen according to the flesh with a brief doxology to the one from whom these privileges derive. God is over and above all these privileges. The doxology, in turn, establishes the theological perspective for considering their fulfillment or non-fulfillment.

9, 6a   It is not that God's word has failed.
    6b   For not all who are from Israel are "Israel,"
    7a   nor because they are Abraham's posterity are all "children,"
    7b   but: "Your posterity shall be [so] called through Isaac."
    8a   That is to say,
    8b   it is not the children of flesh who are children of God,
    8c   but the children of the promise who are reckoned as
                                 descendants.

    9a   For this word was a word of promise:
    9b   "At this time of year I shall come and Sarah will have a son."
    10a   This was shown more strikingly
    10b   when Rebecca conceived by one man, our father Isaac.
    11a   While the twins were still unborn
    11b   and had done nothing good or bad—
    11c   so that God's design would remain according to his own
                                 choice,
    12a   not from [man's] works but from [God's] call—
    12b   she was told:
    12c   "The greater [elder] will serve the lesser [younger]."
    13a   Hence, it is written:
    13b   "Jacob I loved; Esau I hated."

268

14a What then shall we say?

14b Not that there is injustice on God's part?

14c Of course not!

15a   For he says to Moses:

15b   "I will have mercy on whom I have mercy and pity on whom
                  I pity,"

16a   which shows [that everything comes]

16b   not from [man's] willing or trying but from God's showing
                  mercy.

17a   Indeed, scripture says to Pharao:

17b   "It was for this very thing that I raised you up:

17c   to display my power in you

17d   and to spread my name over all the earth,"

18a   which shows

18b   God has mercy on whom he wills

18c   and he hardens whom he wills.

Paul denies that God's word has failed or that his justice can be impugned. His denial stems from his understanding of God's word and God's justice as rooting the particular reasons that he adduces here. The reasons adduced really illustrate Paul's radical understanding of God's word and God's justice. Paul regards God's word as an efficacious promise to which no mere man can lay claim; God's justice consists in his restructuring men's lives to achieve by this re-formation the fulfillment of his promise (cf. Romans 3, 21–4, 25). Paul also presumes here that the over-all divine purpose is salvific: creative election beyond human power or standards of excellence (vv. 9–13), and the exodus experience of deliverance (vv. 14–18). What is more, when Paul surveys God's purpose in fulfilling his promise, he does so not in the metaphysical perspective of knowledge from all eternity but in the metahistorical perspective of God's final glory to be realized according to the pattern established in Christ. To recognize the question of perspective is just as important as to recognize the suppositions for Paul's denial in verse 6b and the implications of the terms he subsequently employs. For, otherwise, we can hardly expect to understand him aright and to avoid a dismal doctrine like that which declares that God predestines some for damnation.

From what we have read in Paul's earlier epistles, it should be clear that his over-all perspective is that of the *end* rather than that of the beginning. Even when he speaks of God's "call" he speaks of a call ordered to final glory (cf. Romans 8, 30; 1 Thessalonians 2, 12). Furthermore, he considers God's action in the dynamic, predominantly functional context of salvation history. Consequently, he does not treat God's action "abstractly" in an essentialistic or conceptualistic manner, for example, by trying to peer into the mind of God as it existed from all eternity "prior" to creation. Since his basic perspective is that of final judgment and salvation rather than that of initial creation, and since this perspective in turn focuses not on God's ideas, but on God's acts in salvation history, it entails certain suppositions concerning the *de facto* human situation. The fundamental supposition in this connection is that man, apart from God's grace through Christ, is a "sinner." He is basically alienated from God, if not by personally committed sins then at least by the condition of his very entry into the human race after mankind had undone itself (cf. Romans 5, 12–21; 7, 7–25). His alienation from God lies radically in this, that he cannot in his slave state under death and sin obtain risen life or fulfill the holy law of God by his own power. God had not made man alienated from himself; man put himself into his present state. In this *de facto* situation, no mere man can lay claim to God's favor.

More particular considerations have usually been offered to obviate a Calvinistic understanding of Paul's words here. While these more particular considerations may perhaps be useful, they seem to have no solid value except in the light of the more general considerations offered above. It is quite true, for instance, that Paul is not considering precisely the ultimate personal salvation of Jacob, Esau, Moses, or Pharao. For one thing, he looks to the role of these personages, notably that of Pharao, in the working out of God's word. Secondly, in line with the role that he indicates for these figures, especially Pharao, Paul can be said to treat them more as types than as individuals. In the last analysis, however, these considerations

270

are merely ways of dodging the difficulty or of obscuring the real issue. For could not what is true of a particular episode in the lives of these personages be true of their whole lives? Could not their own role as types be verified in turn (even as "typical") of the lives of other individual men and women? It is true that the whole of one's life does not amount merely to the sum of particular acts and events, but are not the events mentioned here mentioned precisely as events typical of a whole lived human experience?

Really at stake, however, is the whole understanding of God's word and God's justice. To attempt to minimize or weaken the difficulty from the point of view of man's salvation, even if the attempt could be judged relatively successful, would not be honestly to face the main point at issue. That point is the understanding of God's word and God's justice as achieved through men but not really because of men's actions. The only firm answer to the problem of man's salvation is to take as one's dominant perspective not precisely what will eventually happen to man but how God's word and justice are to be understood. Only the latter perspective is adequately theological, for it alone is properly God-centered. But it is precisely this perspective to which Paul inclines us. Man's salvation will accordingly be found to lie in the divine grace that is shown to him abundantly and without discrimination, even though he cannot lay claim to it.

In 9, 6–13, Paul says that God's word has not failed because it is a word of promise that is realized supernaturally. The supernatural character of the realization is first established by distinguishing between realization on the level of flesh and realization on the level of the promise (v. 8). The genuine Israel is not as such the Israel according to the flesh, those who are physically sons of Abraham. For fulfillment of God's word to Abraham must be understood precisely as fulfillment of what God has promised. The only way to understand the fulfillment of God's word is to recognize it for what it is—and what it is the history of the Patriarchs evinces. The word of

271

personal promise to Abraham (vv. 7, 9) was verified in Isaac, not in Abraham's other son, and it was verified by God in the time divinely designated (v. 9). Turning to the descendants of Isaac (vv. 10–13), Paul devotes his attention to Rebecca, the mother of Esau and Jacob. For this case enables him to illustrate that men's moral works as well as their physical potential are not the determining factors in the realization of God's word. The divine "preference" of one over the other is expressed in the bold Semitic idiom of sharp contrasts. God's "hatred" of Esau is clearly not to be construed in terms of God's personal disposition, but in terms of the functional realization of the promise where, contrary to merely human norms, the greater (elder) was to serve the lesser (younger).

Paul himself senses the difficulty here (v. 14). Is this paradoxical choice in the fulfillment of God's word an injustice on God's part? His reply to the difficulty is to clarify the notion of God's justice and to affirm the basic perspective for understanding it, namely, the realization of God's salvific plan. His argument in defense of God's justice is by no means complete with the end of v. 18; one must not cut him short. For he will go on to show precisely how God's actual conduct at the present time is to be conceived, not as an exercise of brute power but as manifold mercy (9, 19 ff.). He will not concede that God deals with Israel now precisely as he dealt with Pharao. Paul is too keenly aware both of a special manifestation of God's favor to Israel and of the difference between the pre-eschatological period of the law and the eschatological period of the fulfilled promise to make such an error. But at this point he must make quite clear the general understanding of God's justice and the strictly theological perspective for understanding it correctly. God's justice cannot be judged by human standards of greatness, of which Pharao is an outstanding example; it must be judged in terms of God's own sovereign freedom as ordered to the manifestation of his glory. Furthermore, God's justice must be conceived as being one with his mercy.

The first example, which Paul adduces more directly, illus-

272

trates the latter point (vv. 15–16). God's word of promise entails no injustice, for it is displayed as mercy. It is not a giving to men their due but a manifestation of what God is free to give or not, independently of what men want or what they run to accomplish.

In the second example (vv. 17–18), Paul establishes more clearly the perspective of God's action, the demonstration of his own power for spreading his name over all the earth. Pharao's being "raised up" is his exaltation as ruler of Egypt to achieve God's salvific purpose. The "hardening" of Pharao's heart is also attributed to God, not from the moralistic standpoint of responsibility for Pharao's action, but from the standpoint of the total design to be accomplished. Like God's sending a power of deception in 2 Thessalonians 2, 11, the hardening or unrepentance of Pharao's heart supposes Pharao's personal responsibility. But Paul simply takes that point for granted and considers not the aspect of human responsibility but the actual purpose of God in terms of the divine power for deliverance that is to become a reality as a more universal good. The "typology" of human existence is worked out on the level of God's superhuman act of deliverance. Verse 18 must be taken in the light of verse 17. Verse 17 does not say that God raised up Pharao only to harden his heart, but that he raised him up for a purpose that transcends anything that Pharao himself could have accomplished if he had wished to do so. Moreover, verse 18 stands in much the same relationship to verse 17 as verse 16 does in regard to verse 15. As God's freely shown mercy is not to be explained by man's will or effort (though both were evidenced in the case of Moses), God's actual achievement of his salvific design was accomplished through Pharao's obdurateness.

Surely, this statement is a scandal, a stumbling block! Yes, but only for one who does not try to understand it aright. The formulation is no more scandalizing than the fact it affirms, the all-encompassing, absolute power of God's will for the good he designs and deigns to accomplish. To accept both fact and

273

formulation, however, we must learn to understand the will of God as salvific. To indicate the proper understanding of God's will against the background of misunderstanding on the part of a fictitious, scandalized auditor, Paul comes to our aid by stating the obvious objection and his answer to it:

9, 19a	You will say to me, then:
19b	"Why does God still find fault?
19c	For who has stood up to his will?"
20a	Mere man, who are you to answer God back?
20b	"Shall the vessel of clay say to its maker,
20c	'Why did you make me like this?' "
21a	Has not the potter power over his clay
21b	to make from the same mixture
21c	one vessel for noble purposes [honor]
21d	and one for common use [dishonor]?
22a	If God, wishing to display his wrath and make known his power,
22b	has shown great patience in putting up with vessels of wrath
22c	that stand ready for destruction—
23a	and, in order to make known the wealth of his glory
23b	to vessels of mercy
23c	which he has prepared for glory—
24a	such has he actually called us to be,
24b	not only those of us from among the Jews
24c	but those from among the gentiles as well!

The imaginary objector seems at first to have a case, for God's will has been represented as omnipotent. But Paul's response will demolish the very suppositions of the objection. The objector supposes that God's hardening of Pharao's heart as Paul has described it looks to Pharao's moral guilt, whereas it looks more directly to his action in refusing to let the people go and attends to this action only as a part of a total salvific design on God's part. Furthermore, the objector supposes that Paul regards God's will as an overwhelming brute force which no one has resisted or can resist—and such is probably the objector's own understanding of God's will. This is not so. Paul answers with a rhetorical cross-fire employing two complementary arguments.

First, Paul takes the objection not just as a speculative question but as a rhetorical challenge. Just as he presents his own "speculative" problems in a personal, rhetorical context, he takes what we might regard as a "speculative" objection in the personal context of a challenge to God. Hence, his first reaction is to answer rhetorically—*ad hominem*. It is one thing respectfully to search out God's ways, and it is another to challenge them. This distinction is ours and helps clarify Paul's answer. But we must also recognize that Paul simply assumes that the question is indeed a challenge. Even if the suppositions of the objector were legitimate, which Paul will show in effect is not the case, he will not find an answer by challenging God's wisdom. Actually, even in his *ad hominem* answer, Paul is establishing the proper theological perspective and disposition for understanding God's way of acting. The disposition is a humble willingness to start with the facts, with what God has done. The perspective is (at first) God's power as wise creator, and then (almost immediately and with greater emphasis) God's bringing things to judgment or glory. We must be careful not to press the image of the potter, which Paul cites to establish (by a quotation from Jeremiah) the prophetic perspective of God's sovereign power and wisdom in creation. Obviously, man is not a pot. Not so obviously, but of equal importance, is the fact that Paul implies human responsibility as he goes on to speak of God's "enduring" vessels destined ("disposed," *katērtismena;* cf. 1 Corinthians 1, 10; 2 Corinthians 13, 11) for wrath (v. 22b). Furthermore, one must be careful not to allow the image of the potter to lead us to judge God's action simply or primarily from the standpoint of creation, that is, "from the beginning of the world" or from the standpoint of man's responsibility. No sooner has Paul quoted the Old Testament text than he looks to the purpose of God's action in terms of a function to be exercised (v. 21cd). He promptly moves on to the perspective of judgment (immediately connoted by the term "wrath") and of salvation (connoted by the term "glory").

It is in his own exposition of the text concerning the potter (and in his going beyond this text) that we can detect the com-

275

plementary and really more devastating argument in Paul's response. He passes from an argument *ad hominem* to an argument *"ad Deum"*—one that authoritatively centers on what God himself has actually done as the basis for understanding God's will. Now, the norm for understanding Paul's answer resides in the way Paul himself understands God's will on the grounds of what he himself recognizes God has done. The norm for understanding Paul's answer is decidedly not to be found or founded in the mentality of the objector. The function of the objector—who is mainly a rhetorical foil, in the style of the Stoic-cynic diatribe—is but to propose a challenge which furthers Paul's own argumentative exposition of his insight into God's way of acting.

Accordingly, we must beware of what we supply to complete the conditional clause in verse 22 and again in verse 23. Something must indeed be supplied logically, for Paul's own thought is presumably complete even though it is not actually expressed at the points at which the sentence dissolves into an anacoluthon (end of vv. 22c and 23c). But the phrase that we supply logically in following this debater's train of thought must be something that represents Paul's mind as evidenced especially in this context. He alerts us especially in verse 24 as to whither his thought gravitates: to what God has actually done without discriminating between Jews and gentiles. Therefore, Günther Bornkamm is quite right in saying that Paul does not rest his case on abstract possibilities, but on the mercy that God has actually shown. Accordingly, we should heed Bornkamm's caution and not supply to the anacolutha in verses 22c and 23c something like: ". . . is it not *possible* for God to do so?" Nevertheless, we should go further than Bornkamm does. For, in verse 22 Paul expresses God's actual dealings with those vessels that stand ready for destruction: God has shown great patience with them; that is, he has mercifully deferred his wrath. Thus God's power, even with regard to those on whom he could wish (participle) to show his wrath, has been exercised with patience and not as brute force. Accord-

276

ingly, we should not supply to the anacolutha in verses 22 and 23 something like: ". . . who are we to say (that is, to object or complain)? God has the power to do so." More in accord with Paul's thought here would be the conclusion: ". . . how can you, mere man, suppose that God exercises his will in an arbitrary and capricious manner, as though it were brute force?"

We need not insist on the precise formulation of the words we must supply to the anacolutha; not any formulation will do, but a number of formulations could be offered that would do. What is all-important is a formulation construed according to Paul's mind. We could also supply the following: ". . . does he not act freely in so doing?" or: ". . . is this not God's freedom?" In any event, we would not understand God's freedom, as a conceptualistic minded theologian is wont to do, in the perspective of mere speculative possibility or, as the objector does, with the connotation of brute force. A proper understanding of Paul's mind, whatever acceptable formulation is supplied to complete the logic of the sentence, would require this twofold element: 1) a consideration of God's freedom as actually exercised, not as a merely speculative possibility conceived by man (whether validly conceived or not falls beside the point here); and 2) recognition of the qualitative aspect of God's power—a power that is not brute force but merciful even where the sinner is concerned, notably during the present eschatological period (cf. Romans 2, 3–4).

Thus the objector is refuted by being reproved for his insolent assumption that he can challenge the power of God—especially by supposing that God's power is not mercifully exercised. Thus, too, Paul furthers his own exposition of the way God's word has not failed. Truly it has not failed, for it is a word that must be understood as a promise realized according to God's free choice (9, 6–13). God commits no injustice to man in his exercise of this free choice, because the entire choice on God's part can be ordered to nothing less than his own glory and transcends merely human power to achieve it or to frustrate it; God's mercy is sovereignly free (9, 14–18).

277

What is more, his freedom in act cannot be challenged, since it is ordered to universal salvation. Even in the case of those destined for judgment (on the supposition of their own responsibility; cf. Romans 2, 3–5), that freedom has been exercised in a form of mercy, forbearance. Paul will now spell out the mercy God has actually manifested for Jews and for gentiles as well.

9, 25a As he says in Hosea:
25b "I shall call 'Not-my-people' 'My-people,'
25c and 'Unbeloved' 'Beloved,'
26a and in the place where men were told 'You are Not-my-people,'
26b there they will be called 'Sons of the living God'."

27a And on Israel's behalf, Isaiah cries out:
27b "If the number of the sons of Israel [becomes] as the sand of the sea,
27c it is a remnant that will be saved;
28a for by completing his word and shortening it
28b will the Lord execute it upon the earth."
29a Accordingly, Isaiah had said earlier:
29b "If the Lord of Hosts had not left us some posterity,
29c we should have been like Sodom and become like Gomorrah."

In verses 25–26, Paul employs scripture to describe the merciful call of the gentiles. He probably takes the awkward LXX expression in verse 26 in the sense: "in [the] place of being told 'You are Not-my-people,' they will be called 'Sons of the living God'." But there may be an allusion to the universal scope of this call (places other than Israel) by way of an allusion to place. In the Old Testament, of course, the oracle applies simply to Israel. But Paul is not giving an exegesis of the Old Testament; he is illustrating his authoritative understanding of the salvific will of God. Hence, he simply appropriates the passage to express the call of the gentiles. His use of the text will seem less strange if one also recognizes that Paul regards the people of God as *one* precisely because he regards it from the standpoint of the actual fulfillment of God's word. A text which referred to Israel alone could accordingly be used by Paul quite readily even of the non-Jewish element called to belong to the eschatological people of God.

278

The second set of quotations deals with Israel conceived not simply as the Israel according to the flesh but as those prophetically addressed, that is, as called by God (cf. v. 24). God's call of Israel must be understood as the call of a remnant in the last days. The Lord does indeed fulfill his word, but he does so in "shortening" it, that is, by bringing it to pass "quickly" in the "last days." The perspective here is not that of clock-and-calendar time, but the eschatological perspective of fulfillment of the Lord's promise in the "last days" or final stage of salvation history (which is short by theological definition, however long it may last in clock-and-calendar time). The second quotation from Isaiah cues us to note once again that Paul is stressing the actual fulfillment of God's promise as an act of mercy, even though the fulfillment deals with a "remnant."

9, 30a What, then, shall we say?
  30b Why, that gentiles,
  30c   those who did not pursue justice,
  30d   have obtained justice, the justice that is from faith,
  31a whereas Israel,
  31b   pursuing a law of justice
  31c   did not attain law.

  32a Why so?
  32b   because [it was] not from faith but as if from works;
  32c   they tripped against the "stumbling block"
  33a   as it is written:
  33b   "See, I am placing on Sion a stumbling block and a rock to trap them;
  33c   but the man who has faith in him will not be put to shame."

In these verses, Paul concludes the first stage of his defense of the efficacy of the Lord's word by pointing out that its apparent failure is really the failure of some men to grasp it. If Paul's whole argument is difficult to follow at this point, it is largely because he remains true to his initial assertion in 9, 6: "It is not that God's word has failed ["fallen down," *ekpeptōken*]." Rather, some men have stumbled over what God has done. Paul will never compromise his position by saying that God's word has not failed *altogether,* or that it was substantially fulfilled, even though frustrated in some details or to some ex-

279

tent. He concedes no failure whatsoever as far as *God's* word and deed are concerned. The failure he does instance is a failure to grasp what God has done, and this failure is evidenced in false striving. Thus, while implying culpability (or at least what might be termed "objective" guilt), Paul does not really rest content with saying that Israel was at fault or that Israel disbelieved. He endeavors to highlight the element that needed to be grasped by an understanding in faith, and the kind of false perspective that blocked the appreciation of God's powerful word.

Paul's question, "What, then, shall we say?" (v. 30a), places the following remarks in the foregoing context of God's manifest accomplishment. God has not acted according to human expectation or human norms, but by his free choice (9, 6–13). This free choice is by no means unjust, for it is mercy ordered to the realization of God's glory, which cannot as such be affected or frustrated by men (9, 14–18). In the realization of this objective, God cannot be judged to have acted with brute force, but must be acknowledged to have acted according to a creative design finalized in judgment and salvation. Even with regard to those who (on Paul's ever-present practical supposition of their own responsibility) are on the road to destruction, God has shown forbearance; the overriding perspective for understanding God's action, however, is that he prepares men for his glory. This he has done without discriminating between Jew and gentile (9, 19–24). The actual fulfillment accords with the word of God in scripture (9, 25–30). What, then, are we to say to account for the fact of such *paradoxical* fulfillment which has entailed the blessing to gentiles and the disbelief of so many in Israel? What are we to say in the face of what God has actually done insofar as this involves special favor to some men and notable defection on the part of others?

The general response to this question (9, 30b–31) amounts to a further understanding of the way in which God intended to fulfill his word. Paul correspondingly presents in verses

280

32–33 the reason for Israel's defection as an actual and tragic misunderstanding of God's new structure. The contrast in verses 30–31 is somewhat subtle, for it is meant to elucidate the way in which one should understand God's action. It is not really intended to place praise or blame on any group. Paul does not state baldly that the gentiles did not pursue justice, but that Israel did pursue it. Nor does he say that the gentiles have obtained justice whereas Israel has not obtained it. He does say in effect precisely this: a) that in the one case, non-striving actually proved fruitful, because the result obtained was a justice given, a justice from faith; and b) that in the other case, striving was unfruitful, because the object pursued was misunderstood; it was not recognized as a stumbling block, something in the way of man's "running" or achieving justice by his own human efforts. In the case of the gentiles, it is the remarkable effect that stands out: the imparting of justice unaccounted for simply in terms of human striving, for the gentiles had not striven for it. In the case of Israel, it is the non-realization of the law that expressed the ideal and norm of justice. Why? Because Israel pursued a *law* of justice, a formulation of the ideal and norm of justice. In pursuing a law of justice, that is, a formulated pattern of life, Israel did not even attain the standard set by the law itself. The defective factor was not the law nor was it really their striving after the norm and ideal of justice contained in the law. As verse 32 makes clear, their non-attainment of law is to be accounted for by a lack of the proper perspective. They thought of the law of justice as a good which they could accomplish by their merely human striving rather than as an ideal which God alone would make realizable. They did not see that attaining the law meant first obtaining justice demanded by the law but realized in faith (through the person who is the basis for justice and the fulfillment of law; cf. 10, 4).

There is a certain irony in the text concerning the stumbling block of which we must become aware if we are not to misunderstand the Apostle and draw grim conclusions which can beget a gruesome theological outlook. The passage focuses not

281

on God's intention but on God's action and its twofold effect. The irony lies in regarding the result from a point of view (God's intention) that is not really the subject about which the writer is talking. The very abhorrence of attributing to God the intention of trapping his people is part of the theological art of achieving the proper perspective for grasping the mystery; the discerning reader is expected to seek and find the meaning of the statement in the *other* aspect implied. The other aspect here is the twofold effect produced by one and the same thing, depending on men's apprehension or misapprehension of God's action. On the one hand, the stumbling block (which is also the "rock to trap them") is the stone as it trips one who runs his own course mindless of what has been done by the one who placed the stone. On the other hand, the stone (now more clearly to be taken as personified in Christ) serves as the basis for an edifice that will not confound the one who relies on him.

B. *Romans 10*

In the following chapter (Romans 10), Paul expresses his hope for Israel's salvation, but concentrates on the understanding of justice that is needed to guide their zeal, and on the way in which this justice is disclosed. He concludes by saying that it is not really the proclamation of God's justice (through faith) that has been deficient, but Israel's response, in which zeal has been displayed as hostility. Thus, he advances his thesis in defense of God's word by showing that, while it provides the needed fulfillment for Israel's zeal, and while it has not been communicated in a deficient way, God's word of justice has not been acknowledged but has occasioned a "zealous hostility." Paul does not blame, much less excoriate, his kindred, though he does find as the explanation for their conduct the disobedience of which Isaiah spoke. Paul's principal aim, therefore, is not to exercise moral judgment but to propose a doctrinal understanding of that which contributes towards his people's salvation. His exposition in Romans 10 is fully in line with his prayer (Romans 10, 1).

10,	1a	Brothers, my heart's desire and my prayer to God for them
	1b	is that they may be saved.
	2a	I bear them witness
	2b	that they do have zeal for God,
	2c	but a zeal not according to higher knowledge.
	3a	For, not acknowledging God's justice,
	3b	but seeking to set up their own,
	3c	they have not submitted to God's justice.
	4a	The real end of law is Christ
	4b	for justice to everyone who believes.
	5a	For Moses writes of the justice from law that
	5b	"the man who accomplishes will live" by that justice.
	6a	But the justice that comes from faith reads thus:
	6b	"Do not say in your heart, 'Who can go up to heaven?' "
	6c	(meaning to bring Christ down),
	7a	"or, 'Who can go down into the abyss?' "
	7b	(meaning to bring Christ up from the dead).
	8a	How does it read?
	8b	"The message is [quite] near you,
	8c	on your lips and in your heart"
	8d	(meaning the message of faith that we preach).
	9a	Because if you confess with your lips that Jesus is Lord
	9b	and believe in your heart that God raised him from the dead,
	9c	you will be saved.
	10a	One believes in his heart for justification,
	10b	and one confesses with his lips for salvation.
	11a	For scripture says:
	11b	"Anyone who has faith in him will never be put to shame."
	12a	There is indeed no discrimination between Jew and Greek,
	12b	for the same one is Lord over everyone
	12c	and has wealth in abundance for all who call upon him; for
	13	"everyone who calls upon the name of the Lord will be saved."

Although this chapter begins with a recognition of Israel's zeal and ends with an indictment of Israel's disobedience, its main purpose is to indicate how God's justice has been made known (in Christ, involving faith, and therefore through the apostolic preaching). Paul's answer to the apparent non-realization of God's word is to expose further the way in which one should recognize its superlative realization. As ever, Paul's overriding purpose is to bring his readers to a deeper and more appreciative understanding of what God, beyond the measure of human expectation, has actually done. He endeavors to bring his readers to maintain at all time the proper theological perspective in judging the course of events (however tragic) in salvation history personally realized in Christ.

The hope for salvation dominates Paul's exposition from the outset (10, 1). He then mentions Israel's zeal and its false object, setting up a justice according to their own ideas, in order to show how God's justice is effectively realized. Christ is the "end" of law not simply as law's termination, but as its fulfillment, its flowering. For, in him justice is made available to everyone, not just to those who possess the law and vindicate it for themselves. God's justice is fulfilled by being extended beyond the limited framework of the ideal given to one people, especially beyond that ideal as construed to be *theirs* rather than as altogether *God's*.

Israel's defection involves at its most profound level a failure to understand the necessary all-pervasiveness of God's standards and God's action. As long as a man sets his sights on what he himself accomplishes as attributable (in any minuscule measure) ultimately or exclusively to himself and not to God, he will never really attain God's justice according to "higher knowledge." Implicitly, he will think of himself as "adding" to what God has done instead of instrumentalizing God's all-pervading action without ultimately referring the credit to himself. He will therefore tend inevitably to measure fulfillment by works he can do or has done or should accomplish rather than by the activity that God will make really possible for him. When God does something that does not fit into his categorized outlook, he will consequently fall short, that is, fail to accept or recognize the fulfillment (supposing, of course, that he remains fixed in his basic outlook).

The difference of perspective that is entailed in understanding justice is brought out in 10, 5 ff. by means of a citation from Deuteronomy 9, 4 or 30, 12 ff. (Romans 10, 5), and in an interpretative citation of Deuteronomy 30, 11–14 via a targum (a highly interpretative Aramaic translation that reflects a way the text was understood in a living tradition) (Romans 10, 6–8; cf. Lyonnet). What is "written" is contrasted to what the text "says" (that is, "how it reads" in the sense of "what it *means*"). Once again, Paul's standpoint for understanding what the text means is not the Old Testament text itself or the targumic tradition through which he cites the Old Testament, but the actual understanding of fulfillment which he himself possesses. How are we to account, then, for his citing a targum? Part of the answer is that, by citing a targum, Paul appropriately prepares the reader to see the central issue, namely, the way in which justice must be grasped. It must be *understood* (hence it is spoken of by way of an *interpretative* translation of God's word). In the very process that he uses (targumic approach) to indicate *how* justice is realized (in Christ as preached), Paul also indicates that perspective, viewpoint, a *way of understanding* is also absolutely essential. The manner of citation is part of his message.

What Moses *writes* regards the justice from law; there is question here of the "letter." What one *does* (accomplishes) becomes then the key term in this perspective. Paul does not deny that accomplishment is necessary, though it becomes clear from other passages that he thinks that the law cannot of itself make possible the realization of the ideal that it proposes and that man cannot of himself really accomplish what the law sets forth as a norm and ideal of action. In this passage, however, the latter considerations are only implicit suppositions. Paul seems here to cite Moses in order to articulate a perspective that is *inadequate*: the perspective of law, of the letter, of human accomplishment. He goes on to cite the Old Testament again (and, in effect, to cite "Moses," for he is remotely citing Deuteronomy), but he does so in order to bring out a way of understanding justice adequately. To convey this further perspective, he uses a different formula of citation ("says" or "reads" [*legei*] instead of "writes" [*graphei*]), cites the Old

285

Testament through a targum, and refers to the subject of the citation not as "Moses" but as "justice" (thereby indicating that it is not the human speaker but the divine theme or gift that is really in question). Justice from law entails a human perspective and stops short of the adequate perspective; justice from faith involves further understanding focused on the one who realizes the law: justice from faith consists in personal fulfillment of the law in Jesus Christ.

The meaning that Paul discerns in "justice from faith" emerges from his manner of citing the Old Testament text in Romans 10, 6–8, and can more fully be appreciated (though not deduced!) by noting the meaning of the Old Testament text on various levels of its transmission. In the Old Testament text proper, the point is that the law has been given the people so that they can observe it. It stands clearly before them as something to be accomplished. In the targum, the point seems to be that the word of the law is still operative. No further prophetic action, like that of Moses (who went up to heaven) or Jonah (who went into the abyss) is needed to supplement the substantial truth in the law given by Moses. The law as present in the word read in the synagogue adequately expresses God's will. The Jews are not to exonerate themselves from observing it by implying that their present knowledge is not adequate and that they need a prophet to bring to them genuine knowledge (or a fuller share of it).

The targumic view apparently seems to be equally or more at odds with Paul's view than that of Deuteronomy! For the targum seems to imply that the law itself will actually work (which does not seem to be the assumption in key texts of the Deuteronomic history). But Paul finds it useful, for it brings out the truth that the "law" is present in the word that is proclaimed. As "Moses," that is, "law," was present to Jews of later times in the word transmitted to them, so Christ, the fulfillment of the law, is present in the word that is preached, even though he is not present in the flesh. Personal fulfillment of the law is actuated through the communicated word of the authentic

286

speaker. The "justice of faith" is to be understood as accomplishment of God's will in Christ and, at the same time, as the presence of Christ in the word that is preached by the Apostle. The "justice of faith" is present and operative in the "word of faith" that is preached. For both "justice" and "the word" are understood in terms of Christ's being the perfect expression of God's law. The gospel is a personal communication of the definitively personalized law.

Thus Romans 10, 5–8 develops verse 4a ("The real end of law is Christ") by placing "justice" (the ideal of the law) in the perspective of what God has done in Christ rather than in the perspective of what man is to accomplish, and by showing that Christ (and therefore the basis for the realization of justice) is present and operative in the word that is preached. In turn, Romans 10, 9–13 develops verse 4b (". . . for justice to everyone who believes") by showing that justice is now made realizable on a universal scale through profession of faith in the word. Again, the perspective is insistently that of a divine and not a human dimension for fulfillment (cf. v. 3). God's justice is made "fuller" and therefore is "fulfilled" by the realization of his sovereignty over all men, not just over the Jews. For Paul, it goes without saying that the oneness of God stands as the great declaration of the law and that this oneness was to be effectively realized by the allegiance of a people, Israel. Even the oneness of Israel made sense only in terms of the oneness of God, God's being and acting as one over his people. Accordingly, Paul sees the fulfillment of law in the attestation of faith on the part of all men, Greek as well as Jew. The realization of God's universal sovereignty at the present time lies in the recognition as Lord of the one whom he (the Father) has raised from the dead, and who personally guarantees in himself the law of life under God. This recognition, of course, is made in faith, in acclamation of God's power with a view to salvation (risen life in God's Son).

By "salvation" Paul has in mind mainly the culmination of "justice" in the resurrection. He cannot develop the idea of "justice" (v. 4b) without putting it into the context of faith, and he cannot put it into his context without thinking of the full realization in reference to its inchoative realization. That is why he plays on the idea of "lips and heart" (v. 8c), which, together, bring out the total involvement that faith supposes. Both express the confession of faith, but the implications of this confession are spelled out in terms of different persons (Jesus and the Father, v. 9) and different stages of the eschatological period: past and present (God raised him; he is Lord, v. 9ab); present and future (justification and salvation, v. 10ab). Obviously, the distinctions made here are not to lead one to *separate* the elements involved in the distinctions. But the distinctions do highlight the various aspects of the eschaton which are vital if we are to grasp Paul's notion of fulfillment, and they bring out beautifully the way in which faith unifies the understanding of all that God has begun and will fully accomplish in the era of fulfillment.

Thus far in chapter 10, Paul has expressed this hope for Israel's salvation and has shown both the needed perspective for salvation (fulfillment of *God's* justice) and the practical way in which salvation can be attained (through acknowledging God's universal justice in fulfillment of the law *by professing faith in Christ*). He now argues that the good news is there for the hearing (vv. 14–17), but that Israel has not listened to it (vv. 18–21).

10, 14a	Now, how can men call upon one in whom they have not believed?
14b	or believe in one whom they have not heard?
14c	or hear without a preacher?
15a	or preach unless they will have been sent?
15b	Accordingly, scripture says:
15c	"How welcome are the footsteps of those preaching good tidings!"
16a	But not everyone has heeded the good news,
16b	for Isaiah says:
16c	"Lord, who has believed what he has heard from us?"
17a	Faith is therefore something that comes from hearing,
17b	and the hearing in question comes through Christ's message.

18a   I ask, then, have they not heard it?
18b   Of course they have:
18c   "Their voice has gone out through the whole world
18d   and their words to the ends of the earth."
19a   I ask, then, has Israel not recognized it?
19b   Listen first to Moses:
19c   "I shall make you zealous," he says, "against a nation that is
                                no nation;
19d   I shall make you angry with a nation that has no
                         understanding."
20a   And Isaiah even dares to say:
20b   "I have let myself be found by those who did not seek me;
20c   I have shown myself to those who did not ask for me."
21a   Then to Israel he says:
21b   "All day long I have stretched out my hands
21c   to a disobedient and hostile people."

In verses 14–17, Paul first indicates the interrelationship between the profession of faith of which he has just spoken and the apostolic preaching in fulfillment of scripture. The profession of faith depends on acceptance in faith; acceptance in faith depends on hearing (the central point in this series); hearing on preaching; and preaching on one's being sent (v. 14). In effect, hearing is the welcome given the apostolic preaching (v. 15). But "hearing" is not just a physical act. It must be understood as heeding a prophetic word. To underscore this point, Paul cites Isaiah 53, 1 (v. 16) in conjunction with his previous citation of Isaiah 52, 7. The development of thought in verses 14–16 gives special resonance and connotations to Paul's conclusion in verse 17. Faith comes from hearing in the sense that it entails a willingness to listen to the apostolic preaching of the gospel. This preaching, in turn, is one with Christ's own message, so that the "hearing" is a heeding of God's justice in Christ, not radically an obedience to men.

Since the message of salvation according to the higher knowledge of God's justice, that in Christ, has been made available in the apostolic preaching, Israel must have "heard" it, even in the physical sense of the word "to hear" (vv. 18 ff.). To affirm this, Paul once more cites scripture, this time citing a text that implicitly brings out the character of the apostolic preaching as a fulfillment of the law as well as of the prophets. For the psalm cited in verse 19 (Psalms 19, 5) speaks of the declaration of the law in all creation. But Israel has not recognized this fulfillment of the law. To make this concluding point, Paul cites both the law (Moses) and the prophets (Isaiah) (vv. 19–21). The first quotation takes up a theme on which this chapter opened, Israel's "zeal" (*zēlos*), speaking of it now as God's "making them zealous" (*parazēloō*). Paul understands the text in Deuteronomy 32, 21 in the light of Israel's hostility to the gentiles, whom they regard (in the perspective of the old law) as a non-nation (for the gentiles did not acknowledge the one God who really makes a people a people in the adequate, theological sense), and as a nation without understanding (for the gentiles did not have the knowledge of God given in the law). By attributing this hostility to God's action, Paul is obviously neither imputing sin to God nor exonerating Israel of responsibility. Rather, he is placing Israel's non-recognition of the gospel in the perspective of what has actually happened in the working out of God's fulfilling the law. A narrow particularism lies at the root of their non-recognition of the gospel.

It should be noted, however, that Paul is not judging Israel in the sense of accusing Israelites of personal sin. In accord with principles he enunciates elsewhere, he does not presume to judge the way a person actually stands before God. Only God judges the heart. Paul's judgment takes a more objective and doctrinal form, not the form of an individual, personal verdict. He sees at issue in Israel's hostility to those whom they regard as being without understanding a deficiency of understanding precisely within Israel. Their zealous hostility is the way in which their zeal, not according to higher knowledge, has proved itself.

The final quotation is twofold. The first part (v. 20; cf. Isaiah 65, 1) speaks of God's openness to the gentiles and his initiative in manifesting himself to them. This quotation gives the general perspective of prophetic fulfillment as opposed to

290

the particularistic stance of the zealous legalist. The second part of the quotation (v. 21; cf. Isaiah 65, 2) shows that Israel is by no means excluded from God's openness, but that the fault consists in their own disobedience (more precisely, "disbelieving") and hostility ("gainsaying" God's word). Thus, while placing their false zeal in the perspective of events that have come to pass according to God's action (v. 19), Paul does not represent God's own action as hostile. His dominant perspective, established by the stronger ("bolder," "more daring") second statement, is that God is open to all, even to Israel.

Thus, in the first stage of his argument in Romans 9–11, Paul showed that God's word has not failed, but has been realized for the free promise that it is, without injustice, for it expresses God's forbearance and especially his mercy according to the faith that he has made possible, rather than according to man's effort (Romans 9). The "key" to understanding apparent non-fulfillment is to be found in a keener appreciation of how God's past election finds realization in present justice, not in construing God's will as brute force or in regarding his justice as something that is effected by men. In the second stage of his argument (Romans 10), Paul shows that present fulfillment of God's justice is directed to universal salvation. At fault is not God's word (the fulfillment of the law, justice from faith, in Christ), but Israel's false zeal. Again, the "key" to understanding apparent non-fulfillment is to be found in a higher knowledge of fulfillment. Even Israel, however, for all its false zeal, is not excluded from the perspective of justice fulfilled in salvation. In the third stage of his argument (Romans 11), Paul will develop this hope for Israel's salvation, finding the "key understanding" in the mystery of God's creative, universal mercy. The ultimate answer to Job's personal misery lay in the mystery of God's creative power; the ultimate answer to Paul's personal grief over the tragedy of Israel's defection will be found to lie in the mystery of God's creative power for universal salvation, in his bringing about a greater good, namely, mercy to all.

291

C. *Romans 11*

11, 1a I ask, therefore, "Has God repudiated his people?"
   1b By no means!
   1c For I, too, am an Israelite—of the stock of Abraham,
                                   of the tribe of Benjamin.
   2a "God has not repudiated that people of his" he knew of old.
   2b Or do you not know what scripture says in the story of Elijah
   2c as he pleads to God against Israel:
   3a   "Lord, they have killed your prophets,
   3b   they have torn down your altars;
   3c   I alone am left,
   3d   and they are seeking my life."
   4a What is the oracle in answer to him?
   4b   "I have left for myself seven thousand men
   4c   who have not bent the knee to Baal."
   5a Just so, then, even at the present time,
   5b a remnant remains according to the choice of grace.
   6a But if by grace, then not from works;
   6b otherwise grace would no longer be grace.
   7a Well, then?
   7b What Israel has sought for, it has not found;
   7c the chosen [remnant] has found it,
   7d the rest have been dulled.
   8a Accordingly, it is written:
   8b   "God has given them a spirit of numbness,
   8c   eyes that will not see and ears that will not hear,
   8d   even to this very day."
   9a And David says:
   9b   "Let their [sacrificial] table become a snare and a trap,
   9c   their stumbling block and retribution;
  10a   let their eyes be darkened and not see,
  10b   bend their backs down constantly."

In developing his thesis that God has not repudiated his people, Paul argues from what God has actually done in calling Paul himself and a remnant. He judges this event in the light of the fidelity of a small but representatively full number (seven thousand) whom God reserved for himself in the time of Elijah. Paul regards as the crucial element in the understanding of the remnant the fact that it is God's grace and not man's accomplishment that really explains the remnant. The fulfillment of God's election can be grasped only from the standpoint of his special favor. If it were judged from the standpoint of man's achievement, then one would have to say that God's action has been to some extent frustrated; God's grace would not be the sovereign power for fulfillment that it actually is and must be acknowledged to be. While the efficacious grace of election implies human acceptance and "co-working," it is not really explained by human acceptance or human working; though it implies human acts, it is not explained as a human accomplishment.

Paul concludes (vv. 7 ff.) that Israel has "sought" without finding what it really needed, for the goal to be discovered is discernible only by God's disclosure. It is grace that truly accounts for achieving ("finding"), and, therefore, for the constitution of the people devoted to him alone. The fact that Paul does not specify here the objects of "seeking" and "finding"— even though the objects are relatively clear from the preceding discussion—testifies to the fact that he wants to point out the genuinely efficacious factor; his main perspective is that of efficacious action, namely, God's grace. The alternative to attaining or finding by grace is "dullness," lack of perception. In the bold, anthropomorphic imagery of the Old Testament, Paul expresses this dullness in terms of divine deeds and the curse that the psalmist levels against his enemies. In effect, the very absence of grace is the curse.

We would be mistaken were we to construe these quotations as an attribution of hostility to God or as Paul's desire for non-conversion. Such an understanding would fly in the face of Paul's express statements elsewhere and impose contradictions on him. The normative factor for understanding Paul is Paul's own dominant perspective. This perspective is not that of a psychology of God but of understanding the salvific event in terms of God's concrete action according to freely bestowed and fully effective grace, beyond the measure of human accomplishment. Furthermore, the Apostle's principal perspective entails a contrast between what God does and what man cannot do of himself, not a contrast between what God does to some and not to others. The latter perspective would be inadequate and perilous as a *basic* perspective, with the result that all kinds of misconceptions could follow with apparent logic. For, as a basic perspective, it would imply one thing that Paul would find inconceivable, namely, that grace is somehow (of itself or in God's liberality) intrinsically limited in scope. It would imply a limitation (namely, humanly circumscribed definition) of the universal power of grace and of the universal salvific will which God has manifested in Christ (whom Paul does not regard as merely human). As a *secondary* perspective it is admissible, but only if we assume the mystery of human freedom in the non-acceptance of grace. And in this case we must then understand human "freedom" in non-acceptance as a defective freedom, an inadequate response in the face of God's *de facto* achievement.

Paul has not "solved" the mystery of God's choice or grace. The creative mystery of God's power is not a problem like a tangled shoelace, which one "solves" by loosing or cutting it. Nor is it a massive block which our minds whittle into comprehensible shape, lessening its substance in the process. Mystery is more like a fascinating jewel, which must be contemplated from different facets and in varying lights to be appreciated and properly valued. Even this precious-stone image of mystery is woefully deficient, for it omits the element of vital activity. Paul has provided us with the latter, however, because he has provided us with the basic primary perspective for contemplating the mystery: that which God actually works out, and human life in hope of superhuman fulfillment. It is because Paul's basic perspective is that of the power of God's "superhumanizing" grace for all, even those who have stumbled, that he can proceed as he does:

11, 11a I ask, then, have they stumbled so as to fall completely?
   11b Definitely not!
   11c Rather, through their falling away salvation has come for the
                                            gentiles
   11d to rouse their zeal!
   12a If their falling away has meant the world's enrichment,
   12b if their loss has meant the gentiles' gain,
   12c how much more will their fulfillment mean?

294

13a I have a word for you gentiles:
13b   Being Apostle of the gentiles,
13c   I glorify my ministry
14a   in hopes of rousing the zeal of my kindred
14b   and saving some of them.
15a For if their rejection has meant reconciliation of the world,
15b what will their acceptance mean but life from the dead?
16a   If the first loaf is holy, so is the whole batch;
16b   if the root is holy, so are the branches.
17a   If some of the branches have been broken off,
17b   and you, though a wild olive, have been grafted among them
17c   and have become a sharer of the rich sap of the olive tree,
18a   do not boast that you are superior to the branches!
18b   If you do boast, [remember this:]
18c   it is not you who sustain the root;
               the root is sustaining you.
19a   You will say, then:
19b   "But the branches were broken off that I might be grafted on."
20a   That is true.
20b   But they were broken off by disbelief,
20c   and it is by faith that you stand where you do.
20d   Do not think highly [of yourself]; beware!
21a   For if God did not spare the native branches,
21b   neither will he spare you.
22a   Consider, then, the kindness and severity of God:
22b   his severity on those who fell off
22c   and his kindness towards you—
22d   provided you remain [faithful] to his kindness;
22e   otherwise, you, too, will be pruned away.
23a   And the others, if they do not remain in disbelief
23b   will be grafted on again.
23c   God certainly is able to graft them on again!
24a For if you, cut from an olive tree that was by nature wild,
24b   have been grafted, contrary to nature, onto the cultivated
                                                            olive tree,
24c how much more easily will these natural branches
24d   be grafted back onto their own tree?

The reason for Paul's affirmation that Israel's stumbling does not mean a complete fall, a definitive collapse, is once again God's power, as manifested in a process that is basically salvific. That this is Paul's chief perspective in discussing Israel's recovery is borne out by the way Paul reintroduces the expression "to rouse zeal." The salvation that has come to the gentiles can be regarded as "rousing the zeal" of Israel in two different ways.

From the narrow standpoint of their understanding of the law, Israel is roused to a hostile zeal—as already indicated in 10, 19. From the standpoint of the salvific action of God, however, Israel can be roused to a zeal of "emulation" (11, 11d). Thus, from the perspective of God's power for salvation, Israel's "zeal" can be regarded (as here) as instrumental in Israel's recovery.

Paul himself hopes to rouse the zeal of his kindred in this way (11, 14a), that is, by pointing to the more universal good that his apostolate to the gentiles represents. He "glorifies" his ministry by presenting it as God's power for the salvation of all men. His hope for the salvation of his own people is realistic; he says he hopes to save "some," though obviously he would want to save all. Nevertheless, his optimism is doctrinally as strong as is his understanding of God's power for salvation. It is, moreover, an optimism based not on his own efforts or on the period of his own apostolate, but on the total picture of eschatological fulfillment. Perspective, then, is all-important: the perspective of God's power for salvation and the perspective of its total context, the eschatological period.

Paul's optimism in the total perspective of eschatological fulfillment is thrice marked in the thought progression of this passage (vv. 12, 15, and 24). Each of the statements in this series enunciates in an *a fortiori* manner the hope for Israel's recovery. The first statement looks to the "fulfillment" of Israel, to the wholeness of Israel's recovery. But it is no more legitimate to construe this prophetically expressed hope as a guarantee of the salvation of a given percentage in Israel or as an infallible prediction of the conversion of the Jews in large numbers than to construe a similar line of argument in Romans 5, 1–11 as guaranteeing the salvation of all Christians. The grounds for Paul's statements are not to be found in the human potential of Israel itself or in the predicted response on Israel's part, but in the results that God has worked out even with Israel's defection. The more universal good actually accomplished grounds the hope for Israel itself; the benefit for the particular group is seen in the context of the general good, with implicit emphasis on the salvific power of God which accounts for this general good. Significantly, Paul makes no flat statement about what *will* happen but gives an *a fortiori* argument based on God's action against all merely human expectations. His statement is to be taken as a prophetic declaration, not (as Oesterreicher seems to think) as a prediction of specific fact.

In the second statement (v. 15), Paul speaks of the defection of Israel in bolder terms. He does not mention their "falling away" or their own "loss"; he speaks of "rejection" and "acceptance." From his general statement in 11, 11a and especially at the beginning of this chapter (v. 1ab), it is clear that Paul does not understand "rejection" as repudiation by God. But it would seem to be quite out of keeping with his general perspective to try to conceive "rejection" simply in terms of another one-sided action, namely, *Israel's* rejection of God. Paul does not rest his theological understanding on a personal verdict concerning Israel's responsibility, but rather on the concrete situation as evidence of what God has actually done. In this light, Israel's "rejection" is the *de facto* defection that has resulted in the reconciliation of a greater multitude, the whole world. If we take as Paul's basic affirmation and perspective in faith the fact that God is bringing out of this catastrophe a greater good for Israel itself, we can see how his conclusion is that their *de facto* "acceptance" is the prophetically expected manifestation of God's power in the eschatological period: the resurrection, life from the dead.

Paul is not affirming that Israel will be converted at the resurrection; the resurrection lies beyond the time for repentance and conversion. He is judging the real possibility for Israel's conversion in terms of the working out of God's grace. His viewpoint implies the certainty of Israel's salvation as a whole, but the basis of his eschatological hope is resolutely God's power, not Israel's predicted response. Actually, Paul's assertion tells us less about Israel's *de facto* conversion and still less (if anything) about the *time* of Israel's conversion, than

297

about his own vision of God's power for salvation. Perhaps it is inevitable that men want to know what will happen, whether or not this person or that person or a whole people (which is the same problem writ large) will be saved. Paul really offers us no assurance concerning *who* will be saved or even concerning the *de facto* salvation of a given people considered as a collection of individuals. He does provide a hope, and that hope is more than either a velleity or an earnest desire; it is an eschatological and therefore certain hope predicated on the basis of what has already been accomplished in the eschatological process.

But whence does the hope spring? The hope springs from God's power, not from mere man's response. To suppose otherwise would be to reverse Paul's whole fundamental conception of grace. Thus, precisely as he expresses his hope for Israel's salvation, Paul does not really affirm the conversion of a multitude of Jews—much less their conversion shortly before the parousia. Paul affirms his understanding of divine power to bring about their access to God, and the basis for his affirmation of this power (which he obviously yearns to see realized) is that their defection does not weaken it: God's power has already been shown to surpass their expectations, and it is more than enough—just as resurrection follows from the power of reconciliation—to remedy their weakness.

Before stating for the third time (v. 24) his hope of Israel's conversion—rooted not in *Israel's expected response* but in a *fitting exercise of God's power*—Paul cautions the gentiles against a form of self-assertion analogous to the defective outlook of Israel. To attribute to oneself what is really God's favor is a cardinal error. Israel's being rejected is not to be conceived as a total denial of grace on God's part, a complete desacralization. Accordingly, the insertion of the gentiles means that God grants them a share in the grace-determined consecration of Israel. The inserted branches cannot consider themselves better than the others; the point of reference for "boasting" (confident rejoicing in one's present advantage) is the trunk

298

which sustains all the branches. The basic perspective for understanding one's position is not "what we have" as opposed to "what they do not have" but what both have in accordance with God's action. Considering once more the *de facto* situation of the circumstances under which the gentiles have been inserted (vv. 19 f.), and expressing this by way of finality (for he is not considering the fact from the standpoint of God's intention or abstract decree), Paul admits that the branches were broken off so that the gentiles might be grafted on. No sooner does he concede this, however, than he points out how the statement is to be understood: not by supposing an arbitrary whim on God's part, but by recognizing that the very condition for being in the tree (and for being able to boast) is faith. Since faith itself is ultimately to be understood in terms of God's benevolent grace, one cannot look simply to himself. God's "severity" (his "cutting off," *apotomia*) is still to be reckoned with, for it amounts to a pruning of those who do not remain faithful to his kindness.

It should be evident that the metaphor of the olive tree is not to be pressed in a material sense. For instance, we should not suppose that the number of branches is predetermined, so that if some are added others must be cut off, or that if those that have been cut off are added, some of those that have been inserted must be removed to make room for them. Such a literal interpretation of the image that Paul employs is excluded by the Apostle's very understanding of God's power as a vital energy abundantly sufficient for all. It is also excluded by the fact that Paul does not take his own metaphor in a physical sense, but makes some paradoxical alterations to clarify his position. The theological point of view which is at work can be inferred from the violence that Paul does to the image itself.

From the standpoint of horticulture, an inserted branch of a wild olive tree will render the cultivated olive tree fruitful, or an inserted branch of a cultivated olive will become fruitful when grafted onto a wild olive tree. Paul says neither; his own statement simply does not correspond to physical fact. Accord-

299

ingly, a "factual" point of view like that indicated in a literal understanding of the branches numbered in the full olive tree cannot be ascribed to Paul. In verse 24, both the wild and the natural branches survive and become fruitful by reason not of their own properties but by reason of their being in the tree. The precise point that Paul makes along these lines is that an event that seems contrary to nature has actually been accomplished so that the growth that is more fitting to begin with can more certainly be accomplished. Moreover, since the whole process is viewed from this standpoint of grace, Paul does not and cannot introduce into God's activity the note of necessity. Consequently, Paul cannot be regarded as predicting that the Jews will necessarily be reinstated by being converted to Christianity. His hope for the Jews' salvation is perhaps even more optimistic than his hope for the salvation of all the gentiles. Nevertheless, his hope is not a forecast, a prediction of fact; it is a declaration of the fitting and quite possible further exercise of God's revitalizing energy. To move from nothing to something grounds the proportionately lesser expectation of moving from something to everything. The Apostle does not prophesy the personal response in faith to God's own fidelity, and does not even try to do so (nor could he), for he is arguing theologically, centering everything on God's power as man's sole sufficiency. The foundation for his theologically enunciated hope is solely God's power to fulfill abundantly and most fittingly what he has begun.

In the closing lines of this chapter and of this section of Romans, the idea that has ruled Paul's argument from the outset finds its fullest expression: the mystery of God's power to realize an ever greater good. His answer to the problem concerning the fulfillment of God's word comes to full flower in prophetic declaration and prayerful acclaim of God's wisdom. Once again, the prophetic declaration is not as such a prediction of future fact but an enunciation of the mystery of God's creative power, which is the very marrow of the prophet's hope.

11, 25a Brothers, I do not want you to be unaware of this mystery,
   25b   in order that you may not be wise in your own estimation:
   25c   the dulling of Israel has been partial
   25d   until the full number of gentiles come in,
   26a   and thus all Israel will be saved,
   26b   as it is written:
   26c   "From Sion will come the rescuer:
   26d   he will banish impiety from Jacob.
   27a   And this is my covenant with them:
   27b   my taking away their sins."

   28a On the basis of the gospel
   28b   they are enemies [of God] on your account;
   28c on the basis of election
   28d   they are [his] loved ones on account of their fathers.
   29   God's call and gifts of grace are not regretfully revoked.
   30a Just as you formerly refused obedience to God
   30b   but have now been shown mercy
   30c   at their disobedience,
   31a so now have they refused obedience
   31b   at the mercy shown to you
   31c   that they, too, may now be shown mercy.
   32a For God imprisoned all in disobedience
   32b   in order to show mercy to all.

   33a O the depth of God's wealth,
   33b   his wisdom,
   33c   and his knowledge!
   33d   How inscrutable are his judgments
   33e   and untraceable his paths!
   34a   "For who has known the mind of the Lord?
   34b   or who has been his counsellor?
   35   or who has forestalled him in giving and earned a
                          recompense?"
   36a   For from him
   36b   and through him
   36c   and to him are all things;
   36d   glory is his through the ages. Amen.

The strictly theological perspective of God's wisdom and power is evident on a number of counts: the term "mystery" itself in verse 25a, the concluding doxology (vv. 33–36), and Paul's express intention in stating the mystery (v. 25b). Paul's express intention is to bring out the primacy of God's grace for an understanding of the situation of which Paul's gentile

301

hearers are a part. He states the mystery precisely to keep them from being wise in their own estimation, which means that he wants them to recognize the wisdom of God. If this strictly theological perspective is acknowledged, then Paul's enunciation of the mystery will be regarded properly not as an express prediction of future fact (much less with emphasis on the number of the saved) but as the declaration of a process of divine mercy which operates most efficaciously and which stands as the basis for prophetic optimism.

The "mystery" is stated not just in verse 25c (for the sentence is not completed at that point) but in verses 25c–26a, its context as salvation history being given in verses 26c–27b. The "mystery" is not so much a "fact" conceived statically as it is a process manifesting God's universal forgiveness in fulfillment of his word. The whole thrust of Paul's enunciation of the mystery is a thrust towards fulfillment over defection. The defection lies in the dulling of Israel in part. Paul has already asserted that those who have been "dulled" are those of Israel who are not the remnant (11, 7).

Just as his use of the "remnant" idea, however, is primarily a theological use, not a numerical assessment (though it may in fact prove to correspond to a numerical proportion), so his use of the expression "partial dulling" in 11, 25c is a consistent, theological expression (even though the actual number affected seems to be quite larger than this expression would suggest). The "partial" defection is positively related to the "fullness" (*plērōma,* v. 25d; cf. 11, 12c) of the gentiles. Again, this term should not be taken simply or primarily in the sense of a numerical quantity. It may well be a numerical quantity, but it is not to be judged from the standpoint of mathematics or of an historical, arithmetical enumeration. The "full number" (*plērōma*) is a "complement" in the theological sense of a fulfilled people of God. Accordingly, Paul concludes: "and thus all Israel will be saved."

Does "Israel" here refer in Paul's mind to Israel according to the flesh? Such was his view of Israel at the outset of this part of Romans (9, 3), and it would seem unjustified to deny that this sense obtains here as Paul concludes a unified discussion of the problem which affects him personally. Nevertheless, it should be noted that even in the context of Romans 9, 3, Paul considered his kindred according to the flesh not simply from a racist or nationalist standpoint but from the standpoint of those to whom God's favors had been shown, that is, from the standpoint of God's people, not from the standpoint of a people defined in merely human terms. "All Israel" in 11, 26a should be judged at least in the same theological light. It goes without saying that Paul looks for the salvation of the Jews in greater number, but his viewpoint in this regard is resolutely theological: not arithmetical increase as such but their "full complement" (*plērōma,* 11, 12c) is in question.

Paul does not abandon the theological understanding of "Israel" which he has stated at the outset of chapter 9. On the other hand, he does seem to have arrived at an even richer understanding of Israel by the development of thought in the passages preceding 11, 26a, notably in his remarks about the olive tree. In a sense, Israel is not just the native branches (whether remaining on the tree or broken off) as contrasted with the inserted branches of the wild olive tree; Israel is the whole tree, stock and branches. Consequently, while "all Israel" does refer to God's people of old and can therefore be contrasted with "gentiles," it cannot be understood *divisively,* as a separate entity, especially not in 11, 26a. It should be taken more complexively, connoting the incorporation of the gentiles as well as the fulfillment of Israel according to the flesh.

The framework of salvation history is the vital context for grasping this complexive view of Israel's salvation. The rescuer from Sion establishes with Jacob (all Israel) his covenant of forgiveness (vv. 26b–27b). It is God's word promising forgiveness that explains and will explain the whole *de facto* process of fulfillment. Accordingly, we should not conceive fulfillment in terms of the arithmetical number actually saved (which would be the viewpoint of factual history and chronicle

303

rather than the viewpoint of salvation history). Therefore, we should not construe Paul's enunciation of the mystery as a prediction of facts to be verified physically, but as a prophetic declaration of hope that rests totally on the theological perception of God's power and wisdom in accordance with his word. The Apostle is affirming something much more important than what will actually happen to man; he is affirming the salvific will and power of God. Much as the Old Testament prophets themselves, Paul is not disinterested in man's fate, but he does not fix his gaze on man's good as man's good; he focuses on what alone can achieve man's good and what transcends that limited interest, the dynamic salvific power of God. The viewpoint that J. L. McKenzie has predicated of the Old Testament prophets is eminently true of Paul:

God does not, as the Hebrews saw it, bring to pass this judgment and this kingdom in order that men may live the good life. They do, but the prophets were looking to something other than the best thing for man. They looked at the kingdom as a fulfillment in time and space of the divine reality, of the holiness of God Himself. . . . Whatever this may mean for man, he can hope for nothing better; and he must face this future . . . with a sweeping act of faith in the power of God for good.
The Two Edged Sword (Milwaukee, 1956), pp. 209–210.

We may reflect for a moment on the way Paul's vision of God's power for salvation finds fitting if puzzling expression in starkly paradoxical affirmations. Customarily, these are explained as part of his literary heritage from the Old Testament or as characteristic turns of the Semitic mind, in which result is often worded as purpose and nuances of volitive acts (willing, desiring, permitting, tolerating) are not carefully introduced. Factors of literary and cultural heritage surely play a significant part in explaining Paul's paradoxical modes of expression. But do we not need a further explanation—both to explain Paul's deliberate and repeated use of them and to penetrate through "what he says" to "what he sees," which goes beyond the compass of human language? Even after we have "qualified" Paul's

304

"Semitic" statements by distinguishing with a few feeble terms (willing, desiring, permitting, and so forth) or with some notional modifications of an abstractly speculative cast (such as, "according to forseen response") the infinite sweep of God's will, we seem really to be no closer to an understanding of the mystery than was Paul himself. We are probably not even as much attuned to the mystery of God's will as Paul was. In all likelihood, we have done no more than to have rendered Paul's statements more palatable to our own relatively abstract, culturally conditioned habits of thought. The irony in this procedure is that we may have missed capturing the Apostle's vision because we have stopped short with his formulation. We may have missed the sense of mystery which he intends to spark in our minds by the daring contrasts he utters. In any event, we can hardly expect to enter into the mind of the Apostle simply by muting with less disturbing qualifications his apostolically bold utterance of mystery (*parrhēsia*).

How shall we approach, then, such scandalous Pauline paradoxes like that in verse 32 concerning God's "imprisoning all to show mercy to all"? We shall simply have to become alert to the mystery that lies beyond the metaphors of "imprisoning" and "showing clemency" and that transcends human conceptualizations of God's will. The mystery here is that God's dynamic power for salvation is realized in human weakness. Human limitations only serve to disclose its unlimited energy to transform what it touches. Since the heart of the mystery is none other than God's transforming power confronting human limitations, Paul's theological expression takes the form of dialectical contrasts. The transformation amounts to such a radical change of the human condition that only a radical contrast will do to express it: the contrast between imprisonment and unmerited freedom. Since the working out of the transformation must be totally ascribed to God, and since God is considered not in himself (as if created being did not exist), but as he is known by us, in human images, both actions ("imprisoning," "showing mercy"), corresponding to the successive states of mankind in

305

relation to God, are predicated directly of God himself. This dialectical, imaginative description of God's total control of the entire process by no means supposes contrary or contradictory attitudes in God. Conceptualistic opposition of this kind would fall short of the unifying factor of analogy, which preserves the Pauline paradox from a dialectic of notional contradictions (after the manner of Hegel). The factor of analogy consists in this: God's freely bestowed mercy stands as the norm against which any human confinement or new freedom is measured. The total process, which rules our understanding of its dialectically contrasted movements, is not that describing a change in God, but a new relationship of men to God for which he alone actually accounts.

But formulating this unifying principle fittingly requires a kind of unsettling, anthropomorphic imagery. Anthropomorphic, because the formulation is a human attempt to understand God; unsettling, because a kind of awe-provoking shock stands as a prerequisite for understanding a mystery, somewhat as wonder is the beginning of human knowledge. Thus even man's defects are spoken of in terms of God's action, for it is really by God's salvific action that they are to be measured as defects. The defect, viewed theologically (that is, from the standpoint of mystery), serves above all to set in relief vital needs and the means actually offered, operative, and so forth, to provide for them.

The formulation is therefore intended to fix the hearer's attention on God, even though the formulation is spelled out in metaphors of concrete, human circumstances. Now, these concrete, human circumstances also require a twofold aspect in the formula, one of which we may call "negative" (the pejorative aspect, such as imprisoning all men), and the other "positive" (liberation by God's mercy). Paul characteristically views the movement from "negative" to "positive" as a dynamic imbalance; the negative always yields to the positive—not merely being "compensated for" but being "overcome," "surpassed." The dualism that really accounts for this dynamic imbalance

306

is not a dualism in God (Paul's monotheism could not abide this) but a dynamic, relational conception of God's salvific power, together with an awareness of the fact that things do not work out automatically, even though they are being brought to fulfillment. Paul is busy formulating precisely the salvific design of God as it actually works out. His formulation is not concerned simply with God as a kind of being perfectly abstracted from creation, but with the existential, personalistic totality: "God and all men in the working out of his design." To enunciate the all-important totality, it is fitting that there be one subject to the sentence. Since God's action is all-important in understanding what takes place, it is fitting that God be the subject of the verb(s) or of the principal statement. Since there are twofold human aspects to the effect, it is inevitable and even fitting that, for the sake of over-all unity of understanding, both of these, even the "negative" effect, be referred to God. But the dynamic imbalance which so regularly appears underscores what is really essential in understanding God's action: his power for creative fulfillment.

Should our attention focus on God's action as it exists in God himself, we would then have to take only that aspect which really befits God in himself. Paul would already have indicated what this is, namely, the salvific will of God—though even a "salvific will" makes little sense without persons to be saved. Accordingly, we must recognize the fact that Paul is not interested simply in God as existing by himself, perfectly abstracted from creation. The Apostle is interested in "more" than what many theologians who have culled citations from him have tried to understand, that is, the "thing" aspect of God, the "kind of being" that he is. Paul is interested in the relevant, personally existential totality for theological knowledge: who God is as shown in what God personally has done; God together with the whole of creation which he is bringing to fulfillment. I submit that it is only when we have recognized what Paul is treating and what his own basic perspectives are in treating it that we can really accept his statements without being scan-

307

dalized. To try to modify his form of expression all too frequently masks a lack of understanding or a somewhat mechanical attempt to make him over into a theologian of another age. He meant what he said and he said what he meant; we should be able to understand him on his own theological terms. Only once we have done this will we be in in a position to "translate" him into another theological idiom or to make use of his prophetic insights.

We may now return to comment on Romans 11, 28–32, which reaches its crescendo in the paradoxial enunciation of the way God's mercy has been shown. In reference to the gospel (God's power for salvation which they have not accepted), the men of Israel stand at odds with God because of the favor shown to the gentiles. Paul has in the back of his mind, no doubt, the "zeal" of Israel as manifested in their looking down on the gentiles (supposing their concept of a law of justice; cf. 10, 2). But Paul's point here is rather to indicate that their relationship to God has not come up to the standard of God's favor shown in his call of the gentiles. The present, however, is not the sole basis for God's judgment of them and therefore not the sole basis for a prophetic hope for their fulfillment. Accordingly, a further consideration is added in verse 28cd: in reference to God's own election they are beloved. For God has called them in the person of their fathers. These complementary statements are synthesized in a principle which voices Paul's understanding of God's firm will for salvation. God's call and gifts of grace are "irrevocable" in the sense that he does not revoke them as a man might regret offering something that was subsequently not accepted or properly used and then cease to offer it. God's continual personal concern, therefore, grounds optimism. Israel's past is the oracle of God's mercy for the future.

The tension between Israel's being at one time God's enemy and God's loved one arises from two different standpoints, both

308

of which have a common level: the standpoint of *Israel's* being enemy and the standpoint of *Israel's* being loved one, the standpoint of human persons in an historical context. The tension can ultimately be resolved by climbing to a further standpoint, that of *God's* persistent call and gifts of grace, though these, too, are conceived historically as personally bestowed gifts. Similarly, the paradoxical situation in which the gentiles have been shown mercy after disobedience and the Jews have refused obedience at the mercy shown to the gentiles is ultimately resolved not by contrasting what one group has and the other does not, but by relating both groups to the one who showed the favor in the context of salvation history. Disobedience, which is attributed to God's action in order to unify the total and ultimate perspective, is but the negative basis for God's personal achievement in abundance: mercy towards all. The paradoxical dialectic of events is explained from a purely theological standpoint, namely, from God's own accomplishment. Since this theological standpoint takes into account not precisely God's being in himself, but his personally communicated action in salvation history, it is understandable that Paul's formulation of God's actions will entail paradoxical attributions. For Paul is speaking of the total situation in the concrete imagery of personal action and personal response. So long as we do not impose on him a perspective that is alien to him, we need not be repelled or embarrassed by his bold statements. While his own theology is not metaphysical (conceived and enunciated in terms of "being" pure and simple) but metahistorical (conceived and enunciated in terms of personally salvific acts by which God fulfills his people in their lived experience), it implies by its consistent emphasis the basic principle for a metaphysical theology of God (namely, transcendent wisdom according to a totally salvific will of God as a beneficent kind of being).

The closing doxology (vv. 33–36) is much more than a pious appendix to Paul's theological discussion. In other contexts, his prayers enable us to grasp his exhortations more fully as enunciations of an affective theological appreciation of God's

309

grace. In a similar way, this doxology enables us to enter into Paul's personal and profoundly mystical theological outlook. The unifying principle of his whole doctrinal discussion in Romans 9–11 finds its fitting and ultimate formulation in this prayerful acclamation. God's wealth (v. 33a) is not forestalled in anyone else's giving (v. 35); his wisdom (v. 33b) is not to be seen as the result of anyone's counsel (v. 34b); his knowledge (v. 33c) cannot be plumbed by anyone less than the Lord himself (v. 34a). Even in Paul's exploration of it in an attempt at fuller understanding, the mystery remains intact; for all one's attempt to follow it, the mystery remains as rich as before: it is not dissolved or worked out like a mere problem. God's concrete judgments and his ways of working remain beyond human control through human calculation. This is not to say that the mystery admits of no understanding whatever. The foregoing development in three chapters excludes a concept of mystery as pure enigma. But the understanding of the mystery of God's salvific action (which is one way of defining the task of theology) must be suffused with reverence for the one who accounts for it and who cannot be approached as a problem, God himself. Accordingly, Paul moves from God's "attributes" and ways of acting (v. 33e, at the center of the concentric structure in vv. 33–35) to a clearer personal focus on God himself as the subject, means, and object of all things— although, even here (v. 36ac), the stress must fall not on the prepositions but on the personal object, "him." The final word of acclamation (v. 36d: "is" rather than "be") looks to the fulfillment of salvation history in terms of his glory. With that prayerful acclamation of the ultimate subjective principle of all personal fulfillment, we really have the dominant perspective of Paul's entire and quite coherent theological exposition.

310

CHAPTER THREE

PAUL'S GOSPEL

Perhaps the best reason for taking Romans 1, 16–8, 39 as representative of Paul's gospel is that he himself presents it as such. These eight unified chapters stand as the longest formal exposition of Paul's apostolic preaching. From the outset of his letter, he implies that his communication to the Romans is the message that he was called to preach among all the gentiles, including his present audience (1, 1–6). The gospel of God's Son is the spiritual service that he renders to God at all times; his writing the Romans is an advance exercise of the spiritual service that he hopes to perform when he will have been able to reach Rome in person (1, 9–15). The themes that he enunciates in 1, 16–17 and develops at least as far as Romans 8, 39 are prefaced by the statement that he is not ashamed of the gospel—a rhetorical understatement of the fact that he glories in the word of God which he has been commissioned to proclaim. The fuller elaboration of Paul's gospel includes the defense of God's power as sovereign wisdom (Romans 9–11) and an exhortation to the Christian community to respond in understanding love to the gifts of God's grace (Romans 12 ff.). But the first eight chapters are linked together (as we shall see along the course of our exposition) as a somewhat self-contained, doctrinal exposition of the principal themes enunciated in Romans 1, 16–17.

Other formulations of Paul's gospel are evident elsewhere in his works. Actually, his understanding of the gospel is operative in everything he enunciates, just as his apostleship is operative in everything he says and does. At times, however, we find rather explicit reference to basic, catechetical instruction. These references help us focus on the matters that Paul regarded as being of principal importance. They alert us to key elements in the more formal exposition of Romans 1–8 and are in turn illuminated by the fuller development that we find in that more formal exposition.

One of these references to catechetical instruction is found in the kerygmatic statement in 1 Corinthians 15, 1–11. This passage places Paul's gospel firmly in the main current of the apostolic preaching. It highlights the central mystery of the passion and resurrection according to the perspective of God's word in salvation history. "According to the scriptures" imparts to the declaration of Christ's death for our sins and his resurrection the theological context of fulfillment in salvation history. We shall see that in Romans 1–8 the twofold theme of the Christ event and the fulfillment of God's plan according to the scriptures are admirably blended. The twofold theme is evident in the opening lines of the letter (Romans 1, 1–4); it reaches a certain climax in Romans 3, 21–26 and in the pivotal chapter of the first part of the letter (Romans 5, 1–21). In general, by his major development of scriptural texts and themes from Romans 1, 17 through chapter 5, Paul moves back through the LXX text of the Old Testament: the prophets, the psalms, the Pentateuch (the rites indicated in Leviticus, the story of Abraham, the fall of Adam). Paul's perspective of fulfillment covers the whole Old Testament. The death and resurrection of Christ are developed at key points, notably from the point where the contrast with the law (and thus a characteristically Pauline understanding of fulfillment) has been made clear (3, 21 ff.). Since 1 Corinthians 15, 1–11 is meant to enunciate the apos-

312

tolic preaching in general, and is basically a borrowed formula, one does not expect to find in it a characteristic Pauline emphasis. Nevertheless, the characteristic Pauline emphasis in a formal development of the gospel like that in Romans 1–8 can more easily be discerned against the background provided by 1 Corinthians 15, 1–11.

Another reference to catechetical instruction is that given in 1 Corinthians 1, 18 ff., where Paul speaks of the word of the cross. With a paradoxical torque, Paul expresses the message of salvation in the negative terms of God's destruction of the wisdom of wise men of the world. His understanding of the gospel is radicated in a transcendent wisdom which is ultimately God's dynamic power. By his negative approach he intends to jolt his hearers into an awareness of the ultimate mystery to which the cross itself attests. His line of thought in Romans 1–8 is also developed against a starkly negative background involving the power and knowledge of God, and one of the principal points in the development of his announced themes comes with his discussion of Christ's death (Romans 3, 21–26).

In this connection, one should also refer to Galatians 3, 1 f. and Galatians 2, 15–21. For, in Galatians 3, 1 f., Paul alludes to his proclamation to the Galatians and what this implied. In the immediately preceding passage (Galatians 2, 15–21) he had just stated his case with Cephas for understanding the conduct expected in mixed Christian communities, such as at Antioch. Although the circumstances of controversy, whether in Galatia or at Antioch, dictate in large measure what Paul says in both of these passages (as they do in 1 Corinthians 1), Paul's gospel seems to be characteristically voiced in each of them. What is especially noteworthy is that the word of the cross is here more obviously complemented than it is (at first) in 1 Corinthians 1, 18 ff. by the positive themes of life for God and the experience of the spirit. The radical contrast between faith and works of law seems to precipitate this development. These complementary features of Paul's statement of the "word of the cross" should caution us against cutting short his main ex-

313

position of the gospel in the epistle to the Romans, for example, with his thesis on God's justice in Christ. A wider perspective than what God has done in the recent past is entailed in Paul's over-all eschatological outlook. Returning to 1 Corinthians 1, 18, we can see more clearly the scope of this wider perspective: the word of the cross is proclaimed in the face of two kinds of men ("foolish" and "wise"), who indicate its over-all purview in terms which go beyond present justice or condemnation, namely salvation or perdition. Salvation is the fulfillment in risen life of the reconciliation or justification received in Christ (cf. Romans 5, 9–10. 17) and should be regarded as the more ultimate perspective of Paul's gospel. Romans 1, 16 itself testifies to this, for the theme of salvation stands behind that of justice as the more general characterization of the gospel Paul proclaims.

A final passage of no little interest which contains a rather explicit reference to Paul's catechesis is 2 Thessalonians 2 (cf. especially vv. 3–5). As we have argued elsewhere, the strongly apocalyptic language of this passage articulates a fundamental Pauline perspective: that union with the Lord in glory is the consummation of Christian life, and that Christian life as life in faith entails trials to faith for its full realization in triumph. The triumph of faith is to be realized against the background of a mystery of rebellion, anti-faith. Paul's presentation of the theme of salvation in terms of a triumph over vicissitudes of faith reappears to some extent in Romans 9–11. The ultimate answer to the fact of Israel's disbelief lies apocalyptically in the realization of a mystery of God's power. The mystery expressly in question in 2 Thessalonians 2 was the anti-mystery, a process of disbelief, a mystery of rebellion rather than a mystery of fulfillment. But this "negative" mystery is ultimately intelligible as the counterpart of a "positive" mystery which finds expression in the dialectic of Romans 9–11. The differences between the mystery in 2 Thessalonians 2 and that in Romans 9–11 are largely accounted for by the fact that in the former Paul

314

is dealing precisely with a threat to faith within the community, not, as in the latter, with God's power to fulfill his promises to Israel. In both passages, however, Paul enunciates a dialectic of salvation whose warp and woof is mystery, a mystery dealing with the fulfillment of faith.

The apocalyptic dialectic of salvation based on faith which we shall find again in Romans 1–8 can be more readily grasped in the light of Paul's thought as evinced in 2 Thessalonians 2 and Romans 9–11. Thanks to the differences in the pastoral situation, Romans 1–8 is much more positive in character than 2 Thessalonians 2; Paul is dealing with a community whose faith is renowned rather than threatened. But in both cases (as in Romans 9–11), the dialectic of salvation, full union with the risen Lord, remains rooted in faith. Faith through God's justice is the basis for hope of God's glory (and thus of our salvation) through various trials in the life according to the spirit. The exposition in Romans 1–8 is immensely fuller than the contents of a few verses of Paul's earliest epistle; it is also less visually striking and more "interiorized." But 2 Thessalonians 2 alerts us to a basically apocalyptic cast of Paul's thought which can be sensed even in its subsequent modifications in Romans. His stress on universal manifestation of God's sovereignty in a triumph that is at once awesome and heartening, entailing a radical transformation in creation, is one of the most prominent features of Romans 1–8 as a whole. The apocalyptic approach to the gospel is reflected in his very use of the term *apokalyptō* at key points in his exposition: in connection with themes enunciated at the outset (justice and wrath, Romans 1, 17. 18; cf. 2, 5) and in conjunction with the vision of glory given in the last section (Romans 8, 18–19).

The foregoing brief survey of some of the clearer references in Paul's writings to his own catechesis obviously cannot serve as a rigid model for understanding the development of his gospel in Romans 1–8. Paul is not a man accustomed to rest content with set forms. But the survey may put one in the proper dis-

315

position of mind to grasp more easily the exposition that Paul does offer in Romans 1–8. To understand him, one must simply "catch" his mind by a kind of inductive process of reading him consistently. The best way to do this seems to be to focus on passages where he himself refers more clearly to his own basic instruction. Our aim in recalling these passages is simply to dispose the reader to interpret Paul through Paul himself. Accordingly, we have deliberately avoided two other basic approaches which, for all their acknowledged value, do not seem to provide the most fruitful standpoint for understanding Romans 1–8.

One of these approaches is to read Paul in the light of his speeches in Acts (notably those given at length in a missionary context: Acts 13, 16–41, where Paul, on Mission I, speaks to the Jews in Pisidian Antioch; and Acts 17, 22–31, where Paul, waiting in Athens on Mission II, speaks to the pagans. There is a certain Pauline flavor to each of these speeches. In Acts 13, for instance, Paul stresses God's election (v. 17) and justification offered beyond what can be effected by the law of Moses (vv. 38–39); in Acts 17 there is a certain polemic against idol worship (v. 29), a stress on judgment to be exercised by Christ (v. 31), and the mention of faith consequent on the resurrection (v. 31). But the speeches can hardly be taken as Pauline compositions. Their proper context is that of their present redactional placement, namely, Luke's theology. In Acts 13, 24–25, for example, John the Baptist is a key transitional figure in the whole exposition of salvation history; Paul himself, however, never mentions John, much less in a way that represents a peculiarly Lucan view of John (*met' eme*, v. 25, which avoids a "spatial" concept of discipleship; cp. Luke 3, 16 and Mark 1, 7). The speech in Acts 17 seems strangely irenic for Paul, and curiously muted in point of apocalyptic imagery— considering the fact that he had shortly before preached to the predominantly gentile Thessalonians in boldly apocalyptic imagery which he repeats and develops in a letter written from Corinth not long after his visit to Athens. In the speeches that

316

Luke has given us as "typical" we do not have the kind of speech that Paul himself must have given, especially at this early period.

The approach to Paul through Luke no longer enjoys much favor, and rightly so, though it does have the advantage of putting one in touch with Paul by putting him in touch with one who knew Paul and was more immediately acquainted with his work. Another major approach to Paul is more critical but more conjectural. Through biblical and extra-biblical evidence, one arrives at a certain reconstruction of Paul's background and/or of the kind of preaching of the period which may, we hope, shed light on what Paul is doing. Some very helpful insights have been provided by this method. We have come to recognize, for instance, the "diatribe" style in much of Paul's argumentation, a certain indebtedness to popular categories of virtues and vices, a tradition of apocalyptic polemic against idol worship, and so forth. But, in proportion as any given author is a brilliant and original thinker, he will be less easily explained by his environment or background. And in proportion as his most fundamental convictions (for example, in the area of faith) are new and sharply at variance with those of his earlier training, he may be expected to be outstanding for his differences from reconstructed background or environment rather than for his conformity to it. As far as determining Paul's basic judgments is concerned, we simply cannot rest with considerations of background, literary form and mode of expression, and so forth. We must ground our interpretation of Paul's mind in nothing short of Paul's basic outlook itself. The proof of a solid interpretation of Paul's mind and thought will accordingly lie in a certain inner consistency of interpretation of what he himself, in a representative bulk of material, has consistently expressed. The key to the consistency will not be found simply in formulation, but in the basic perspectives of Paul himself.

Our interpretation of Paul's gospel in Romans 1–8, therefore, supposes for its validation mainly the perspectives already

317

noted in the course of reading 1 Thessalonians through Romans. Whatever other considerations must be weighed, the basic test of an interpretation of Paul is whether or not Paul himself seems to speak more clearly, consistently, and effectively in the *total* interpretation provided.

STRUCTURE OF ROMANS 1—8

The structure of the first eight chapters of Romans should not be conceived univocally. Like the kerygma of the early Church in general, Romans 1–8 proclaims salvation in Christ—according to the scriptures. A twofold aspect rather than a single, clear-cut concept is evident from the outset. Paul allows us no doubt that his gospel is a gospel of fulfillment (1, 1–4) as well as a message of salvation (1, 16). Any division of the letter should respect these complementary aspects of the Apostle's preaching by distinguishing them without confusing or separating them.

The theme of scriptural fulfillment, in its over-all lines, is developed retrospectively. A dominant theme is the fulfillment of sonship not according to the flesh but according to the spirit, as in Christ. This keynote is sounded in the very introduction of the speaker (Romans 1, 1–4). In the main body of Paul's epistolary discourse (Romans 1, 16–8, 39), Paul proceeds from a citation of Habakkuk (Romans 1, 17), back through major prophets (2, 24) and psalms (3, 4. 10–20), through allusions to the rite of expiation in Leviticus 16 (3, 21–26), to the story of Abraham (Romans 4) and Adam (Romans 5) in Genesis. Following his general review of the whole Old Testament, he discusses the consequences of life with or without Christ, the new mankind (Romans 5–7), and presents with markedly apocalyptic features the life in the spirit ordered to the new creation (Romans 8).

The message of salvation, in turn, is developed in a multiple perspective which looks radically to the "apocalypse" or manifestation of a salvific mystery of justification against the back-

318

ground of a process of judgment. The latter is developed first, in a temporal dimension which attends mainly not to the past but to the present and future. "Wrath" is manifested in the apocalyptically viewed "fullness of evil" in the world of Paul's day, and it is seen as ordered to *final* wrath in Christ's judgment (on condition of non-repentance—though repentance is expected precisely because the ultimate realization of wrath has been deferred in this time of God's forbearance). Against this terrifying theme of judgment is counterweighted in a dynamic imbalance the manifestation of God's salvific justice. This is now available through a bond of faith in Christ, and it is ordered to the manifestation of God's glory in the new creation. Christian experience both in its personal aspects and in the dimension of a cosmic overthrow of the reigns of death and sin (the former implemented by Adam, the latter by law) is central to this whole process. The ultimate basis for understanding the whole process is the unmerited gift of God to both Jew and gentile, a gift that lies beyond the proportion of their reasonable expectations.

Understanding the message of salvation entails an over-all twofold perspective on a number of counts. A few of the more important ones may be sketchily mentioned here, though they can be explained only in the course of a reading of St. Paul himself:

The Ages up to the Present..............The Eschaton (now to the parousia)

Present Aspects of the Eschaton....Future Aspects of the Eschaton

(for instance)

Present Wrath........Wrath to Come (judgment)

Justice Now..........Salvation (fulfillment of justice)

Within these perspectives of salvation history, though not in schematic correspondence to them, are considerations of the relationships between God and man, Jew and gentile, personal

Christian experience and cosmic fulfillment, law and grace, flesh and spirit, and so forth. Understanding the message of salvation entails above all a recognition of God's effective sovereignty over all men, of merely human impotence with regard to salvific efficacy. The lack of human claims, even those allegedly founded in God's law, must be stated emphatically, both with regard to gentile and to Jew and with regard to man's present guilt (for there are no real grounds for his protesting innocence) or his alleged merits in a graceless state (for there are here no grounds for boasting, for rejoicing confidently in one's strength or accomplishments).

In working out these perspectives, Paul has alternated between exposition (indictment or proof) and debate with an imagined adversary. But even this literary development is not altogether simple; it becomes complicated by the insertion of hortatory passages in the closing expositions and controversy (Romans 5–8). Nevertheless, together with the enunciation and development of themes and perspectives which we have already noted, this alternation of genres seems to provide a solid literary basis for an "outline" of Romans 1, 16–8, 39. The following outline, then, will serve as the basic structure for our comments on these chapters.

Romans

1, 1–7		ADDRESS AND GREETING	
1, 8–15		THANKSGIVING AND PRAYER	
1, 16–17		ENUNCIATION OF THEMES	
1, 18–32	I.	EXPOSITION	God's wrath . . . man's injustice
2, 1—3, 20	II.	CONTROVERSY	excluding man's *defense* before God
3, 21–26	III.	EXPOSITION	God's *justice* . . . for all men
3, 27—4, 25	IV.	CONTROVERSY	excluding man's *boast* in what he has done or can contribute
5, 1–21	V.	EXPOSITION	God's *salvation* in continuity with God's justice . . . for us; some EXHORTATION (cf. vv. 1–11: to *boast*)

THE APOSTLE'S GREETINGS
TO THE FAITHFUL (1, 1–7)

As one can learn from many of Paul's opening lines, the Apostle is accustomed to sound certain keynotes for what he later writes at length. Here he introduces himself to a largely unknown audience by appealing to a common faith and shared call in the messianic message of God's gospel:

1, 1a Paul, a servant of Jesus Christ,
  1b   called to be an apostle,
  1c   set apart for the gospel of God
  2a   which was promised long ago
               through the prophets
  2b   in holy scriptures
  3a   concerning his Son,
  3b   descended from David
  3c   according to the flesh,
  4a   constituted God's Son in power
  4b   according to a spirit of sanctification following
                    resurrection from the dead,
  4c   Jesus Christ our Lord,
  5a   through whom we have received grace and apostleship
  5b   for obedience of faith
  5c   among all the gentiles
  5d   for the honor of his name,
  6a   among whom are you, too,
  6b   those called for Jesus Christ;

  7a to all God's beloved who are in Rome,
  7b   to those called holy ones:

  7c grace to you and peace
  7d   from God our Father and Jesus Christ, Lord.

Greeting the Roman community (Romans 1, 1–7), Paul thrice mentions a "call": his own call to be an Apostle (v. 1b),

321

the Romans' being called with all nations to belong to Jesus Christ (v. 6b), and their being called to be holy (v. 7b). The theme of a calling helps weld together this lengthy address and greeting. In particular, it helps establish in the address proper (vv. 1–7b) the bond in God's gospel concretized in Jesus Christ which links Paul with those to whom he writes. Paul's calling is distinctive, but it stands as a shared call nonetheless. For Paul's being called an Apostle means precisely his being selected for God's prophetic gospel concerning his Son, Jesus Christ "our" Lord. Picking up the theme of apostleship in verse 5a, after developing the transition between "his Son" (v. 3a) and "our Lord" (v. 4c), Paul anchors it once more in the theme of a shared vocation in Jesus Christ (v. 6b). Paul's apostolic role for all gentiles to bring honor to Jesus' name (that is, to help initiate or further men's acknowledging and under-standing Christ as Lord) means that he can address the Romans who are Christ's called ones. Thus Paul addresses the Romans on the basis of their common faith in Christ at the same time that he addresses them according to his apostolic commission; his apostolic destiny is one with their vocation. In verse 7ab, Paul complements the Christological emphasis of verses 1–6 by speaking of the Romans' being "called holy ones." "Christ's called ones" (v. 6b) are thus viewed as those whom God has loved and whom he regards both as men consecrated to him in the risen Lord (who has the spirit of holiness, v. 4b) and men who are to become fully what they are by his love.

As Paul dictates these opening lines, then, he identifies himself with his addressees in point of a shared vocation in faith. If we recognize this, we shall find it easier to grasp the mystery Paul thrusts at us in verses 3b–4b. The Apostle is probably citing a credal formula which is already known to the Roman community. He makes it his own and finds place for it here in order to achieve a twofold objective: first, by citing it promi-nently, he establishes a rapport in faith with those whom he addresses; second, he also enunciates a central perspective for the subsequent exposition of his gospel, namely, faith in the

322

risen Lord. He finds place for this credal formula in a larger perspective, that of a personalized salvation history. Although he does not cite the credal formula parenthetically, he does subsume it into a larger whole by assimilating it into a lengthy introductory sentence. If he mystifies the modern reader by formulating his Christology functionally, Paul also aids him in interpreting the formula by providing a context for it.

The immediate context is formed by the transition from "his Son" to "Jesus Christ our Lord." We are so accustomed to think of the two phrases as one (as in the liturgical refrain "through Jesus Christ your Son our Lord") that we may miss the mystery of grace hidden in their combination. "God's Son" is not automatically "our Lord." The second title supposes something that the first does not, namely, that God raised Jesus from the dead. Moving from one title to the other entails the whole mystery of God's grace, a grace shown in the fulfillment of salvation history and bestowed as a personal favor to us.

Within this thought context, one can grasp what Paul intends us to understand when he says that God's Son (v. 3a) was constituted God's Son in power. He is not implying that a mere man became God. If anything, by designating one and the same person as God's Son and Jesus Christ our Lord, and by designating him as Son as he begins to speak of the way he became our Lord, Paul implies that Jesus was divine to begin with, even before becoming a descendant of David according to the flesh. Paul intends us to understand that for "his Son" to become "our Lord" a transformation took place. Transformation—not simply "incarnation," but rather "eschatologically realized incarnation"—is the point that emerges from contrasting the two principal groupings in verses 3b–4b. The "descendant of David" (v. 3b) is, of course, a kingly figure. But a king "according to the flesh" (v. 3c) does not measure up to what has actually been accomplished in God's Son. That accomplishment is stated in verse 4a. Here one must beware of taking the words in this verse singly. The whole phrase must be contrasted with the parallel expression in verse 3b, which reads literally: "become from David's seed." Thus, although there is an implied contrast between "being" and "becoming" in verses 3a and 4c (being his Son; becoming our Lord), the contrast between verses 3bc and 4ab is not one between "being" and "becoming." Rather, the contrast is between two states of royal existence, the second of which is more actual than the first: "becoming" David's descendant and "being fully empowered as king." The fullness of Christ's kingship is not seen in his incarnation but in the further stage of his existence to which it served as prologue, his enthronement in power as a fuller king. The "constitution" of God's Son is to be taken existentially as the fulfillment of his becoming man. "Being manifested" or "being marked out" are acceptable translations only if they relay a further note of existential realization.

The same existential note is reflected in the second paralleled phrase of each grouping, verses 3c and 4b. Here, again, one has to beware of atomizing the text, as even the most respected commentators (such as O. Michel) are wont to do. If the basis for Christ's being a descendant of David is the "flesh," a properly earthbound principle of life, the basis for Christ's being constituted God's Son in power is something that derives from elsewhere. To spell out more fully how the Messiah's power is to be understood, Paul speaks of it in terms of a fullness of holiness (*'agiōsynē*) achieved after the resurrection. Again, a dynamic concept of "holiness" is implied, and one which befits the king as ruling rather than as one who is himself supposed to be in need of holiness. The full power to sanctify is his to exercise. Accordingly, Paul speaks of those whose Lord he is (v. 4c), as those "called for Jesus Christ" (v. 6b), and equivalently as those "called holy ones" (v. 7b). As "his Son" is "our Lord," so the explanation of *how* he is our Lord (that is, by his resurrection with this power) explains how we can be called his and be called holy. The mystery of his transformation explains the mystery of what we are before God. The basic reason for Paul's speaking of the "spirit of sanctification" is not

324

really to show something that Christ himself received but to declare the way in which God's Son can rule effectively on our behalf.

In retrospect, the tripartite address and greeting is beautifully unified. The standardly enunciated messianic blessings of grace and peace, which suggest the total perspective of God's initiative and its full realization, are charged with fuller, interpersonal meaning in the light of what Paul has said at length. The grace Paul wishes for the Romans (v. 7cd) is a participation in the grace he himself has received through the mystery of faith which makes God's Son his Lord and theirs (cf. v. 5a). The messianic blessings of grace and peace with which he greets the Romans are expected from God the Father and from Jesus Christ as from a kind of common source of blessing (v. 7d)— which is clearer in the light of the fact that God's Son is our Lord by a spirit of abundant holiness. Those addressed (v. 7ab) are God's beloved, called holy ones. For the divine gospel of how God's Son became our Lord, fulfilling the prophetic word, proves God's love—a point which Paul will have made more forcefully by the time he writes the closing phrase of Romans 8: ". . . the love of God which is in Christ Jesus our Lord." By way of explanation, those who are beloved of God are said to be "called holy ones." For they are Jesus Christ's called ones (cf. v. 6b) whose holiness can be grasped in terms of the spirit of holiness which Jesus possesses effectively as the risen Lord—and all this, again, comes through the prophetic, apostolic gospel of God. Lastly, the one who addresses the Romans (vv. 1–6) is also one called, but as an apostle consecrated ("set apart," v. 1c) for the gospel of their common faith in Christ (vv. 1–4). Through Christ the Lord as their common bond Paul has received the commission "for obedience of faith." That is, the Apostle is expected to strive to bring all men to that allegiance to God which consists radically in faith that Jesus is Lord. This commission has a universal scope (v. 5c), further to be understood not just as bringing about initial conversion but as directed to "the honor of his name," that is, to an effective profession of faith in the Lord to whom those of the gentiles in Rome have already given their allegiance.

THANKSGIVING AND OFFERING (1, 8–15)

First and foremost Paul then thanks God for the Romans' faith, going on to express his prayer and longing to impart to them a richer understanding in faith according to what God expects of him.

1, 8a To begin with, I thank my God through Jesus Christ
   8b concerning all of you;
   8c for your faith is renowned throughout the world.

   9a God is my witness,
   9b he whom I render religious service
   9c in my spirit [charismatic understanding]
   9d in [preaching] the gospel of his Son,
   9e how unceasingly I remember you,
  10a constantly asking in my prayers
  10b that if God so wills, by some means, now at last,
  10c I may successfully make my way to you.

  11a I am really longing to see you
  11b in order to impart to you some spiritual gift for strengthening
                              you,
  12a that is, to share in your consolation
  12b through the faith [that links us] to one another
  12c your [faith] and mine.
  13a I should like you to know, brothers,
  13b that I have often intended to come to you
  13c (but so far have always been prevented)
  13d in order to have a harvest among you, too,
  13e as among the rest of the gentiles;
  14a to Greeks and non-Greeks alike,
  14b to wise and foolish alike,
  14c I have my duty.
  15a Thus, for my part, I am eager to preach the gospel
  15b to you who are in Rome as well.

The passage falls into three main sections: Paul's thanksgiving, his attested prayer, and his longstanding personal intention to preach at Rome. The thanksgiving is relatively brief. Paul is not concerned with describing the Romans' progress but with indicating the grounds on which he hopes to communicate with them, their universally known faith. Accordingly, Paul voices his prayer as God's witness of his desire to come to them. God's witness is borne out in Paul's priestly service, which has a prophetic cast (preaching, not baptizing; cf. 1 Corinthians 1, 17). He renders this service in and through his charismatic understanding ("his spirit"); he exercises it in and through the gospel. The gospel is Paul's way of life, his way of communicating the understanding that he received. God's witness, therefore, explains Paul's prayerful desire to come to them, for Paul's coming is in hope of fulfilling his prophetic role in preaching the gospel. In the closing third of this passage, Paul really explains his prayer—his desire according to God's will. His whole intention is to effect a fuller sharing in the spirit through a common faith. Rome seems to represent to Paul more than a common faith, however. If he yearned to come there, it was to reap a harvest from the gentile city par excellence. His yearning found motivation principally in his understanding of the work of the spirit that God expected of him as Apostle of the gentiles.

EVANGELICAL THEMES (1, 16–17)

With the next few lines, Paul states the basic theme of the gospel which he is proud to preach, and the thematic standpoint from which he will develop it positively in this letter. Before coming to Rome, he probably wanted to prepare the community for understanding his position as a whole. In the light of his previous missionary problems with Jew and Greek, in line with his attempt to adapt himself to all men (cf. 1 Co-

327

rinthians 9, 19–23), and in view of the Romans' reputation as men who knew law (cf. Romans 7, 1), he probably decided to elaborate his theme in a somewhat juridical way, offering a kind of *sui generis* defense and vindication of God's universal gospel.

1, 16a For I am not ashamed of the gospel.
16b For it is a divine power for salvation to everyone who believes,
16c   to the Jew primarily but to Greek as well.
17a For in it divine justice is revealed from faith to faith,
17b as Scripture says: "He who is just will live from faith."

Having given his apostolic qualifications and interests (1, 1–7), Paul states what the gospel means for him (1, 8 ff.). He is "confessing the faith" in the form of apostolic *parrhēsia* (full franchise of speech in declaring the mystery of salvation), though he begins by rhetorically understating this *parrhēsia*. His dynamic conception of the gospel is evident. It is not so much a truth to be accepted and understood (though it is also this) as it is a vital power at work among men. Not all men, nor automatically! The power is for everyone who believes; its universality in act is conditioned on faith. No one is excluded from it, yet this power is shown "primarily" to the Jew. Priority here is not measured by worth (cf. Romans 2, 9–11; 3, 9; 10, 12) but by expected order of fulfillment. God's word is a word of promise. Paul will discuss in Romans 9–11 the apparent reversal of this order, only to probe further the mystery of salvation for all believers, the principal thrust of his gospel.

Though salvation stands as the overriding theme of Paul's gospel, he will not begin formally to develop it until the pivotal point of Romans 1–8, that is, Romans 5. His concept of salvation is so strongly eschatological in the epistles up to and including Romans that he reserves the term to describe not the state of the Christian in the whole eschaton but his state at the final climax of this end time, the resurrection. While the gospel is a power for salvation, it does not come to its dynamic term in all men at once. Concerning God's Son, the gospel has been realized fully in resurrection from the dead; concerning men, this is not yet the case. Accordingly, the working out of God's power for salvation must first be developed from the standpoint of the present stage of the eschaton which gravitates towards the future stage. That present stage, in its positive, salvific aspect, is the apocalypse (revelation) of God's justice. God's "justice" (*dikaiosynē*) is clearly to be distinguished from God's "judgment" (*krima*) or "just judgment" (*dikaiokrisia*). For Paul, "judgment" is condemnatory, synonymous with "wrath," which has a twofold perspective corresponding to the two poles of the eschaton: wrath now and wrath to come. "Justice" is paradoxically no condemnation of man whatsoever, but the present aspect of a life which, it is hoped, terminates in salvation. "Just judgment" marks that point at which final wrath and fulfilled justice (salvation) are effected; it is a more complexive term in content (looking to wrath as well as to salvation), though more restricted in temporal perspective (looking to the moment of final consummation).

The basis of justice is none other than that for salvation, faith. At this point, Paul gives us a slogan more than an explanation: "from faith to faith." The form of this expression should be considered in explaining it. On the basis of form, as seen in the light of Psalm 83 (84), 8; 2 Corinthians 2, 16; 3, 18; 4, 17; *4 Esdras* 6, 8, two views commend themselves. One is that Paul simply stresses the *sole condition* in terms of the *terminus a quo* and the *terminus ad quem*. This is acceptable, understanding faith in the way that Paul understands it, as an eschatological bond in Christ. *Faith alone*—not in a divisive sense but in an all-inclusive sense as the basic structure permeating all God's gifts of grace—builds the context for the revelation of God's justice. Another view complements the preceding rather than contradicts it. The form ("from . . . to . . .") suggests a dynamic perspective, that of incipient and full realization of God's justice and of faith itself. This view is undergirded by many if not all of the parallel expressions adduced above, and particularly by the apocalyptic perspective explicitly men-

329

tioned here in Romans ("is revealed," *apokalyptetai*). "Revelation" means for Paul a dynamic process, not a statically conceived fact. Revelation is effective manifestation of power (cf. v. 16b).

Thus, God's justice is revealed in a dynamic context of faith, from faith received to faith fulfilled in eternal life. Paul's quotation from Habakkuk 2, 4 (v. 17b) supports this view. The stress is clearly on faith. Hence it is somewhat misleading to ask first whether "from faith" goes with "just" or with "will live"—though an option must be made in translating the ambiguous Greek. But, given the emphasis on faith, the quotation is meant to explain how divine justice is *revealed*. For the quotation to make much sense, faith must therefore be taken dynamically, in which case the logical secondary stress falls on living. Paul's point is not so much who will live and who will not live (as if he were saying that one who is just from *faith* will live), but on what basis the just man will live, and therefore how God's justice must be understood as manifested effectively: on the basis of life-giving faith. Justice is to be understood in terms of the whole context of faith, from beginning to fulfillment, and faith as entailing life. The development of this thought will not be completed before Romans 5.

I. EXPOSITION OF GOD'S WRATH AND MAN'S INJUSTICE (1, 18–32)

Yet another step is needed for Paul to proclaim the gospel of salvation in which God's justice is revealed. To proclaim it for the sovereign favor that it is, and as a favor not automatically received, he must proclaim its opposite, the revelation of God's wrath. He begins with an indictment ostensibly leveled against the gentiles, but in reality leveled against all men, including the Jew who does as the gentiles do:

1, 18a   Indeed, divine wrath is revealed from heaven
  18b   against every impiety and injustice of men
  18c   who seize [or possess, hold fast] the truth unjustly.
  19a   For what can be known of God is clear among them;

19b	God has made it clear to them.
20a	From the foundation of the world, his invisible nature
20b	has, through his works, been visible to men's minds—
20c	his eternal power and divinity—
20d	so that they are without defense.
21a	For,

knowing God,

21b	they have not glorified him as God
21c	or given him thanks;
21d	instead, they have been frustrated in their own rationalizations
21e	and their uncomprehending hearts have been darkened.
22a	Claiming to be wise,
22b	they have become fools
23a	and have given up the glory of the incorruptible God in exchange
23b	for the very image of corruptible man,
23c	and of birds and beasts and reptiles!

24a	That is why God has given them up to the lusts of their hearts,
24b	to defilement, to dishonoring their bodies one with another:
25a	because they are people who have given up God's truth in exchange for falsehood,
25b	and have offered reverence and worship to a creature in contempt of the creator
25c	(be he blessed forever. Amen.)!

26a	That is why God has given them up to shameful passions.
26b	Their women have given up natural relationships in exchange for unnatural ones,
27a	and the men, too, have given up natural relations with women
27b	and blazed with passion for one another—
27c	men perpetrating shame on men
27d	and receiving in their own persons the due recompense of their perversion!

28a	And as they have not seen fit to hold God in true knowledge,
28b	God has given them up to misfit judgment to do what is unsuitable [immoral].
29a	They are filled with every form of injustice: malice, rapacity, evil;
29b	full of jealousy, murder, quarreling, treachery, spite;
30a	backbiters, slanderers, haters of God, arrogant, proud, braggarts;
30b	plotters of evil, disobedient to parents;
31	without conscience, without honor to their word, without affection, without pity—
32a	people who know the just decree of God,
32b	that those who so act deserve to die,
32c	yet not only do they do so themselves,
32d	but they likewise deem it fit for those so doing.

331

The general form of this passage is that of Christian missionary preaching bolstered by traditional Jewish polemic against idol worship. Paul indicts men on the grounds of their not properly responding to the knowledge God has given them. His indictment is at the same time a verdict, a declaration of God's wrath. For God's wrath, which is to some extent an apocalyptic synonym for hell, is really no added sanction. It is not something that God imposes on men but rather something that they bring on themselves: God hands them over to the consequences of their own folly. Vice, in a sense, is its own punishment, and personal degradation the consequence of personal, culpable ignorance of God. There is worse to come, namely, final wrath in judgment on condition of non-repentance (Romans 2, 1–16); but even now God's wrath is effectively manifested in widespread perversion. Paul speaks here basically of "the present evil age" (cf. Galatians 1, 4). He is not castigating the vices of his Christian audience at Rome, nor those of Romans in general—as if the latter were other than representative of mankind at the time. Paul provides here a typological, that is, representative, picture of perverse humanity, of man under God's wrath by man's fault, not by God's initial dealings with him. Verses 18–23 spell out the basis for this wrath in men's unjust (self-centered) grasping hold of God's truth; verses 24–32, in three major stages, indicate the penalty in moral degradation suffered even now (whether those involved are aware of the fact or not).

In verse 18b, Paul declares a twofold basis for God's wrath: impiety and injustice. The first of these, godlessness, false worship, seems to be spelled out in the second, a generic term for wickedness, and one that more clearly suggests the tribunal of God's judgment. Verse 18c clarifies this twofold sin in terms of man's injustice in his way of handling God's truth. The term *katechontōn,* which is preferably translated "possess," "hold fast," or "seize," is often translated here as "suppress" or "hold fettered." Surprisingly, the common interpretation need not greatly be affected. In either event, Paul indicts a distortion of the clear knowledge of God. But the translation that we

332

prefer seems to safeguard the more normal sense of the Greek verb and enjoys the advantage of focusing attention on the self-centeredness of men's injustice. Men's crime is not to have hindered initial knowledge of God; that knowledge is supposed as known from the outset and as being at hand to convict them (cf. vv. 19 ff.). Men's crime is rather to have taken that knowledge for their own use "in injustice," wrongly. They have wickedly appropriated for self-centered ends the truth that God has given; they have not really suppressed that truth itself. Verses 19–23 then spell out this crime. Verses 19–20 speak of God's action in making the truth known, and thus establish the culpability of those accused; verses 21–23 speak of men's action consequent upon the knowledge of God (v. 21) and upon their own self-styled wisdom (vv. 22–23), thus spelling out men's injustice and impiety. Men's basic sin is that of selfish, foolish distortion of knowledge of God rather than simple, much less initial, repression of this knowledge. Their injustice consists in the way they have arrived at false worship of man and of corruptible creatures.

The Apostle is not speaking here about the knowledge of God through reason alone, nor is he speaking of a knowledge through faith, as that term is generally understood by Catholic dogmatic theologians. We must understand Paul in line with his own categories as an apostolic, eschatological-minded preacher. He is speaking of a knowledge of God that was given men from the foundation of the world and is still attainable through the mind's eye on the basis of God's works (a complexive term covering more than inanimate or brute creation). This knowledge, had it been properly (and not unjustly) held fast, could presumably have saved men from the wrath that is now upon them. Thus, the knowledge in question was a salvific knowledge, and could have been so effectively but for men's injustice. Accordingly, it may not be judged as a purely rational knowledge, a knowledge of the natural law by unaided reason. Paul's statement does indeed suppose that men's minds have not been utterly incapable of grasping God's power and divinity.

333

But Paul is really not proclaiming a "natural law" in the sense of a knowledge attainable by human reason pure and simple. He recognizes no law but that which can be ultimately subsumed into the law and justice of Christ or which is the standard of God's judgment as executed through Christ (cf. Galatians 2, 11–21 and Romans 2, 16 as completing Romans 2, 12–15).

On the other hand, Paul is not speaking here precisely of a knowledge in faith, even though he is speaking of a knowledge that presumably could have saved men from God's wrath. To many a dogmatic theologian, this may sound like nonsense, for he himself thinks in categories of reason and faith as principles of understanding. He does not really think eschatologically. But Paul does. For Paul, "faith" is the eschatological knowledge of God in Christ. Thus, he does not use the term "faith" in this context. For, in this context, he is speaking of wrath as consequent on a knowledge regarded mainly as hitherto available to men.

The dogmatic theologian, to answer the problem of the salvation of those who lived before Christ or who live now without acknowledging Christ, has extended the concept of "faith" to cover an illumination and assent by which, mysteriously, men living before Christ (or after him and for one reason or another not formally acknowledging him) could be saved. For the dogmatic theologian rightly holds that without faith there is no salvation. Paul, however, does not directly face this problem of the salvation of those before Christ and of those who sincerely do not think they acknowledge him but who should not be judged as shut out from salvation. His theological standpoint is more historical than psychological. Given Paul's whole eschatological position, one may see how it lies open to further development according to what the Apostle affirms concerning God's salvific purpose, a knowledge always offered to all men, and concerning definitive manifestation of salvific knowledge in Christ.

But one only confuses the question and confounds the solution by judging Romans 1, 18 ff. mainly from the standpoint of a metaphysically or psychologically oriented theology, without first having grasped Paul's eschatological, metahistorical position. In eschatological perspective, Paul reserves the term "faith" for the *historically fulfilled* knowledge of God now given in Christ (cf. Romans 3, 21 ff.). He always regards things primarily from a kind of functional standpoint, the standpoint of existential fulfillment in the perspective of salvation history. Thus, Paul is not speaking in Romans 1, 18–32 of a knowledge "in faith," nor is he speaking here of a knowledge of the "natural law"—as these terms are understood by the dogmatic theologian. The dogmatic theologian, given an awareness of Paul's own perspective and terminology, may nonetheless appeal to Paul for light on his own discipline. In this event, and in terms of his own discipline rather than in terms of biblical exegesis, he should call the knowledge given all men a kind of knowledge in faith, one that can be attained in the use of reason, though hardly through "unaided" reason.

More strikingly than he speaks about God's making himself known and man's foolish bartering of this knowledge for the products of his own rationalizations, Paul speaks of God's wrath. The wrath of God consists in his giving men up to their own way of acting with its degrading consequences. In verses 24–25, the punishment (v. 24) and its basis (v. 25) are stated. The "lusts of their hearts" are not just sexual urges. "Lusts" (*epithymiai*) are desires of a much wider scope; "heart" looks to the center of the whole personality rather than simply to the seat of the affections. Nevertheless, Paul obviously regards the "lusts of their hearts" as typified concretely in sexual abuses. The cult of the creature consequent on the idolatry of man (cp. vv. 23a and 25ab) bears with it the wrath of God. Wrath revealed from heaven lies in men's hearts and bodies in a kind of self-worship on their part. The wrath is restated again in verses 26–27, this time in terms of both sexes and their perversion. Sin brings about the disintegration of tne race, a degrading disintegration which stands as symptom of the religious malady and proof of God's wrath. Lastly, in verses 28–32,

335

Paul concludes, and in concluding summarizes his declaration of God's wrath. He seems to play on a Greek word for judgment or opinion (vv. 28ab, 32d) to bring out the inner sequence between crime and punishment befitting the crime. As he had charged men with taking hold of (*katechein*) the truth unjustly (v. 18c), he now repeats the charge as their not seeing fit to hold (*echein*) God in "higher knowledge" (*epignōsis*). In an effort to possess God's truth on their own self-centered terms, they have lost hold of the knowledge that they needed and that lay beyond them. Thus, their judgment in other matters leads to a fullness of evil in their own lives and approval of it in the lives of others. In all this, however, they cannot plead simple ignorance (v. 32ab); Paul supposes responsible recognition of the demand of God's just law (*dikaiōma,* "just decree") and its full consequence. What is presented as outstandingly typified in sexual abuse (vv. 24–25), especially homosexuality (vv. 26–27), is seen to be true of all other vices (vv. 28–32— where no "sexual" sin is even mentioned): perversion of desire and judgment is verified in perversion of conduct and moral values, and everything is reduced to the basic sin of idolatry.

Men's injustice is equivalently defined as a denial of glory to the invisible but self-revealing God. Their cultic disorientation from God brings with it human self-worship and degradation to life on the level of animal existence or worse. Thus, God's wrath is existentially revealed in their becoming sinful fools by their own self-centeredness.

II. CONTROVERSY EXCLUDING MAN'S DEFENSE BEFORE GOD (2, 1—3, 20)

After this blistering indictment, Paul turns to an imaginary hearer who would righteously dissociate himself from such an indictment. The genre of Paul's writing thus changes from exposition to controversy. From 2, 1 to 3, 20, Paul excludes the defense of any man against God's wrath and equivalently excludes any claim on God's salvific justice. At first, Paul seems to be speaking to a gentile, but he is really speaking to *any* man who judges (2, 1a). His polemic is throughout a hidden polemic against the Jew as well. That he has both in mind is attested not only by the statement of his general theme in Romans 1, 16, but by his résumé ("to the Jew primarily, but to the Greek as well") in 2, 9–10, by his presumed audience in speaking of those without the law (2, 14), and by his conditional introduction of the defenseless man in 2, 17. Thus, the "any man who judges" of 2, 1 typologically represents more than the gentile as distinguished from the Jew. He represents, quite simply, any man who sets himself up as a judge of others but in reality falls under the same condemnation. The hidden polemic against the Jew (who of all people was especially privileged and might consider himself an exception) becomes a direct polemic in 2, 17 ff. But the conclusion to this whole controversy supplies us with the basic line of Paul's argument (3, 19–20): every mouth is to be closed—no man has any defense against God's judgment and thus no man, not even the Jew, has a claim on God's justice.

Glory, associated with incorruptibility, honor, and peace (Romans 2, 7. 10), figures as the object to be sought through patient endurance in good work, and as the reward itself for those who meet the standards of God's just judgment. This ideal of glory, however, is practically unattainable. For man has no defense, on the score of his own works, against an adverse judgment. Glory sought (for which the reward is eternal life) and glory achieved on a universal scale (for Jew and gentile alike) is unattainable by merely human efforts. The sinfulness of even God's own privileged people serves to set in relief God's unique justice and fidelity, for his glory; that is, for his being shown to be the only one who of himself is just and good (3, 7).

2, 1a   Thus, you are without defense, every man of you who judges.
1b   For in judging another, you condemn yourself—
1c   for you who judge do the very same things.
2a   We know, indeed, that God's judgment falls unerringly

2b   on those who do such things.

3a   Do you think, then, you man who judge those who do such things

3b   and do the very same things yourself,

3c   that you will escape God's judgment?

4a   Or do you scorn his wealth of goodness

4b   and forbearance

4c   and longsuffering,

4d   unmindful of the fact that God's goodness leads you to
                                         repentance?

5a   Through the hardness of your unrepentant heart

5b   you are storing up for yourself wrath

5c   for the day of wrath and of God's just judgment.

6   He will render to every man according to his works:

7a   to those who by perseverance in good works

7b   seek glory, honor, and immortality,

7c   eternal life;

8a   but for those who, out of selfishness,

8b   are disobedient to the truth

8c   and obey injustice,

8d   there will be wrath and anger.

9a   There will be affliction and anguish

9b   for every human being who does what is evil,

9c   Jew primarily, but Greek as well;

10a   glory and honor and peace

10b   for everyone who does good,

10c   Jew primarily, but Greek as well.

11   For there is no "going by appearances" with God.

12a   Whoever have sinned lawlessly

12b   will perish lawlessly

12c   and whoever have sinned under law

12d   will be judged by law;

13a   for it is not those who hear the law

13b   who are just in God's sight,

13c   but those who do the law [are they who]

13d   will be declared just.

14a   Indeed, whenever the gentiles, who do not have the law,

14b   do by nature what the law enjoins.

14c   they are a law to themselves;

14d   then, although they do not have law,

15a   they are people who show the work of the law

15b   written in their hearts—

15c   their conscience bearing witness

15d   as do their discursive judgments

15e   of blame

15f   or even of exoneration

16a   for the day on which God will judge men's secrets

16b   as my gospel proclaims he will do

16c   through Christ Jesus.

338

In the opening lines (2, 1–4), Paul is trying to destroy a sense of false security. The missionary must show that his message is personally relevant, and to do this he must somehow rouse his complacent, self-satisfied listener. Such, at least, was Paul's approach, in line with that of the prophets. But his technique is radically positive, even here. Paul demolishes man's defense only to bring him to look to God's mercy. The wrath of God, though it already lies on men in their sins, has been mercifully deferred inasmuch as it entails final wrath to come; there is still time for repentance.

The wrath to come, mercifully deferred in this time of God's forbearance, serves as the thematic framework for 2, 5–16. The genre is still that of controversy, not exposition, for Paul directly confronts defenseless man with the picture of God's judgment in Christ (cf. v. 5; cp. v. 5c and v. 16). God's judgment will be according to works (vv. 6–10) and, impartially, according to liability to law's demands (vv. 11–15). In dealing with the former of these classical prophetic categories of judgment, Paul speaks first mainly of interior good or evil dispositions (vv. 7–8) and then of actual execution of what is evil or good (vv. 9–10). Of special interest in verses 7–8 is the way Paul speaks of disobedience. It is allied with selfishness and is at least implicitly opposed to justice. As present wrath lies on men for their injustice (Romans 1, 18), so wrath to come in judgment will look to the interior lack of response to truth and justice. Response to the gospel might seem more clearly implicated here than it was in the discussion of God's present wrath in the light of knowledge hitherto available. Nevertheless, Paul does not specify the "truth" in verse 8b as the truth of the gospel. He allows for a certain vagueness in "everyman's" understanding of the truth, even as he confronts every man liable to judgment with the vision of a final, impartial judgment by Christ. In verses 9–10, the prospects of judgment are explicitly enlarged by the mention of Jew and Greek: universal judgment is in question as well as final judgment. In turn, this explicit expanding of perspective prepares us for Paul's handling of the second major criterion of God's judgment (the ultimate basis of the first), namely, God's law. For works are judged according to law. Law, as a known norm of responsible action, is the norm of judgment for all men.

Impartial judgment entails, besides a norm, recognition by the judge of the degree of personal responsibility in following the norm. Paul insists on a universal judgment and therefore on a universal norm, so he must show that this norm is present even among persons who do not have the Mosaic law. From the preceding development, vv. 6–10, he supposes God's knowledge of interior dispositions as well as external actions. But he now insists on a norm that is present as a criterion for these interior dispositions and external actions even in those who cannot be said to have the Mosaic law. He begins with a distinction that shows that law is basic to judgment. The first part of this distinction may somewhat puzzle the reader, for it involves a play on the word "lawlessly" (*anomōs*). In a sense, those who have sinned outside the (Mosaic) law will perish outside the (Mosaic) law. But Paul will go on to show that they will not perish without any law whatsoever. He does not take the Mosaic law (as the dictum of verse 12a–d might have been understood in Jewish circles) as the sole kind of law, or as actually the law by which God will judge. Rather, he speaks of "sinning lawlessly" in the sense of acting against that law which is acknowledged and of "perishing lawlessly" in the sense of perishing as one who has been disobedient to the law which he knew. The force of the whole dictum is that law, as known and as followed or not followed, stands as the criterion of judgment. This meaning is borne out by verse 13, which represents real knowledge (acknowledgment) of law as *effective, productive* knowledge.

In verses 14–15, Paul then argues that even the gentiles, who do not have the law (in the sense of the Mosaic law, as supposed in one understanding of the dictum in v. 12) do indeed fall under law in another valid sense. Paul says that the gentiles do not "have" law. That is, they do not possess for use a set of

340

formulated principles and norms given them by God. The expression also indicates that Paul does not regard the gentiles as finding a natural law "out there" in creation and learning to pattern themselves after it. Rather, he sees the "natural law" as something interior and personal, verified primarily in acts conformed to God's demands. The gentiles *are* a law when they do "by nature" (*physei,* that is, without benefit of an added external norm such as the Mosaic law) "the things of the law" (that is, what the formulated revealed law demands—even though the gentiles do not have, that is, employ this law or know it as Mosaic). In doing the things of the law they show that what the law wants done (its "work," v. 15a) is written interiorly, at the center of their personal being. Paul then indicates to some extent how the gentiles are aware of law (v. 15c–f). In "conscience," an awareness of their moral standing before God, and by discursive judgments of accusation or defense, they show how the law which they do not possess as an external norm to which they can conform is personally inscribed in their hearts. This present knowledge, however, will not of itself acquit or condemn them; it is ordered to God's judgment in Christ, the final, penetrating judgment of the heart (v. 16).

Thus, in verses 11–16, Paul speaks of the impartial, all-penetrating judgment of God according to law. Beginning with a dictum that sets law as the criterion for judgment (v. 12), Paul interprets the criterion as actual performance of the law's demands (v. 13), and argues that the gentiles, though they do not "have" law (as a revealed and external norm which they can use) *are* the law, that is, effectively measure up to the criterion, when they do it. They have within themselves a forum for being aware of the way they stand with God for the day on which God will judge according to law, through Christ. Paul is not speaking precisely of the law of the spirit when he speaks of the work of the law written in the heart. What we said of "faith" apropos of Romans 1, 18–32 is likewise to be said of "spirit": for Paul, "spirit" is to be understood eschatologically,

341

in terms of Christ's resurrection and faith itself. The law which the gentiles are to themselves is a law ordered to judgment through Christ. Therefore, it is not a "natural law" in the sense of a law known by unaided reason alone, a law conceived as perfectly distinct from revelation in Christ. On the other hand, it is not precisely a law known in faith—as Paul understands faith. It is "natural" in the sense of being not formally revealed (as was the Mosaic law), and it is truly (*effectively*) law not so much by the way it is known (though it is known in conscience), as by being *done*. The law which is the criterion for God's eventual judgment in Christ is a law in the functional, practically operative sense, a law *performed* or *not performed* by the person concerned.

Before leaving this part of Paul's attack on the defense of any man who sits in judgment, a word is in order on judgment in Christ. The gospel of Paul, the "good news of salvation," comprises more than the message of salvation for men. It proclaims God's sovereignty in Christ. Thus, surprisingly only to those who view the gospel from the standpoint of man's expectations, the gospel includes a declaration of wrath against sin and a warning of wrath to come on condition of non-repentance. Hell is part of the revelation of the gospel. The focus of the good news lies clearly on the message of salvation. But the fact that a revelation of wrath and insistence on God's prerogative of judgment in Christ figure so strikingly in Paul's proclamation of the gospel proves that one cannot understand the gospel adequately without taking a further standpoint, the standpoint of God's sovereignty. Paul himself settles for no less. Thus, Paul's view of the gospel is thoroughly one with that of the rest of the New Testament and of Christ himself: the reign of God in Christ, ordered to just judgment (whether of condemnation—on those who have not responded to the knowledge of God and repented as they were given a chance, or of salvation—intended for all who believe) governs the total perspective of the gospel.

342

2, 17	But if you bear the title of "Jew,"	and rest confidently on law,
18a	and boast of God,	and know his will,
18b	and possess discernment,	being instructed by the law,
19a	and thus believe yourself to be	
19b	a guide to the blind,	a light for those in darkness,
20a	and educator of the foolish,	a teacher of mere children,
20b	having in the law the perfect	pattern of knowledge and truth—
21a	well, then, teacher of others,	do you not [need to] teach yourself?
21b	preacher against stealing,	do you [yourself] steal?
22a	denouncer of adultery,	do you commit adultery?
22b	abhorrer of idols,	do you swindle [rob temples, treasuries]?
23	You who boast in the law—	through your transgression of the law,
		you dishonor God;
		as scripture says:
24	"Among the gentiles, thanks to you, God's name is in disgrace!"	
25a	Circumcision is of value	if you do what the law requires.
25b	But if you are a transgressor of the law, your circumcision is undone.	
26a	If, then, one who is uncircumcised keeps the commandments of the law,	
26b	will not his uncircumcision be reckoned as circumcision?	
27a	and will not he who is physically uncircumcised yet fulfills the law	
27b	judge you, who with the law's letter and circumcision transgress the law?	
28a	For the [true] Jew is not the man who is outwardly such,	
28b	nor is the [true] circumcision that which appears outwardly in flesh;	
29a	no, the [real] Jew is he who is such inwardly,	
29b	and circumcision is of the heart, spiritual, not literal,	
29c	that of one whose "praise" is not from men but from God.	
3, 1a	What, then, is the advantage of being a Jew,	
1b	or what is the value of circumcision?	
2a	Great in every respect!	
2b	First and foremost, they [the Jews] were entrusted with God's oracles.	
3a	What if some were unfaithful?	
3b	Surely their unfaithfulness does not annul God's fidelity?	
4a	Never! God is to be found true, though every man is false;	
4b	as scripture says:	
4c	"As you are to be justified in your words	
4d	and will be vindicated when called to account."	

343

5a   But if our injustice serves to prove God's justice,

5b   what then?

5c   Surely God is not unjust when he exercises wrath (I speak in
                     human fashion).

6   Of course not! Else how will God judge the world?

7a   But if through my falseness God's truthfulness
       has redounded abundantly to his glory,

7b   then why am I still condemned as a sinner?

8a   And why not—as some libelously report us to say—

8b   do what is evil that good may come of it?

8c   The condemnation for those people [who so act or argue]
                     is quite deserved.

The second major movement of this section begins with Romans 2, 17. Even the Jew is to be "convinced of sin" before Paul can declare God's paradoxical justice. In verses 17–29, Paul interprets the privilege of the Jews existentially, as discerned according to actual fulfillment of the law, interiorly. In the last analysis, the Jew is one whose "praise" (a play on the popular etymology of the term "Jew") comes from God on the basis of actual performance according to the heart. The argument gravitates towards what the Jew (addressed honorably by this religious and national title) knows from God's law (cf. vv. 17, 18b, 20b). But a rhetorical twist at verse 19a points up the scope of Paul's address. He suggests the basic vice of self-assurance on the grounds of this law and knowledge. Accordingly, he places on his hearer the burden of recognizing the discrepancy between what he says and boasts of and what he does (vv. 21–23). In an interpretative citation of Isaiah 52, 5 (v. 24) along rabbinical lines ("When Israel does the will of God his name is blessed, and when not his name is, as it were, blasphemed": Simeon ben Yohai, *circa* A.D. 150), Paul declares that God is far from praised by their conduct. The privilege of the law is thus judged existentially and theologically in the perspective of actual fulfillment to God's honor. The sign of adherence to the law is circumcision, the topic which Paul immediately discusses, then, in verses 25–29. Again, he judges this practice in terms of actual fulfillment of that for

344

which it stands, the keeping of God's commands. He understands circumcision in accord with the prophetic view of interior conformity to God, phrasing this understanding in terms of his own distinction between the spirit and the letter, and insisting on God's judgment as the ultimate criterion.

Thus far in 2, 17 ff., Paul feels that he has brought his self-assured adversary to become aware of conduct radically at variance with his vaunted title, and even to recognize that circumcision (which the adversary might claim he had practiced in fulfillment of the law) means nothing as mere external compliance. In doing this, Paul has really argued from the standpoint of God's honor (v. 24) and God's personal judgment (v. 29c). Accordingly, he now affirms privilege in the light of God's fidelity to his word, not in the light of human performance. The advantage of title (cp. 3, 1a and 2, 17. 29c) and the usefulness of circumcision (cp. 3, 1b and 2, 25a)—in the sense of the special thing one gains—are examined together. "First and foremost" (there is no subsequent enumeration; cf. Romans 1, 8), the gainful privilege is to be found in the legacy that God has entrusted to the Jews. God's gift—concretely, his oracles, not their possession of them—is the ultimate criterion of privilege. For Paul, anything "objectively better" is judged in the strictly theological perspective of what God has given, not as what man takes as being exclusively, even minimally, his own. Without this rigorous perspective of God's sole absolute right, nothing in Paul makes much sense. By appealing to this perspective in this context, Paul demolishes the last line of man's defense against God's judgment. Not only what man has done, even if he is a Jew, but what he does not have except by God's fidelity, leaves him without any claim on God for justice, for special personal consideration instead of judgment.

The purpose of the rapid-fire questions at this juncture is to establish God's right to judgment precisely in view of privileges he has bestowed. The "advantage" is immediately contrasted to the infidelity of "some" (litotes, considering the previous de-

345

velopment and subsequent statements in 3, 9–20). Infidelity on man's part is then supposed for the subsequent argumentation. Thus, Paul can simply overrule the objection in verses 7–8 which, to a speculative-minded questioner not convinced of his own guilt, might seem to be a legitimate objection. For Paul supposes that the objector is himself responsible and really a sinner. On this supposition (bolstered by the whole previous discussion in Romans 1, 18–32 and 2, 1 ff.), the objection is irresponsible—a judgment borne out by the fact that it is tied in with an evidently irresponsible charge against the Apostle's doctrine. In verses 3–4, however, infidelity is adduced to bring out God's fidelity and consequent right to judgment. *He* has not failed (a point that Paul will develop at length in Romans 9–11). Accordingly, he has the right to display his justice in judgment—though Paul will show in 3, 21–26 that he has not thus displayed it. The words of Psalm 50 (LXX), 6, part of the oracles that God entrusted to his people, vindicate him on this score.

In verses 5–6 and 7–8 Paul quickly answers two objections in such a way as to undergird his main point, God's right to judgment. Our injustice (in sin) puts in relief God's justice (fidelity to his word), yet this does not mean that God would be unjust if he showed wrath (judgment) instead of justice (further fidelity and mercy). Paul even apologizes somewhat for the inference, necessitated by human language, that God might be conceived as unjust in any way. He then affirms a tenet that he feels all will take for granted, that God is expected to judge the world for its sins. The second objection takes a somewhat different standpoint. Though it is clear that no objection can rest on the score of our injustice (vv. 5–6), what of an objection on the score of God's truthfulness (fidelity to his word)? Why am I judged a sinner if I serve to extol his fidelity? As we said above, the objector ignores the fact of his own responsibility. He has not really done anything for God's glory if he is a sinner. Paul feels that he has only to spell out the objection in terms of irresponsible assertion in order to let it fall as self-refuted (though he will return to similar objections in Romans 6, 1 and 9, 19).

346

3, 9a   What then? Do we [Jews] have a real advantage?
  9b   Absolutely not.
  9c   For we have already charged all men,
  9d   Jews and Greeks alike,
  9e   that they are under [the power of] sin;
 10a   as scripture says:
 10b   "There is no just man, not even one;
 11a   there is none who understands,
 11b   there is none who seeks the Lord.
 12a   All have gone astray, all alike have become worthless;
 12b   there is none who shows kindness,
 12c   not even one.

 13a   Their throats are open graves,
 13b   with their tongues they have wrought deceit.
 13c   The venom of adders is beneath their lips,
 14   their mouths are full of bitter curses.

 15   Their feet hasten to shed blood;
 16   ruin and misery lie in their paths,
 17   and they have not known the way of peace;
 18   the fear of God is not before their eyes."

 19a   We know that whatever the law says,
 19b   it says to those subject to the law.
 19c   Let every mouth be silenced, then,
 19d   and the whole world stand liable to God's judgment;
 20a   for from works of law
 20b   "*no* human being will be justified in his sight."
 20c   Through the law, you see, comes full knowledge of sin.

In view of God's unassailable right to judgment, then, in accordance with the words to which he alone has remained faithful, there is *de facto,* that is, effectively, no advantage which the Jews can claim (3, 9 ff.). They fall under the charge laid against all men and can raise no voice to plead special defense. To make his point tellingly, especially where his people themselves are concerned, Paul cites a combination of scripture texts (basically that of Ps. 13 [14], 1–3). Paul's addition, which helps us to discern with certainty the main point of his citation, is found in verse 10b (cf. Ps. 13, 3): ". . . just man, not even one!" That there is no exception to injustice stands as the salient point of the first stanza (vv. 10b–12c). The second stanza spells out human corruption by stressing faculties of speech (vv. 13a–14). The third stanza (vv. 15–18) speaks of men's miserable destiny in the light of their conduct, that is, their "way of walking" and its lack of proper direction. These words of the law (in the wide sense of Old Testament wisdom) are relevant to the Jew—they "speak to him"—with the result that he, like the gentile (and perhaps even like Job; cf. Job 40, 3–4) must give up his defense. No one will be found in the right from "works of law," that is, from actual performance of the law, human efforts of man understood as things that man has done of himself that stand as a claim against God. Law has actually served to bring out a real knowledge (*epignōsis*) of sin. The law, a universal criterion of judgment, stands of itself as an unrealizable ideal. Paul has stated his case dogmatically and has proved it rhetorically.

III. EXPOSITION OF GOD'S JUSTICE FOR ALL MEN (3, 21–26)

The human judges have been silenced. God's justice can now be heard, and Paul proclaims it in Romans 3, 21–26, a quite brief but highly important and concentrated exposition.

The universal need on man's part for glory denied in man's injustice (§ I) and glory to be sought or achieved by doing good—though had by God alone (§ II) is met, beyond all reasonable expectation, by God's redemptive act in Christ's death (§ III). By a public declaration, promulgated in Jesus as the point of contact in the cultic rite of expiation, God justifies man. With forbearance, he drops the charges and establishes a new bond for one who belongs to Jesus.

3, 21a   Now, though independently of law, God's justice has been made
manifest,

21b   witnessed to by the law and the prophets—

22a   God's justice, I say, through Jesus Christ's faith

22b   to all those who believe.

22c   There is, indeed, no discrimination.

23   For all sinned and are in need of God's glory

348

24a   while being justified freely by his personal favor
24b   through the redemption in Christ Jesus
25a   whom God set forth as expiation center
25b   through faith in his blood,
25c   for a clear indication of his justice
25d   with regard to a remission of past sins
26a   in God's forbearance,
26b   for that clear indication of his justice
26c   in the present time,
26d   for his being just precisely as justifying one of Jesus' faith.

The leading verses of this passage (vv. 21–22) embody the basic affirmation developed in those which follow (vv. 22–26). Though justice cannot be expected on the basis of law as fulfilled by men, it is attested by the law and the prophets. For it comes by way of divine fulfillment, not human expectation or compliance. Paul says that God's justice "has been made manifest" (*pephanerōtai*)—a synonym for its "being revealed" (*apokalyptetai;* Romans 1, 17), but a word which perhaps is more appropriate when speaking of a definitive, clear-cut event against the negative background of law's role. He speaks of this justice insistently (cp. vv. 21a and 22a) as God's justice, indicating particularly its manner of coming (through Christ's faith) and its universal scope (again on the basis of faith). Every word in these opening lines is operative in the exposition which follows, but perhaps the whole can be grasped more effectively by interweaving three specific topics: the justice of God, the perspective of universal expiation, and the meaning of "Christ's faith."

God's justice must be understood as salvific, not condemnatory. The whole point of the preceding controversy was to exclude man's defense against God's judgment, legitimately shown in wrath. The point now is not to affirm God's judgment, but to point out a new reality which does not follow precisely on law (though witnessed to by the Mosaic law and the prophets). Thus, God's justice is to be conceived as other than the consequences which follow on law as a criterion of sin; justice is not judgment but its paradoxical contrary. Yet its coming is attested by the Old Testament ("law and prophets") as the fulfillment of the covenant in a rite of expiation, as Paul will shortly explain. God's justice is not only dissociated from law (in point of effective manifestation; Romans 3, 21a), it is also realized through faith (v. 22ab), ordered to the glory that sinners lack (vv. 23–24a), and is associated with a rite of expiation (v. 25a) and a form of remission of sins (v. 25de). Verse 22 focuses justice on faith, which is certainly the basis for salvation and, as focused on faith, justice is universal in scope (just as its opposite, wrath, was universal in scope—both in its present manifestation according to sin and in its prospective manifestation according to law). Justice stands as the initial positive step towards God's glory. In verses 23–24, Paul subordinates the participle "being justified" to the fact of sin and the need for God's eschatological glory (the glory of the resurrection, not that of the first Adam, but that to come). He does not say "*but* are justified"—for this would stress simply the change of man's state. He looks as ever to the ultimate prerogative of God which establishes the total perspective of what he is speaking about. What is more, verse 24a contains an interesting pleonastic expression which highlights the salvific and non-legal character of God's justice: "freely [*dōrean*] by his personal favor [*tē autou chariti*]." God is under no constraint in giving; he gives freely. But that free giving is "by his grace," by way of personal favor; it is not according to law (which stands as the basis for impartial judgment). This is not to say that justice is not a juridical notion, or that it is not manifested juridically. But "law" is not the whole of juridical relationships. Law can attest to something other than itself (v. 21b), and juridical bonds can be of another kind than those involving works and claims based on works. Paul will later clarify this juridical aspect of justice as a kind of "trust." Here he develops mainly its cultic aspect, a liberation from sin (vv. 24b ff.).

The expiation center of the old law which witnesses to God's justice was the *'ilastērion* (cf. Leviticus 16, 2–17; Exodus 25, 16–22; Numbers 7, 89), the gold paten covering the ark and the place on which the blood, symbolizing vital contact between

God and the people, was sprinkled on the day of expiation (*Yôm Kippûr*). The sins of the whole people were thus expiated, washed away, in an act by which the covenant was rendered effective. In Paul's theology, Christ himself is this *'ilastērion,* the instrument of deliverance from sin. Not an instrument in a crass sense, but an instrument nonetheless, a means of expiation for the whole people. The sense in which Christ is *'ilastērion* is principally qualified by the whole of verse 25b (which cannot easily be taken in smaller units without coming to O. Michel's conclusion that "through faith" seems to disrupt the sequence of thought). Christ is *'ilastērion* not automatically or simply by his own death, but by way of God's establishing a covenant bond of a new kind, faith, in his life blood. This act of expiation is represented as the Father's public act (a kind of proclamation) with juridical effects. The first of these, which we may term somewhat "negative," is described in verses 25c–26a. God manifests his justice by dropping the case against men for the sins committed in the context of God's forbearance (that is, for sins committed even in the present time, namely, that prior to the *final* wrath of God; cf. 2, 4). He has effected a remission of sins as *paresis,* dropping the case against men for sins which he had abided thus far. This is the salvific but still relatively negative side of God's justice. The positive side is given more emphatically in verse 26b–d. In setting forth Christ as expiation center through faith in his blood, God proved his justice as a reality here and now, a justice shown precisely in his effecting a new bond in Christ. Justice through expiation amounts to remitting past sins effectively (under the image of dropping the charge, vv. 25c–26a) and to establishing a new eschatological and juridical bond in Christ (v. 26b–d).

By "Jesus Christ's faith" Paul does not intend to attribute to Jesus himself a subjective "act of faith" by which he believed in God, accepting revelation on God's word. Paul presumes that Christ is himself the revealer and the revelation (cf. 2 Corinthians 3, 14–18). The believers are other men (cf. v. 22b); the paradigm of the believers is not Christ but Abraham (Romans 4; Galatians 3, 6 ff.). But neither does Paul intend to describe this faith simply in terms of a subjective act on the part of men, simply a "commitment" or "personal assent." The whole context for his argumentation thus far (and in subsequent chapters) is juridical as well as personal, for it is *inter*personal, not individualistically personal. Even the cultic image underlying 3, 25 evokes a covenant notion, the expiation of the sins of a people through a certain "objective" as well as subjective bond which, though not law, is not non-juridical. Paul's use of the genitive case ("faith of Christ"), as Otto Schmitz noted almost fifty years ago, involves a kind of objective juridical bond, further brought out in Paul's discussion of Abraham (for example, Romans 4, 16). Perhaps the clearest formulation in Romans 3, 21–26 is that in verse 26d, "one of Jesus' faith," *ton ek pisteōs Iēsou,* which echoes and illumines expressions in verses 22a and 25b. When the article (usually in the plural) is used with a following prepositional phrase governed by *ek* ("of," "from"), a certain "party" or group of "affiliates" is designated. For instance, "those of law" (*'oi ek nomou*) in Romans 4, 14 are those whose status or condition is defined by the bond which is the law—not precisely "those individuals who appeal to law" but "those who are heirs on the grounds of law," "those of the law party." Similarly, in the singular, "one from law" (Romans 4, 16c) means one whose juridical position is that of law, and "one from faith" (Romans 4, 16d) means one whose juridical position is that of a kind of trust. The juridical aspect of faith makes it possible to see how Paul can call faith itself a "law" in a real but unique sense (Romans 3, 27). "Faith" is analogous to "law"—simply different (for it is a blessing pure and simple, a benefice like a trust), yet somehow the same (for it is a cultic, juridical bond for a whole people). Recognizing the juridical aspect of law does not really contradict the prevailing interpretation of "Jesus' faith" as personal, individual faith in act, but it considerably enriches the interpretation. For one then grasps better the "institutional" aspect of faith, and can perceive more clearly how it is that Paul is able to oppose law and faith while at the same time he can find the

352

law fulfilled in faith and employ juridical terms (like *paresis*, 3, 25d) in presenting faith.

A final word is called for apropos of the translation given for verse 26d. God proves his justice precisely to show himself just—not precisely to meet a human need, for the latter interpretation of God's justice would be radically man-centered. Thus, it is no tautology but an insistence on strictly theological perspective that accounts for Paul's saying that God clearly indicates his justice for *his being just*. But Paul goes even further than this; he characterizes that justice as salvific and as realized in the bond of faith in Christ. The participle in verse 26d ("justifying") is coordinated with an adjective expressing the same idea and even using the same root ("just") by the conjunction "and" (*kai*), which we have translated by "precisely as." For the coordination is rather curious and seems to require that one take *kai* as explicative. The expression is not unparalleled. Isaiah 16, 5 speaks of "a judge and one seeking judgment and hastening justice," that is, an effective judge, a judge precisely as one who is honest and efficient. Psalm 3, 4 speaks of "My glorious one and lifting high my head," that is, my glory precisely as lifting me up. The "selfish, malicious group" in Romans 2, 8 (*tois de ex eritheias*) seems to be specified by *kai* and the participle as precisely those who disbelieve (*kai apeithousin . . .*). In Romans 3, 26d, the sense would be that God is just precisely in this (positive) way, by establishing man in a salvific relationship to himself (as justifying), and by doing this to one who belongs to Jesus in a bond of faith. Thus, God's salvific justice is effectively manifested in a new juridical, interpersonal relationship in Christ.

IV. CONTROVERSY EXCLUDING MAN'S BOAST BEFORE GOD (3, 27—4, 25)

Having declared God's salvific justice against the background of God's right to exercise wrath, Paul enters the lists of controversy once more. This time, he strikes at man's boast, as hitherto (in Romans 2, 1–3, 20) he struck mainly at man's alleged defense. What God has actually done, even though on men's behalf, leaves man no grounds for confidently rejoicing in his own achievement (boasting). Paul will subsequently (Romans 5) encourage boasting, though he rules it out here (Romans 3, 27–4, 25). For subsequently it will be clear that one boasts only in God's power and glory (cf. 1 Corinthians 1, 30–31) and thus, as far as one himself is concerned, only in his own weaknesses (cf. 2 Corinthians 12, 6–10) as God's theater of operation. In the passage immediately before us, any vestige of self-centered satisfaction must yet be demolished; the fact of justice instead of judgment does not change this need. As Paul excluded man's defense from God's wrath in judgment, he must exclude man's self-centered boast in escaping judgment and obtaining justice.

Achievement by God alone rules out a boast by mere man on the score of mere man's works. For this achievement amounts to the establishment of a definitive principle or law (faith) that is superior to the law (of works) which measures man's efforts. The superiority of the law of faith is substantiated by the case of Abraham. Abraham's act of faith, the grounds for his justification, was his giving glory to God by acknowledging a promise efficacious beyond human hope (4, 18–22). In giving glory to God (professing God's acting aright), Abraham was empowered by faith with new life; his case typifies the Christian's glorification of God; as it typifies the Christian's faith in the Father who empowers us by having enlivened Jesus as our Lord.

3, 27a Where, then, [is our] boast?
27b It has been locked out.
27c Through what kind of law?
27d that of works?
27e No, through law of faith!

28a We argue, you see, that a man is justified by faith
28b independently of works of law.
29a Or is God God of Jews alone? not of gentiles, too?
29b Yes, of gentiles too,
30a since God is *one,*

30b   who will justify the circumcised from faith
30c   and the uncircumcised through the [same] faith.
31a   Are we nullifying law, then, by the faith?
31b   By no means! We are establishing law.

The genre of controversy is established with the opening questions (3, 27–31) and evidently continues into the argument concerning Abraham (for example, 4, 9. 10) (cf. p. 359). The dominant theme, exclusion of man's boast on the basis of law and of what scripture says relevant to Abraham (and to us), requires that we conclude the whole argumentative section only at 4, 25, and that we begin it at 3, 27. The major break within this section occurs with the introduction of the test case, that of Abraham, at 4, 1. Other noteworthy divisions may be placed at 4, 13 (cf. p. 362) and 4, 23 (cf. p. 362).

To exclude man's boast, to "rule it out of court," Paul appeals to what we would call a "principle," and what he, in the juridical framework of Romans, calls a "law." The law adduced to exclude boasting (*kauchēsis*) is the law of faith. How so? It is a superior, definitive law vis-à-vis the law of works. In appealing to the law of faith instead of that of works, Paul feels, moreover, that he is really establishing law, that is, that he is radicating law in an absolute, that he is showing just how law must be conceived eschatologically—which is the same as affirming the law of faith.

To follow Paul in this argument, we should recall that, for him, law was defined mainly in terms of the power and nature of the exalted ruler. That is most sovereignly law which most accurately represents the actual power of the lawgiver; law is the manifest will of the sovereign (who, outside of a strictly human understanding of the ruler, is not in the last analysis one of the people). Moreover, we should recall that Paul judges law and power, as he judges almost everything, in a concrete, dynamic sense, not from the standpoint of the conceptualistic philosopher or theologian. When he grounds his theological arguments in God, he regularly does so in the functional perspective of that which God has done—how God *is effectively* what he is believed to be.

355

Accordingly, Paul launches his argument (v. 28) with an appeal to the fact that he has just declared in 3, 21–26, that God has shown salvific justice in a bond of faith, a juridical arrangement other than that of fulfillment of the law by man's own efforts (for it is a justice involving forgiveness of sins). After reasserting the way in which man is actually justified, Paul hurries on to declare in functional terms the nature of the one who so justified man. God is not to be understood in a limited way; he is God of *all* men. Thus, his law must be understood universally, as *manifestly* universal (in the light of 3, 20–21) and therefore as a law of faith. For God is *one*— not simply in a static, numerical sense, but in the dynamic, functional sense as *effectively* one over all. Law attests God's oneness; the law of faith attests that he will justify all, that he is therefore effectively one over all by faith, and that the law of faith itself is thus definitive and final law, overruling the law of works. Law itself finds its fullest and most definitive expression in the law of faith, because law must be understood in terms of the exalted lawgiver, who is one. Thus Paul proves several things at once: the law of faith is the supreme and definitive law which excludes man's boasting; the law of faith is grounded in God's being effectively one over all men; Paul himself, in appealing to the law of faith, is establishing law in its fullest and proper sense.

In the second main subdivision of this section, Romans 4, 1–25, Paul takes up the case of Abraham. He argues not only that Abraham had no boast (because he was justified by receiving in faith a blessing typifying forgiveness of sins), but that by being justified as an uncircumcised believer, he fulfilled his role as father of many nations (inheriting the world), and serves as a paradigm or type of those whose faith is centered on the giver of risen life in Jesus our Lord. Thus, Paul excludes grounds for boasting by appealing to a key scriptural example which he uses to develop the theme of God's transforming power in justification by faith.

Some background may facilitate one's understanding of this

356

complicated passage. In the first place, Paul presumes but adapts or criticizes certain Jewish views concerning Abraham. The Jews not only regarded Abraham as their forefather and spiritual paradigm, but as one who "inherited the world" and who did so by "meriting" before God. They were accustomed to expound their view of Abraham's merit by linking Genesis 15, 6 with Genesis 22, where Abraham's faith is tested and he offers Isaac (cf. Sirach 44, 20; 1 Maccabees 2, 52). Thus, they read Genesis 22 back into Genesis 15 and considered Abraham's encounter with God and his faith as being a meritorious act, a "work" for which Abraham deserved credit. In effect, Paul insists that Genesis 15 is, as far as Genesis 22 is concerned, an independent context. He argues from a "prior" text. He cites Genesis 15, 6 in Romans 4, 3. 9. 18 (and in 4, 18 moves back to Genesis 15, 5); 4, 22. 23. In Romans 4, 11 and 4, 17 he moves on as far as Genesis 17 (the sign of circumcision), but only to insist that Genesis 17 does not change Genesis 15. In Romans 4, 18, he cites Genesis 15, 5 with Genesis 17 in order to tie these two texts together in terms of the promised inheritance. He sedulously avoids combining a further text (Genesis 22) with that which he regards as basic. On the other hand, he uses a rabbinical approach to interpret a text from the law (Genesis 15, 6) in the light of a text from the Psalms (Psalms 32, 1; cited in Romans 4, 7–8). In doing this, he employs a principle of rabbinic exegesis, *gᵉzērā šāwā'*, by which two texts are joined on the basis of similar terms. The device is a rather artificial one by which the exegete gets a "middle term" for his argument. The same word, "reckon" (*logizomai*), is used (in antithetical phrases) in Genesis 15, 6 and Psalm 32, 1: "not reckon sin" (that is, "forgive," as the parallel stitch of the psalm verse indicates) is taken as the equivalent of "reckon for justice."

A second set of observations deserves even more attention. While Paul supposes the Jewish views given above and employs rabbinical techniques in dealing with them, his argument really rests on an insight into the mystery of justification by

357

faith. The perennial value of his remarks, then, is not to be discerned in the suppositions of his time or in the communications media of the day which he employs in dealing with these suppositions, though one must advert to these communications media in order to disengage Paul's real affirmations. The emerging affirmation of lasting importance is Paul's understanding of justification as an unmerited blessing, forgiveness of sins and an empowering with life, typified in Abraham, but realized eminently in the Christian faithful without discrimination. Paul may seem to be giving an exegesis of Old Testament texts, and thus may seem to be attributing actual sinfulness to Abraham or at least to require us to suppose that Abraham actually existed as an individual. Neither Abraham's sinfulness nor his existence as an individual need be affirmed as actual fact in order to accept Paul's theological affirmations. For Paul presents Abraham basically as a type, as an Old Testament figure understood primarily from the Christian standpoint of fulfillment in Christ and serving to spell out concretely the meaning of this fulfillment. Abraham is not called a type (as is Adam in Romans 5, 14), but he is clearly regarded as one (cf. the contrasts between Romans 4, 23a and 4, 24a, plus the use of the verb *mellein* in 4, 24b and 5, 14). Paul is reading back into the Old Testament example which he adduces the mystery of justification in Christ as he understands it, in order rhetorically and pedagogically to communicate his understanding of the mystery. Paul is no philosopher, one who expects his arguments to stand on their own merit as rational arguments. He is a theologian of a rhetorical persuasion who tries to bring his hearers to accept and understand through dialectical argumentation his own faith insight into the mystery of justification by faith.

A third set of preliminary remarks may also prove helpful in following Paul's argument here. In Paul's use of the term "faith," as Greer Taylor has suggested, there seems to be a juridical notion, that of "a trust." This metaphorical understanding of faith can be of great assistance in making good sense out of what Paul says—providing one does not press it. For Paul never uses metaphors at length without radically altering them. When invoking the metaphor of a "trust," one must recognize the meaning with which Paul invests it thanks to his insight into the mystery of justification in Christ. Thus, one will have to combine with the popular understanding of a trust some distinctive elements of Pauline theology. We hope to indicate a number of these in the course of our exposition.

4, 1a What, then, shall we say about what Abraham found,
   1b   our forefather according to the flesh?
   2a For if Abraham was justified by works, he has grounds for
                                                    boasting.
   2b Not before God!

   3a For what does scripture say?
   3b   "Abraham believed God, and it was *reckoned* to him for justice."
   4a To a man who performs work,
   4b   wages are not reckoned as a gift but as something owed;
   5a to a man who does not work, however,
   5b but simply relies on [believes] one who justifies the godless,
   5c   the faith of this man is reckoned for justice.
   6a Accordingly, David speaks of the blessing of the man
   6b to whom God reckons justice independently of works
                                          [accomplished]:
   7   "Blessed are they whose iniquities are forgiven and whose sins
                                          are covered,
   8·   blessed the man whose sin the Lord will not reckon."
   9a Now, does this blessing apply only to the circumcised
   9b   or to the uncircumcised as well?
   9c For we say that Abraham's *faith* was reckoned for justice.
   10a How, then was it reckoned?
   10b   to one who was [at the time] circumcised
   10c   or uncircumcised?
   10d   Not circumcised
   10e   but uncircumcised!
   11a And he received the *sign* of circumcision
   11b as a seal on the justice from faith had while uncircumcised,
   11c so he would be
   11d   father of all uncircumcised believers
   11e   so that justice could be reckoned to them, too,
   12a   and father of circumcised [descendants], who were not just
                                          circumcised
   12b   but were also those who walked in the footsteps of the faith
   12c   had by our father Abraham when uncircumcised.

                                                    359

Paul begins (4, 1) with a question concerning what Abraham "found." The verb is ambivalent; it could refer to a reward or to an unmerited blessing. He also introduces the topic of Abraham's relationship to us ("our forefather"), though he develops this only subsequently (vv. 11 ff.) and then by equivalently correcting "forefather according to flesh" to "forefather according to faith." He then situates the argument quite squarely in the context of 3, 27 ff., the exclusion of boasting (here, the exclusion not only of the act of boasting, *kauchēsis,* but of grounds for boasting, *kauchēma*). Characteristically, Paul rules out boasting by measuring man's act vis-à-vis God (v. 2b), and proceeds with his argument in this strictly God-centered perspective.

Paul then goes to God's word. Each key term in his citation, "believed," "was reckoned," and "justice," will figure prominently in Paul's argument. But he takes up first the term "was reckoned," proceeding immediately to the possible grounds for a "reckoning." Fittingly, Paul focuses attention on this particular term. Not only will it prove to be the "middle term" to be interpreted in the light of a text from the psalms, but it is a verb in the passive, and makes us advert to what "happened to" Abraham rather than to what Abraham himself did. The image behind the term "reckon" is that of a person's regarding or considering something, such as an action, either by judging it valuable itself (worthwhile, as Philippians, 4, 8, or worthy of compensation) or by judging it to be an occasion for bestowing something of value. In the case of one who "does work" (*ergazomai*), that is, who not only places an act but accomplishes something, the reckoning is something owed for value received (v. 4). But this is not the case with one who has nothing to offer and who, as a debtor, must in fact throw himself on the mercy of the judge. The term "reckon" is thus distinguished by the use of two images. In verse 4, the image is that of a transaction, a "work contract." In verse 5, the image is that of a courtroom decision regarding one who is guilty of sin. Paul boldly supposes as fact conduct which the Old Testament regards as an abomination among human judges, "justify-

360

ing the godless." When a human judge so acts, because he is moved by bribe or plea, the Old Testament regards him in horror (cf. Genesis 18, 23. 25; Exodus 23, 7; Isaiah 5, 23). But Paul supposes a different situation, one in which the divine judge, unmoved by bribe or plea, decides to forgive a man what he owes the judge himself and to grant this same person (who has trustfully thrown himself on the mercy of the judge) a benefice. The benefice will subsequently be shown to be forgiveness of sins and the gift of life—for the one faced with judgment and for his descendants. Such a reckoning is clearly not necessarily the case! But Paul's point in verses 4–5 is to distinguish two kinds of reckoning in view of two different situations.

The second kind of reckoning is then affirmed (vv. 6–8) via a quote from Psalm 32. Such a reckoning is forgiveness of sin, a blessing pure and simple. In not reckoning sin, God reckons forgiveness as a blessing quite independently of the return that a man deserves for accomplishments. Nor is the blessing conditioned on privileged status any more than it is conditioned on accomplishment. To establish this point, Paul moves on (v. 9) to discuss the circumstances of the one who received the blessing; at the same time, he shows the universal scope of the blessing. The circumstances highlight the faith of the one to whom the reckoning was made. Abraham was uncircumcised (which, in this context of a kind of rabbinical argumentation, is probably part of the reason why Paul supposes him to be "godless" and a sinner). Thus Abraham had not performed that work basic to a law of works and could only trust. He received circumcision as a sign, a verification of his relationship to God already had by his justification from faith. Accordingly, he is father in a twofold but radically single sense, father of the uncircumcised and father of the circumcised—but of the latter (as of the former) precisely on the basis of faith. In short, the blessing which Abraham was reckoned (that is, "into which" or "for which" the reckoning was made to him) applies to everybody according to the basis on which Abraham himself received it, not circumcision but faith.

Thus far, then, Paul has argued that "our forefather Abraham" had no grounds for boasting. For Abraham simply received a blessing (forgiveness of sins) while uncircumcised (not marked out as God's possession under a law of works) on the occasion of his trusting in God. This biblical type of God's people is thus our forefather in justice according to faith.

4, 13a   It was not on the grounds of law
13b   that the promise was made to Abraham or to his posterity
13c   that he would inherit the world,
13d   but on the grounds of justice from faith.
14a   For if those who are of law are heirs,
14b   the faith [the trust] is emptied of meaning
14c   and the promise is nullified.
15a   For the law produces wrath;
15b   you see, where there is no law, there is no transgression either.
16a   This is why it is conditioned on faith: that it may come as a
                   personal favor
16b   so that the promise would be valid for all [Abraham's] posterity,
16c   not to one simply under law ["of law"],
16d   but to one, too, who is of Abraham's faith, [Abraham]
17a   who is father of all of us,
17b   as it is written:
17c   "I have made you father of many nations,"
17d   [when Abraham stood] before the God in whom he
                   believed,
17e   who gives life to the dead
17f   and calls non-beings to exist;
18a   who believed with hope against [normal] hope
18b   that he would become a father of many nations
18c   according to what was spoken [to him]:
18d   "Thus [as the stars] will your posterity be."
19a   Not faltering in [his] faith, he understood quite well
19b   that his own body was dead [he was some hundred years
                   of age]
19c   and that Sarah's womb was dead,
20a   but at God's promise he did not waver with disbelief;
20b   instead, he was empowered by faith,
20c   giving glory to God
21a   and being filled with assurance
21b   that what he has promised [God] is able to accomplish.
22   That is why it was reckoned to him for justice!

23a   But it was not for his sake alone
23b   that it was reckoned to him;
24a   rather, it was for us, too,
24b   to whom it was going to be reckoned,

24c	to those who believe [rely on]
24d	him who raised from the dead Jesus our Lord,
25a	who was delivered up for our sins
25b	and was raised to effect our justification.

The previous discussion (vv. 1–2) has led Paul to treat more fully (vv. 13 ff.) the implications of Abraham's fatherhood, namely the inheritance he received for his sons. These implications, because of "groups" involved, require a certain escalation of terms used thus far. "Works" are now treated more institutionally as "law" (namely, law of works). Faith is treated in a corresponding way, a different kind of juridical arrangement, but one involving certain rights. The promise to Abraham of a universal inheritance was not grounded in a legal claim, but was given in justice as a trust. Paul supposes a kind of forensic situation in which one group advances a claim to inheritance differently. If those of the law party are heirs, then the trust makes no sense, nor does the promise which is part and parcel of the trust (v. 14). Law implies sanction, judgment against a transgressor. In view of Paul's argument earlier in Romans, it should be obvious that no one can lay claim to a gift, but can expect only judgment against his transgressions when he takes his stand on law. On the other hand, in an arrangement which is not that of lawful claims, then transgression is no real obstacle to acquiring an inheritance. The benefice comes not on the basis of claim but on the basis of a trust, precisely to bring out its nature: it is a personal favor (v. 16a). As a personal favor given by way of trust, the promised inheritance can hold for everybody associated with the beneficiary in the trust, even to one in the law party (provided he does not expect it on the grounds of law). But by a trust, as understood at the time, one's heirs can be sons other than those born to one according to flesh. In fact, it seems that only by a trust is such a wider inheritance juridically possible, and that the metaphor of a trust underlies Paul's argument here, especially his remark in verse 16b.

The trust as understood here is nevertheless a unique arrangement. It is a juridical arrangement between the judge himself and those who stand before him not simply as persons without a claim but as guilty parties. The benefice conferred is not a sum of money or a legal title to material goods, but forgiveness and life itself. What is more, Abraham's inheritance was not only for his sons, it consisted in sons—all nations—for the inheritance was life itself.

If the promise is a bequest pure and simple to everyone who follows Abraham in believing, how did Abraham believe? In verses 17–22 Paul gives us a vivid picture of our father in faith. With the first relative clause (v. 17), Paul shows that Abraham received this stupendous blessing as a nobody. Then, in verses 18 ff., he shows that, in believing, Abraham looked beyond what was humanly possible. His faith was itself an empowering by God (not just Abraham's commitment) to hope according to God's word. He was not blind to the difficulties, but was enabled to give glory to God, that is, to recognize God's power in his own weakness, and to be fully assured of fulfillment on the basis of that power. That is what is meant, Paul concludes, by saying "it was reckoned to him for justice" (v. 22). Thus Paul has complemented his earlier explanation of this key text with a picture of Abraham's personal faith.

The Apostle now brings to bear on the Christian community this text and the whole explanation which stands with it (vv. 23–25). What is written of Abraham finds its full import and ultimate relevance in the mystery of Christians' justification in Christ. Paul does not concentrate on describing a similarity in human acts, but maintains his theological perspective, that governed by God's acts. God gave Abraham a certain kind of life, but he gives risen life in Jesus. As Abraham's faith must ultimately be understood in terms of God's power, so Christians' faith makes sense in terms of God's life-giving power in Jesus. Man's boasting is excluded by God's way of justifying all in faith; man's grounds for boasting are excluded as in Abraham's case by the fact that actual life-giving power is clearly God's alone.

364

V. EXPOSITION AND EXHORTATION REGARDING GOD'S SALVIFIC POWER
(5, 1–21)

Having excluded man's defense against judgment and any self-centered boast in the justice he has paradoxically been shown, Paul now embarks on an exposition of the prospects for salvation based on what God has already done on our behalf. The messianic blessing of "peace" is already a reality, though it remains to be realized fully in God's "glory" at the resurrection. Paul encourages his hearers to rejoice confidently (boast) in hope of this full realization. The twofold boast, which dominates the general structure of Romans 5, has two principal stages. From verse 3 to verse 10 it focuses on the Christian experience in present trials working out, thanks to God's love, for salvation. From verse 11 onwards, it focuses even more intently on God's action, this time in the perspective of historical fulfillment in the overthrow of the reigns of death and sin through the establishment of the reign of grace in Christ.

5, 1a Justified, then, by faith, we are at peace with God
1b   through our Lord Jesus Christ
2a   through whom we have obtained direct access
2b   to our present state of grace.

2c Yes, let us boast in the hope of God's glory—
3a what is more, while boasting, too, in our trials,

3b   knowing quite well that
3c   tribulation produces patient endurance
4a   and patient endurance, proved character,
4b   and proved character, hope,
5a   hope that does not disappoint
5b   because God's love has been poured out into our hearts
5c   through [the] Holy Spirit given us.

6a For, you see, if Christ, while we were yet weak,
6b still, at the time appointed, died for godless men—
7a   surely, one would scarcely die for a just man,
7b   yet, for a really good man one might find courage to die,
8a   though to us God clearly demonstrates *his* love
8b   in that, while we were yet sinners, Christ died for us!—

9a   how much more certainly, then, now that we have been
                                    justified in his blood,
9b   will we be saved through him from the Wrath!

10a   Indeed, if, while we were enemies,
10b   we were reconciled to God through his Son's death,
10c   how much more certainly, once reconciled,
10d   will we be saved in his risen life!   -
11a   What is more, [let us boast in this hope] while boasting, too, in God
11b   through our Lord Jesus Christ,
11c   through whom we have obtained the reconciliation at this
                                    present time.

"Peace" is the establishment of the messianic reign through
justice, reconciliation with God. This peace, Paul declares, is
now ours through Christ. He has given us access to God's personal favor, in which we now stand. Instead of judgment and
wrath, against which man was defenseless, we have obtained
personal justice. Paul will end this chapter on a note recalling
that with which he has commenced it: a messianic reign of grace
through justice obtained through Christ our Lord.

Since this triumph has been achieved through our Lord, we
can and should boast. What renders possible such confident
rejoicing is clearly what God alone effects in us. The boast in
general is oriented to God's glory, the fulfillment of justification
and the reign of grace. In the first movement in which Paul develops this theme (vv. 3–10), however, he commences with the
role of human adversity in the eschatological period. Unlike sin,
which is a hostile force to be overthrown, tribulation positively
contributes to the realization of hope. It is not simply a trial to
be endured, much less a hurdle to be avoided, but the struggle
through which God's glory is realized. Interior power for the
realization of hope through trials is that of God's love operative
in the Holy Spirit.

To explain how such a boast in adversity makes sense, one
must have recourse to the mystery of Christ's own death. The
power of God's love in the Holy Spirit is demonstrated in what
has happened to us through Christ. This power, in turn, is to be
appreciated not only as a present reality but as grounds for

366

abundant fulfillment. In two parallel sections (vv. 6a–9b and 10a–10d), each with its own condition (vv. 6a, 10a) and *a fortiori* conclusion (vv. 9ab, 10cd), Paul explains this power in terms of the cross and the resurrection at the same time that he explains it in terms of the present and future state of Christians.

A point of special interest to the reader of these two parallel sections is the way in which Paul moves from a more juridical way of speaking to a more personal tone and focus. Neither form of utterance perfectly abstracts from the other. But Paul evinces a marked tendency, observable in other passages as well (Galatians 2, 16–17 in relation to Galatians 2, 18–21; Romans 6–7 [service] in relation to Romans 8 [sonship]), to move from the more juridical to the more personal, intimate, and intense. Consider the following progressions (from *A to B*):

A		B	
6, 6a	weak (*asthenōn*)	6, 10a	enemies (*echthroi*)
6b	godless (*asebōn*)		
8b	sinners (*'amartōlōn*)		
9a	justified	10bc	reconciled
9a	his (cf. vv. 6a, 8b, *Christ's*) blood	10b	death of his *Son*
9b	saved through him from the Wrath	10d	saved in his life

Similarly, even God's love, affirmed in verse 5b, finds more striking personal expression in verse 8ab. By dialectical progressions of this kind, Paul endeavors to bring his readers to a keener appreciation of God's achievement, to a deeper sense of personal involvement, and to a richer optimism in the Lord. His theological thinking in the proclamation of the gospel of salvation is closely attuned to the pastoral situation as he sees it: the need for him to communicate a spiritual gift of understanding for the Romans' encouragement (cf. Romans 1, 11–12).

5, 12a	For this reason,	
12b	as through one man	sin entered the world
12c		and through sin, death,
12d	even so into all men	did death spread
12e		by which } all "sinned."
	[or:	by one by whom]}

13a   (For up to law, sin was there in the world,
13b   though [I grant] sin is not "invoiced' when there is no law;
14a   but death reigned supreme from Adam up to Moses
14b   even over those who did not commit sin after the pattern of
          the transgression of Adam)

14c   who is the counterpart of him who was to come:

15a   But the gracious gift is not at all comparable to the falling away;
15b   for if, by that one man's fall,
15c   the multitude perished,
15d   how much more did the grace of God,
15e   and the free gift which is that of the one man Jesus Christ
15f   well over into the multitude!

16a   Nor is this free grant comparable to the results of one man's
          sinning.
16b   For then: an indictment, after one [act], for general
          condemnation;
16c   but now: a gracious gift, after many sins, for acquittal.
17a   For if, by the sin of one man, death reigned supreme through
          [that] one,
17b   how much more will those who accept the fullness of grace
17c   and of the free gift, justification,
17d   reign supreme in life through the one Jesus Christ!

18a   To sum up, then:
18b   As one man's falling away [affected] all men for general
          condemnation,
18c   so, too, one man's act of justice [affects] all men for a verdict
          granting life
19a   For just as through the disobedience of one
19b   the multitude was constituted sinners,
19c   so, too, through the obedience of one
      will the multitude be constituted just men.

20a   Law, you see, made its entrance later to increase the falling
          away,
20b   though, where sin increased, grace really passed all bounds,
21a   so that
21b   just as sin reigned supreme in death,
21c   so, too, grace would reign supreme, through justification,
          for life eternal
         through Jesus Christ our Lord!

The second movement of Paul's boast begins in verse 11, a verse which should hardly be thought to stand by itself without subsequent development. The boast in verse 3a began with our trials and moved towards the hope of our future salvation (vv.

9ab, 10cd) on the basis of God's present love. The boast in verse 11 (which is closely parallel in form to that of v. 3a) begins with God and focuses on the reconciliation at this present time. God's achievement through Christ would seem by the emphatically placed *nyn* ("at this present time") to be given a historical setting. Would Paul leave this topic without further explanation and simply turn to another topic? Most editors and commentators seem to suppose so when they begin a major part of the epistle or a major subdivision at 5, 12. The grammatically self-contained structures of 5, 12–21 must be recognized. But it seems preferable to construe verses 12–21 as the very grounds for the boast in God stated in verse 11—the grounds in salvation history which account for the present reconciliation and the reign of grace.

Reconciliation at the present time as God's achievement through Christ really accounts for the catastrophe of the reign of death (and subsequently of sin) in the past. For, in Paul's line of thought, fulfillment of a paradoxical cast (most paradoxical when the era preceding the eschaton is contrasted with the eschaton itself) accounts for the course of events which has preceded it. Within the period of eschatological trials, God's love to be fulfilled in salvation gives meaning to our tribulations and thus grounds our confident rejoicing (boast). Within the whole of salvation history, God's triumph in Christ, the new Adam, makes sense of the catastrophe reversed in present reconciliation in a reign of grace, and thus grounds our confident rejoicing in God. The leading words in verse 12a, *dia touto* ("for this reason") have the force of an emphatic "thus" introducing an explanation.

The explanation goes through four stages. First, Paul presents the catastrophic fact of the reign of death through one, accounting for the sin of all (v. 12a-e). He does so in a tightly articulated sentence; *kai 'outōs* in verse 12d is not to be translated "so, too," as if it introduced a comparative clause, but as "even so," introducing a demonstrative clause of result. Second, Paul explains parenthetically (vv. 13a–14b) what he means in verse

369

12d by saying that all "sinned." Third, having established a universal bent towards sin under the reign of death, even apart from the subsequent role of law, Paul proceeds to contrast the picture of universal catastrophe with its opposite by contrasting the effects of two men's actions (taken complexively, with their implications) (vv. 14c–17d). Fourth, he sums up and advances his previous antitheses by making comparisons (vv. 18–21) which take account of the later role of law in turning the reign of death into a veritable reign of sin, so that the victory of the reign of grace stands out as all the more evident and secure for the future.

In the first stage (v. 12), Paul obviously thinks of Adam as an individually existing man. But this supposition, inevitable in Paul's time, does not really enter into his basic affirmation (any more than, as we saw before, do questions like Abraham's existence as an individual, quantitative, clock-and calendar aspects of the parousia, or the actual percentage of Israel who are saved). Adam is presented not precisely as an individual, but as a type, a literary figure intelligible mainly in terms of his counterpart, Christ. The universal scope of redemption in Christ is ultimately the basis for discerning what need be said of Adam ("Man") from a theological standpoint.

Paul does imply a real causality, however, in the role of Adam: "even thus" (v. 12d). The action of "one" (however that "oneness" be construed in phenomenological history) adversely affected "all." The sequence for Adam was sin—death; the sequence for all men was then death—sin. Both death and sin should be taken here as apocalyptic personifications and therefore in a complexive, typological sense. They "enter" (*eisēlthen*), or "spread" (*diēlthen*), and "rule." Like law, which "entered later" (*pareisēlthen,* v. 20a) they are power figures of a mythical rather than strictly conceptualistic cast. This is not to say they are unreal; it is to recognize their intrinsic vagueness and help one see how they must be discussed. Death, for instance, should not be taken as merely physical death (cf. Wisdom 1, 12 ff.; 2, 24; Hosea 13, 14 and 1 Corinthians 15, 54–

370

57), though physical death is part of the features of this personification. Death and sin are causally connected, but death more than sin seems to be what Adam transmitted directly (cf. v. 12d after v. 12bc). It was in conjunction with the spread of death that all "sinned" (v. 12e).

The connective here, *eph' 'ọ* (translated as "by which" or "by [one by] whom"), indicates for all its ambiguity some loose causal connection involving in one way or another both Adam and death. We shall not pretend to be able exactly to fix its meaning. But the interpretation that seems most plausible to us is that it is not a conjunction (such as "inasmuch as") but a preposition followed by a relative pronoun, whose antecedent is more likely "death" than "one." F. W. Danker has demonstrated (from Menander) the grammatical basis for another likely interpretation, namely, that *eph' 'ọ* refers to a kind of juridical basis, the "terms" for the subsequently described condition. But the juridical basis, in our view, would have to be interpreted as a kind of "law of death" (cf. Romans 7, 23–24; 8, 2b), by which all "sinned" and became liable to condemnation. The "juridical basis" would not (and could not, in view of 5, 13–14) be taken as the law of Moses, the law which "entered later" (5, 20). However *eph' 'ọ* is interpreted, it should not be taken in such a way as to make the spread of death consequent on the "sinning of all." The translation "inasmuch as" (favored by Lyonnet) at least tends to reverse the line of thought in this way; it does not do justice to the term "even so," which introduces the *demonstrative result* (on a universal scale —cf. "into *all*") of Adam's act. Nor does the translation "inasmuch as" help us make sense out of the subsequent parenthesis, which explains the kind of sin that is attested by the reign of death (not how death subsequently spread by personal sins like Adam's). In short, Paul says that by Adam's opening the door to sin and thus to death, death was able to spread into all men and by weakening them make them "sin."

We may understand this weakening or deleterious effect, death's spreading into all, as the cause of further sin (in which

371

case the further sin is personal sin) or as itself a kind of sin, a being guilty or a being sin-bent (in which case it is sin in an analogous sense—not as personally committed but as being a kind of natural or *de facto* inheritance). Before pursuing the details of the text, it helps to recall that, for Paul, alienation from God as a gentile sinner is alienation from the *living* God (cf. 1 Thessalonians 1, 9; Romans 9, 26; 2 Corinthians 6, 16). We need not be surprised, in view of what he says elsewhere, to find him here regarding "death" as "sin" of a real but analogous kind. Now, the term which is used for "sinned" in verse 12e is not the same aorist type as that which is used for a sinful act in verses 14b and 16a. This of itself proves nothing but the possibility that another sense may be intended in this context. Ligier, however, has argued well that the second aorist of verse 12e can be taken in the sense of "being sinful" without the connotation of personally committed sin. This analogous notion of sinfulness (which is traditionally that of a Catholic theology of original sin concerning those afflicted by it consequent upon Adam) seems to be what Paul himself endeavors to bring out in the parenthesis of verses 13a–14b. Apparently he perceives the vagueness of his own statement about death's spreading into all men by which they all sinned (v. 12de). He also recalls the fact that he has tied sin to law (3, 20), and in the perspective of salvation history which he gives in Romans 5, 12 ff. he adverts to the fact that law (as a power figure in this epic drama) is not yet on stage. He therefore explains himself before continuing with a contrast between Adam and Christ.

The *second* stage of Paul's explanation, the parenthesis of verses 13a-14b, illuminates quite well the meaning of "sinned" in verse 12e. Indeed there was sin in the world even prior to the coming of law (v. 13a), but sin is not present as "invoiced" when there is no law (v. 13b, *ouk ellogeitai*, "not invoiced"; cf. Philemon 18–19, where Paul uses the very term *ellogein* just before penning a personal I.O.U.). Sin without law is not "chalked up" as a personal debt.

Now, we must recognize that, in speaking of law here, Paul

372

prescinds from the subjective, interior knowledge of law which he sometimes describes or supposes elsewhere (Romans 2, 14–16; 7, 7–25). In Romans 5, he is treating salvation history, and therefore law, in a more epic perspective; law is a power figure which enters later (v. 20a). Accordingly, Paul's perspective here in verse 13 is not that of sins as recognized in conscience. Consequently, we cannot construe his words as a denial that there were personal sins during the period prior to law, that is, prior to Moses. He is simply explaining how he can affirm the presence of real sin without bringing law into the picture. The sin is one which is not "invoiced," that is, not personally reckoned.

How is the sin to be understood then? As death. This is the point of verse 14ab. After saying that sin was there—but not an invoiced sin—Paul affirms that death reigned supreme in the whole period prior to law and subsequent to Adam, even over those who did not commit *personal* sins after the pattern of the *transgression of a precept* (a *law*), as was the case with Adam himself. Thus verse 14 shows that everyone is one with Adam in being subject to "death" even though one did *not* sin as Adam did, namely, by transgressing a precept, a law (as conveyed in the sense of the term transgression, *parabasis*). Far from saying that everybody sinned as Adam sinned, Paul says that everybody suffered what Adam suffered even without having committed sin as Adam did. But what everybody suffered as Adam and in consequence of Adam's act is nevertheless a kind of sinfulness, an alienation from the living God which is equivalently condemnation, liability to wrath. In short, the parenthesis (vv. 13–14) explains "all 'sinned' " as referring to real sin consequent upon Adam even though that sin was not personal sin (transgression of a precept). Paul does not say that there were no personal sins from Adam to Moses, but he affirms that there was universal sinfulness which was not personal. He does not limit this real non-personal sinfulness to the period between Adam and Moses, but argues from this period to affirm its existence. This non-personal sinfulness will be articulated by law (vv. 16c, 20), which will escalate the reign of death (v. 14a) into a reign of sin in death (v. 21b).

It is important not to inject into Paul's perspective of epic catastrophe a specific problem which is alien to it, namely, how those before Christ, especially infants, are saved. Undoubtedly they could be saved by God through Christ. Precisely how they could be saved involves a psychologically or sociologically oriented theology which goes beyond that of Paul himself. What is more, Paul is dealing here not with the problem of how these people could be saved but with the way they can all be said to have sinned and thus be open to redemption by God's grace. He explains this universal sin quite well, by distinguishing it from men's actions under law (their personal sins) and thus by rooting it somehow in their natural (or *de facto*) state subsequent to Adam. Modern theologians questing further will no doubt have to mythologize (construct a model solution) in their own way as did the medievals who mythologized to convey to men of their own day Paul's basic insight into universal need for redemption in Christ. But by mythologizing in his own way, the Apostle does provide some solid indications of the way in which "original sin" in men subsequent to Adam can be understood as truly sin but not personal sin. He also seems to require that we affirm a universal sinfulness, even apart from personal sinfulness, in order properly to understand redemption in Christ, which he sees as a total restructuring of humanity, a radical reorientation to life. The rest of this chapter and subsequent passages from Romans (such as 7, 7–25) confirm the longstanding recognition that what has come to be called the doctrine of original sin is fundamental to Pauline theology. Through an original personal sin committed by man, the whole of humanity has become radically alienated from the living God and lies prone to personal sins leading to condemnation; this catastrophic situation is that which has been triumphantly undone through Christ, the new Adam.

From the parenthetical explanation of universal sinfulness, Paul sweeps into his dominant contrast. The *third* stage of his

374

explanation, the contrast between type and fulfillment figure, entails two complexive situations in a kind of dynamic imbalance. In verse 15, Paul declares that the gracious personal favor of God and the concrete manifestation of this favor in Christ has already outweighed the effects of Adam's sin. A certain corporate situation is implied by the use of the term "multitude" in each case. Although the "multitude" (*'oi polloi*) is generally taken to mean "all" (cf. vv. 12de and 18, *pantes*), it more exactly conveys (in Greek or in its Hebrew and Aramaic equivalents) the image of a community, a collectivity, thus adding the note of some kind of corporate identity. With regard to this corporate situation, Paul does not say that Christ restored what Adam lost; he says that Christ was the way God *abundantly* manifested his favor in the multitude who died. The contrasted effects are unequally weighted. What is more, the contrast here does not rest with a double "one/many" antithesis. Paul does not contrast the fall through one with the restoration by another; he contrasts the fall through one with God's personal gift freely bestowed in another. Thus, Paul is speaking of God's new constitution of humanity in Christ, a kind of new creation after death, highlighting God's sovereign freedom on men's behalf.

In a second contrast (vv. 16–17), Paul moves to the further consequences in each series. Once again a striking upset is underscored; after one sin came condemnation, but acquittal has come after many sins. What man has brought on himself by one act, God has superabundantly outdone by granting favor after many sins. His power for forgiveness is greater than man's power for failure. Here again Paul makes a curious contrast which brings out a dynamic imbalance in power. He does not contrast the reign of death with the reign of life, but the reign of death with those who will by the abundance of grace reign in life (v. 17). *Abundance* (*perisseia*) of grace is underscored in verse 17b as it was in verse 15d-f (where the verbal form is used: *eperisseusen*, "welled over") and as it will be in verse 20b (where a still more emphatic verbal form appears: *'ypereperisseusen*, "passed all bounds"). But the freely bestowed gift of

375

God, for all its power, is not forced on men. Paul supposes that the reign in life means that people will have taken what was given (cf. v. 17b). Thus, while the consequences in each series entail a reign, a kingdom, the grace series is not automatic, but supposes free acceptance of a freely bestowed favor.

At the *fourth* stage of his exposition in 5, 12–21, Paul formulates his main constructions as comparisons. These are more regular than his sharp contrasts in verses 15–17 and easier to follow, the contrasts in verses 18–21 being contained mainly in the particular phrases employed. The condemnation suffered by all as the result of Adam's sin was death—not only in the physical sense but in the sense in which it has been offset by the effective verdict granting life (*dikaōsin zōēs,* v. 18c). The parallelism here (cp. the end of b with the end of c in v. 18) as earlier (cp. vv. 16b and 17a with vv. 16c and 17d) bears out our earlier observation that Paul considers the sin of Adam to the extent that it automatically affected all as bringing on a state of death. Additional confirmation of this view can be found in verse 19, which is introduced as a further explanation of verse 18 ("For," *gar*). Condemnation on all (v. 18b) is paralleled by the constitution of the multitude as sinners (v. 19b), whereas the constitution of the multitude as just men (v. 19d) is paralleled by the verdict granting life (literally: justification of life, v. 18c), so that being sinners and being condemned is seen not only in contrast to being just but to having life. Therefore, being constituted sinners is equivalently being made a community under the reign of death.

Further nuances are introduced in verse 19, but they do not seem to alter the interpretation that Paul sees the sinfulness of all in connection with Adam as a state of death rather than as a reckoning of personal sins. By the time justification arrived, there were also numerous personal sins (cf. v. 16c), but insofar as the personal disobedience of one had an effect on all, the sinfulness was a state of death which gravitated towards condemnation. It was law, which entered later, that increased sinfulness and made the reign of death into a reign of sin in death (vv.

376

20–21). The constitution of a community of the just is expressed in a future tense. With W. Thüsing, it seems best to take the verb not only as a logical future ("would be constituted") but as a real future ("will be constituted"). Paul sees the new reign in the light of its consummation as well as in the light of its present inauguration. In verse 15d-f he indicates that grace is a present reality; in verse 17b-d and again in verse 19d he at least strongly hints at its future permanence, and in verse 21c, by the addition of the word "eternal" Paul certainly indicates the overall futuristic thrust of his thought.

The epic triumph which has been achieved in Christ is the reign of God's grace for eternal life where before there had been a reign of death and of sin in death. This epic divine achievement is the historical grounds for our boast in God's reconciliation here and now (Romans 5, 11) as basing in turn our confident hope for the full realization of his glory (Romans 5, 2). Our boastful hope lies in the power of the grace he has shown us in Christ.

VI. CONTROVERSY AND EXHORTATION APROPOS OF ROMANS 5, 12–21: SIN, DEATH AND LAW (6, 1—7, 25)

In the following two chapters, Paul once again enters into controversy with an imagined adversary. He debates points which arise directly from what he has said in the second half of Romans 5, probing especially the theme of freedom from sin (leading to death) and the deadly role of law. In effect, he argues that this divine triumph of grace in Christ, which he has presented as the grounds for our boast in hope, entails a restructuring of our lives through an identification with Christ's death and resurrection (6, 1–14), a new service at odds with sin (6, 15–23) precisely because we have been made dead to law for a new bond with Christ (7, 1–6), though God's law itself was not sinful, but only the catalyst for sin, death, and despair under a law of sin within me (7, 7–25). The resurrection of Christ, as an act of consummate power in the new reign or kingdom of grace for eternal life, has been effected through the Father's glory (6, 4). Thus, the divine glory on which our hope is centered (5, 2) is already inaugurated and Christologically defined: it is the glory in the risen Lord with whom the Christian is already vitally united—through baptism into his death. From this mystical union there follows death to sin and law (§ VI) and a new life in the Spirit (§ VII) leading to the glory to be revealed in us.

6, 1a What, then, shall we say?
 1b Are we to remain in sin that grace may increase?
 2a By no means!
 2b We are people who have died to sin; how shall we still live in it?
 3a   Or are you unaware
 3b   that all of us when we were baptized into Christ Jesus
 3c   were baptized into his death?
 4a   We were buried with him, then, by our baptism into [his] death,
 4b   in order that just as Christ was raised from the dead through the Father's glory,
 4c   so we, too, may walk in newness of life.

 5a For if we have become vitally united with the very likeness of his death,
 5b   we shall also be [vitally united with the very likeness] of his resurrection,
 6a   recognizing
 6b   that our old self was crucified with him
 6c   completely to withdraw our body from sin's influence, from ever again being slaves to sin;
 7   for one who has died has been absolved [justified] from sin.

 8a If, then, we have died with Christ,
 8b we understand by faith [believe] that we shall live with him,
 9a   knowing quite well
 9b   that Christ risen from the dead dies no more;
 9c   death no longer exercises dominion over him;
 10a   as to his death, he died to sin once and for all;
 10b   as to his life, he lives for God.

 11a   So, too, must you reckon yourselves to be
 11b   fully dead to sin
 11c   but living for God in Christ Jesus.

 12a   Therefore, do not let sin reign in your mortal bodies

12b	so as to obey its lusts,
13a	and do not keep surrendering your limbs to sin as arms for injustice,
13b	but surrender yourselves to God as men raised from the dead to life,
13c	and your limbs to God as arms for justice.
14a	For sin is not to have any dominion over you;
14b	since you are not subject to law but to grace.

The first objection (6, 1) which Paul answers is that of a spectator who feels that in view of what God has done he need not change his way of life. Paul replies that our lives have been totally restructured in Christ through baptism; we are ordered to a new way of life (6, 1–4). The Apostle develops this point in two similarly constructed passages (vv. 5–7 and vv. 8–10). The first of these stresses the fact that Christ's death and resurrection shape Christian existence as a whole. Through baptism (supposed from what was said in vv. 3–4) we have taken on a form that is radically at odds with sin, the form of the Servant's obedience (as subsequent remarks suggest). But the very likeness of Christ's death which becomes the shape of our lives expresses a mysterious ontological union, not just a moral disposition. The sacrament of baptism itself is not this "very likeness" (v. 5a) but finds its deepest meaning in this mysterious existential conformity which it effectively signifies. Ontological conformity with the mystery of Christ's death and resurrection will be fulfilled only with our own resurrection (v. 5b), though our being shaped by his death already achieves a total break with sin (vv. 6–7).

The second passage restates and builds upon the first. In our understanding in faith of what this ontological conformity implies, we see that death with Christ means life with him—life which he enjoys now and forever. Verses 8–10 focus not on the negative effect (justification from sin) but on the positive aspect of the same mystery (eternal life), not on the effect in us (v. 7) but on the reality in Christ (v. 10), especially in its positive, God-centered aspect of life for the Father (v. 10b). Accordingly, Paul exhorts his hearers to a present life in Christ which, though not exactly the same as that of the resurrection in verse 13b (he uses '*ōsei,* literally, "as if"), is clearly a participation in Christ's risen life.

6, 15a	What then?
15b	Are we to sin because we are not subject to law but to grace?
15c	By no means!
16a	Do you not know
16b	that when you surrender yourselves in servitude to anyone's obedience,
16c	you are slaves of the one you obey?
16d	either slaves of sin for death
16e	or [slaves] of obedience for justice?
17a	Thanks be to God
17b	that you [who] were slaves to sin
17c	have become sincerely obedient to that model of training to which [or: to whom] you have been entrusted;
18a	having been emancipated from sin,
18b	you have become slaves to justice.
19a	I am speaking in human fashion because of your human limitations [the weakness of your flesh]:
19b	just as in the past you surrendered your limbs
19c	to be slaves to impurity and wickedness for further wickedness,
19d	so now you are to surrender your limbs
19e	to be slaves to justice to [advance in] holiness.
20a	For when you were slaves of sin,
20b	you were free from [the control of] justice.
21a	What return did you then have from deeds
21b	for which you are now ashamed?
22a	But now that you have been made free of sin's control,
22b	and are enslaved to God,
22c	the return which you have leads to holiness
22d	and the end is life everlasting.
23a	For death is the wages [paid by] sin,
23b	but eternal life is the gracious gift of God
23c	in Christ Jesus our Lord.

The next objection which Paul forfends (6, 15) is not that of a diffident man (as in 6, 1) but that of an antinomian, one who thinks that this new subjugation to grace which has shaped his life releases him from any obligation because it releases him from law. Paul argues that there is question of a new service.

380

Human freedom is not in his eyes an absolute. From his Old Testament background, being a "slave of God" is an honorific title quite compatible with the notion of genuine freedom. As an Apostle, free as any man (cf. 1 Corinthians 9, 1. 19), Paul himself is the "slave of Jesus Christ" (cf. Romans 1, 1; Galatians 1, 10; Philemon 1, 1). Realistically, Paul judges that some service is inevitable for man, and that what is of decisive importance is the one whom one ultimately serves. In verse 17, he speaks of an object of service contrasted with sin, the "model of training" (*typos didachēs*). Perhaps this refers to the form of baptismal teaching which spells out one's allegiance to Christ the Lord. The Master himself is present in the apostolic word in other respects (for example, as salvific power, Romans 10, 6–10), and the word of this gospel is an object of obedience (cf. Romans 10, 16; 1, 5; 2 Corinthians 10, 5; 2 Thessalonians 1, 8). Reductively, at least, the expression would seem to refer to Christ himself. Paul regularly uses the term *typos* of persons, and just as one can be said to learn teaching (Romans 16, 17), which is contrasted with not serving Christ (Romans 16, 18), one can be said to learn Christ himself (Ephesians 4, 20). In any event, the abstract "service of justice" is ultimately seen concretely and personally as service to God (cp. vv. 20ab and 22ab). Wickedness itself is not so much transgression of precept as it is rebellion (*anomia*, v. 19c, "lawlessness" in the sense of personal hostility to God, as regularly understood in New Testament eschatology). The end of the old service is a wage paid; the end of the new service is not an impersonal remuneration but the personal gift of God, eternal life in Christ our Lord.

7, 1a Or are you unaware, brethren (I am speaking to men who
                                        understand law),
1b   that law has dominion over a man [only] just as long as he lives?
2a   A married woman is bound by law to her husband while he lives;
2b   but if her husband dies, she is freed from the law of her husband.
3a   To put it succinctly:
3b   While her husband lives she is called an adulteress
3c   if she becomes [the possession] of another man,

3d   but if her huband dies, she is free from the law,
3e   so as not to be an adulteress when becoming another man's.
4a   So, my brethren,
4b   you, too, have been made dead to the law through Christ's body,
4c   for becoming [the possession] of another, the one raised from the dead,
4d   that we may bear fruit for God.
5a   For when we were in the flesh,
5b   our sinful passions, those [stirred up] through the law
5c   were operative in our limbs
5d   for bearing fruit for death.
6a   But now we are completely withdrawn from the law,
6b   having died to that by which we were held [possessed for service]
6c   with the result that we are to serve
6d   in the new order of the spirit,
6e   not in the old order of the letter.

The break with sin as entailing a new, fruitful service which is not service under law forms the topic of Paul's explanation in 7, 1–6. He first gives the example of the married woman who is free for a new bond (vv. 2–3). She is bound by the law of her husband, that is, by her husband himself (as her "lord" in the Semitic way of thinking) until his death; then she is free for a new union. Secondly, Paul applies his metaphor, doing considerable violence to it, in order to indicate the distinctive character of the new bond (vv. 4–6). The metaphor will simply not bear the full force of Paul's conception of the totally new bond in Christ and of the way this new bond arose. He does not say, therefore, "you were wedded to the law (namely, that under which you sinned), but that law is effectively dead and now you are wedded to Christ (to bear according to the spirit for life)." Why not? The preceding formulation, which Paul does not use, might imply that one relationship ceased and another arose without any internal connection—but this does not fit the facts of salvation history. What is more, it might imply that the basis for the new bond really lay in the freedom of the woman and not in what took place in the dominant partner with whom she is united. Precisely to bring out the theological understanding of *how* the *total* change in the woman's status has been effected,

382

Paul must do violence to his own metaphor. Christ must figure prominently in both stages of the transformation of the woman's status. In applying the metaphor, Paul attributes the whole change of the woman's status (and thus her freedom) to one and the same person, Christ. The "law of the husband" is dissolved by the death of the husband, Christ, and the new union is not only possible but abundantly fruitful by the fact that he, as risen, is the "new husband." One must be careful not to press the metaphor even along the lines by which Paul changes it. For instance, one should not identify the law as oppressive with Christ himself, or regard the law as identified with Christ at the time of his public life and passion. Paul's point in identifying Christ with law is simply to explain Christologically the termination of the old order at the same time that he extols the superiority of the new bond in the risen Christ by which one's freedom is realized. This freedom is a service in the newness of the spirit, for the spirit derives from the risen Christ, whose indivisible paschal mystery accounts for the whole process of transformation in us.

7, 7a   What, then, shall we say?
    7b   [That] the law is sin[ful]?
    7c   Absolutely not!
    7d   But I would not have known sin
    7e   were it not for law;
    7f   and indeed I would not have known covetousness
    7g   unless the law said "You shall not covet!"
    8a   But sin, seizing the occasion provided by the explicit injunction
    8b   produced in me every illicit desire [kind of covetousness];
    8c   since without law sin is dead.

    9a   Once upon a time I lived without law.
    9b   But when the explicit injunction came along, sin sprang to life,
   10a   and I died.
   10b   And the injunction that was to [point the way to] life
   10c   was found to be for me [the occasion] for death.
   11a   For sin, seizing the occasion provided by the explicit injunction
   11b   deceived me, and through that [injunction] slew me.
   12a   Consequently, the law [itself] is holy,
   12b   and the injunction is holy and just and altogether good.
   13a   Was it then a good thing that caused my death?

13b By no means!
13c It was sin,
13d   sin that was to manifest itself as sin
13e   by using a good thing to bring about my death,
13f   sin that was to become superlatively sinful
13g   by means of the injunction.
14a For we know quite well that the law is spiritual,
14b but I am flesh and blood, sold into slavery to sin.
15a   I do not acknowledge my actions as my own.
15b   For it is not what I wish that I do.
15c   It is what I hate that I do.
16a   But if I do not do what I wish,
16b   I agree with the law that [the law] is good.
17a   But, as it is, it is no longer I who effect the deed,
17b   it is rather sin dwelling within me.
18a I know by experience that in me, that is, in my flesh, good does not
                                                                        dwell.
18b   For to wish lies in my power,
18c   but to effect what is noble does not.
19a   For I do not do good, which is what I want to do,
19b   but what I do not want to do, evil, that is what I do.
20a   And if I do what I do not want,
20b   then it is no longer I who effect the deed
20c   but sin dwelling within me.
21a In a word, I find the law as I want to do what is noble
21b   to the effect that in my power is evil.
22   I am pleased with the law of God according to the inner man,
23a   but I see another law in my limbs,
23b   doing battle with the law of my intelligence
23c   and taking me captive for the law of sin that is in my limbs.
24a Miserable man that I am!
24b Who will rescue me from this body doomed to death?
25a Thanks be to God through Jesus Christ our Lord!
25b To sum up: I myself by my intelligence render service to God's
                                                                        law,
25c   but in my flesh [I serve] the law of sin.

In extolling this new bond, Paul refuses to condemn the law
itself (7, 7–25). His main concern throughout this section of
Romans has been to show the practical consequences of the
new reign of grace (Romans 5, 21) over that of sin, abetted by
law, in death. The reign of grace means a complete break with
sin and therefore with that situation in which sin is inescapable,
a situation in which law articulates sin but does not and cannot
effectively stop it, because law in this deathbound situation is

not a dominant power. Concretely, law only serves as the tool of sin when it does not remedy man's basic need by giving life, an interior power to resist sin. The role of law must be discussed in this epic framework of human devolution, and it must be judged to be a starkly negative one. The epic global standpoint of apocalyptic (which sidesteps the way in which law was accompanied by grace, which was operative not by reason of law but by reason of the way law would be fulfilled) admittedly oversimplifies the role of law. But it does not really falsify it— so long as one retains Paul's eschatological perspective in which the primary distinction falls between old and new epochs of salvation history and everything is judged from the standpoint of creative fulfillment.

Thus, before God's grace was operative through Christ, man was not internally fortified in that way in which he would be fortified in Christ. Even in an initial state of favor with God, prior to sin, he was more vulnerable to sin given a confrontation with God's law. He was vulnerable to deception, though not yet a slave to sin. Once man had committed sin, he became subject to it in a state of death which led to further sin at every confrontation with the holy law of God that lay beyond his power of effective action. The result was the emergence of a counter-law or pattern within man's personal actions, the law of sin dooming him to death. In the new epoch of salvation history, as Paul will show in Romans 8, the "spiritual law" of God (v. 14a) can be fulfilled by a connatural *internal* principle which man did not have before, even when he was in a state of rapport with God prior to confrontation with the law. The "law of the spirit giving life" of the epoch of fulfillment is more than man (Adam) had even *prior* to his sin, not to say much more than he had in the state of death and sin in which he put himself. What dogmatic theologians would call the "grace of Christ" was qualitatively different from what, in a dogmatic context, would be called the "grace of Adam" (prior to his sin). Paul expresses this truth in his own way, namely, in the perspective of eschatological fulfillment by the advent of a new,

385

internal power which was not operative even prior to man's self-inflicted alienation from God, and which became the only hope in view of the consequences of self-inflicted and progressive alienation from God.

Throughout most of 7, 7–25, Paul speaks in the first person. His "I" is not biographical, nor is it as psychologically introspective as men in the West have thought from Augustine to Luther and beyond (cf. K. Stendahl). He speaks in a kind of dramatic monologue, and in the person of Adam, "Man," rather than in his own person (cf. Lyonnet); it is typological, not autobiographical. His monologue has a typological cast precisely because it evokes the image of Adam, which means, however, that it cannot be taken in a merely univocal way, for example, as a picture of "Everyman." For one thing, it is clearly not the picture of man in grace, but that of man without Christ, man who voices a cry of desperation at the end of this section (v. 24) and receives his answer in terms of the law as fulfilled through Christ (7, 25 plus 8, 1–2). Furthermore, Paul presents us with a situation which is in some respects unique: life in halcyon days apart from law (7, 9a). Understood in terms of epic salvation history described in Romans 5, this situation might be thought to refer to the period before Moses. But the personal flavor of the monologue itself suggests that we understand this situation of the life of Adam prior to temptation. For the "law" he knew was the "precept" or "injunction" enunciated subsequently to his first idyllic days in paradise. He alone truly lived "once upon a time without law." What is said in this typological monologue may be understood proportionately of every adult in a graceless state, but only proportionately, so that not every detail can be verified of every graceless man. Not to observe this caution would be to turn type into definition, literary portraiture into logic.

Within this typological picture, Paul leaves room for affirming that man is not sold into slavery to sin simply by being flesh and blood (v. 14b). What accounts for this *slavery* to sin is the state of death resulting from a kind of first sin (vv. 9b, 10a,

11b, 13a, 13e). Given death through sin, one is under the sway of sin. What accounts for the first sin by which this hopeless situation arises? Paul mentions only the presence of law by way of a precept typical of law—an injunction against self-centered fulfillment. Paul certainly does not suppose any special "glory of Adam," but at the same time he seems not to suppose any prior state of alienation from the living God. His presumed source, Genesis, would indicate more positively a state of familiarity with God and an original (though pre-eschatological) state of being wholly good. Thus, the dogmatic theologian may well argue that what Paul says implies that Adam lived in a state of favor with God. From the dogmatic theologian's standpoint, in which biblical terms are redefined for a new universe of metaphysical discourse, the idyllic state could be called a state of grace. Paul, of course, would not call this state "grace," for "grace," like "faith" and "spirit" are, for him, eschatological concepts proper to the state of Christian existence (life in the era of fulfillment). The Apostle thinks metahistorically, not metaphysically; accordingly, all his terms are employed in an eschatological perspective of fulfillment. What is more, he certainly does not mythically develop the image of Adam's felicity prior to the first sin. Man from the outset is quite liable to deception; he does not have the outlook of the spirit (cf. 8, 2–7), an eschatological reality. What Paul says of Adam before his sin could easily be said of one or more emerging human beings on the lowest evolutionary rung of the species. No special gifts of wisdom or understanding are implied in Adam in contrast to Christians of Paul's own day; in fact, less is implied, even when Adam is considered as sinless.

On the other hand, even after sin, and when living in a state of death and moral impotence, man is not depicted as wholly corrupt. Paul says not: "no good dwells in me," but: "in my flesh good does not dwell." Man is not wholly corrupt, for even when in sin he can still recognize what he is expected to do, and recognize it appreciatively. Nor, for all his misery in being unable to fulfill the law he recognizes as holy, would this man rightly be judged free from responsibility for his actions. For, ultimately, he becomes powerless through his own doing. Responsibility, however, is not the precise issue here; the monologue depicts rather a desperate situation in which one has been imprisoned by sin and death and cannot extricate himself. Man's desperate state under sin, death, and law is now ready to be contrasted with the prospects of an eschatological hope in Christ. To join these contrasting pictures of despair and hope, Paul sheds a ray of thankful hope into the picture of anguished despair (v. 25), and then restates in less anguished, juridically formulated terms, the plight of one whom he will answer directly and juridically at the beginning of the next section (8, 2).

VII. EXPOSITION AND EXHORTATION APROPOS OF ROMANS 5, 1–11: NEW CREATION THROUGH THE SPIRIT (8, 1–39)

With Romans 8, we come to the grand climax of the juridically phrased Pauline apocalypse of God's gospel. The chapter is not without numerous ties to what precedes, especially to Romans 5, 1–10, with its triumphant description of the Christian experience as grounds for eschatological hope of God's glory—the experience of trials leading to triumph through the love of God experienced in the working of the spirit which God has given in Christ. God's justice through a bond of faith in Christ, which is achieved through a death that proves God's love and imparts it to us through the spirit of the risen Lord, grounds our hope for the achievement of God's glory—the new creation that is our inheritance in his Son's life.

In Romans 8, Paul declares that the apocalyptic condemnation has actually fallen on sin existing in human disorientation from God, not on those who are in Christ Jesus (Romans 8, 1–4). The latter are now able to fulfill the just conduct of the law by the interior principle of the spirit, provided they walk according to the spirit by the power which now dwells in them (8, 5–13), which was not previously the case (7, 7–25). In being guided by the spirit of God, they are sons, not just servants (8, 14 ff.; cf. Romans 6, 15–7, 6), much less slaves out of fear (8, 15), and can look forward to the inheritance of sons which will be the full proof of their sonship according to the pattern of the mystery of Christ's life (8, 14–17; cf. 6, 1–14). That consummation of sonship implies a whole new order of creation achieved through tribulations in confident hope overcoming all frustration (8, 18–25; cf. Romans 5, 2–21), for it is achieved by the spirit of God (8, 23. 26; cf. 5, 5. 15–17) according to the salvific design which is at work in those who love God by virtue of his effective action on their behalf (8, 26–30). No condemnation or obstacle is to be feared in view of the love of God shown us in Christ Jesus our Lord (8, 31–39). Thus, Paul's good news of God's power of salvation exercised universally through justification by faith (Romans 1, 16–17; 3, 21–26; 5, 1) is completed in firm hope for the permanence and fulfillment of God's love as shown in the messianic Lord whom we acknowledge.

In Romans 1–8, an apocalypse of salvific power is cast against the negative background of expected judgment on a universal scale (and with no defense) as a paradoxically manifested personal justice that is to be fulfilled in risen life according to the sovereign power of God's grace juridically manifested in the law of faith and the law of the spirit of life realized through Christ. An ontological transformation, the new creation, is being achieved juridically—by an act which is, however, not legalistic (narrowed by human claims or accomplishments) but sovereignly personal and gracious, a stupendous act of love disproportionate to mankind's legitimate expectations (that is, "supernatural" in an eschatological sense).

8, 1   But there is now no condemnation awaiting those who are in
                                           Christ Jesus.
  2a   For the law of the spirit bringing life in Christ Jesus
  2b   has emancipated you [singular] from the law of sin and death.

389

3a   As to what the law could not do, because it was incapacitated by
          the flesh—

3b   God, sending his own Son in the very likeness of sinful flesh

3c   to deal with sin,

3d   passed condemnation on sin in the flesh [of men]

4a   in order that the just conduct which the law demanded might
          be fulfilled

4b   in us, men who walk not according to the flesh,

4c   but according to the spirit.

5a Those who live according to the flesh desire fleshly things,

5b but those who live according to the spirit [desire] spiritual things.

6a Indeed, the desire of the flesh leads to death,

6b whereas the desire of the spirit looks to life and peace.

7a This is why the desire of the flesh is hatred towards God;

7b   it does not yield itself to the law of God, and cannot;

8   and those who are in the flesh cannot please God.

9a But you are not in the flesh; you are in the spirit,

9b   since God's spirit is dwelling within you.

9c   If one does not have Christ's spirit,

9d   this one does not belong to him.

10a On the other hand, if Christ is in you,

10b   then the body is dead as far as sin goes

10c   and the spirit is alive for [fulfilling] justice.

11a And if the spirit of him who raised Jesus from the dead is
          dwelling in you,

11b   then he who raised from the dead Christ Jesus

11c   will enliven your mortal bodies, too,

11d   through his own spirit that is dwelling within you.

12a So, then, brethren,

12b we are not indebted to the flesh

12c   to live according to the flesh.

13a   For if you live according to the flesh,

13b   you are going to die.

13c   But if by the spirit you put to death the deeds of the body,

13d   you will live.

This chapter begins with an answer to the condemned man speaking in Romans 7, 7–25, which opens out into a consideration of two basic outlooks and tendencies that are a matter of death or life (8, 1–13). It then turns into a development of the Christian experience of life in the spirit given to God's sons, stressing the prospects for future glory in a new creation (8, 14–30) (cf. p. 392). Concluding the chapter and the proclamation of the gospel in the whole first part of Romans is a peroration insistently demanding whether anyone can judge us adversely or whether anything in creation can separate us from the salvific love of God in Christ Jesus our Lord (8, 31–39) (cf. p. 397).

In verses 1–13, Paul first explains the transformation of the existence of the doomed man by showing the freedom effected by the law of the spirit of life in Christ. The verdict of condemnation, thanks to God's sending his Son, is not passed on man but on sin, so that what the law demands can indeed be fulfilled when one no longer lives according to the death principle (flesh). The law itself could not effect a transformation, for it remained exterior and flesh was not capable of meeting the demands of the "spiritual" law (cf. 7, 14a). But Christ was sent in the very likeness of sinful flesh, that is, his mission was effected in weak human nature as subject to the effect of sin, death. "Sinful flesh" is deathbound flesh. Thus, a reconstitution of human nature from within could be effected by Christ's dealing with sin in this concrete form. He "dealt" with it by undergoing death and, in the same process of one mystery, by outdoing death in resurrection. As Paul has done so often before (for instance, 3, 27–4, 25; 5, 1–21), he now blends juridical and ontological aspects in the mystery of grace by which we receive justification instead of judgment.

Then, in verses 5–13, Paul spells out the respective tendencies of flesh and spirit, accounting for the latter in terms of Christ, and closing with a brief admonition to live according to the spirit (vv. 12–13). The "desire" in each case (vv. 5–8) is not just an urge but a whole "mind" or outlook (*phronēma;* cf. Philippians 2, 2–6), a basic orientation of thought and action. Flesh is not hateful to God, but the *phronēma* of the flesh, self-centered interest taken as the basic norm and ceiling of man's own way of life, effectively means hatred of God. On the other hand, once man has been placed in the spirit by the risen Christ, then he has dwelling within him (8, 9b, as opposed to 7, 18a) an altogether new and dominant principle. Possession of the spirit is decisive in belonging to Christ (v. 9cd). To be in Christ and

391

to belong to Christ are the same (Galatians 3, 28–29); to belong to Christ and Christ's being in us are also the same (Romans 8, 9d. 10a). Through this mystical identification with Christ (cf. Thüsing), Paul can speak of "the body" and "the spirit" (v. 10bc) without the use of personal pronouns like "your" body and "your" spirit, even though one's personal conduct is implied. For, if Christ is in us, we are one with his body and his spirit, and our identification with him is what really explains our stance towards sin and justice. What is more, our existence in Christ and his in us not only accounts for our being able to please God in the present, but firmly grounds our hope for resurrection (v. 11). Basing the "imperative" of Christian life in the present foregoing "indicative," Paul closes by speaking of our radical obligation according to the law of the spirit. The same spirit that is the principle of resurrection is the principle of "mortification" of deeds representing a lower ceiling of human activity. Given Paul's awareness of the oneness of Christ's death and resurrection, it should come as no surprise that the spirit that he has transmitted to us by this mystery has a single thrust (towards life in resurrection) through the two-fold movement of death-life in the process of our own Christ-formed transformation. The law of the spirit, which is none other than the spirit himself had in Christ, and which was given by God in and through Christ, is that one live according to the spirit by subordinating everything else to that vital principle of activity. As Paul had blended ontological and juridical aspects of transformation through Christ, he here blends the ontological and moral aspects of the transformation.

8, 14a   Those who are guided by the spirit of God,
  14b   they are the sons of God.
  15a   You have not received a spirit of slavery [to lead you] back into
                                      fear;
  15b   you have received the spirit of sonship by which we cry, "Father!"
  16a   The spirit himself joins with our spirit in bearing witness
  16b   that we are God's children.
  17a   If we are his children, then we are heirs, too,
  17b   heirs of God,

17d   co-heirs with Christ,
17c   seeing that we share his sufferings
17e   in order to be sharers in his glory.
18a   I reckon the sufferings of the present time of no account
18b   in comparison with the glory that will one day be revealed in us.

19a   Creation is awaiting with eager expectation
19b   the revelation of [the glory of] God's sons.
20a   For creation has been subjected to frustration—
20b   not by her choice, but on account of him who made her
                                        subject—
20c   yet with hope,
21a   whereby she, too, will be emancipated from decay
21b   to enter upon the freedom of the glory that belongs to God's
                                        children.
22a   For we know
22b   that the whole of creation is groaning in birth pangs even to
                                        this hour.
23a   And, what is more,
23b   we ourselves, while having the first-fruits of the spirit,
23c   we, too, groan inwardly,
23d   while we await our [full] sonship, the deliverance [given] our
                                        bodies,
24a   For it is in [this] hope we are saved.
24b   Hope that sees for itself is not really hope;
24c   for why should one look forward to what he already sees?
25a   But if we look forward to what we do not see,
25b   we await it with patient endurance.

26a   Here, too, the spirit comes to the aid of our weakness.
26b   For we do not know how and what to ask as we ought.
26c   But the spirit himself makes intercession for us by wordless
                                        groanings,
27a   and he who searches hearts knows what is the spirit's desire,
27b   because it is according to God['s will] that he intercedes for
                                        the saints.

28a   We know that in all respects he works to the good with those
                                        who love God,
28b   those who are called according to [God's] decree:
29a   because those whom he lovingly knew from the first
29b   he also predestined to bear the very image of his Son,
29c   so that he would be the firstborn among many brothers.
30a   The same whom he has predestined, he has also called;
30b   the same whom he has called, he has also justified;
30c   and the same whom he has justified, he has also glorified.

The Apostle now takes up the more positive side of freedom through the spirit (8, 14–30; cf. 8, 2). At the same time, he advances from the theme of service (Romans 6–7) to that of sonship, thus bringing his proclamation of the gospel into its fullest personal perspective. First (vv. 14–17), with attention to the trinitarian character of Christian life, he speaks of the familiar converse in prayer to the Father which the spirit makes possible and which attests to divine sonship. The liturgical address (to which Paul alludes by adding the Aramaic form, *Abba*) voices God's witness as well as our own that we belong to him as sons. But real sonship means more than a title or state of being, even one prayerfully attested; it means actual enjoyment of the fullness of sonship, that is, inheritance, according to the very basis of that sonship, Christ himself. The future inheritance is inescapably bound up with the present, for both are one in the mystery of Christ's death and resurrection.

The mystery of sufferings consummated in glory (v. 17) serves as the springboard (v. 18) for Paul's eschatological hope —a hope which will not be disappointed, because God's love has been proved to us in Christ through the Holy Spirit given us (cp. Romans 8, 24–25 and Romans 5, 2–10). At least two major sections may conveniently be distinguished in verses 19–30. The first (vv. 19–25) moves from the hope of all creation to its grounds in our own hope for deliverance through patient endurance; the second (vv. 26–30) stresses the inner direction of the spirit which accounts for the efficacy of this hope according to God's will. "Groanings," an apocalyptic image of eager yearning with patient endurance of sufferings of the present time (cp. vv. 18a, 22b, 23c), find efficacious utterance in the spirit (v. 26c); the glory to be revealed (cp. vv. 18b, 19b, 21b, 23d) is the climax of an entire series of salvific acts (v. 30c) according to God's will which the spirit desires to bring about (v. 27 f.).

Paul sees the whole of creation made subject to frustration by Adam's sin (v. 20b). From this apocalyptic perspective one should not conclude that Paul affirms that the physical world prior to Adam's fall was a different kind of physical universe. The apocalyptic perspective is fundamentally theological, not

394

phenomenological or physical. Paul supposes a certain frustration of the powers of God placed in creation without supposing an initial transfiguration of creation. On the other hand, he does seem to suppose a future transfiguration proportioned to that which he expects for the risen sons of God. Nevertheless, even here he does not launch out with sails full set into a sea of apocalyptic imagery. He shows considerable restraint in speculation which might be construed too physically; he hopes for things unseen, affirming a transformation in resurrection which he makes no pretense to sketch in phenomenological detail. Suffice it to say that the physical transformation is not envisaged as a "return to paradise." Adam was not glorified, but "earthly," even as he came from God's hand, whereas the new Adam is the glorified Christ. Accordingly, the creation "subjected" by Adam (8, 20b) is not to be taken as the norm for imagining the glory to be revealed in the brothers of the new Adam and shared by all creation. The norm for imagining the new creation is the risen Jesus and those raised to join him.

Since even as we yearn for that which we do not as yet fully possess we have the first-fruits of the spirit (v. 23b), we have the aid of the spirit in patient endurance (v. 25b; cf. Romans 5, 3b–5c). Accordingly, Paul can speak in verse 26a of a *further* aid from the spirit in our weakness (that is, in our not having as yet the full sonship which consists in the inheritance of a risen body like that of God's Son). This further aid lies in something unheard but working efficaciously within us, since it is in line with the Father's manifest will. Those who love God (v. 28a) are those who have the spirit of God as the proof of God's own love (Romans 5, 5; cf. 2 Corinthians 13, 14). In all respects, even in our struggles (cf. 5, 3), it is the spirit who works to the good with those who love God. The spirit is the unnamed subject of the verb in verse 28a, as recent exegesis has pointed out (cf. M. Black). Although we do not know how and what to ask as we ought, we do know that in all respects the articulate spirit is at work within us for good. He who intercedes for the saints according to God's

395

will (v. 27b) is at work for those called according to God's decree (v. 28b).

In expressing God's "decree," or elective love, Paul does not soar into a psychological analysis of God's decree from all eternity. Rather, he enumerates from the standpoint of salvation history the successive steps by which God realizes our love for him. Foreknowledge is to be understood as an act of love by which God sets us on the way to full union with his Son. The standpoint from which Paul views predestination itself is not that of a kind of vacuum prior to creation but that of the resurrection of God's Son. Predestination of men is ordered to Christ's being the firstborn (from the dead) of many brothers. God's elective love (foreknowledge, v. 28b) is one with his setting the ideal to be realized (predestination, v. 29b), a new creation of men in the likeness of his Son and in union with him (*symmorphous,* v. 29b). This new creation, which is the dominant perspective of historically conceived predestination, then accounts for the other steps in the achieving of God's design: call in faith, justification, glorification. Paul certainly does not regard this progression as automatic, for it is a progression achieved in the spirit by God's grace. But he certainly affirms a kind of predestination to glory with his Son. Paul predicts no one's salvation or damnation, but simply declares that God's intention, centered on his Son, is realized in a whole integrated series of salvific acts. One would more accurately characterize verses 29–30 not as a picture of "predestination and its consequences" but as a complexively stated picture of God's actual governance of the world. Note that even glorification to come is expressed in the past tense ("has glorified," v. 30c) to make it accord with the rest of the verbs in the series. Paul has one total picture in mind. To express these aorists in a way that would less awkwardly express the total perspective of God's achievement of his love in us by the working of the spirit, one might well translate them as presents: ". . . knows from the first . . . predestines . . . calls . . . justifies . . . glorifies."

Thus, the coming glory for which we hope (§ V) and in view of which we are justified (§ III) is a glory patterned on Christ's own lived experience (passion—death—resurrection), intended on a cosmic scale, liberating the whole world from the slavery of corruption, and fulfilling inanimate and otherwise inarticulate yearnings. God's design for the new creation is our redemptive liberation, which, in its fullest sense, means our transformation into the image of his Son (8, 29). All the salutary acts of God, the expressions of his operative intention for man's reconstitution in life, are finalized in this personal working out of our glorification in his Son.

8, 31a	What, then, shall we say in the face of all this?	
31b	If God is for us, who [can be] against us?	
32a	God, you see, did not spare his own Son,	
32b	but gave him up for us all!	
32c	How can he do anything but give us everything else along with him?	
33a	Who will dare accuse God's chosen ones?	
33b	God who acquits [them]?	
34a	Who will condemn [us]?	
34b	Christ Jesus who has died?	
34c	Or, rather, who has been raised from the dead,	
34d	who is at God's right hand	
34e	and who even intercedes for us?	
35a	Who will separate us from the love of Christ?	
35b	tribulation? or distress? or persecution?	
35c	or hunger? or destitution? or peril? or the sword?	
36a	Just as scripture says:	
36b	"For your sake we are being put to death all day long;	
36c	we have been reckoned as sheep for slaughter."	
	[Psalms 43 (LXX), 23]	
37a	And yet in all these trials we conquer and more than conquer	
37b	through him who has loved us.	

38a	I am fully convinced that	
38b	neither death	nor life,
38c	nor angels,	nor dominions,
38d	nor things present,	nor things to come,
38e	nor powers,	
39a	nor height,	nor depth,
39b	nor anything else in creation	
39c	will be able to separate us from the love of God	
39d	[given us] in Christ Jesus our Lord!	

In a series of rhetorical questions, Paul defends the Christian as one not only fully acquitted but secure from any unfavorable judgment in point of salvation. The prospect of grace in the future rests on the love of God in Christ (cf. vv. 35a, 37b, 39cd). Worldly perils (v. 35bc) will be no obstacle: Paul cites Psalm 43 (LXX), 23 to prove that worldly tribulation does not mean that God does not love the persecuted; rather, such tribulation is precisely a sign of that love. Even cosmic forces, imaginatively sketched in the closing lines of Paul's apocalyptic defense of the gospel, cannot disrupt the union which God has lovingly effected in Christ Jesus our Lord.

Boastful "triumphalism," like baroque, may perhaps not appeal to the democratic mind. But perhaps the democratic mind thinks too humanly in the forum of the spirit, where God is the only sovereign. Paul's triumphalistic presentation of the gospel makes sense on the grounds of the actual triumph he proclaims, the sovereign grace of God in our risen Lord Jesus Christ. For all its pomp and rhetorical flourish, the Apostle's message of God's power for salvation is radically a message of love in the life of the spirit through one who died for us and rose to effect our transformation. With or without the appeal of triumphalistic rhetoric, this stands as a triumphant fact which should suffuse the Christian's heart with eager hope and persevering joy in the face of all obstacles to his fuller union with the risen Lord.

CHRONOLOGICAL TABLE

For a concise discussion of the chronology of Paul's life and works, cf. J. A. Fitzmyer, "A Life of Paul," *The Jerome Biblical Commentary* (Englewood Cliffs, N.J.: Prentice-Hall, 1968), #46, II, 215–222. The table given below follows Fitzmyer's chronology quite closely.

A.D.

ca. 10	Paul is born at Tarsus in Cilicia.
ca. 30	Paul studies under Gamaliel.
36	Paul at the stoning of Stephen; activity as a persecutor. Paul's conversion; journey to "Arabia" (the Nabataean Kingdom in Transjordan).
37	Paul returns from Arabia and spends about three years in Damascus.
40	Paul visits Jerusalem to ask information from Cephas and has an ecstasy in the temple. A Hellenist plot makes him withdraw to Tarsus, where he apparently remains until 44; vision at Tarsus.
44	Barnabas brings Paul from Tarsus to Antioch. Agabus prophesies a famine.
46	Paul's second visit to Jerusalem (during the famine).

46–49	Paul's first missionary journey (that in the company of Barnabas) (see map).
49	Paul visits Jerusalem for the "Council."
(autumn)	Paul confronts Peter at Antioch.
49–52	Paul's second missionary journey (see map). 1 and 2 Thessalonians written from Corinth. Paul is haled before the proconsul L. Junius Gallio towards the end of his eighteen-month stay in Corinth. He visits Jerusalem on his way back to Antioch.
52 (autumn)– 54 (spring)	Paul stays at Antioch.
54–58	Paul's third missionary journey (see map). For three years his missionary activity is centered in Ephesus. Galatians and Philippians written from Ephesus (ca. 54 and 56, respectively). Corinthian correspondence dates from this period (especially ca. 56–57).
57–58	Paul arrives in Corinth (winter, 57) and stays for three months in Achaea. Romans written from Corinth in early 58. A plot forces Paul to return to Jerusalem overland, by way of Macedonia; he spends Passover at Philippi (58).
58 (late spring)	Paul's last visit to Jerusalem. Protective arrest; confinement at Caesarea under Felix (58–60).
60	Paul's "appeal to Caesar" under Festus. Journey to Rome (see map); shipwreck on Malta (late autumn). Arrival in Rome (spring, 61).
61–63	House arrest in Rome for two years. Philemon, Colossians, and Ephesians written from Rome (ca. 63).
63–67	Freedom? Trip to Spain as planned? Arrest on a trip to the East (Troas), or in Rome? If 1 Timothy, Titus, and 2 Timothy are genuinely Paul's work, they must have been written in this period (1 Timothy and Titus from Macedonia, ca. 65; 2 Timothy from Rome as Paul faced death, ca. 67).

67 (?)   Martyrdom of Paul in Rome; beheaded under Nero (whose persecution lasted from the summer of 64 to the emperor's death in June, 68). Paul buried on the Via Ostiensis.

PAUL'S FIRST MISSION 46-49

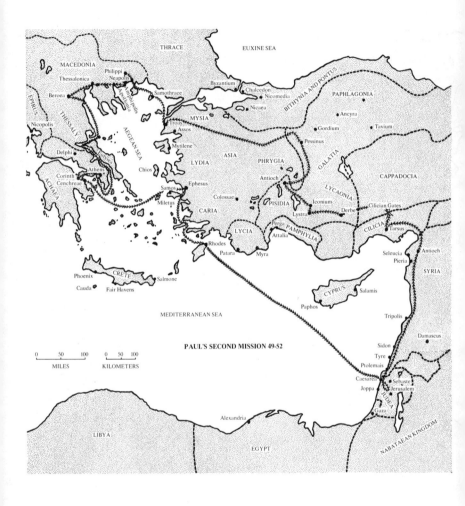

THRACE   EUXINE SEA

MACEDONIA
Thessalonica   Philippi
Beroea   Neapolis   Samothrace   Byzantium   Chalcedon   Nicomedia   PAPHLAGONIA
EPIRUS   Amphipolis   Apollonia   Nicaea

THESSALI   MYSIA   BITHYNIA AND PONTUS   Ancyra
Nicopolis   Troas   Gordium   Tavium
    Assos   Pessinus

Delphi   AEGEAN SEA   Mytilene   LYDIA   ASIA   PHRYGIA   GALATIA   CAPPADOCIA
Corinth   Athens   Chios   Antioch
Cenchreae   Samos   Ephesus   LYCAONIA
ACHAIA   Miletus   Colossae   Iconium   Cilician Gates
    CARIA   PISIDIA   Derbe   CILICIA   Tarsus
    Lystra

    LYCIA   Perga   PAMPHYLIA
Rhodes   Attalia   Seleucia   Antioch
Patara   Myra   Pieria   SYRIA

Phoenix   CRETE   Salmone   CYPRUS   Salamis
Cauda   Fair Havens   Paphos   Tripolis   Damascus

MEDITERRANEAN SEA   Sidon
    Tyre
PAUL'S SECOND MISSION 49-52   Ptolemais

0   50   100   0   50   100   Caesarea   Sebaste
MILES   KILOMETERS   Joppa   Jerusalem
    JUDEA

    Gaza
Alexandria

LIBYA   NABATAEAN KINGDOM

EGYPT

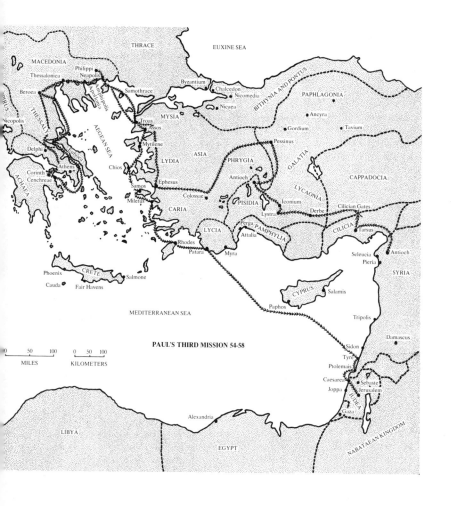

PAUL'S THIRD MISSION 54-58

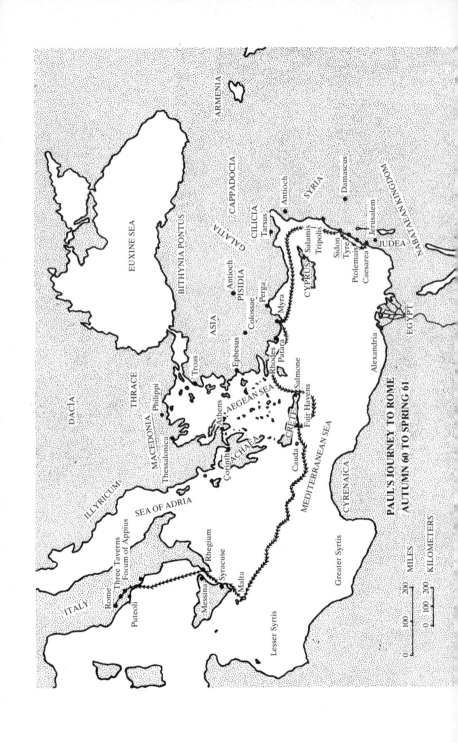

PAUL'S JOURNEY TO ROME
AUTUMN 60 TO SPRING 61

BIBLIOGRAPHY

This select bibliography contains some recommendations for further reading or, in a few cases, references to works of authors expressly discussed in this book. For more complete information, the reader is referred to the following: *Elenchus Bibliographicus Biblicus,* published annually by the Pontifical Biblical Institute, Rome; *New Testament Abstracts,* published thrice yearly at Weston College School of Theology, Cambridge, Mass.; introductory works such as that of Paul Feine, J. Behm, and W. G. Kümmel, *Introduction to the New Testament* (Nashville: Abingdon Press, rev. ed., 1966); verse-by-verse commentaries such as those in *The Jerome Biblical Commentary* (Englewood Cliffs, N.J.: Prentice-Hall, 1968) II, 227–331.

1 THESSALONIANS

Baltensweiler, H., "Erwägungen zu 1 Thessalonians 4, 3–8," *Theologische Zeitschrift*, 19 (1963), 1–13,

Fitzmyer, J. A., "New Testament Epistles," *The Jerome Biblical Commentary* (Englewood Cliffs, N.J.: Prentice-Hall, 1968), II, 223–226.

Funk, R. W., ed., *Apocalypticism (Journal for Theology and the Church, 6)* (New York: Herder and Herder, 1969).

Gatzweiler, K., "La conception paulinienne du miracle," *Ephemerides Theologicae Lovanienses,* 37 (1961), 813–846.

Munck, J., "I Thessalonians i. 9–10 and the Missionary Preaching of Paul. Textual Exegesis and Hermeneutic Reflections," *New Testament Studies,* 9 (1962 f.), 95–110.

Schippers, R., "The Pre-synoptic Tradition in I Thessalonians ii:13–16," *Novum Testamentum,* 8 (1966), 223–234.

Sint, J., "Awaiting and Deferment of the Parousia in Paul," *Theology Digest,* 13 (1965), 214–220.

Stempvoort, P. A. van, "Eine stilistische Lösung einer alten Schwierigkeit in I Thessalonians v. 23," *New Testament Studies,* 7 (1960 f.), 262–265.

Stuhlmacher, P., "Erwägungen zum Problem von Gegenwart und Zukunft in der paulinischen Eschatologie," *Zeitschrift für Theologie und Kirche,* 64 (1967), 423–450.

2 THESSALONIANS

Giblin, Charles H., *The Threat to Faith. An Exegetical and Theological Re-examination of 2 Thessalonians 2* (Rome: Pontifical Biblical Institute, 1967).

GALATIANS

Burtschaell, J., "A Theology of Faith and Works. The Epistle to the Galatians—A Catholic View," *Interpretation,* 17 (1963), 39–47.

Fitzmyer, J. A., "Saint Paul and the Law," *The Jurist,* 27 (1967), 18–36.

Giblin, C. H., "Why Jesus Spoke in Parables—an Answer from Luke 15" (interesting as a Lucan parallel to the Pauline notion of justice), *Chicago Studies* (Autumn, 1968), 213–220.

Kilpatrick, G., "Galatians 1:18 *'istorēsai Kēphan,*" *New Testament Essays. Studies in Memory of T. W. Manson,* ed. A. J. B. Higgins (Manchester: Manchester University Press, 1959), 144–149.

Le Déaut, R., "Traditions targumiques dans le Corpus Paulinien? (Hébreux 11, 4 et 12, 24; Galates 4, 29–30; 2 Corinthiens 3, 16)," *Biblica,* 42 (1961), 28–48.

Lyonnet, S., "St. Paul: Liberty and Law," *The Bridge,* 4 (1961–1962), 229–251.

Sanders, J. T., "Paul's 'Autobiographical' Statements in Galatians 1–2," *Journal of Biblical Literature,* 85 (1966), 335–343.

Stanley, D. M., "Judaism and Christianity," *Thought,* 37 (1962), 330–346.

Stuhlmacher, P., "Erwägungen zum ontologischen Charakter der *kainē ktisis* bei Paulus," *Evangelische Theologie,* 27 (1967), 1–35.

Taylor, Greer M., "The Function of PISTIS CHRISTOU in Galatians," *Journal of Biblical Literature,* 85 (1966), 58–76.

PHILIPPIANS

Ahern, Barnabas M., " 'The Fellowship of His Sufferings' (Philippians 3, 10)," *Catholic Biblical Quarterly,* 20 (1960), 1–32.

Käsemann, Ernst, "A Critical Analysis of Philippians 2:5–11," *God and Christ, Existence and Province (Journal for Theology and the Church,* 5) (New York: Harper and Row, 1968), 45–88.

Klijn, A. F. J., "Paul's Opponents in Philippians iii," *Novum Testamentum,* 7 (1965), 278–284.

Koester, Helmut, "The Purpose of the Polemic of a Pauline Fragment (Philippians III)," *New Testament Studies,* 8 (1961 f.), 317–332.

Talbert, C. H., "The Problem of Pre-existence in Philippians 2, 4–11," *Journal of Biblical Literature,* 86 (1967), 141–153.

1 CORINTHIANS

Barrett, C. K., "Christianity at Corinth," *Bulletin of the John Rylands Library, Manchester,* 46 (1964), 269–297.

Boucher, Madeleine, "Some Unexplored Parallels to 1 Corinthians 11, 11–12 and Galatians 3, 28: The NT on the Role of Women," *Catholic Biblical Quarterly,* 31 (1969), 50–58.

Coune, M., "Le problème des Idolothytes et l'éducation de la *Syneidêsis,*" *Recherches de Science Religieuse,* 51 (1963), 497–534.

Cullmann, O., "All Who Call on the Name of Our Lord Jesus Christ," *Journal of Ecumenical Studies,* 1 (1964), 1–21.

Feuillet, A., "The Enigma of 1 Corinthians 2:9," *Theology Digest,* 14 (1966), 143–148.

Furnish, V. P., " 'Fellow Workers in God's Service,' " *Journal of Biblical Literature,* 80 (1961), 364–370.

Giblin, C. H., "1 Corinthians 7—A Negative Theology of Marriage and Celibacy?" *Bible Today,* 41 (March, 1969), 2839–2855.

Hooker, M. D., "Authority on Her Head: An Examination of I Corinthians xi. 10," *New Testament Studies,* 10 (1963 f.), 410–416.

Hurd, J. C., Jr.,*The Origin of I Corinthians* (London: SPCK, 1965).

Johannson, N., "I Corinthians xiii and I Corinthians xiv," *New Testament Studies,* 10 (1963 f.), 383–392.

Käsemann, Ernst, "The Pauline Doctrine of the Lord's Supper," *Essays on New Testament Themes* (London: SCM, 1964), 108–135.

Leaney, A. R. C., "The Doctrine of Man in 1 Corinthians," *Scottish Journal of Theology,* 15 (1962), 394–399.

Le Déaut, R., "The Paschal Mystery and Morality," *Doctrine and Life,* 18 (1968), 202–210, 262–269.

Léon-Dufour, X., "Mariage et virginité selon saint Paul," *Christus,* 11 (1964), 179–194.

Malherbe, A. J., "The Beasts at Ephesus," *Journal of Biblical Literature,* 87 (1968), 71–80.

Maly, K., "1 Kor 12, 1–3, eine Regel zur Unterscheidung der Geister?" *Biblische Zeitschrift,* 10 (1966), 82–95.

Mueller, H., "The Ideal Man as Portrayed by the Talmud and St. Paul," *Catholic Biblical Quarterly,* 28 (1966), 278–291.

Navone, J. J., "Love in the Message of Paul," *Worship,* 40 (1966), 437–444.

Osborne, R. E., "Paul and the Wild Beasts," *Journal of Biblical Literature,* 85 (1966), 225–230.

Sanders, J. T., "First Corinthians 13. Its Interpretation Since the First World War," *Interpretation,* 20 (1966), 159–187.

Schlier, H., *Der Brief an die Epheser* (Düsseldorf: Patmos-Verlag, rev. ed., 1958), 272 n. 2.

Schneider, B., "The Corporate Meaning and Background of 1 Corinthians 15, 45b—'o eschatos adam eis pneuma zōopoioun," *Catholic Biblical Quarterly,* 29 (1967), 450–467.

Schütz, J. H., "Apostolic Authority and the Control of Tradition: I Corinthians xv," *New Testament Studies,* 15 (1968 f.), 439–457.

Smalley, S. S., "Spiritual Gifts and 1 Corinthians 12–16," *Journal of Biblical Literature,* 87 (1968), 427–433.

Sweet, J. P. M., "A Sign for Unbelievers: Paul's Attitude to Glossolalia," *New Testament Studies,* 13 (1966 f.), 240–257.

Wilson, J. H., "The Corinthians Who Say There Is No Resurrection of the Dead," *Zeitschrift für die Neutestamentliche Wissenschaft,* 59 (1968), 90–107.

2 CORINTHIANS

Allmen, D. von, "Réconciliation du monde et christologie cosmique, de II Corinthiens 5:14–21 à Colossiens 1:15–23," *Revue d'Histoire et de Philosophie Religieuses,* 48 (1968), 32–45.

Bornkamm, G., "The History of the Origin of the So-called Second Letter to the Corinthians," *New Testament Studies,* 8 (1961 f.), 258–264.

Carrez, M., "La confiance en l'homme et la confiance en soi selon l'apôtre Paul," *Revue d'Histoire et de Philosophie Religieuses,* 44 (1964), 191–199.

Feuillet, A., "The Christ-Image of God According to St. Paul (2 Corinthians 4:4)," *Bible Today,* 21 (1965), 1409–1414.

Fitzmyer, J. A., "Qumrân and the Interpolated Paragraph in 2 Corinthians 6, 14–7, 1," *Catholic Biblical Quarterly,* 23 (1961), 271–280.

Hill, E., "The Construction of Three Passages from St. Paul (Romans 8, 20–21; 2 Corinthians 1, 20; 2 Corinthians 3, 10)," *Catholic Biblical Quarterly,* 23 (1961), 296–301.

Leivestad, R., " 'The Meekness and Gentleness of Christ' II Corinthians x. 1," *New Testament Studies,* 12 (1965 f.), 156–164.

McNamara, Martin, *The New Testament and the Palestinian Targum to the Pentateuch* (Rome: Pontifical Biblical Institute, 1966), 168–188.

Thierry, "Der Dorn im Fleische (2 Kor. xii, 7–9)," *Novum Testamentum,* 5 (1962), 301–310.

Wagner, G., "Le tabernacle et la vie 'en Christ,' Exégèse de 2 Corinthiens 5:1 à 10," *Revue d'Histoire et de Philosophie Religieuses,* 41 (1961), 379–393.

ROMANS 12–16

Cranfield, C. E. B., "*Metron pisteōs* in Romans xii. 3," *New Testament Studies,* 8 (1961 f.), 345–351.

Klassen, W., "Coals of Fire: Sign of Repentance or Revenge?" *New Testament Studies,* 9 (1962 f.), 337–350.

Knox, J., "Romans 15:14–33 and Paul's Conception of His Apostolic Mission," *Journal of Biblical Literature,* 83 (1964), 1–11.

Stendahl, Krister, "Hate, Non-Retaliation, and Love. 1 QS X, 17–20 and Romans 12, 19–21," *Harvard Theological Review,* 55 (1962), 343–355.

Stoessel, H. E., "Notes on Romans 12:1–2. The Renewal of the Mind and Internalizing the Truth," *Interpretation,* 17 (1963), 161–175.

PAUL'S APOSTOLIC CONSCIOUSNESS

Ahern, Barnabas M., "The Christian's Union with the Body of Christ in Corinthians, Galatians, and Romans," *Catholic Biblical Quarterly,* 23 (1961), 199–209.

Allo, E.-B., "L'évolution de l'évangile de Paul," *Mémorial Lagrange* (Paris: Gabalda, 1940), 259–267; cf. *Vivre et penser* (= *Revue Biblique,* 1941–1944), 1 (1941), 48–77, 165–193.

Bernard, C.-A., "Expérience spirituelle et vie apostolique en Saint Paul," *Gregorianum,* 49 (1968), 38–57.

Cerfaux, L., *The Spiritual Journey of Saint Paul* (New York: Sheed and Ward, 1968).

————"La vocation de saint Paul," *Euntes Docete,* 14 (1961), 3–35.

Conzelmann, H., "Current Problems in Pauline Research," *Interpretation,* 22 (1968), 171–186.

Culliton, J. B., "Lucien Cerfaux's Contribution concerning 'The Body of Christ'," *Catholic Biblical Quarterly,* 29 (1967), 41–59.

Davies, W. D., "Paul and Judaism," *The Bible in Modern Scholarship,* ed. J. Philip Hyatt (Nashville: Abingdon Press, 1965), 178–186.

Denis, A.-M., "L'investiture de la fonction apostolique par 'apocalypse'. Etude thématique de Galates 1:16," *Revue Biblique,* 65 (1957), 335–362.

Grassi, J. A., "An Apostle of Christ: Paul's Criterion," *Bible Today,* 24 (April, 1966), 1578–1582.

Holtz, T., "Zum Selbstverständnis des Apostels Paulus," *Theologische Literaturzeitung,* 91 (1966), 321–330.

Jeremias, J., "The Key to Pauline Theology," *Expository Times,* 76 (1964 f.), 27–30.

Kamlah, E., "Wie beurteilt Paulus sein Leiden? Ein Beitrag zur Untersuchung seiner Denkstruktuur," *Zeitschrift für die Neutestamentliche Wissenschaft,* 54 (1964), 217–232.

Koester, Helmut H., "Paul and Hellenism," *The Bible in Modern Scholarship,* ed. J. Philip Hyatt (Nashville: Abingdon Press, 1965), 187–195.

Menoud, P.-H., "Revelation and Tradition; The Influence of Paul's Conversion on His Theology," *Interpretation,* 7 (1953), 131–141.

Munck, J., *Paul and the Salvation of Mankind* (London: SCM, 1959).

————"Pauline Research Since Schweitzer," *The Bible in Modern Scholarship,* ed. J. Philip Hyatt (Nashville: Abingdon Press, 1965), 166–177.

Schweizer, E., "The Church as the Missionary Body of Christ," *New Testament Studies,* 8 (1961 f.), 1–11.

Spicq, C., "Our Lord in the Scripture. St. Paul's Epistles," *Doctrine and Life,* 11 (1961), 246–253, 292–299.

Whiteley, D. E. H., *The Theology of St. Paul* (Oxford: Blackwell, 1964).

Wikenhauser, A., *Pauline Mysticism* (New York: Herder and Herder, 1960).

Wood, H. G., "The Conversion of St. Paul," *New Testament Studies,* 1 (1954 f.), 276–282.

PAUL'S THEOLOGICAL PERSPECTIVES
(especially ROM. 9–11)

Barth, M., "Jews and Gentiles: The Social Character of Justification in Paul," *Journal of Ecumenical Studies,* 5 (1968), 241–267.

Benoit, P., "The Theologies of Paul and John," *Theology Digest,* 13 (1965), 135–141; digest of "Paulinisme et Johannisme," *New Testament Studies,* 9 (1962 f.), 193–207.

Blackman, E. C., "Divine Sonship and Missionary Strategy in Romans 9–11," *Canadian Journal of Theology*, 11 (1965), 124–134.

Bornkamm, G., "Paul's Christology," *Perspective*, 4 (1963), 11–24.

―――"Paulinische Anakolouthe im Römerbrief," *Das Ende des Gesetzes* (Munich: Kaiser-Verlag, 1952), 76–92.

Bouttier, M., *Christianity According to Paul* (London: SCM, 1966).

Bultmann, R., *Theology of the New Testament*, Vol. I (London: SCM, 1952), 185–352.

Cerfaux, L., *Christ in the Theology of St. Paul* (New York: Herder and Herder, 1959).

―――*The Church in the Theology of St. Paul* (New York: Herder and Herder, 1959).

―――*The Christian in the Theology of St. Paul* (New York: Herder and Herder, 1967).

Delling, G., "Zum neueren Paulusverständnis," *Novum Testamentum*, 4 (1960), 95–121.

Dion, H.-M., 'Predestination in St. Paul," *Theology Digest*, 15 (1967), 144–149; digest of "La prédestination chez saint Paul," *Recherches de Science Religieuse*, 53 (1965), 5–43.

Fitzmyer, J. A., *Pauline Theology. A Brief Sketch* (Englewood Cliffs, N.J.: Prentice-Hall, 1967).

―――"The Use of Explicit Old Testament Quotations in Qumran Literature and in the New Testament," *New Testament Studies*, 7 (1960 f.), 297–333.

Grundmann, W., "Überlieferung und Eigenaussage im eschatologischen Denken des Apostels Paulus," *New Testament Studies*, 8 (1961 f.), 12–26.

Leaney, A. R. C., "The Experience of God in Qumran and in Paul," *Bulletin of The John Rylands Library*, 51 (1969), 431–452.

Lyonnet, S., "Saint Paul et l'exégèse juive de son temps. A propos de Romans, 10, 6–8," *Mélanges Bibliques rédigés en l'honneur de André Robert* (Paris: Bloud et Gay, 1957), 494–506.

Oesterreicher, J. M., "Israel's Misstep and Her Rise—The Dialectic of God's Saving Design in Romans 9—11," *Bible Today*, 12 (April, 1964), 768–774.

Thüsing, Wilhelm, *Per Christum in Deum. Studien zum Verhältnis von Christozentrik und Theozentrik in den paulinischen Hauptbriefen* (Münster: Aschendorff, 1965).

414

PAUL'S GOSPEL (especially ROM. 1–8)

Black, M., "The Interpretation of Romans viii, 28," *Studia Neo-testamentica et Patristica* (*O. Cullmann Festschrift*) (Leiden: E. J. Brill, 1962), 166–172.

Blackman, C., "Romans 3, 26b: A Question of Translation," *Journal of Biblical Literature,* 87 (1968), 203–204.

Bonnard, P., "La justice de Dieu et l'histoire. Remarques exégétiques sur une controverse récente," *Etudes Théologiques et Religieuses,* 43 (1968), 61–68.

Bourke, Myles M., "St. Paul and the Justification of Abraham," *Bible Today,* 10 (February, 1964), 643–649.

Bultmann, R., "Adam and Christ According to Romans 5," *Current Issues in New Testament Interpretation* (*O. Piper Festschrift*) (London: Harper, 1962) 143–165.

————"DIKAIOSYNĒ THEOU," *Journal of Biblical Literature,* 83 (1964), 12–16.

Cranfield, C. E. B., "St. Paul and the Law," *Scottish Journal of Theology,* 17 (1964), 43–68.

Danker, F. W., "Romans v. 12. Sin under Law," *New Testament Studies,* 14 (1967 f.), 424–439.

Goppelt, L., "Paul and Heilsgeschichte. Conclusions from Romans 4 and I Corinthians 10, 1–13," *Interpretation,* 21 (1967), 315–326.

Howard, G., "On the 'Faith of Christ'," *Harvard Theological Review,* 60 (1967), 459–465.

Hunter, A. M., "The Hope of Glory: The Relevance of the Pauline Eschatology," *Interpretation,* 8 (1954), 131–141.

Käsemann, Ernst, "God's Righteousness in Paul," *The Bultmann School of Biblical Interpretation: New Directions?* (*Journal for Theology and the Church,* 3) (New York: Harper and Row, 1967), 1–13.

Kümmel, W. G., "*Paresis* and *endeixis.* A Contribution to the Understanding of the Pauline Doctrine of Justification," *Distinctive Protestant and Catholic Themes Reconsidered* (*Journal for Theology and the Church,* 3) (New York: Harper and Row, 1967), 1–13.

Ligier, L., " 'In quo omnes peccaverunt' Actes ou État (Romans 5, 12)?" *Nouvelle Revue Théologique,* 82 (1960), 337–348.

415

Lyall, F., "Roman Law in the Writings of Paul—Adoption," *Journal of Biblical Literature,* 88 (1969), 458–466.

Lyonnet, S., "History of Salvation in Romans 7," *Theology Digest,* 13 (1965), 35–38; digest of "L'histoire du salut selon le chapître VII de l'épître aux Romains," *Biblica,* 43 (1962), 117–151.

Malina, Bruce, "Some Observations on the Origin of Sin in Judaism and St. Paul," *Catholic Biblical Quarterly,* 31 (1969), 18–34.

Rosin, H., *"To gnōston tou Theou," Theologische Zeitschrift,* 17 (1961), 161–165.

Schnackenburg, R., *Baptism in the Thought of St. Paul* (Oxford: Blackwell, 1964).

Schweizer, E., "Dying and Rising with Christ," *New Testament Studies,* 14 (1967 f.), 1–14.

Stendahl, Krister, "The Apostle Paul and the Introspective Conscience of the West," *Harvard Theological Review,* 56 (1963), 119–216.

Stuhlmacher, P., "Glauben und Verstehen bei Paulus," *Evangelische Theologie,* 26 (1966), 337–348.

INDEX OF AUTHORS

417

INDEX OF BIBLICAL TEXTS

This index is intended primarily to supplement the Pauline texts already indicated in the Table of Contents (pp. v–viii); page reference follows colon after biblical reference.

418

INDEX OF SUBJECTS

The more important references are in italics.